CHILTON'S
REPAIR & TUNE-UP GUIDE
GM
J-CAR
1982

Chevrolet **CAVALIER** • Oldsmobile **FIRENZA**
Buick **SKYHAWK** • Pontiac **J-2000** • Cadillac **CIMARRON**

CAVALIER

Managing Editor KERRY A. FREEMAN, S.A.E.
Senior Editor RICHARD J. RIVELE, S.A.E.
Editor DEAN F. MORGANTINI, S.A.E.

President WILLIAM A. BARBOUR
Executive Vice President JAMES. A. MIADES
Vice President and General Manager JOHN P. KUSHNERICK

CHILTON BOOK COMPANY
Radnor, Pennsylvania
19089

SAFETY NOTICE

Proper service and repair procedures are vital to the safe, reliable operation of all motor vehicles, as well as the personal safety of those performing repairs. This book outlines procedures for servicing and repairing vehicles using safe, effective methods. The procedures contain many NOTES, CAUTIONS and WARNINGS which should be followed along with standard safety procedures to eliminate the possibility of personal injury or improper service which could damage the vehicle or compromise its safety.

It is important to note that repair procedures and techniques, tools and parts for servicing motor vehicles, as well as the skill and experience of the individual performing the work vary widely. It is not possible to anticipate all of the conceivable ways or conditions under which vehicles may be serviced, or to provide cautions as to all of the possible hazards that may result. Standard and accepted safety precautions and equipment should be used when handling toxic or flammable fluids, and safety goggles or other protection should be used during cutting, grinding, chiseling, prying, or any other process that can cause material removal or projectiles.

Some procedures require the use of tools specially designed for a specific purpose. Before substituting another tool or procedure, you must be completely satisfied that neither your personal safety, nor the performance of the vehicle will be endangered.

Although the information in this guide is based on industry sources and is as complete as possible at the time of publication, the possibility exists that the manufacturer made later changes which could not be included here. While striving for total accuracy, Chilton Book Company cannot assume responsibility for any errors, changes, or omissions that may occur in the compilation of this data.

PART NUMBERS

Part numbers listed in this reference are not recommendations by Chilton for any product by brand name. There are references that can be used with interchange manuals and aftermarket supplier catalogs to locate each brand supplier's discrete part number.

ACKNOWLEDGMENTS

The Chilton Book Company expresses its appreciation to the General Motors Corporation for their generous assistance.

Information has been selected from General Motors shop manuals, owners manuals, service bulletins and technical training manuals.

Copyright © 1981 by Chilton Book Company
All Rights Reserved
Published in Radnor, Pa., by Chilton Book Company
and simultaneously in Ontario, Canada
by Nelson Canada, Limited

Manufactured in the United States of America

1234567890   098765432

Chilton's Repair & Tune-Up Guide: GM J-Car 1982
ISBN 0-8019-7059-8 pbk.
Library of Congress Catalog Card No. 81-66634

CONTENTS

1 General Information and Maintenance
- **1** How to Use this Book
- **2** Tools and Equipment
- **7** Routine Maintenance and Lubrication
- **30** How to Buy a Used Car

2 Tune-Up

- **33** Tune-Up Procedures
- **34** Tune-Up Specifications

3 Engine and Engine Rebuilding
- **48** Engine Electrical System
- **56** Engine Service and Specifications
- **69** Engine Rebuilding

4 Emission Controls and Fuel System
- **91** Emission Control System and Service
- **108** Fuel System Service

5 Chassis Electrical
- **119** Accessory Service
- **122** Instrument Panel Service
- **125** Lights, Fuses and Flashers

100 Chilton's Fuel Economy and Tune-Up Tips

6 Clutch and Transaxle

- **129** Manual Transaxle
- **135** Clutch
- **136** Automatic Transaxle

7 Suspension and Steering
- **141** Front Suspension
- **149** Rear Suspension
- **151** Steering

8 Brakes
- **162** Front Brakes
- **165** Rear Brakes
- **169** Brake Specifications

9 Body
- **176** Repairing Scratches and Small Dents
- **180** Repairing Rust
- **186** Body Care

10 Troubleshooting
- **190** Problem Diagnosis

- **223** Appendix
- **226** Index

Quick Reference Specifications For Your Vehicle

Fill in this chart with the most commonly used specifications for your vehicle. Specifications can be found in Chapters 1 through 3 or on the tune-up decal under the hood of the vehicle.

 ## Tune-Up

Firing Order_____

Spark Plugs:

    Type_____

    Gap (in.)_____

Point Gap (in.)_____

Dwell Angle (°)_____

Ignition Timing (°)_____

    Vacuum (Connected/Disconnected)_____

Valve Clearance (in.)

    Intake_____ Exhaust_____

 ## Capacities

Engine Oil (qts)

    With Filter Change_____

    Without Filter Change_____

Cooling System (qts)_____

Manual Transmission (pts)_____

    Type_____

Automatic Transmission (pts)_____

    Type_____

Front Differential (pts)_____

    Type_____

Rear Differential (pts)_____

    Type_____

Transfer Case (pts)_____

    Type_____

FREQUENTLY REPLACED PARTS

Use these spaces to record the part numbers of frequently replaced parts.

PCV VALVE   **OIL FILTER**   **AIR FILTER**

Manufacturer_____   Manufacturer_____   Manufacturer_____

Part No._____   Part No._____   Part No._____

General Information and Maintenance

HOW TO USE THIS BOOK

Chilton's Repair and Tune-Up Guide for the GM J-car is intended to teach you more about the inner workings of your automobile and save you money on its upkeep. Chapters 1 and 2 will probably be the most frequently used in the book. The first chapter contains all the information that may be required at a moment's notice—information such as the location of the various serial numbers and the proper towing instructions. It also contains all the information on basic day-to-day maintenance that you will need to ensure good performance and long component life. Chapter 2 covers tune-up procedures which will assist you not only in keeping the engine running properly and at peak performance levels, but also in restoring some of the more delicate components to operating condition in the event of a failure. Chapters 3 through 11 cover repairs (rather than maintenance) for various portions of the car, with each chapter covering either one system or two related systems. The appendix then lists general information which may be useful in rebuilding the engine or performing some other operation on any car.

In using the Table of Contents, refer to the bold listings for the beginning of the chapter. See the smaller listings or the index for information on a particular component or specifications.

In general, there are three things a proficient mechanic has which must be allowed for when a nonprofessional does work on his car. These are:

1. A sound knowledge of the construction of the parts he is working with, their order of assembly, etc.
2. A knowledge of potentially hazardous situations.
3. Manual dexterity, which includes the ability to put the right amount of torque on a part to ensure that it will not be damaged or warped.

This book provides step-by-step instructions and illustrations wherever possible. Use them carefully and wisely—do not just jump headlong into disassembly. Where you are not sure about being able to readily reassemble something, make a careful drawing of the component before taking it apart. Assembly always looks simple when everything is still assembled.

Cautions and notes will be provided where appropriate to help prevent you from injuring yourself or damaging your car. Therefore, you should read through the entire procedure before beginning the work, and make sure that you are aware of the warnings. Since no number of warnings could cover

2 GENERAL INFORMATION AND MAINTENANCE

every possible situation, you should work slowly and try to envision what is going to happen in each operation ahead of time.

When it comes to tightening things, there is generally a slim area between too loose to properly seal or resist vibration and so tight as to risk damage or warping. When dealing with major engine parts, or with any aluminum component, it pays to procure a torque wrench and go by the recommended figures.

When reference is made in this book to the "right side" or "left side" of the car, it should be understood that the positions are always to be viewed from the front seat. Thus, the left side of the car is always the driver's side and the right side is always the passenger's side, even when facing the car, as when working on the engine.

We have attempted to eliminate the use of special tools whenever possible, substituting more readily available hand tools. However, in some cases the special tools are necessary. These can be purchased from your General Motors dealer, or an automotive parts store.

Always be conscious of the need for safety in your work. Never get under the car unless it is firmly supported by jackstands or ramps. Never smoke near or allow flame to get near the battery or the fuel system. Keep your clothing, hands and hair clear of the fan and pulleys when working near the engine, if it is running. Most importantly, try to be patient; even in the midst of an argument with a stubborn bolt, reaching for the largest hammer in the garage is usually a cause for later regret and more extensive repair. As you gain confidence and experience, working on your car will become a source of pride and satisfaction.

TOOLS AND EQUIPMENT

It would be impossible to catalog each and every tool that you may need to perform all the operations included in this book. It would also not be wise for the amateur to rush out and buy an expensive set of tools on the theory that he may need one of them at some time. The best approach is to proceed slowly, gathering together a good quality set of those tools that are used most frequently. Don't be misled by the low cost of bargain tools. It is far better to spend a little more for quality, name brand tools. Forged wrenches, 12 point sockets and fine-tooth ratchets are a better investment than their less expensive counterparts. As any good mechanic can tell you, there are few worse experiences than trying to work on a car or truck with bad tools. Your monetary savings will be far outweighed by frustration and mangled knuckles.

Begin accumulating those tools that are used most frequently: those associated with routine maintenance and tune-up. In addition to the normal assortment of screwdrivers and pliers, you should have the following tools for routine maintenance jobs:

1. Metric and SAE wrenches, sockets and combination open end/box end wrenches;
2. Jackstands—for support;
3. Oil filter wrench;
4. Oil filler spout or funnel;
5. Grease gun—for chassis lubrication;
6. Hydrometer—for checking the battery;
7. A low flat pan for draining oil;
8. Lots of rags for wiping up the inevitable mess.

In addition to these items there are several others which are not absolutely necessary, but handy to have around. These include a transmission funnel and filler tube, a drop light on a long cord, an adjustable wrench and a pair of slip-joint pliers.

A more advanced set of tools, suitable for tune-up work, can be drawn up easily. While the tools are slightly more sophisticated, they need not be outrageously expensive. The key to these purchases is to make them with an eye towards adaptability and wide range. A basic list of tune-up tools could include:

1. Tachometer/dwell meter;
2. Spark plug gauge and gapping tool;
3. Feeler gauges for valve and point adjustment;
4. Timing light.

A tachometer/dwell meter will ensure accurate tune-up work on cars without electronic ignition. The choice of a timing light should be made carefully. A light which works on the DC current supplied by the car battery is the best choice; it should have a xenon tube for brightness. Since all J-cars have an electronic ignition system, the timing light should have an inductive pickup which clamps around the No. 1 spark plug cable (the timing light illustrated has one of these pickups).

In addition to these basic tools, there are several other tools and gauges which, though not particularly necessary for basic tune-up

GENERAL INFORMATION AND MAINTENANCE 3

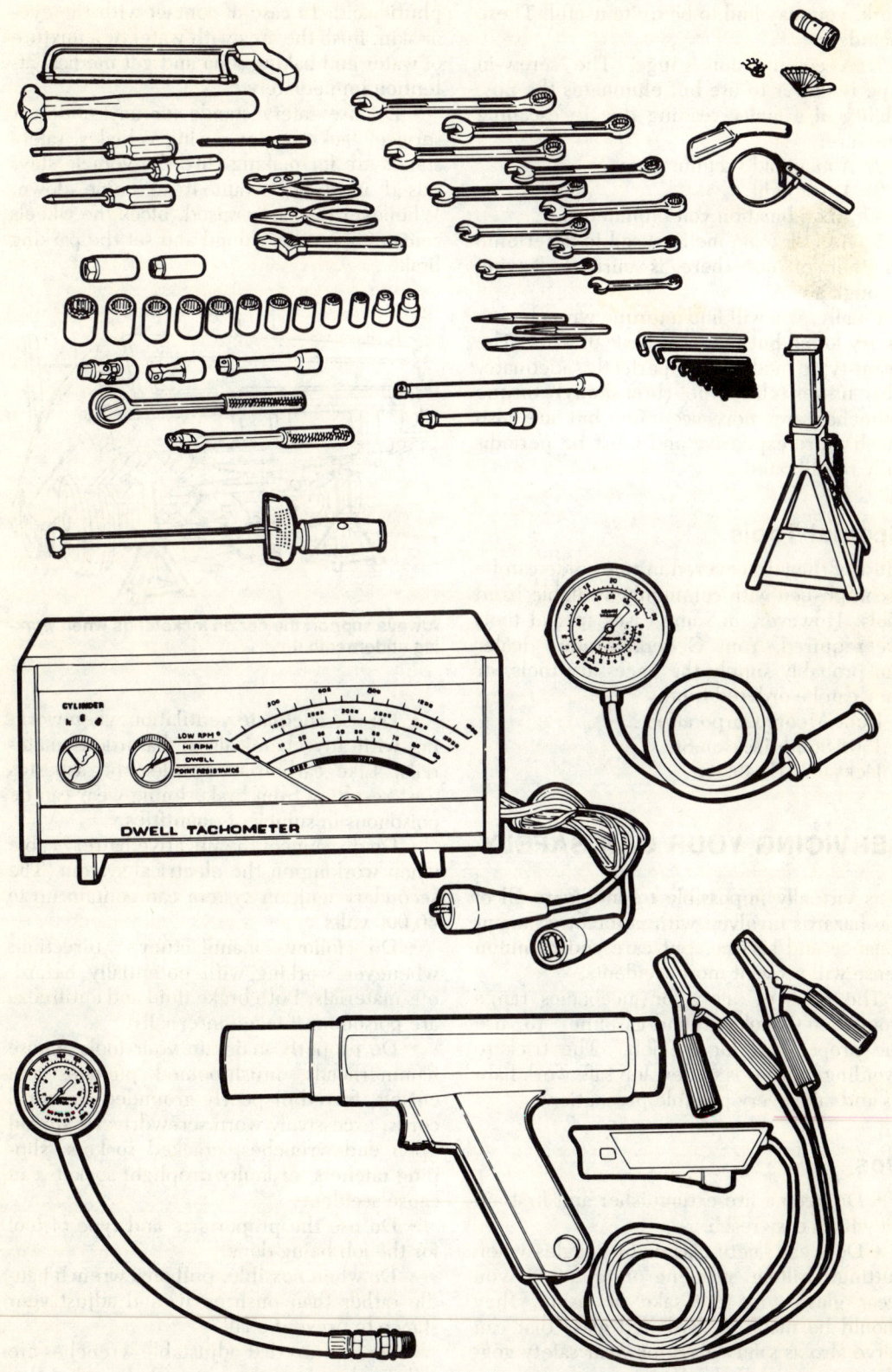

You need only a basic assortment of hand tools for most maintenance and repair jobs

4 GENERAL INFORMATION AND MAINTENANCE

work, you may find to be quite useful. These include:

1. A compression gauge. The screw-in type is slower to use but eliminates the possibility of a faulty reading due to escaping pressure;
2. A manifold vacuum gauge;
3. A test light;
4. A combination volt/ohmmeter;
5. An induction meter, used to determine whether or not there is current flowing through a wire.

Finally, you will find a torque wrench necessary for all but the most basic of work. The beam-type models are perfectly adequate. The newer click-type (breakaway) torque wrenches are more accurate, but are also much more expensive and must be periodically recalibrated.

Special Tools

Most of the jobs covered in this guide can be accomplished with commonly available hand tools. However, in some cases special tools are required. Your General Motors dealer can probably supply the necessary tools, or they can be ordered from:

Kent-Moore Corporation
1501 South Jackson St.
Jackson, MI. 49203

SERVICING YOUR CAR SAFELY

It is virtually impossible to anticipate all of the hazards involved with automotive maintenance and service, but care and common sense will prevent most accidents.

The rules of safety for mechanics range from "don't smoke around gasoline," to "use the proper tool for the job." The trick to avoiding injuries is to develop safe work habits and take every possible precaution.

Dos

• Do keep a fire extinguisher and first aid kit within easy reach.
• Do wear safety glasses or goggles when cutting, drilling, grinding or prying. If you wear glasses for the sake of vision, they should be made of hardened glass that can serve also as safety glass, or wear safety goggles over your regular glasses.
• Do shield your eyes whenever you work around the battery. Batteries contain sulphuric acid. In case of contact with the eyes or skin, flush the area with water or a mixture of water and baking soda and get medical attention immediately.
• Do use safety stands for any undercar service. Jacks are for raising vehicles; safety stands are for making sure the vehicle stays raised until you want it to come down. Whenever the car is raised, block the wheels remaining on the ground and set the parking brake.

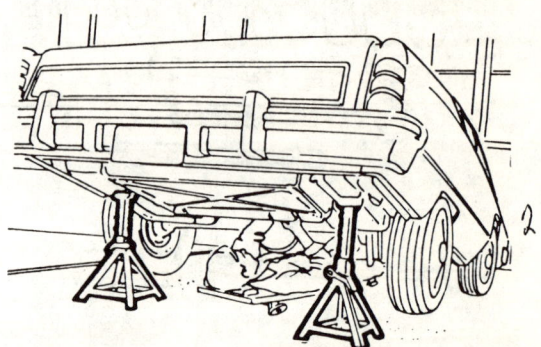

Always support the car on jackstands when working underneath it

• Do use adequate ventilation when working with any chemicals or hazardous materials. Like carbon monoxide, the asbestos dust resulting from brake lining wear can be poisonous in sufficient quantities.
• Do disconnect the negative battery cable when working on the electrical system. The secondary ignition system can contain up to 40,000 volts.
• Do follow manufactuer's directions whenever working with potentially hazardous materials. Both brake fluid and antifreeze are poisonous if taken internally.
• Do properly maintain your tools. Loose hammerheads, mushroomed punches and chisels, frayed or poorly grounded electrical cords, excessively worn screwdrivers, spread open end wrenches, cracked sockets, slipping ratchets, or faulty droplight sockets can cause accidents.
• Do use the proper size and type of tool for the job being done.
• Do when possible, pull on a wrench handle rather than push on it, and adjust your stance to prevent a fall.
• Do be sure that adjustable wrenches are tightly closed on the nut or bolt and pulled so that the face is on the side of the fixed jaw.
• Do select a wrench or socket that fits the

GENERAL INFORMATION AND MAINTENANCE

nut or bolt. The wrench or socket should sit straight, not cocked.
- Do strike squarely with a hammer; avoid glancing blows.
- Do set the parking brake and block the drive wheels if the work requires the engine running.

Don'ts

- Don't run an engine in a garage or anywhere else without proper ventilation—EVER! Carbon monoxide is poisonous; it takes a long time to leave the human body and you can build up a deadly supply of it in your system by simply breathing in a little every day. You may not realize you are slowly poisoning yourself. Always use power vents, windows, fans or open the garage doors.
- Don't work around moving parts while wearing a necktie or other loose clothing. Short sleeves are much safer than long, loose sleeves; hard-toed shoes with neoprene soles protect your toes and give a better grip on slippery surfaces. Jewelry such as watches, fancy belt buckles, beads or body adornment of any kind is not safe working around a car. Long hair should be hidden under a hat or cap.
- Don't use pockets for toolboxes. A fall or bump can drive a screwdriver deep into your body. Even a wiping cloth hanging from the back pocket can wrap around a spinning shaft or fan.
- Don't smoke when working around gasoline, cleaning solvent or other flammable material.
- Don't smoke when working around the battery. When the battery is being charged, it gives off explosive hydrogen gas.
- Don't use gasoline to wash your hands; there are excellent soaps available. Gasoline may contain lead, and lead can enter the body through a cut, accumulating in the body until you are very ill. Gasoline also removes all the natural oils from the skin so that bone dry hands will suck up oil and grease.
- Don't service the air conditioning system unless you are equipped with the necessary tools and training. The refrigerant, R-12, is extremely cold when compressed, and when released into the air will instantly freeze any surface it contacts, including your eyes. Although the refrigerant is normally non-toxic, R-12 becomes a deadly poisonous gas in the presence of an open flame. One good whiff of the vapors from burning refrigerant can be fatal.

MODEL IDENTIFICATION

NOTE: *Illustrations of the Oldsmobile Starfire and the Buick Skyhawk were not available at the time of publication.*

1982 Cavalier

1982 Cimarron

1982 J2000

SERIAL NUMBER IDENTIFICATION

Vehicle

The vehicle identification number is a seventeen place sequence stamped on a plate attached to the left front of the instrument panel, visable through the windshield.

Body

The body style identification plate is located on the front bar, just behind the right headlamp.

Engine

The engine VIN code is stamped on a pad at the front (right side of car) of the cylinder block, just below the cylinder head.

6 GENERAL INFORMATION AND MAINTENANCE

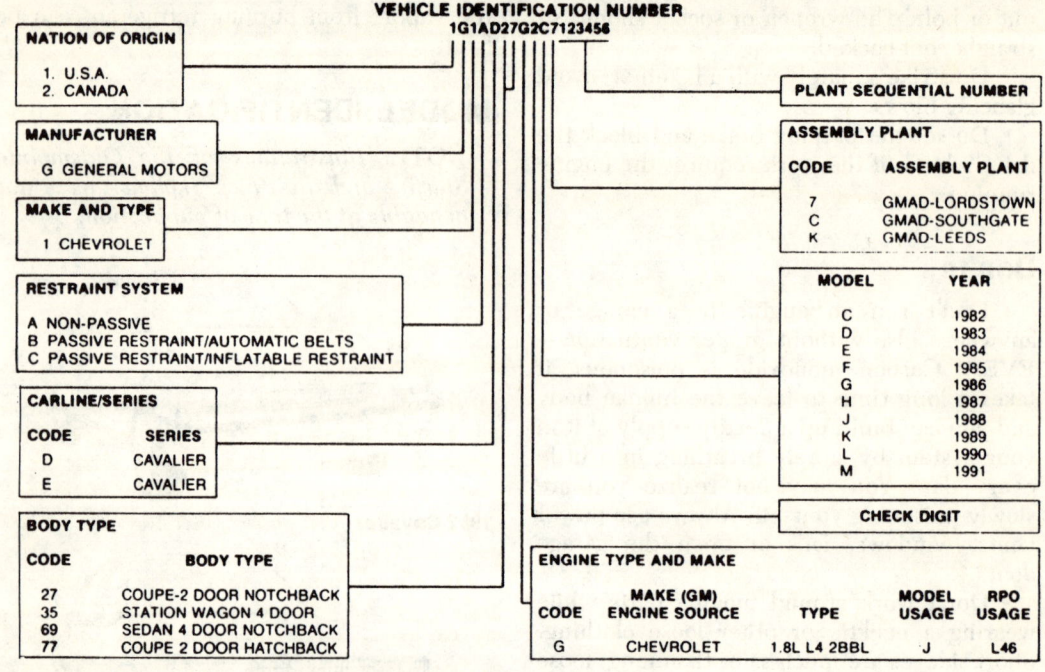

Vehicle identification number

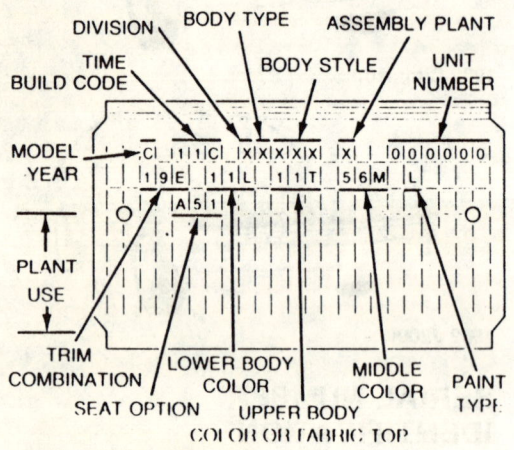

The body identification plate looks like this

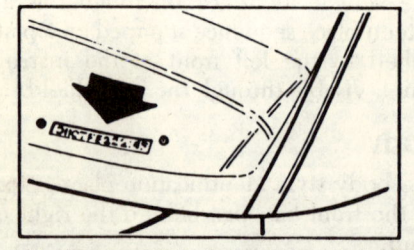

The VIN plate is visible through the windshield

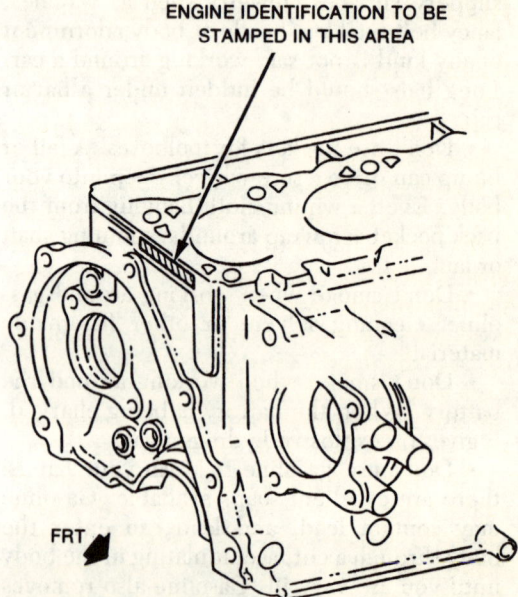

Engine serial number location

Transaxle

The manual transaxle identification number is stamped on a pad on the forward side of the transaxle case, between the upper and middle transaxle-to-engine mounting bolts. The automatic transaxle identification number is stamped on the oil flange pad to the right of the oil dipstick, at the rear of the transaxle. The automatic transaxle model code tag is on top of the case, next to the shift lever.

GENERAL INFORMATION AND MAINTENANCE 7

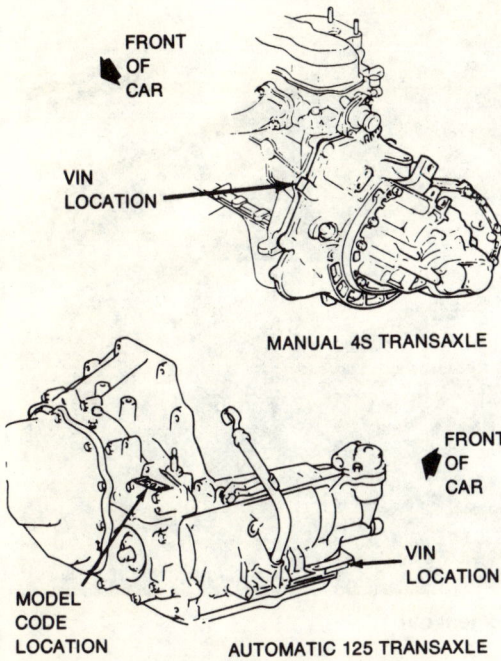

Transaxle serial number and code locations

ROUTINE MAINTENANCE

Routine maintenance is the self-explanatory term used to describe the sort of periodic work necessary to keep a car in safe and reliable working order. A regular program aimed at monitoring essential systems ensures that the car's components are functioning correctly (and will continue to do so until the next inspection, one hopes), and can prevent small problems from developing into major headaches. Routine maintenance also pays off big dividends in keeping major repair costs at a minimum, extending the life of the car, and enchancing resale value, should you ever desire to part with your new J-car.

The J-cars require less in the way of routine maintenance than any cars in recent memory. However, a very definite maintenance schedule is provided by General Motors, and must be followed not only to keep the new car warranty in effect, but also to keep the car working properly. The "Maintenance Intervals" chart in this chapter outlines the routine maintenance which must be performed according to intervals based on either accumulated mileage or time. Your J-car also came with a maintenance schedule provided by G.M. Adherence to these schedules will result in a longer life for your car, and will, over the long run, save you money and time.

The checks and adjustments in the following sections generally require only a few minutes of attention every few weeks; the services to be performed can be easily accomplished in a morning. The most important part of any maintenance program is regularity. The few minutes or occasional morning spent on these seemingly trivial tasks will forestall or eliminate major problems later.

Air cleaner

All the dust present in the air is kept out of the engine by means of the air cleaner filter element. Proper maintenance is vital, as a clogged element not only restricts the airflow, and thus the power, but may also cause premature engine wear.

The filter element should be cleaned at least every 15,000 miles and replaced every 50,000 miles; more often if the car is driven in dry, dusty areas. The condition of the element should be checked periodically; if it appears to be overly dirty or clogged, shake it, if this does not help, the element should be replaced.

NOTE: *The paper element should never be cleaned or soaked with gasoline, cleaning solvent or oil.*

CLEANING OR REPLACING THE FILTER ELEMENT

The air cleaner is located in the center of the engine compartment, on top of the engine.
1. Unscrew the wing nut on top of the air cleaner and then lift off the housing lid.

Unscrew the wingnut and remove the air cleaner housing lid

8 GENERAL INFORMATION AND MAINTENANCE

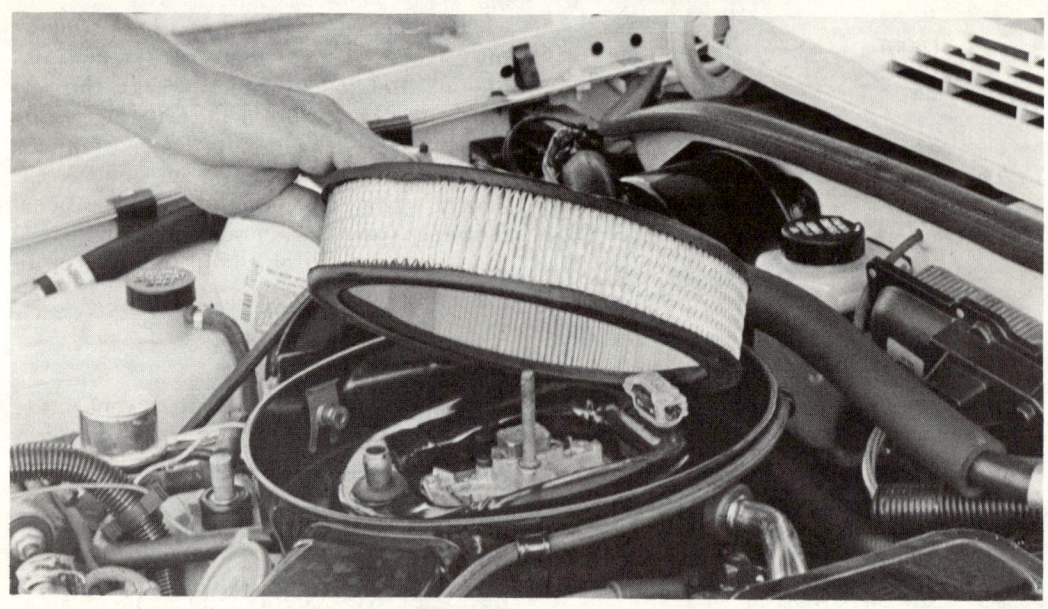

Lift the old filter element out

2. Lift out the filter element and shake the dirt out of it. If it remains clogged, replace it with a new one.

3. Before reinstalling the filter element, wipe out the housing with a damp cloth. Check the lid gasket to ensure that it has a tight seal.

Always wipe out the inside of the housing before installing a new element

4. Position the filter element, replace the lid and tighten the wing nut.

PCV Valve

The Positive Crankcase Ventilation (PCV) valve regulates crankcase ventilation during various engine running conditions. At high vacuum (idle speed and partial load range) it will open slightly and at low vacuum (full throttle) it will open fully. This causes vapors to be drawn from the crankcase by engine vacuum and then sucked into the combustion chamber where they are dissipated.

The PCV valve must be replaced every 30,000 miles. Details on the PCV system, including system tests, are given in Chapter Four.

The valve is located in a rubber grommet in the valve cover, connected to the air cleaner housing by a large diameter rubber hose. To replace the valve:

1. Pull the valve (with the hose attached) from the rubber grommet in the valve cover.
2. Remove the valve from the hose.
3. Install a new valve into the hose.
4. Press the valve back into the rubber grommet in the valve cover.

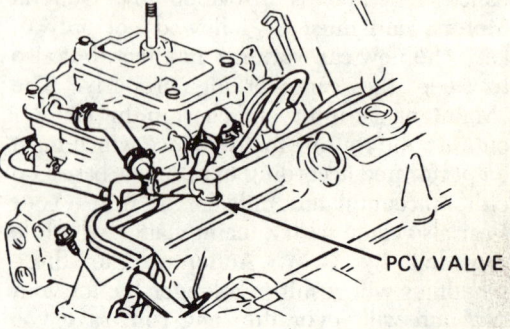

PCV valve

GENERAL INFORMATION AND MAINTENANCE

PCV FILTER

The PCV filter is located in the air cleaner housing and must be replaced every 50,000 miles.

1. Remove the air cleaner housing lid.
2. Slide back the filter retaining clip and remove the old filter.
3. Install the new filter, replace the retaining clip and replace the housing lid.

Evaporative Emissions System

Check the evaporative emission control system every 15,000 miles. Check the fuel vapor lines and the vacuum hoses for proper connections and correct routing, as well as condition. Replace clogged, damaged or deteriorated parts as necessary.

For more details on the evaporative emissions system, please refer to Chapter Four.

Battery

The J-cars have a "maintenance free" battery as standard equipment, eliminating the need for fluid level checks and the possibility of specific gravity tests. Nevertheless, the battery does require some attention.

Once a year, the battery terminals and the cable clamps should be cleaned. Remove the side terminal bolts and the cables and the battery terminals with a wire brush until all corrosion, grease, etc. is removed and the metal is shiny. It is especially important to clean the inside of the clamp thoroughly, since a small deposit of foreign material or oxidation there will prevent a sound electrical connection and inhibit either starting or charging. Special tools are available for cleaning the side terminal clamps and terminals.

Before installing the cables, loosen the battery hold-down clamp, remove the battery, and check the battery tray. Clear it of any debris and check it for soundness. Rust should be wire brushed away, and the metal given a coat of anti-rust paint. Replace the battery and tighten the hold-down clamp securely, but be careful not to overtighten, which will crack the battery case.

After the clamps and terminals are clean, reinstall the cables, negative cables last. Give the clamps and terminals a thin external coat of grease after installation, to retard corrosion.

Check the cables at the same time that the terminals are cleaned. If the cable insulation is cracked or broken, or if the ends are frayed, the cable should be replaced with a new cable of the same length and gauge.

NOTE: *Keep flame or sparks away from the battery; it gives off explosive hydrogen gas. Battery electrolyte contains sulphuric acid. If you should get any on your skin or in your eyes, flush the affected areas with plenty of clear water; if it lands in your eyes, get medical help immediately.*

Drive Belts

BELT TENSION

Every 12 months or 15,000 miles, check the water pump, alternator, power steering pump (if so equipped), and air conditioning compressor (if so equipped) drive belts for proper tension. Also look for signs of wear, fraying, separation, glazing and so on, and replace the belts as required.

Belt tension should be checked with a gauge made for the purpose. If a gauge is not available, tension can be checked with moderate thumb pressure applied to the belt at its longest span midway between pulleys. If the belt has a free span less than twelve

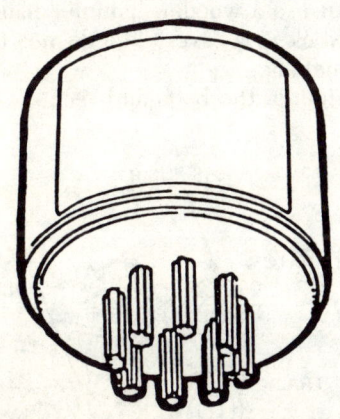

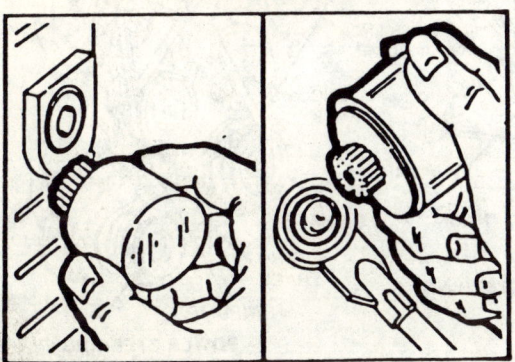

A special tool is available for cleaning the side terminals and clamps

10 GENERAL INFORMATION AND MAINTENANCE

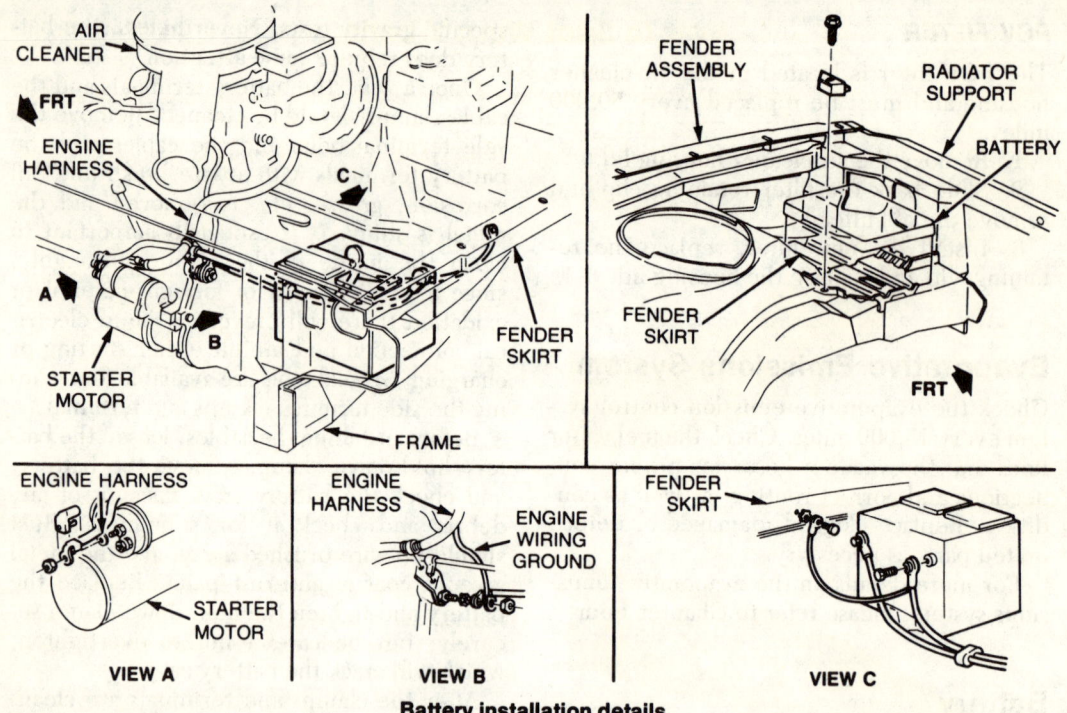

Battery installation details

inches, it should deflect approximately ⅛–¼ inch. If the span is longer than twelve inches, deflection can range between ⅛ and ⅜ inches.

1. Loosen the driven accessory's pivot and mounting bolts.

2. Move the accessory toward or away from the engine until the tension is correct. You can use a wooden hammer handle or a broomstick as a lever, but do not use anything metallic.

3. Tighten the bolts and recheck the ten-

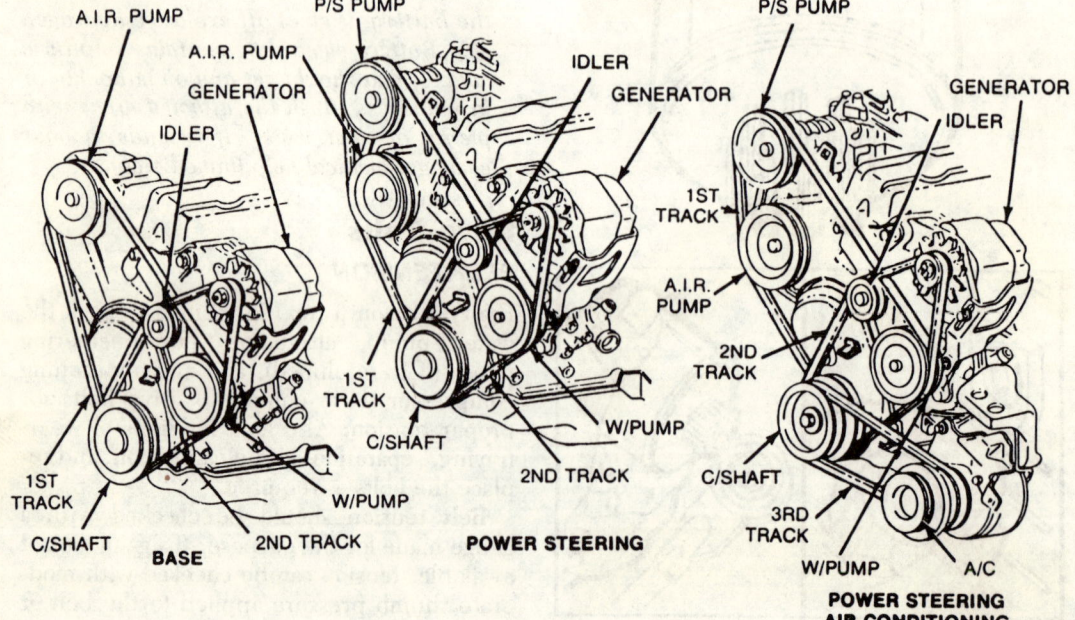

Drive belt and pulley diagram

GENERAL INFORMATION AND MAINTENANCE

How to Spot Worn V-belts

V-Belts are vital to efficient engine operation—they drive the fan, water pump and other accessories. They require little maintenance (occasional tightening) but they will not last forever. Slipping or failure of the V-belt will lead to overheating. If your V-belt looks like any of these, it should be replaced.

Cracking or weathering

This belt has deep cracks, which cause it to flex. Too much flexing leads to heat build-up and premature failure. These cracks can be caused by using the belt on a pulley that is too small. Notched belts are available for small diameter pulleys.

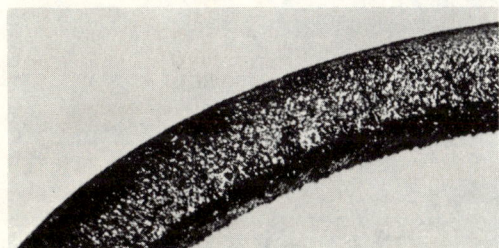

Softening (grease and oil)

Oil and grease on a belt can cause the belt's rubber compounds to soften and separate from the reinforcing cords that hold the belt together. The belt will first slip, then finally fail altogether.

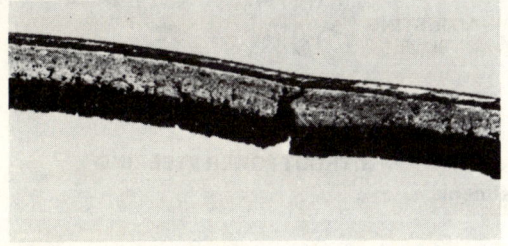

Glazing

Glazing is caused by a belt that is slipping. A slipping belt can cause a run-down battery, erratic power steering, overheating or poor accessory performance. The more the belt slips, the more glazing will be built up on the surface of the belt. The more the belt is glazed, the more it will slip. If the glazing is light, tighten the belt.

Worn cover

The cover of this belt is worn off and is peeling away. The reinforcing cords will begin to wear and the belt will shortly break. When the belt cover wears in spots or has a rough jagged appearance, check the pulley grooves for roughness.

Separation

This belt is on the verge of breaking and leaving you stranded. The layers of the belt are separating and the reinforcing cords are exposed. It's just a matter of time before it breaks completely.

12 GENERAL INFORMATION AND MAINTENANCE

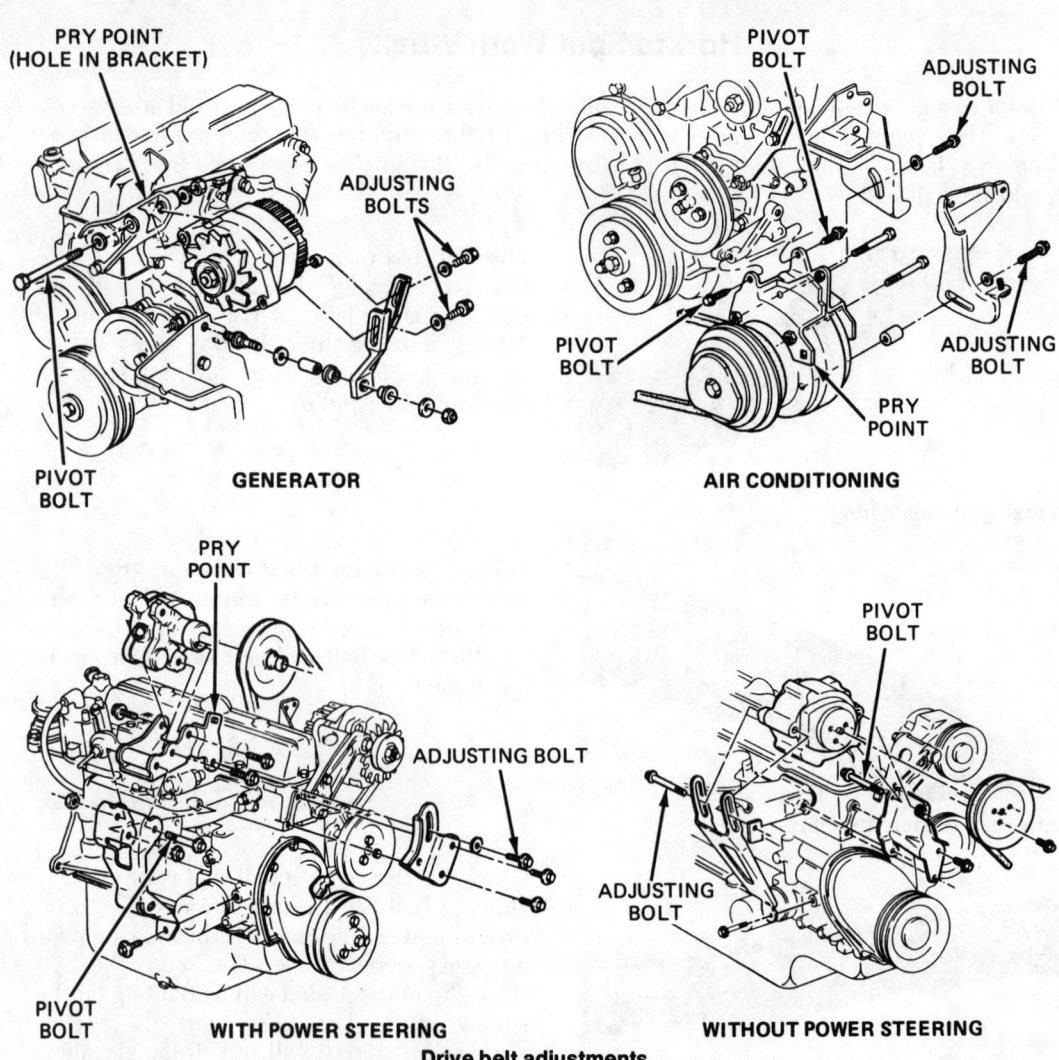

Drive belt adjustments

Engine	Tensioning	Generator	Power Steering	Air Conditioning	A.I.R. Pump
L-4	New Used	146LB(650N) 67LB(300N)	146LB(650N) 67LB(300N)	168LB(750N) 90LB(400N)	146LB(650N) 67LB(300N)

When adjusting a belt with a gauge, tension to these specifications

sion. If new belts have been installed, run the engine for a few minutes, then recheck and readjust as necessary.

It is better to have belts too loose than too tight, because overtight belts will lead to bearing failure, particularly in the water pump and alternator. However, loose belts place an extremely high impact load on the driven component due to the whipping action of the belt.

Hoses

Upper and lower radiator hoses and all heater hoses should be checked for deterioration, leaks and loose hose clamps every 15,000 miles. To remove the hoses:

1. Drain the radiator as detailed later in this chapter.
2. Loosen the hose clamps at each end of the hose to be removed.

GENERAL INFORMATION AND MAINTENANCE

3. Working the hose back and forth, slide it off its connection and then install a new hose if necessary.

4. Position the hose clamps at least ¼ in. from the end of the hose and tighten them.

NOTE: *Always make sure that the hose clamps are beyond the bead and placed in the center of the clamping surface before tightening them.*

Cooling System

Once a month, the engine coolant level should be checked. This is quickly accomplished by observing the level of coolant in the recovery tank, which is the translucent tank mounted to the right of the radiator, and connected to the radiator filler neck by a length of hose. As long as coolant is visible in the tank between the "Full Cold" and "Full Hot" marks the coolant level is OK.

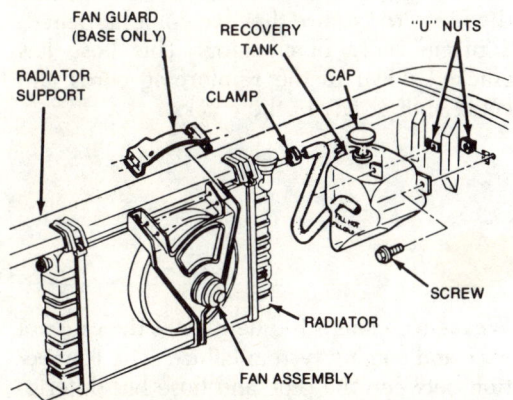

The coolant recovery tank is at the right front of the engine compartment

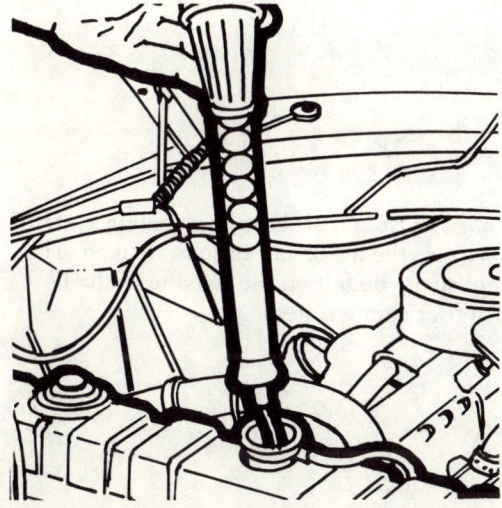

You can use an inexpensive tester to check antifreeze protection

If coolant is needed, a 50/50 mix of ethylene glycol-base antifreeze and clear water should always be used for additions, both winter and summer. This is imperative on cars with air conditioning; without the antifreeze, the heater core could freeze when the air conditioning is used. Add coolant to the recovery tank through the capped opening; make additions only when the engine is cool.

The radiator hoses, clamps, and radiator cap should be checked at the same time as the coolant level. Hoses which are brittle, cracked, or swollen should be replaced. Clamps should be checked for tightness (screwdriver tight only—do not allow the clamp to cut into the hose or crush the fitting). The radiator cap gasket should be checked for any obvious tears, cracks or swelling, or any signs of incorrect seating in the radiator neck.

CAUTION: *To avoid injury when working with a hot engine, cover the radiator cap with a thick cloth. Wear a heavy glove to protect your hand. Turn the radiator cap slowly to the first stop, and allow all the pressure to vent (indicated when the hissing noise stops). When the pressure has been released, press down and remove the cap the rest of the way.*

The cooling system should be drained, flushed and refilled every two years or 30,000 miles, according to the manufacturer's recommendations. However, many mechanics prefer to change the coolant every year; it is cheap insurance against corrosion, overheating or freezing.

1. Remove the radiator cap when the engine is cool. See the preceding "CAUTION" about removing the cap.

2. With the radiator cap removed, run the engine until heat can be felt in the upper hose, indicating that the thermostat is open.

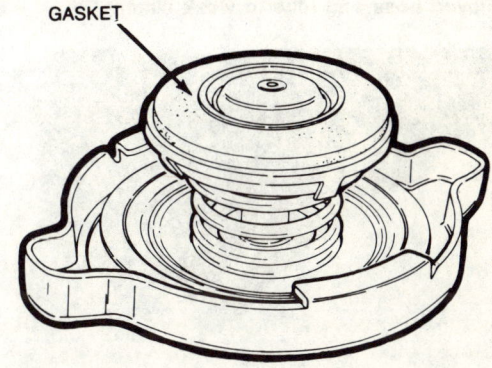

Check the condition of the radiator cap gasket

GENERAL INFORMATION AND MAINTENANCE

How to Spot Bad Hoses

Both the upper and lower radiator hoses are called upon to perform difficult jobs in an inhospitable environment. They are subject to nearly 18 psi at under hood temperatures often over 280°F., and must circulate nearly 7500 gallons of coolant an hour—3 good reasons to have good hoses.

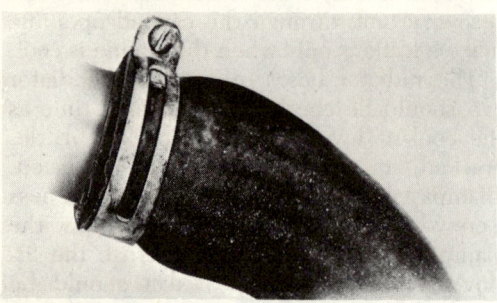

Swollen hose

A good test for any hose is to feel it for soft or spongy spots. Frequently these will appear as swollen areas of the hose. The most likely cause is oil soaking. This hose could burst at any time, when hot or under pressure.

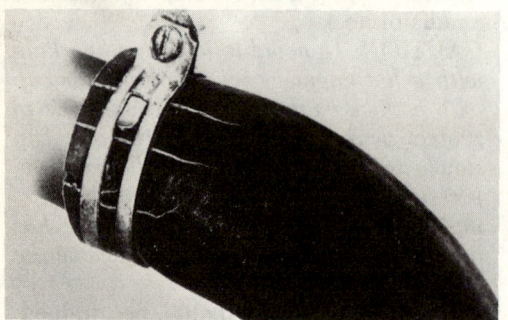

Cracked hose

Cracked hoses can usually be seen but feel the hoses to be sure they have not hardened; a prime cause of cracking. This hose has cracked down to the reinforcing cords and could split at any of the cracks.

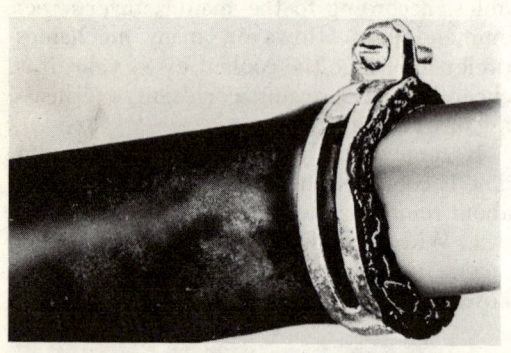

Frayed hose end (due to weak clamp)

Weakened clamps frequently are the cause of hose and cooling system failure. The connection between the pipe and hose has deteriorated enough to allow coolant to escape when the engine is hot.

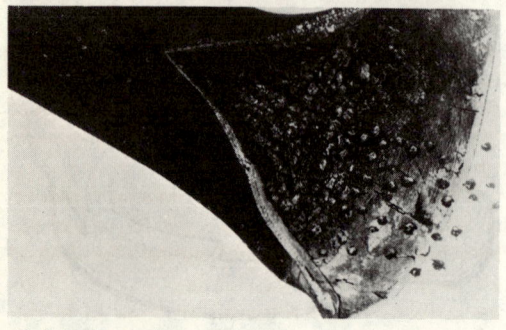

Debris in cooling system

Debris, rust and scale in the cooling system can cause the inside of a hose to weaken. This can usually be felt on the outside of the hose as soft or thinner areas.

GENERAL INFORMATION AND MAINTENANCE

The heater should be turned on to its maximum heat position, so that the core is flushed out.

3. Shut off the engine and open the drain cock in the bottom of the radiator. Drain the radiator.

4. Close the drain cock and fill the system with clear water. A cooling system flushing additive can be added, if desired.

5. Run the engine until it is hot again.

6. Drain the system, then flush with water until it runs clear.

7. Clean out the coolant recovery tank: remove the cap leaving the hoses in place. Remove the tank and drain it of any coolant. Clean it out with soap and water, empty it, and install it.

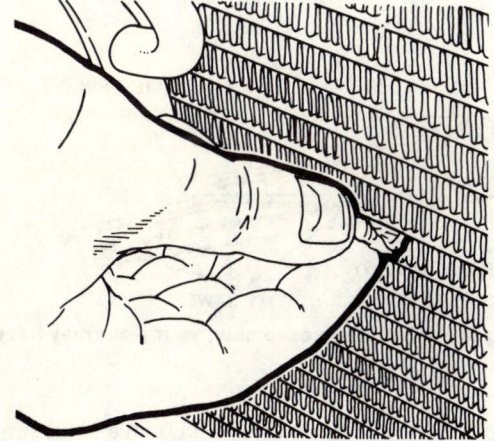

Clean the front of the radiator of any bugs, leaves, or other debris at every yearly coolant change

8. Close the drain cock and fill the radiator with a 50/50 mix of ethylene glycol-base antifreeze and water to the base of the radiator filler neck. Fill the coolant recovery tank with the same mixture to the "Full Hot" mark. Install the recovery tank cap.

9. Run the engine until the upper radiator hose is hot again (radiator cap still off). With the engine idling, add the 50/50 mix of antifreeze and water to the radiator until the level reaches the bottom of the filler neck. Shut off the engine and install the radiator cap, aligning the arrows with the overflow tube. Turn off the heater.

Air Conditioning System

The air conditioning system requires no routine maintenance, except for periodic belt tension adjustment, as outlined previously. The air conditioning system should be operated for about five minutes each week, even in winter. This will circulate lubricating oil within the system to prevent the various seals from drying out.

The factory-installed air conditioning unit has no sight glass for system checks. It is recommended that all air conditioning service work be entrusted to a qualified mechanic. The system is a potentially hazardous one.

CAUTION: *Do not attempt to charge or discharge the refrigerant system unless you are thoroughly familiar with its operation and the hazards involved. The compressed refrigerant used in the air conditioning system expands and evaporates (boils) into the atmosphere at a temperature of $-21.7°F$ ($-29.8°C$) or less. This will freeze any surface that it contacts, including your eyes. In addition, the refrigerant decomposes into a poisonous gas in the presence of flame.*

Windshield Wipers

For maximum effectiveness and longest element life, the windshield and wiper blades should be kept clean. Dirt, tree sap, road tar and so on will cause streaking, smearing and blade deterioration if left on the glass. It is advisable to wash the windshield carefully with a commercial glass cleaner at least once a month. Wipe off the rubber blades with the wet rag afterwards.

If the blades are found to be cracked, broken or torn, they should be replaced immediately. Replacement intervals will vary with usage, although ozone deterioration usually limits blade life to about one year. If the wiper pattern is smeared or streaked, or if the blade chatters across the glass, the elements should be replaced. It is easiest and most sensible to replace the elements in pairs.

The wiper blades are retained to the wiper arms by one of two methods. One uses a press-type release tab, which, when depressed, allows the blade to be separated from the arm. The other uses a coil spring retainer. By inserting a screwdriver on top of the spring and pressing downward, the blade can be separated from the arm.

The rubber wiper element can be replaced separately from the blade, which is usually less expensive than replacing both blade and element. As with the blades, two methods are used to retain the rubber element to the blade. On one, a press-type button is used

16 GENERAL INFORMATION AND MAINTENANCE

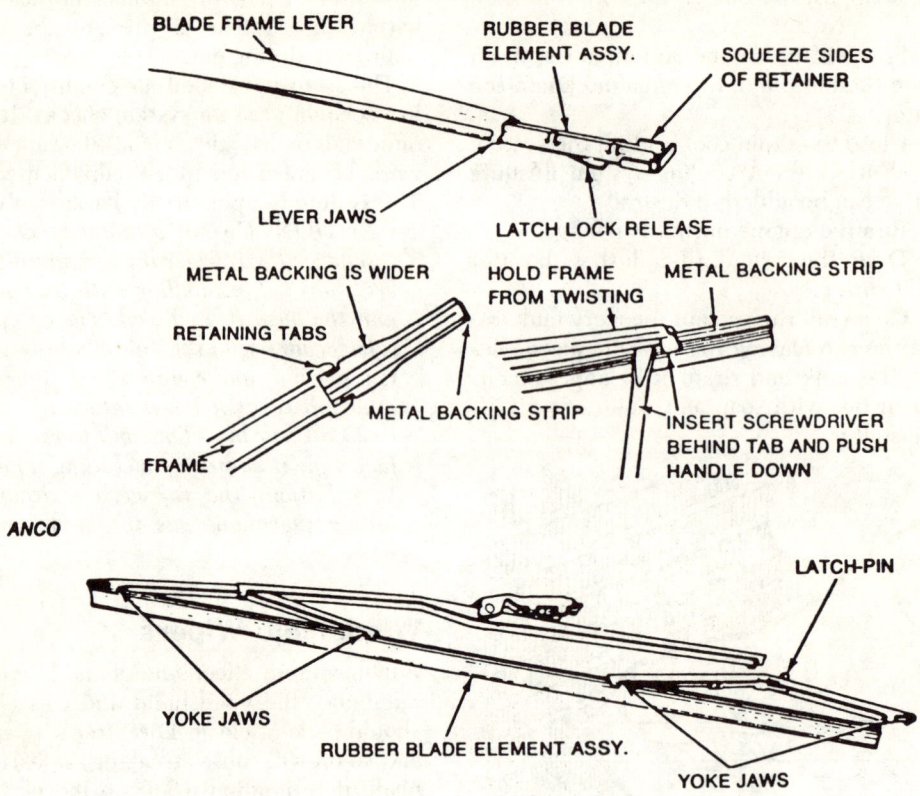

The rubber element can be changed without replacing the entire blade assembly; your J-car may have either one of these types of blades

which, when depressed, releases the element, which can be slid off the blade. On the other, a squeeze clip is used; squeezing the clip allows the element to be pulled from the blade. Replacements are simply slid back into place; be sure all the arms are engaged.

Fluid Level Checks
ENGINE OIL

The engine oil level should be checked at every fuel stop, or once a week, whichever occurs more regularly. The best time to check is when the engine is warm, although checking immediately after the engine has been shut off will result in an inaccurate reading, since it takes a few minutes for all of the oil to drain back down into the crankcase. If the engine is cold, the engine should not be run before the level is checked. The oil level is checked by means of a dipstick, located at the front of the engine compartment:

1. If the engine is warm, it should be allowed to sit for a few minutes after being shut off to allow the oil to drain down into the oil pan. The car should be parked on a level surface.

2. Pull the dipstick out from its holder, wipe it clean with a rag, and reinsert it firmly. Be sure it is pushed all the way home,

Oil dipstick location

GENERAL INFORMATION AND MAINTENANCE

The oil level on the dipstick must always be above the 'ADD' line. 1 quart will raise the level from the 'ADD' line to the 'FULL' line

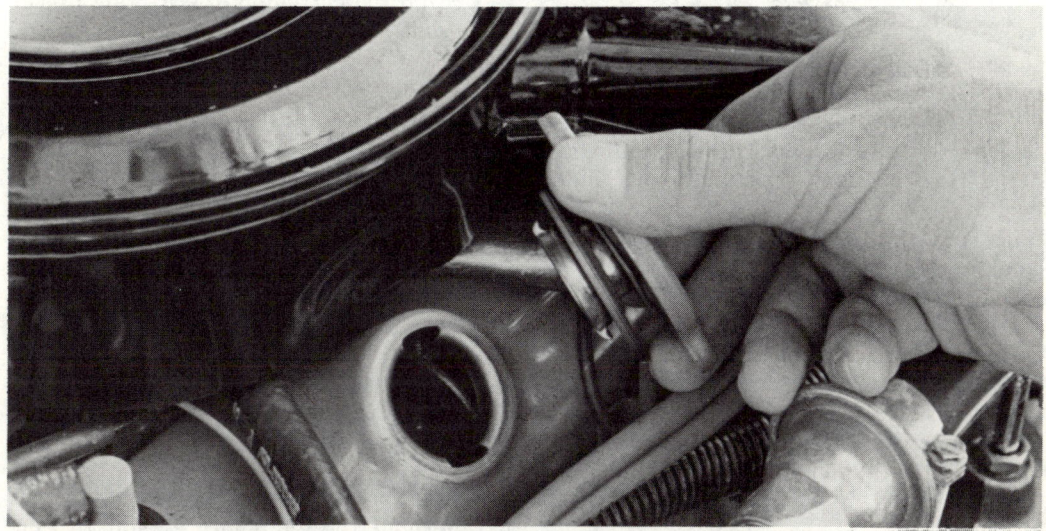

Add oil through the capped filler hole in the cylinder head cover

or the reading you're about to take will be incorrect.

3. Pull the dipstick again and hold it horizontally to prevent the oil from running. The dipstick is marked with "Add" and "Full" lines. The oil level should be above the "Add" line.

4. Reinstall the dipstick.

If oil is needed, it is added through the capped opening in the cylinder head cover. One quart of oil will raise the level from "Add" to "Full." Only oils labeled "SF" should be used; select a viscosity that will be compatible with the temperatures expected until the next drain interval. See the "Oil and Fuel Recommendations" section later in this chapter if you are not sure what type of oil to use. Check the oil level again after any additions. Be careful not to overfill, which will lead to leakage and seal damage.

TRANSAXLE
Manual

The fluid level in the manual transaxle should be checked every 12 months or 7,500 miles, whichever comes first.

NOTE: *Certain models may be equipped with a dipstick for checking the fluid level. If so, remove the dipstick when the transaxle is cold and check the level.*

1. Park the car on a level surface. The transaxle should be cool to the touch. If it is hot, check the level later, when it has cooled.

2. Slowly remove the filler hole plug from

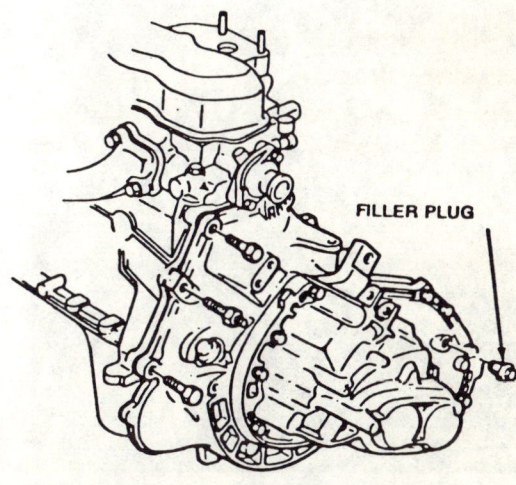

Some models use a filler plug to check the level of the manual transaxle lubricant

18 GENERAL INFORMATION AND MAINTENANCE

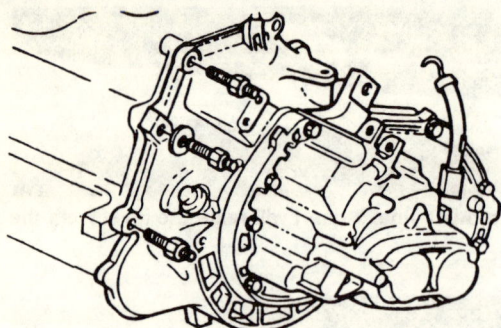

Some models use a dipstick to check the level of the manual transaxle lubricant

the left side of the transaxle. If lubricant trickles out as the plug is removed, the fluid level is correct. If not, stick in your finger (watch out for sharp threads); the lubricant should be right up to the edge of the filler hole.

3. If lubricant is needed, add DEXRON® II automatic transmission fluid until the level is correct. The use of a manual transmission lubricant is specifically *not* recommended.

4. When the level is correct, install the filler plug and tighten until snug.

Automatic

The fluid level in the automatic transaxle should be checked every 12 months or 7,500

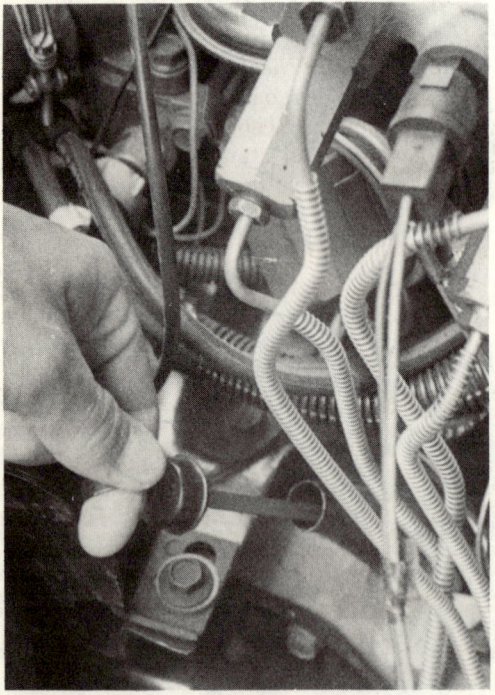

Automatic transaxle fluid dipstick and filler tube location

miles, whichever comes first. The transaxle has a dipstick for fluid level checks.

1. Drive the car until it is at normal operating temperature. The level should not be checked immediately after the car has been driven for a long time at high speed, or in city traffic in hot weather; in those cases, the transaxle should be given a half hour to cool down.

2. Stop the car, apply the parking brake, then shift slowly through all gear positions, ending in Park. Let the engine idle for about five minutes with the selector in Park. The car should be on a level surface.

3. With the engine still running, remove the dipstick, wipe it clean, then reinsert it, pushing it fully home.

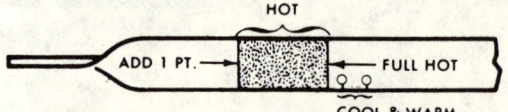

Automatic transaxle dipstick markings

4. Pull the dipstick again and, holding it horizontally, read the fluid level.

5. Cautiously feel the end of the dipstick to determine the temperature. Note that on the J-cars the cool and warm level dimples are above the hot level area. If the fluid level is not in the correct area, more will have to be added.

6. Fluid is added through the dipstick tube. You will probably need the aid of a spout or a long-necked funnel. Be sure that whatever you pour through is perfectly clean and dry. Use an automatic transmission fluid marked "DEXRON® II." Add fluid slowly, and in small amounts, checking the level frequently between additions. Do not overfill, which will cause foaming, fluid loss, slippage, and possible transaxle damage. It takes only one pint to raise the level from "Add" to "Full" when the transaxle is hot.

BRAKE FLUID

Once a month, the fluid level in the brake master cylinder should be checked.

1. Park the car on a level surface.
2. Clean off the master cylinder cover before removal.
3. The cover simply snaps onto the master cylinder body. Use your thumbs to press up on the two tabs on the side of the cover to unsnap it. Remove the cover, being careful not to drop or tear the rubber diaphragm underneath. Be careful also not to drip any

GENERAL INFORMATION AND MAINTENANCE

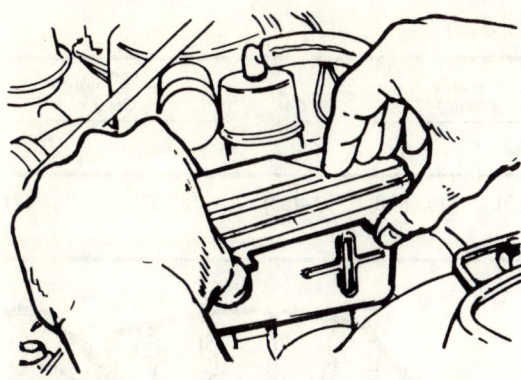

Use thumb pressure to remove the brake master cylinder cover

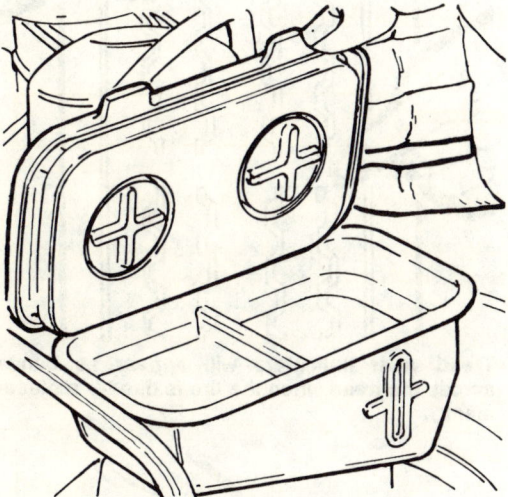

The proper brake fluid level is approximately ¼ in. below the lip of master cylinder

brake fluid on painted surfaces; the stuff eats paint.

NOTE: *Brake fluid absorbs moisture from the air, which reduces effectiveness, and will corrode brake parts once in the system. Never leave the master cylinder or the brake fluid container uncovered for any longer than necessary.*

4. The fluid level should be about ¼ inch below the lip of the master cylinder well.

5. If fluid addition is necessary, use only extra heavy duty disc brake fluid meeting DOT 3 specifications. The fluid should be reasonably fresh because brake fluid deteriorates with age.

6. Replace the cover, making sure that the diaphragm is correctly seated.

If the brake fluid level is constantly low, the system should be checked for leaks. However, it is normal for the fluid level to fall gradually as the disc brake pads wear; expect the fluid level to drop not more than ⅛ inch for every 10,000 miles of wear.

STEERING GEAR

The rack and pinion steering gear used on the J-cars is a sealed unit; no fluid level checks or additions are ever necessary.

POWER STEERING FLUID

The power steering hydraulic fluid reservoir is attached to the firewall at the back of the engine compartment. It is a translucent plastic container with fluid level markings on the outside. Check the fluid level every 12 months or 7,500 miles, whichever comes first. If the level is low, add power steering fluid until it is correct. Be careful not to overfill as this will cause fluid loss and seal damage.

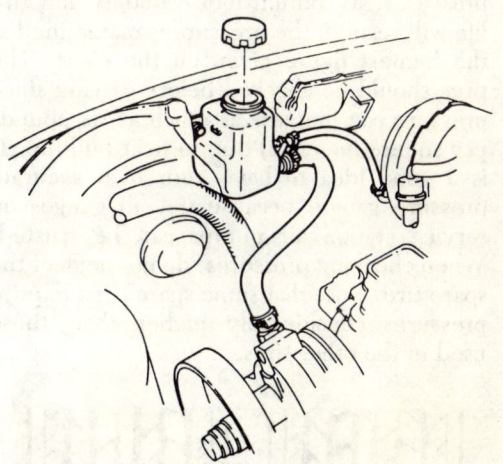

The power steering pump reservoir is located at the back of the engine compartment

COOLANT LEVEL

Coolant level checks are covered earlier in this chapter, under "Cooling System." Check the coolant level every month.

BATTERY

The J-cars have a "Maintenance Free" battery which does not require periodic additions of water thus eliminating fluid level checks. See the "Battery" section earlier in this chapter for regular maintenance.

WINDSHIELD WASHER FLUID

Check the fluid level in the windshield washer tank at every oil level check. The fluid can be mixed in a 50% solution with water, if desired, as long as temperatures re-

20 GENERAL INFORMATION AND MAINTENANCE

Capacities

Year	Engine Displacement Cu In. (cc)	Crankcase Quarts (Liters) w/filter	Crankcase Quarts (Liters) wo/filter	Transaxle Pints(L) 4 speed	Transaxle Pints(L) Auto	Gas Tank Gal (L)	Cooling System Qts (L) w/heater	Cooling System Qts (L) w/AC
1982	112 (1840)	4.0(3.8)	4.0(3.8)	5.9(2.8)	10.5(5.0)	14(53)	8.0(7.57)	8.0(7.57)

main above freezing. Below freezing, the fluid should be used full strength. Never add engine coolant antifreeze to the washer fluid, because it will damage the car's paint.

Tires

Tires should be checked weekly for proper air pressure. A chart, located at the left front door edge, gives the recommended inflation pressures. Maximum fuel economy and tire life will result if the pressure is maintained at the highest figure given on the chart. The tires should be checked before driving since pressure can increase as much as six pounds per square inch (psi) due to heat buildup. It is a good idea to have your own accurate pressure gauge, because not all gauges on service station air pumps can be trusted. When checking pressures, do not neglect the spare tire. Note that some spare tires require pressures considerably higher than those used in the other tires.

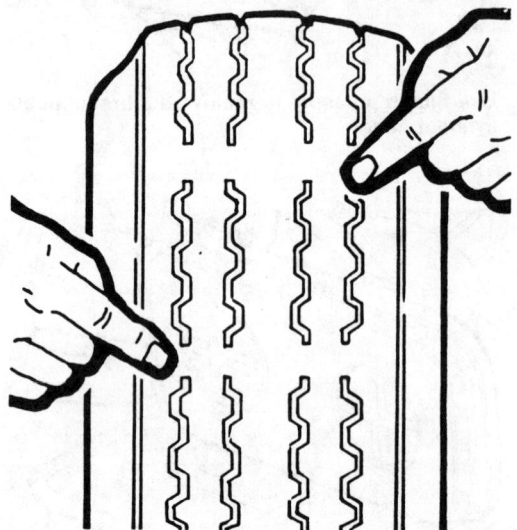

Tread wear indicators will appear as bands across the tread when the tire is due for replacement

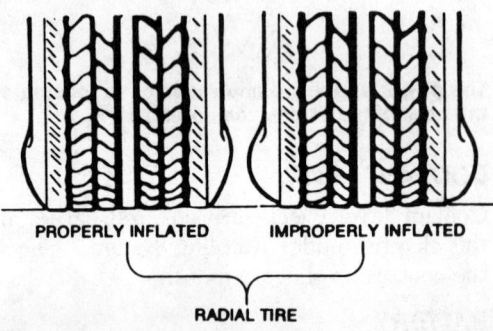

Don't judge a radial tire's pressure by its appearance. An improperly inflated radial tire looks similar to a properly inflated one

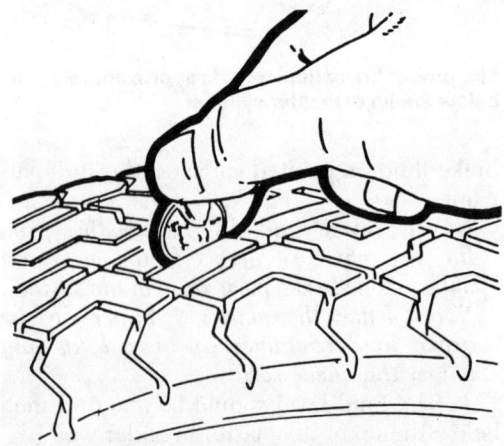

You can use a penny for tread wear checks; if the top of Lincoln's head is visible in two adjacent grooves, the tire should be replaced

While you are about the task of checking air pressure, inspect the tire treads for cuts, bruises, and other damage. Check the air valves to be sure that they are tight. Replace any missing valve caps.

Check the tires for uneven wear that might indicate the need for front end alignment or tire rotation. Tires should be replaced when a tread wear indicator appears as a solid band across the tread.

When buying new tires, give some thought to the following points, especially if you are considering a switch to larger tires or a different profile series:

GENERAL INFORMATION AND MAINTENANCE

1. All four tires should be of the same construction type. Radial, bias, or bias-belted tires must not be mixed.
2. The wheels must be the correct width for the tire. Tire dealers have charts of tire and wheel rim compatibility. A mismatch can cause sloppy handling and rapid tread wear. The tread width should match the rim width (inside bead to inside bead) within an inch. For radial tires, the rim width should be 80% or less of the tire (not tread) width.
3. The height (mounted diameter) of the new tires can change speedometer accuracy, engine speed per given road speed, fuel mileage, acceleration, and ground clearance. Tire manufacturers furnish full measurement specifications.
4. The spare tire should be usable, at least for low speed operation, with the new tires.
5. There shouldn't be any body interference when the car is loaded, on bumps or in turning.

All of these problems can be avoided by replacing the tires with new ones of the same type and size. The P-metric radials installed as standard equipment on the J-cars are particularly fuel-efficient; you can expect some reduction on fuel mileage if, when they wear out, they are replaced with conventional radials, or tires of other construction types. One other thing to remember when buying new tires: always have the dealer install new valve stems. Few things are more aggravating than having a new tire go flat because of an old, leaky valve stem.

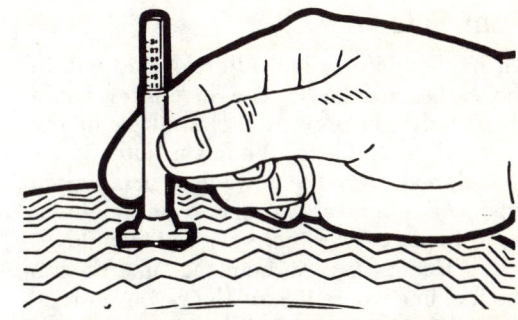

Inexpensive gauges are also available for measurement of tread wear

TIRE ROTATION

Tire rotation is recommended every 7,500 miles or so, to obtain maximum tire wear. The pattern you use depends on whether or not your car has a usable spare. Radial tires should not be cross-switched (from one side of the car to the other); they last longer if their direction of rotation is not changed. Snow tires sometimes have directional arrows molded into the side of the carcass; the arrow shows the direction of rotation. They will wear very rapidly if their rotation is reversed. Studded tires will lose their studs if their rotational direction is reversed. Mark the wheel position or direction of rotation on radial tires or studded snow tires before removing them to avoid these problems.

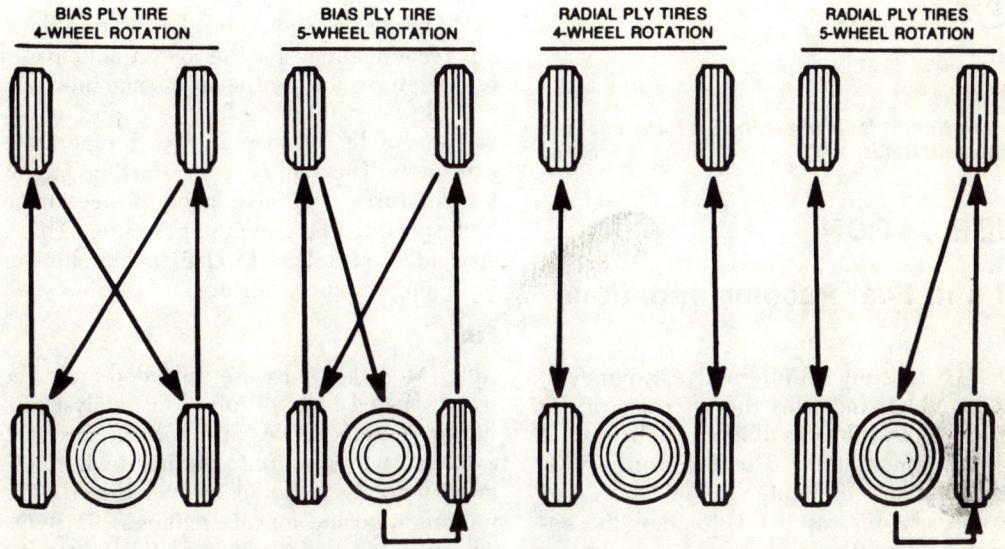

Tire rotation diagrams; radials must never be cross switched

22 GENERAL INFORMATION AND MAINTENANCE

Fuel Filter

All models have a fuel filter located within the carburetor body. The fuel filter has a check valve to prevent fuel spillage in the event of an accident. When the filter is replaced, make sure the new one is of the same type. All filters are of the paper element type. Replace the filter every 15,000 miles.

1. Place a few absorbent rags underneath the fuel line where it joins the carburetor.
2. Disconnect the fuel line connection at the fuel inlet nut.
3. Unscrew the fuel inlet nut from the carburetor. As the nut is removed, the filter will be pushed partway out by spring pressure.
4. Remove the filter and spring.
5. Install the new spring and filter. The hole in the filter faces the nut.
6. Install a new gasket on the inlet nut and install the nut into the carburetor. Tighten securely.
7. Install the fuel line. Tighten the connector to 18 ft. lbs. (24 Nm.) while holding the inlet nut with a wrench.
8. Start the engine and check for leaks.

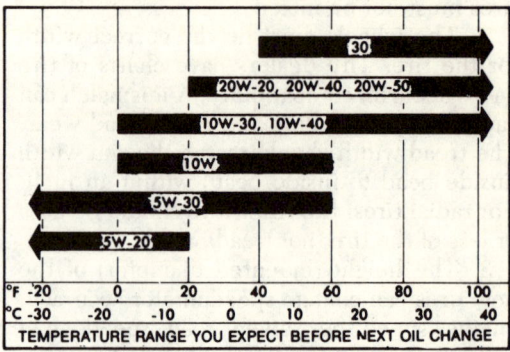

Oil viscosity chart; multi-viscosity oils offer greater temperature latitude

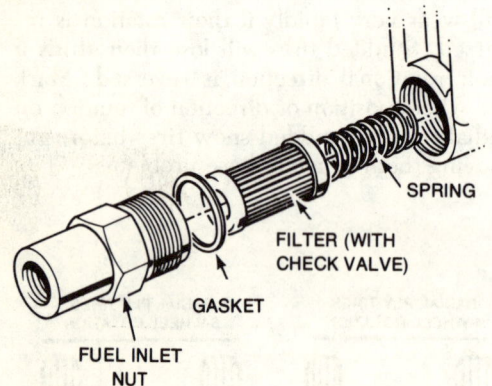

The fuel filter is located behind the large inlet nut on the carburetor

LUBRICATION

Oil and Fuel Recommendations

OIL

The SAE (Society of Automotive Engineers) grade number indicates the viscosity of the engine oil, and thus its ability to lubricate at a given temperature. The lower the SAE grade number, the lighter the oil; the lower the viscosity, the easier it is to crank the engine in cold weather.

The API (American Petroleum Institute) designation indicates the classification of engine oil for use under given operating conditions. Only oils designated for use "Service SF" should be used. Oils of the SF type perform a variety of functions inside the engine in addition to the basic function as a lubricant. Through a balanced system of metallic detergents and polymeric dispersants, the oil prevents the formation of high and low temperature deposits, and also keeps sludge and dirt particles in suspension. Acids, particularly sulfuric acid, as well as other byproducts of combustion, are neutralized. Both the SAE grade number and the API designation can be found on the top of the oil can.

NOTE: *Non-detergent or straight mineral oils must never by used.*

Oil viscosities should be chosen from those oils recommended for the lowest anticipated temperatures during the oil change interval.

Multi-viscosity oils offer the important advantage of being adaptable to temperature extremes. They allow easy starting at low temperatures, yet give good protection at high speeds and engine temperatures. This is a decided advantage in changeable climates or in long distance touring.

FUEL

All G.M. J-cars must use unleaded fuel. The use of leaded fuel will plug the catalyst rendering it inoperative, and will increase the exhaust back pressure to the point where engine output will be severely reduced. The minimum octane for all engines is 91 RON. All unleaded fuels sold in the U.S. are required to meet this minimum octane rating.

GENERAL INFORMATION AND MAINTENANCE

Maintenance Intervals Chart

Intervals are for number of months or thousands of miles, whichever comes first.
NOTE: *Heavy-duty operation (trailer towing, prolonged idling, severe stop and start driving) should be accompanied by a 50% increase in maintenance. Cut the interval in half for these conditions.*

Maintenance	Service Interval
Air cleaner (Replace)	30,000 mi. (48,000 km.)
PCV filter element (Replace)	50,000 mi. (48,000 km.)
PCV valve (Replace)	30,000 mi. (48,000 km.)
Power steering (Check)	12 mo/7,500 mi. (12,000 km.)
Belt tension (Adjust)	12 mo/15,000 mi. (24,000 km.)
Engine oil and filter (Change)	12 mo/7,500 mi. (12,000 km.)
Fuel filter (Change)	15,000 mi. (24,000 km.)

Manual transaxle
  Check
  Change
	
	12 mo/7,500 mi. (12,000 km.)
	100,000 mi. (160,000 km.)

Automatic transaxle
  Check
  Change (including filter)
	
	12 mo/7,500 mi. (12,000 km.)
	100,000 mi. (160,000 km.)

Engine coolant
  Check
  Change
	
	Weekly
	24 mo/30,000 mi. (24,000 km.)

Chassis lubrication	12 mo/7,500 mi. (12,000 km.)
Rotate tires	7,500 mi. (12,000 km.)
Brake fluid (Check)	12 mo/7,500 mi. (12,000 km.)
Spark plugs and wires, ignition timing, idle speed	30,000 mi. (48,000 km.) See Chapter Two

Use of a fuel too low in octane (a measurement of anti-knock quality) will result in spark knock. Since many factors affect operating efficiency, such as altitude, terrain, and air temperature and humidity, knocking may result even though the recommended fuel is being used. If persistent knocking occurs, it may be necessary to switch to a slightly higher grade of unleaded gasoline. Continuous or heavy knocking may result in serious engine damage, for which the manufacturer is not responsible.

NOTE: *Your car's engine fuel requirement can change with time, due to carbon buildup, which changes the compression ratio. If your car's engine knocks, pings, or runs on, switch to a higher grade of fuel, if possible, and check the ignition timing. Sometimes changing brands of gasoline will cure the problem. If it is necessary to*

24 GENERAL INFORMATION AND MAINTENANCE

retard timing from specifications, don't change it more than a few degrees. Retarded timing will reduce power output and fuel mileage, and will increase engine temperature.

Lubricant Changes

ENGINE OIL AND FILTER

If you purchased your J-car new, the engine oil and filter should be changed at the first 7,500 miles or 12 months (whichever comes first), and every 7,500 miles or 12 months thereafter. You should make it a practice to change the oil filter at every oil change; otherwise, a quart of dirty oil remains in the engine every other time the oil is changed. The change interval should be halved when the car is driven under severe conditions, such as in extremely dusty weather, or when the car is used for trailer towing, prolonged high speed driving, or repeated short trips in freezing weather.

1. Drive the car until the engine is at normal operating temperature. A run to the parts store for oil and a filter should accomplish this. If the engine is not hot when the oil is changed, most of the acids and contaminants will remain inside the engine.

2. Shut off the engine, and slide a pan of at least six quarts capacity under the oil pan. Throw-away aluminum roasting pans can be used for this.

3. Remove the drain plug from the engine oil pan, after wiping the plug area clean. The drain plug is the bolt inserted at an angle into the lowest point of the oil pan.

4. The oil from the engine will be HOT. It will probably not be possible to hold onto the drain plug. You may have to let it fall into the pan and fish it out later. Allow all the oil to drain completely. This will take a few minutes.

5. Wipe off the drain plug, removing any

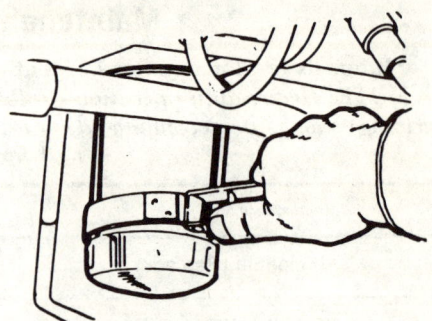

Use an oil filter strap wrench to remove the oil filter; install the new filter by hand

traces of metal particles. Pay particular attention to the threads. Replace it, and tighten it snugly.

6. The oil filter is at the back of the engine. It is impossible to reach from above, and almost as inaccessible from below. It may be easiest to remove the right front wheel and reach through the fender opening to get at the four cylinder oil filter. Use an oil filter strap wrench to loosen the oil filter; these are available at auto parts stores. It is recommended that you purchase one with as thin a strap as possible, to get into tight areas. Place the drain pan on the ground, under the filter. Unscrew and discard the old filter. It will be VERY HOT, so be careful.

7. If the oil filter is on so tightly that it collapses under pressure from the wrench, drive a long punch or a nail through it, across the diameter and as close to the base as possible, and use this as a lever to unscrew it. Make sure you are turning it counterclockwise.

8. Clean off the oil filter mounting surface with a rag. Apply a thin film of clean engine oil to the filter gasket.

9. Screw the filter on by hand until the gasket makes contact. Then tighten it by hand an additional ½ to ¾ of a turn. *Do not overtighten.*

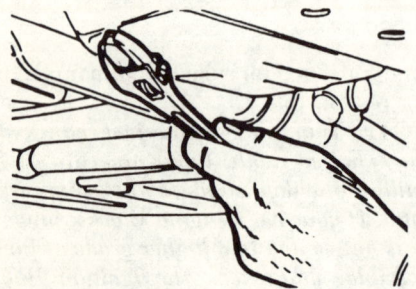

The oil drain plug is located at the lowest point of the oil pan

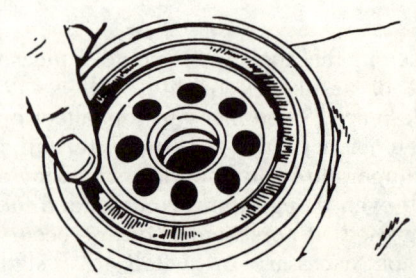

Apply a thin film of clean oil to the new gasket to prevent it from tearing upon installation

Recommended Lubricants

Lubricant	Classification
Engine Oil	SF, SF/CC or SF/CD
Engine Coolant	Mixture of water and a good quality Ethylene Glycol base anti freeze
Brake System and Master Cylinder	DOT 3
Parking Brake Cables	Chassis grease meeting requirements of GM 6031-M
Power Steering System & Pump Reservoir	GM Power Steering Fluid, Part No. 1050017 or equivalent
Manual Steering Gear	Chassis grease meeting requirements of GM 6031-M
Automatic Transaxle	DEXRON® II Automatic Transmission Fluid
Automatic Transaxle Shift Linkage	Engine oil
Manual Transaxle	DEXRON® II Automatic Transmission Fluid
Clutch Linkage Pivot Points	Engine oil
Floor Shift Linkage	Engine oil
Chassis Lubrication	Chassis grease meeting requirements of GM 6031-M
Windshield Washer Solvent	GM Optikleen Washer Solvent, Part No. 1051515 or equivalent
Hood Latch Assembly a. pivots and spring anchor b. release pawl	a. Engine oil b. Chassis grease meeting requirements of GM 6031-M
Hood and Door Hinges	Engine oil
Body door hinge pins, station wagon tailgate hinge and linkage, station wagon folding seat, fuel door hinge, rear compartment hinges	Engine oil
Key Lock Cylinders	WD-40 Spray lubricant or equivalent

10. Remove the filler cap on the rocker (valve) cover, after wiping the area clean.

11. Add the correct number of quarts of oil specified in the "Capacities" chart. If you don't have an oil can spout, you will need a funnel. Be certain you do not overfill the engine, which can cause serious damage. Replace the cap.

12. Check the oil level on the dipstick. It is normal for the level to be a bit above the full mark. Start the engine and allow it to idle for a few minutes.

CAUTION: *Do not run the engine above idle speed until it has built up oil pressure, indicated when the oil light goes out.*

Check around the filter and drain plug for any leaks.

13. Shut off the engine, allow the oil to drain for a minute, and check the oil level.

After completing this job, you will have

GENERAL INFORMATION AND MAINTENANCE

several quarts of filthy oil to dispose of. The best thing to do with it is to funnel it into old plastic milk containers or bleach bottles. Then, you can either pour it into the recycling barrel at the gas station (if you're on good terms with the attendant), or put the containers into the trash.

MANUAL TRANSAXLE

The fluid in the manual transaxle should be changed at the interval specified in the "Maintenance Intervals" chart, or more often if the car is used under severe conditions. You may also want to change it if you have purchased your J-car used, or if it has been driven in water deep enough to reach the transaxle case.

1. The fluid should be hot before it is drained. If the car is driven until the engine is at normal operating temperature, the fluid should be hot enough.

2. Remove the filler plug (or dipstick) from the left side of the transaxle to provide a vent.

3. The drain plug is located on the bottom of the transaxle case. Place a pan under the drain plug and remove it.

CAUTION: *The fluid will be HOT. Push up against the threads as you unscrew the plug to prevent leakage.*

4. Allow the fluid to drain completely. Check the condition of the plug gasket, and replace it if necessary. It will probably be ok. Clean off the plug and replace, tightening until snug.

5. Fill the transaxle with fluid through the filler hole or dipstick tube (the car may be equipped with either) in the left side. Use only DEXRON® II automatic transmission fluid to fill the transaxle. DO NOT use conventional manual transmission lubricants. You will need the aid of a long necked funnel or a funnel and a hose to pour through.

6. If the car has a filler hole, the fluid should come right up to the edge of the filler hole. You can stick your finger in to verify this (watch out for sharp threads).

If the car has a dipstick tube, use the dipstick to gauge the level of fluid.

7. Replace the filler plug or the dipstick. Dispose of the old fluid in the same manner as you would old engine oil. Take a drive in the car, stop on a level surface, and check the fluid level.

AUTOMATIC TRANSAXLE

The fluid should be changed according to the schedule in the "Mintenance Intervals"

chart. If the car is normally used in severe service, such as stop and start driving, trailer towing, or the like, the interval should be halved. If the car is driven under especially nasty conditions, such as in heavy city traffic where the temperature normally reaches 90°F, or in very hilly or mountainous areas, or in police, taxi, or delivery service, the fluid should be changed every 15,000 miles (24,000 km.).

The fluid must be hot before it is drained; a 20 minute drive should accomplish this.

1. There is no drain plug; the fluid pan must be removed. Place a drain pan underneath the transaxle pan and remove the pan attaching bolts at the front and sides of the pan.

2. Loosen the rear pan attaching bolts approximately four turns each.

3. Very carefully pry the pan loose. You can use a small prybar for this if you work CAREFULLY. Do not distort the pan flange, or score the mating surface of the transaxle case. You'll be very sorry later if you do. As the pan is pried loose, all of the fluid is going to come pouring out.

4. Remove the remaining bolts and remove the pan and gasket. Throw away the gasket.

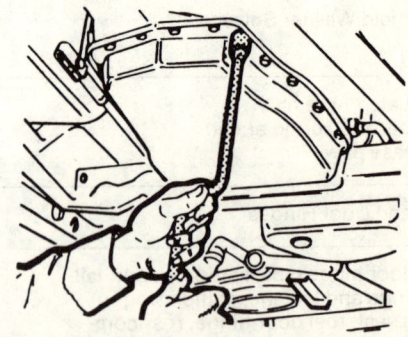

Loosen the pan bolts and allow one corner of the pan to tilt slightly to drain the fluid

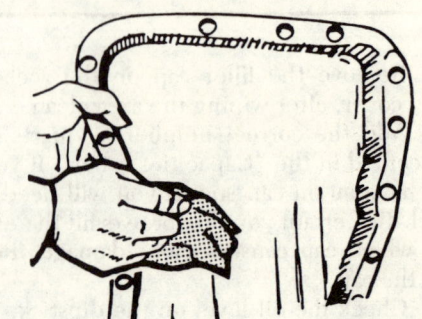

Clean the pan thoroughly with gasoline and allow it to air dry completely

GENERAL INFORMATION AND MAINTENANCE 27

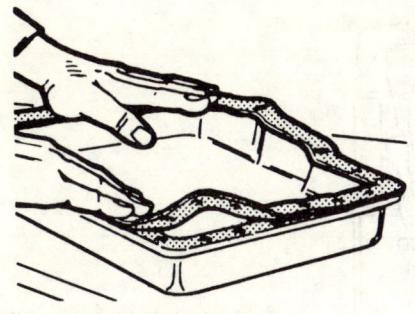

Install a new gasket on the pan

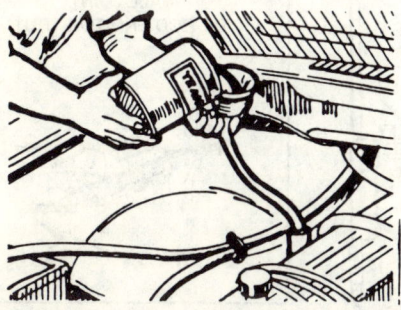

Fill the transaxle with the required amount of fluid. Do not overfill. Check the fluid level and add fluid if necessary

5. Clean the pan with solvent and allow it to air dry. If you use a rag to wipe out the pan, you risk leaving bits of lint behind, which will clog the dinky hydraulic passages in the transaxle.

6. Remove and discard the filter and the O-ring seal.

7. Install a new filter and O-ring, locating the filter against the dipstick stop.

8. Install a new gasket on the pan and install the pan. Tighten the bolts evenly and in rotation to 12 ft. lbs. (16 Nm.). Do not overtighten.

9. Add approximately 4 qts. (3.8 L) of DEXRON® II automatic transmission fluid to the transaxle through the dipstick tube. You will need a long necked funnel, or a funnel and tube to do this.

10. With the transaxle in Park, put on the parking brake, block the front wheels, start the engine and let it idle. DO NOT RACE THE ENGINE. DO NOT MOVE THE LEVER THROUGH ITS RANGES.

11. With the lever in Park, check the fluid level. If it's ok, take the car out for a short drive, park on a level surface, and check the level again, as outlined earlier in this chapter. Add more fluid if necessary. Be careful not to overfill, which will cause foaming and fluid loss.

NOTE: *If the drained fluid is discolored (brown or black), thick, or smells burnt, serious transmission troubles, probably due to overheating, should be suspected. Your car's transaxle should be inspected by a reliable transmission specialist to determine the problem.*

Chassis Greasing

There are only two areas which require regular chassis greasing: the front suspension components and the steering linkage. These parts should be greased every 12 months or 7,500 miles (12,000 Km.) with an EP grease meeting G.M. specification 6031M.

If you choose to do this job yourself, you will need to purchase a hand operated grease gun, if you do not own one already, and a long flexible extension hose to reach the various grease fittings. You will also need a cartridge of the appropriate grease.

Press the fitting on the grease gun hose onto the grease fitting on the suspension or steering linkage component. Pump a few shots of grease into the fitting, until the rubber boot on the joint begins to expand, indicating that the joint is full. Remove the gun from the fitting. Be careful not to overfill the joints, which will rupture the rubber boots, allowing the entry of dirt. You can keep the grease fittings clean by covering them with a small square of tin foil.

Chassis Lubrication

Every 12 months or 7,500 miles (12,000 km.), the various linkages and hinges on the chassis and body should be lubricated, as follows:

TRANSAXLE SHIFT LINKAGE

Lubricate the manual transaxle shift linkage contact points with the EP grease used for chassis greasing, which should meet G.M. specification 6031M. The automatic transaxle linkage should be lubricated with clean engine oil.

HOOD LATCH AND HINGES

Clean the latch surfaces and apply clean engine oil to the latch pilot bolts and the spring anchor. Use the engine oil to lubricate the hood hinges as well. Use a chassis grease to lubricate all the pivot points in the latch release mechanism.

DOOR HINGES

The gas tank filler door, car door, and rear hatch or trunk lid hinges should be wiped

28 GENERAL INFORMATION AND MAINTENANCE

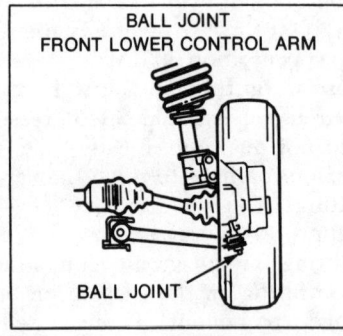

BALL JOINT FRONT LOWER CONTROL ARM

BALL JOINT

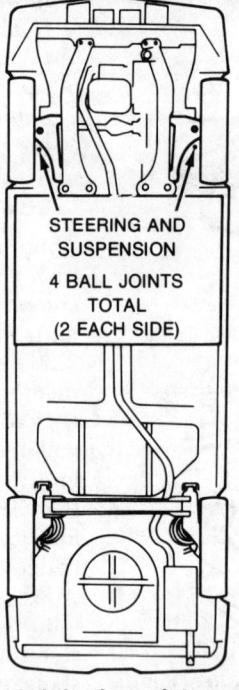

STEERING AND SUSPENSION

4 BALL JOINTS TOTAL (2 EACH SIDE)

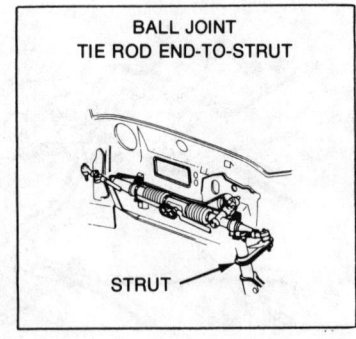

BALL JOINT TIE ROD END-TO-STRUT

STRUT

Lubrication points

clean and lubricated with clean engine oil. Silicone spray also works well on these parts, but must be applied more often. Use engine oil to lubricate the trunk or hatch lock mechanism and the lock bolt and striker. The door lock cylinders can be lubricated easily with a shot of silicone spray or one of the many dry penetrating lubricants commercially available.

PARKING BRAKE LINKAGE

Use chassis grease on the parking brake cable where it contacts the guides, links, levers, and pulleys. The grease should be a water resistant one for durability under the car.

ACCELERATOR LINKAGE

Lubricate the carburetor stud, carburetor lever, and the accelerator pedal lever at the support inside the car with clean engine oil.

PUSHING AND TOWING

The J-cars may not be pushed or towed to start, because doing so may cause the catalytic converter to explode. If the battery is weak, the engine may be jump started, using the procedure outlined in the following section.

Your J-car may be towed on all four wheels at speeds less than 35 mph (60 km/h) for distances up to 50 miles (80 km). The driveline and steering must be normally operable. If either one is damaged, the car may not be flat-towed. If the car is flat-towed (on all four wheels), the steering must be unlocked, the transaxle shifted to Neutral, and the parking brake released. Towing attachment must be made to the main structural members of the chassis, not to the bumpers or sheetmetal.

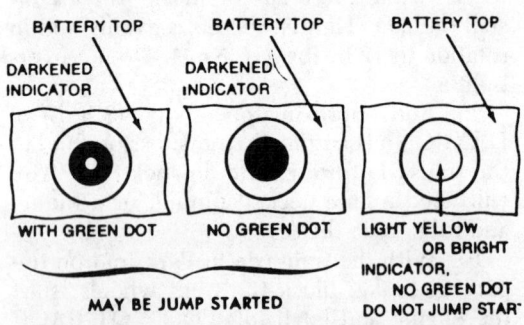

Check the appearance of the charge indicator on top of the battery before attempting a jump start; if it's not green or dark, do not jump start the car

The car may be towed on its rear wheels by a wrecker; make sure that safety chains are used. J-cars with manual transaxles may be towed on their front wheels, for short distances and at low speeds. Be sure the transaxle is in Neutral. Cars with automatic trans-

GENERAL INFORMATION AND MAINTENANCE

Jump Starting a Dead Battery

The chemical reaction in a battery produces explosive hydrogen gas. This is the safe way to jump start a dead battery, reducing the chances of an accidental spark that could cause an explosion.

Jump Starting Precautions

1. Be sure both batteries are of the same voltage.
2. Be sure both batteries are of the same polarity (have the same grounded terminal).
3. Be sure the vehicles are not touching.
4. Be sure the vent cap holes are not obstructed.
5. Do not smoke or allow sparks around the battery.
6. In cold weather, check for frozen electrolyte in the battery.
7. Do not allow electrolyte on your skin or clothing.
8. Be sure the electrolyte is not frozen.

Jump Starting Procedure

1. Determine voltages of the two batteries; they must be the same.
2. Bring the starting vehicle close (they must not touch) so that the batteries can be reached easily.
3. Turn off all accessories and both engines. Put both cars in Neutral or Park and set the handbrake.
4. Cover the cell caps with a rag—do not cover terminals.
5. If the terminals on the run-down battery are heavily corroded, clean them.
6. Identify the positive and negative posts on both batteries and connect the cables in the order shown.
7. Start the engine of the starting vehicle and run it at fast idle. Try to start the car with the dead battery. Crank it for no more than 10 seconds at a time and let it cool off for 20 seconds in between tries.
8. If it doesn't start in 3 tries, there is something else wrong.
9. Disconnect the cables in the reverse order.
10. Replace the cell covers and dispose of the rags.

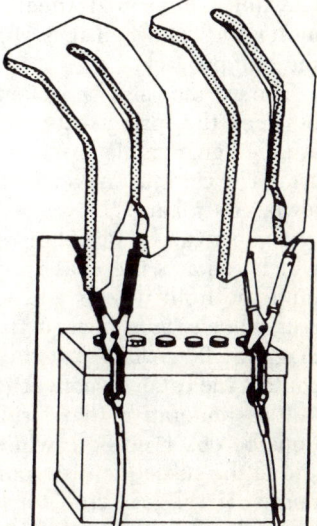

Side terminal batteries occasionally pose a problem when connecting jumper cables. There frequently isn't enough room to clamp the cables without touching sheet metal. Side terminal adaptors are available to alleviate this problem and should be removed after use

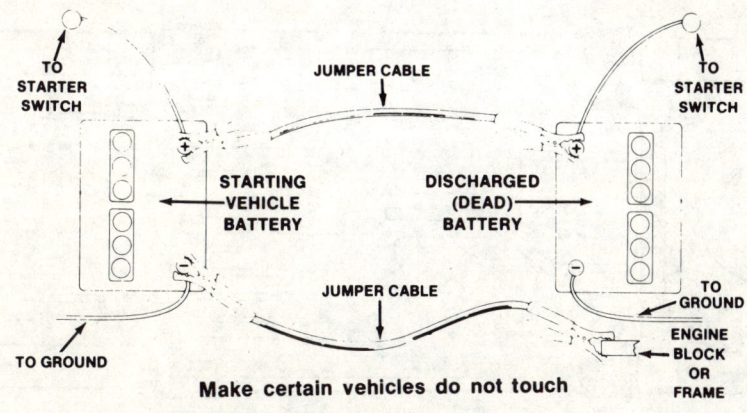

Make certain vehicles do not touch
This hook-up for negative ground cars only

GENERAL INFORMATION AND MAINTENANCE

axles should not be towed on their front wheels; transaxle damage may result. If it is impossible to tow the car on its rear wheels, place the front wheels on a dolly.

JACKING AND HOISTING

The J-cars are supplied with a jack for changing tires. This is a bumper jack, engaging slots in the bumpers by means of a hook. This jack is satisfactory for its intended purpose; it is not meant to support the car while you go crawling around underneath it. *Never* crawl under the car when it is supported by only the bumper jack.

The car may also be jacked at the rear axle between the spring seats, or at the front end at the engine cradle crossbar or lower control arm. The car must never be lifted by the rear lower control arms.

The car can be raised on a four point hoist which contacts the chassis at points just behind the front wheels and just ahead of the rear wheels, as shown in the accompanying diagram. Be certain that the lift pads do not contact the catalytic converter.

It is imperative that strict safety precautions be observed both while raising the car and in the subsequent support after the car is raised. If a jack is used to raise the car, the transaxle should be shifted to Park (automatic) or First (manual), the parking brake should be set, and the opposite wheel should be blocked. Jacking should only be attempted on a hard level surface.

HOW TO BUY A USED CAR

Many people believe that a two or three year old used car is a better buy than a new car. This may be true; the new car suffers the heaviest depreciation in the first two years, but is not old enough to present a lot of costly repair problems. Whatever the age of the used car you might want to buy, this section and a little patience will help you select one that should be safe and dependable.

TIPS

1. First decide what model you want, and how much you want to spend.
2. Check the used car lots and your local newspaper ads. Privately owned cars are usually less expensive, however you will not get a warranty that, in most cases, comes with a used car purchased from a lot.
3. Never shop at night. The glare of the lights make it easy to miss faults on the body caused by accident or rust repair.
4. Try to get the name and phone number of the previous owner. Contact him/her and ask about the car. If the owner of the lot refuses this information, look for a car somewhere else.

A private seller can tell you about the car and maintenance. Remember, however, there's no law requiring honesty from private citizens selling used cars. There is a law that forbids the tampering with or turning back the odometer mileage. This includes both the private citizen and the lot owner. The law also requires that the seller or anyone transferring ownership of the car must provide the buyer with a signed statement indicating the mileage on the odometer at the time of transfer.

5. Write down the year, model and serial number before you buy any used car. Then dial 1-800-424-9393, the toll free number of the National Highway Traffic Safety Administration, and ask if the car has ever been in-

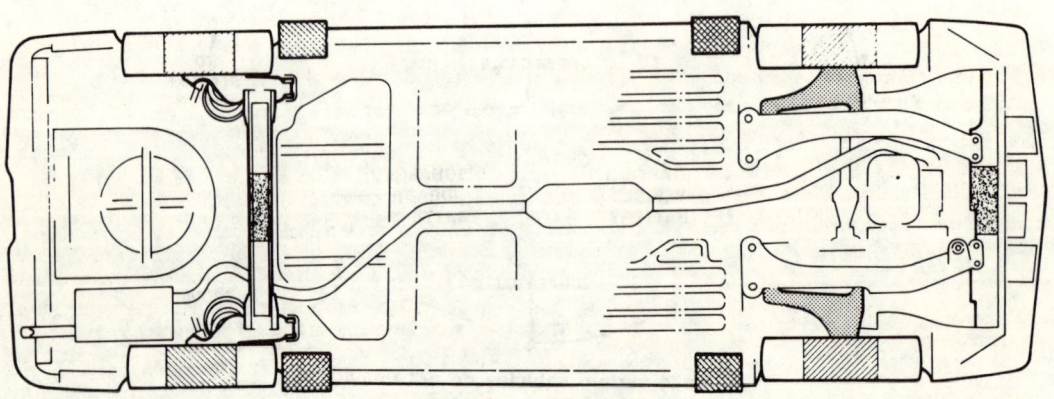

Jacking and hoisting locations

GENERAL INFORMATION AND MAINTENANCE

cluded on any manufacturer's recall list. If so, make sure the needed repairs were made.

6. Use the "Used Car Checklist" in this section and check all the items on the used car you are considering. Some items are more important than others. You know how much money you can afford for repairs, and, depending on the price of the car, may consider doing any needed work yourself. Beware, however, of trouble in areas that will affect operation, safety or emission. Problems in the "Used Car Checklist" break down as follows:

1-8: Two or more problems in these areas indicate a lack of maintenance. You should beware.

9-13: Indicates a lack of proper care, however, these can usually be corrected with a tune-up or relatively simple parts replacement.

14-17: Problems in the engine or transmission can be very expensive. Walk away from any car with problems in both of these areas.

7. If you are satisfied with the apparent condition of the car, take it to an independent diagnostic center or mechanic for a complete check. If you have a state inspection program, have it inspected immediately before purchase, or specify on the bill of sale that the sale is conditional on passing state inspection.

8. Road test the car—refer to the "Road Test Checklist" in this section. If your original evaluation and the road test agree—the rest is up to you.

USED CAR CHECKLIST

NOTE: *The numbers on the illustrations refer to the numbers on this checklist.*

1. *Mileage:* Average mileage is about 12,000 miles per year. More than average mileage may indicate hard usage. 1975 and later catalytic converter equipped models may need converter service at 50,000 miles.

2. *Paint:* Check around the tailpipe, molding and windows for overspray indicating that the car has been repainted.

3. *Rust:* Check fenders, doors, rocker panels, window moldings, wheelwells, floorboards, under floormats, and in the trunk for signs of rust. Any rust at all will be a problem. There is no way to check the spread of rust, except to replace the part or panel.

4. *Body appearance:* Check the moldings, bumpers, grille, vinyl roof, glass, doors, trunk lid and body panels for general overall condition. Check for misalignment, loose holdown clips, ripples, scratches in glass, rips or patches in the top. Mismatched paint, welding in the trunk, severe misalignment of body panels or ripples may indicate crash work.

5. *Leaks:* Get down and look under the car. There are no normal "leaks", other than water from the air conditioning condenser.

6. *Tires;* Check the tire air pressure. A common trick is to pump the tire pressure up to make the car roll easier. Check the tread wear, open the trunk and check the spare too. Uneven wear is a clue that the front end needs alignment. See the troubleshooting chapter for clues to the causes of tire wear.

7. *Shock absorbers:* Check the shock absorbers by forcing downward sharply on each corner of the car. Good shocks will not allow the car to bounce more than twice after you let go.

8. *Interior:* Check the entire interior. You're looking for an interior condition that agrees with the overall condition of the car. Reasonable wear is expected, but be suspicious of new seatcovers on sagging seats, new pedal pads, and worn armrests. These indicate an attempt to cover up hard use. Pull back the carpets and look for evidence of water leaks or flooding. Look for missing hardware, door handles, control knobs etc. Check lights and signal operations. Make sure all accessories (air conditioner, heater, radio etc.) work. Check windshield wiper operation.

9. *Belts and Hoses:* Open the hood and check all belts and hoses for wear, cracks or weak spots.

10. *Battery:* Low electrolyte level, corroded terminals and/or cracked case indicate a lack of maintenance.

11. *Radiator:* Look for corrosion or rust in the coolant indicating a lack of maintenance.

12. *Air filter:* A dirty air filter usually means a lack of maintenance.

13. *Ignition Wires:* Check the ignition wires for cracks, burned spots, or wear. Worn wires will have to be replaced.

14. *Oil level:* If the oil level is low, chances are the engine uses oil or leaks. Beware of water in the oil (cracked block), excessively thick oil (used to quiet a noisy engine), or thin, dirty oil with a distinct gasoline smell (internal engine problems).

15. *Automatic Transmission:* Pull the transmission dipstick out when the engine is running. The level should read "Full", and

32 GENERAL INFORMATION AND MAINTENANCE

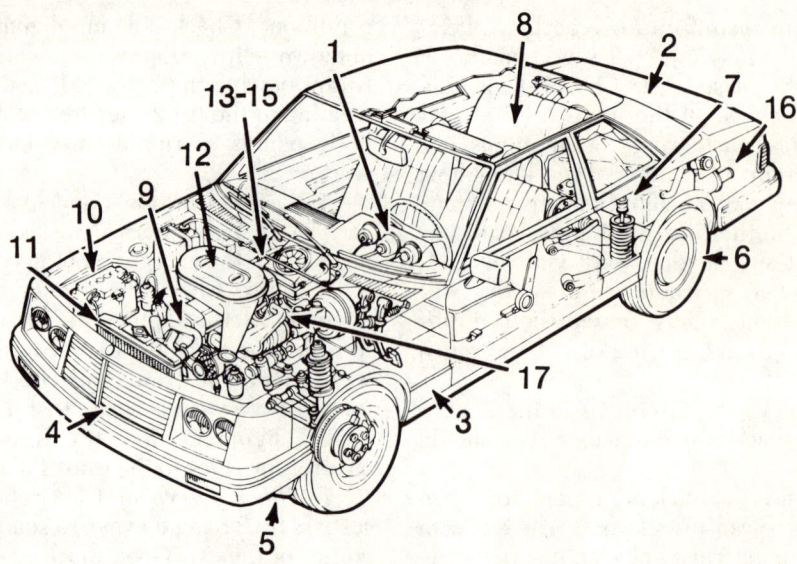

You should check these points when buying a used car. The "Used Car Checklist" gives an explanation of the numbered items

the fluid should be clear or bright red. Dark brown or black fluid that has distinct burnt odor, signals a transmission in need of repair or overhaul.

16. *Exhaust:* Check the color of the exhaust smoke. Blue smoke indicates, among other problems, worn rings; black smoke can indicate burnt valves or carburetor problems. Check the exhaust system for leaks; it can be expensive to replace.

17. *Spark Plugs:* Remove one of the spark plugs (the most accessible will do). An engine in good condition will show plugs with a light tan or gray deposit on the firing tip. See the color Tune-Up tips section for spark plug conditions.

ROAD TEST CHECK LIST

1. *Engine Performance:* The car should be peppy whether cold or warm, with adequate power and good pickup. It should respond smoothly through the gears.

2. *Brakes:* They should provide quick, firm stops with no noise, pulling or brake fade.

3. *Steering:* Sure control with no binding, harshness, or looseness and no shimmy in the wheel should be expected. Noise or vibration from the steering wheel when turning the car means trouble.

4. *Clutch (Manual Transmission):* Clutch action should give quick, smooth response with easy shifting. The clutch pedal should have about 1–1½ inches of free-play before it disengages the clutch. Start the engine, set the parking brake, put the transmission in first gear and slowly release the clutch pedal. The engine should begin to stall when the pedal is one-half to three-quarters of the way up.

5. *Automatic Transmission:* The transmission should shift rapidly and smoothly, with no noise, hesitation, or slipping.

6. *Differential:* No noise or thumps should be present. Differentials have no "normal" leaks.

7. *Driveshaft, Universal Joints:* Vibration and noise could mean driveshaft problems. Clicking at low speed or coast conditions means worn U-joints.

8. *Suspension:* Try hitting bumps at different speeds. A car that bounces has weak shock absorbers. Clunks mean worn bushings or ball joints.

9. *Frame:* Wet the tires and drive in a straight line. Tracks should show two straight lines, not four. Four tire tracks indicate a frame bent by collision damage. If the tires can't be wet for this purpose, have a friend drive along behind you and see if the car appears to be traveling in a straight line.

Tune-Up

TUNE-UP PROCEDURES

In order to extract the full measure of performance and economy from your car's engine it is essential that it be properly tuned at regular intervals. Although the tune-up intervals for the 1982 J-cars have been stretched to limits which would have been thought impossible a few years ago, periodic maintenance is still required. A regularly scheduled tune-up will keep your car's engine running smoothly and will prevent the annoying minor breakdowns and poor performance associated with an untuned engine.

A complete tune-up should be performed at the interval specified in the "Maintenance Intervals" chart in Chapter One. This interval should be halved if the car is operated under severe conditions, such as trailer towing, prolonged idling, continual stop-and-start driving, or if starting and running problems are noticed. It is assumed that the routine maintenance described in the first chapter has been kept up, as this will have a decided effect on the results of a tune-up. All of the applicable steps should be followed in order, as the result is a cumulative one.

If the specifications on the tune-up label in the engine compartment of your J-car disagree with the "Tune-Up Specifications" chart in this chapter, the figures on the sticker must be used. The label often reflects changes made during the production run.

Spark Plugs

Spark plugs ignite the air and fuel mixture in the cylinder as the piston reaches the top of the compression stroke. The controlled explosion that results forces the piston down, turning the crankshaft and the rest of the drive train.

The average life of a spark plug in a J-car is 30,000 miles. Part of the reason for this extraordinarily long life is the exclusive use of unleaded fuel, which reduces the amount of deposits within the combustion chamber and on the spark plug electrodes themselves, compared with the deposits left by the leaded gasoline used in the past. An additional contribution to long life is made by the HEI (High Energy Ignition) System, which fires the spark plugs with over 35,000 volts of electricity. The high voltage serves to keep the electrodes clear, and because it is a "cleaner" blast of electricity than that produced by conventional breaker-points ignitions, the electrodes suffer less pitting and wear.

Nevertheless, the life of a spark plug is dependent on a number of factors, including

TUNE-UP

Tune-Up Specifications

When analyzing compression test results, look for uniformity among cylinders rather than specific pressures.

Year	Engine No. Cyl Displacement (cu in.)	hp	Spark Plugs Orig Type	Gap (in.)	Distributor Point Dwell (deg)	Point Gap (in.)	Ignition Timing (deg)▲● Man Trans	Auto Trans	Valves Intake Opens (deg)■	Fuel Pump Pressure (psi)	Idle Speed (rpm)▲ Man Trans	Auto Trans
1982	4-112	88	R-42TS	0.045 ①	Electronic		12B	12B	30	4.5–6.0	②	②

NOTE: *The underhood specifications sticker often reflects tune-up specification changes made in production. Sticker figures must be used if they disagree with those in this chart.*
▲ See text for procedure
● Figure in parenthesis indicates California and High Altitude engine
■ All figures Before Top Dead Center
B Before Top Dead Center
Part numbers in this chart are not recommendations by Chilton for any product by brand name.
① Certain models may use 0.035 in. Gap — see underhood specifications sticker to be sure
② See underhood specifications sticker

TUNE-UP 35

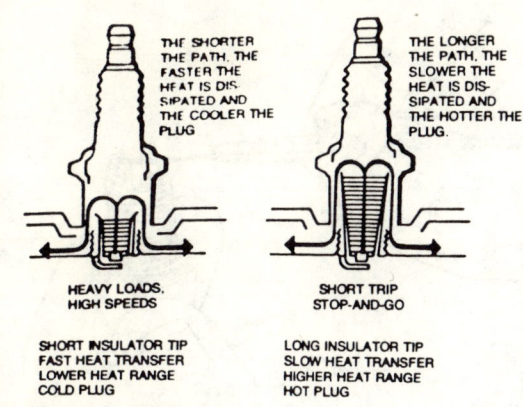

Spark plug heat range

Left diagram labels: THE SHORTER THE PATH, THE FASTER THE HEAT IS DISSIPATED AND THE COOLER THE PLUG. HEAVY LOADS, HIGH SPEEDS. SHORT INSULATOR TIP / FAST HEAT TRANSFER / LOWER HEAT RANGE / COLD PLUG

Right diagram labels: THE LONGER THE PATH, THE SLOWER THE HEAT IS DISSIPATED AND THE HOTTER THE PLUG. SHORT TRIP STOP-AND-GO. LONG INSULATOR TIP / SLOW HEAT TRANSFER / HIGHER HEAT RANGE / HOT PLUG

the mechanical condition of the engine, driving conditions, and the driver's habits.

When you remove the plugs, check the condition of the electrodes; they are a good indicator of the internal state of the engine. Since the spark plug wires must be checked every 15,000 miles, the spark plugs can be removed and examined at the same time. This will allow you to keep an eye on the mechanical status of the engine.

A small deposit of light tan or rust-red material on a spark plug that has been used for any period of time is to be considered normal. Any other color, or abnormal amounts of wear or deposits, indicates that there is something amiss in the engine.

The gap between the center electrode and the side or ground electrode can be expected to increase not more than 0.001 in. every 1,000 miles under normal conditions.

When a spark plug is functioning normally or, more accurately, when the plug is installed in an engine that is functioning properly, the plugs can be taken out, cleaned, re-gapped, and reinstalled in the engine without doing the engine any harm.

When, and if, a plug fouls and begins to misfire, you will have to investigate, correct the cause of the fouling, and either clean or replace the plug.

There are several reasons why a spark plug will foul and you can learn which is at fault by just looking at the plug. A few of the most common reasons for plug fouling, and a description of the fouled plug's appearance, are listed in Chapter Ten, which also offers solutions to the problems. Also see the "Color Insert" section of Chapter Four.

Spark plugs suitable for use in your car's engine are offered in a number of different heat ranges. The amount of heat which the plug absorbs is determined by the length of the lower insulator. The longer the insulator, the hotter the plug will operate; the shorter the insulator, the cooler it will operate. A spark plug that absorbs (or retains) little heat and remains too cool will accumulate deposits of oil and carbon, because it is not hot enough to burn them off. This leads to fouling and consequent misfiring. A spark plug that absorbs too much heat will have no deposits, but the electrodes will burn away quickly and, in some cases, preignition may result. Preignition occurs when the spark plug tips get so hot that they ignite the fuel/mixture before the actual spark fires. This premature ignition will usually cause a pinging sound under conditions of low speed and heavy load. In severe cases, the heat may become high enough to start the fuel/air mixture burning throughout the combustion chamber rather than just to the front of the plug. In this case, the resultant explosion (detonation) will be strong enough to damage pistons, rings, and valves.

In most cases the factory recommended heat range is correct; it is chosen to perform well under a wide range of operating conditions. However, if most of your driving is long distance, high speed travel, you may want to install a spark plug one step colder than standard. If most of your driving is of the short trip variety, when the engine may not always reach operating temperature, a hotter plug may help burn off the deposits normally accumulated under those conditions.

REMOVAL

1. Number the wires with pieces of adhesive tape so that you won't cross them when you replace them.

2. The spark plug boots have large grips to aid in removal. Grasp the wire by the rubber boot and twist the boot ½ turn in either direction to break the tight seal between the boot and the plug. Then twist and pull on the boot to remove the wire from the spark plug. Do not pull on the wire itself or you will damage the carbon cord conductor.

3. Use a ⅝ inch spark plug socket to loosen all of the plugs about two turns. A universal joint installed at the socket end of the extension will ease the process.

If removal of the plugs is difficult, apply a few drops of penetrating oil or silicone spray to the area around the base of the plug, and allow it a few minutes to work.

4. If compressed air is available, apply it

TUNE-UP

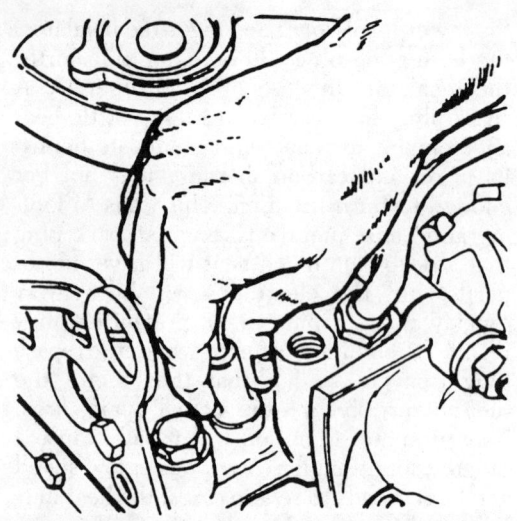

Twist and pull on the rubber boot to remove the spark plug wires; never pull on the wire itself

to the area around the spark plug holes. Otherwise, use a rag or a brush to clean the area. Be careful not to allow any foreign material to drop into the spark plug holes.

5. Remove the plugs by unscrewing them the rest of the way.

INSPECTION

Check the plugs for deposits and wear. If they are not going to be replaced, clean the plugs thoroughly. Remember that any kind of deposit will decrease the efficiency of the plug. Plugs can be cleaned on a spark plug cleaning machine, which can sometimes be found in service stations, or you can do an acceptable job of cleaning with a stiff brush.

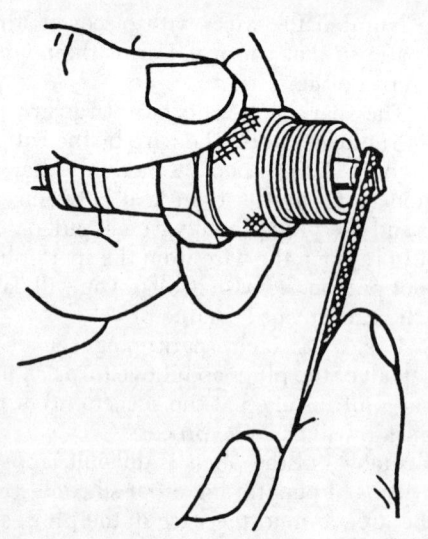

Plugs that are in good condition can be filed and reused

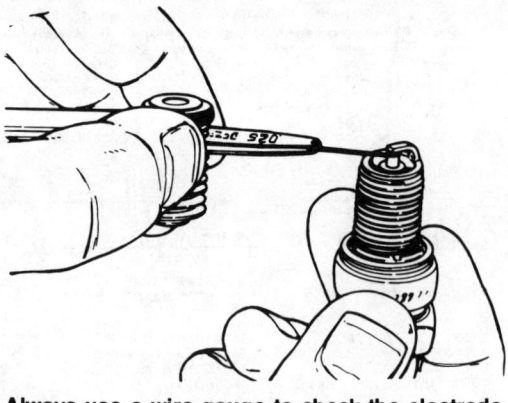

Always use a wire gauge to check the electrode gap

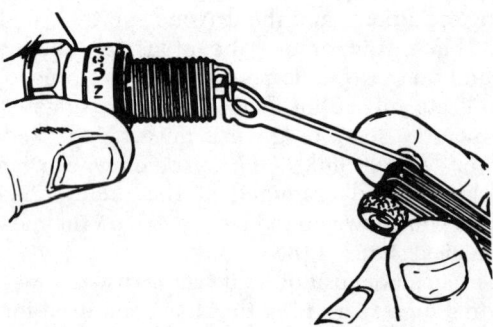

Adjust the electrode gap by bending the side electrode

If the plugs are cleaned, the electrodes must be filed flat. Use an ignition points file, not an emery board or the like, which will leave deposits. The electrodes must be filed perfectly flat with sharp edges; rounded edges reduce the spark plug voltage by as much as 50%.

Check the spark plug gap before installation. The ground electrode must be parallel to the center electrode and the specified size wire gauge should pass through the gap with a slight drag. Always check the gap on new plugs, too; they are not always correctly set at the factory. Do not use a flat feeler gauge when measuring the gap, because the reading will be inaccurate. Wire gapping tools usually have a bending tool attached. Use that to adjust the side electrode until the proper distance is obtained. Also, be careful not to bend the side electrode too far or too often; it may weaken and break off within the engine, requiring removal of the cylinder head to retrieve it.

INSTALLATION

1. Lubricate the threads of the spark plugs with a drop of oil or a shot of silicone spray.

TUNE-UP 37

Install the plugs and tighten them handtight. Take care not to cross-thread them.

2. Tighten the spark plugs with the socket. Do not apply the same amount of force you would use for a bolt; just snug them in. These spark plugs do not use gaskets, and over-tightening will make future removal difficult. If a torque wrench is available, tighten to 7–15 ft. lbs.

NOTE: *While over-tightening the spark plug is to be avoided, under-tightening is just as bad. If combustion gases leak past the threads, the spark plug will overheat and rapid electrode wear will result.*

3. Install the wires on their respective plugs. Make sure the wires are firmly connected. You will be able to feel them click into place. Spark plug wiring diagrams are in Chapter Three if you get into trouble.

CHECKING AND REPLACING SPARK PLUG WIRES

Every 15,000 miles, inspect the spark plug wires for burns, cuts, or breaks in the insulation. Check the boots and the nipples on the distributor cap. Replace any damaged wiring.

Every 45,000 miles or so, the resistance of the wires should be checked with an ohmmeter. Wires with excessive resistance will cause misfiring, and may make the engine difficult to start in damp weather. Generally, the useful life of the cables is 45,000–60,000 miles.

To check resistance, remove the distributor cap, leaving the wires in place. Connect one lead of an ohmmeter to an electrode within the cap; connect the other lead to the corresponding spark plug terminal (remove it from the spark plug for this test). Replace any

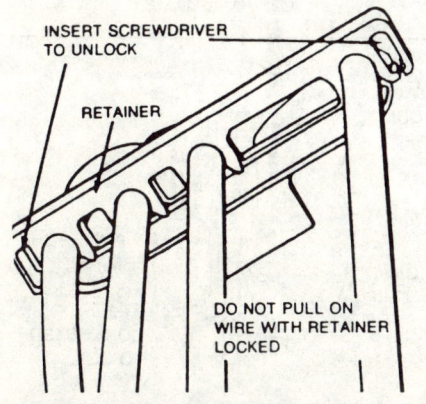

Unlock the plastic retainers to replace the spark plug wires

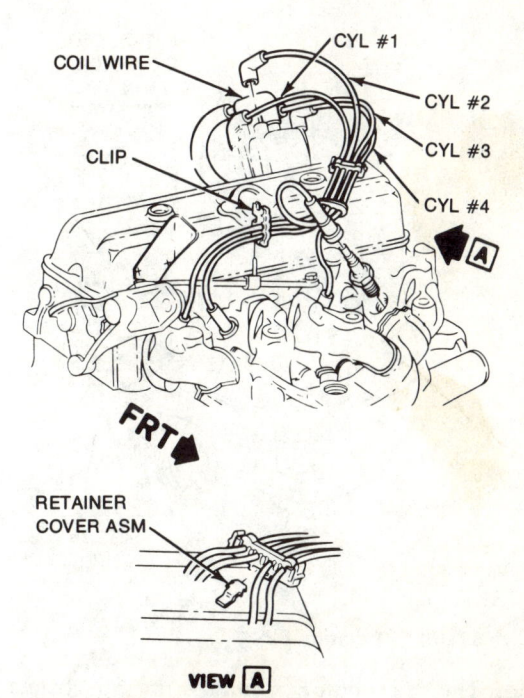

Spark plug wire routing

wire which shows a resistance over 30,000 ohms. The following chart gives resistance values as a function of length. Generally speaking, however, resistance should not be considered the outer limit of acceptability.

- 0–15 inches—3,000–10,000 Ω;
- 15–25 inches—4,000–15,000 Ω;
- 25–35 inches—6,000–20,000 Ω;
- Over 35 inches—25,000 Ω.

It should be remembered that resistance is also a function of length; the longer the wire, the greater the resistance. Thus, if the wires on your car are longer than the factory originals, resistance will be higher, quite possibly outside these limits.

When installing new wires, replace them one at a time to avoid mixups. Start by replacing the longest one first. Install the boot firmly over the spark plug. Route the wire over the same path as the original. Insert the nipple firmly onto the tower on the distributor cap, then install the cap cover and latches to secure the wires.

High Energy Ignition (HEI) System

The General Motors HEI system for 1982 is a pulse-triggered, transistor-controlled, inductive discharge ignition system. It is a completely self-contained unit—all parts are contained within the distributor.

38 TUNE-UP

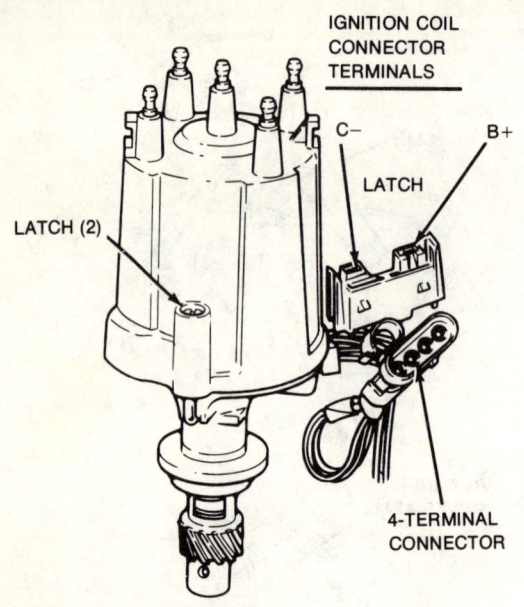

1982 HEI EST distributor

The distributor contains the electronic control module, and the magnetic triggering device. The magnetic pick-up assembly contains a permanent magnet, a pole piece with interal "teeth," and a pickup coil (not to be confused with the ignition coil).

An HEI distributor with Electronic Spark Timing is used (for more information on EST, refer to Chapter 4). Unlike most other HEI distributors, an externally mounted ignition coil is used; connected to the distributor by means of a high tension wire.

All spark timing changes are done electronically by the Electronic Contol Module (ECM) which monitors information from various engine sensors, computes the desired spark timing and then signals the distributor to change the timing accordingly. No vacuum or mechanical advance systems are used whatsoever.

In the HEI system, as in other electronic ignition systems, the breaker points have been replaced with an electronic switch—a transistor—which is located *within* the control module. This switching transistor performs the same function the points did in a conventional ignition system; it simply turns coil primary current on and off at the correct time. Essentially then, electronic and conventional ignition systems operate on the same principle.

The module which houses the switching transistor is controlled (turned on and off) by a magnetically generated impulse induced in the pick-up coil. When the teeth of the rotating timer align with the teeth of the pole piece, the induced voltage in the pick-up coil signals the electronic module to open the coil

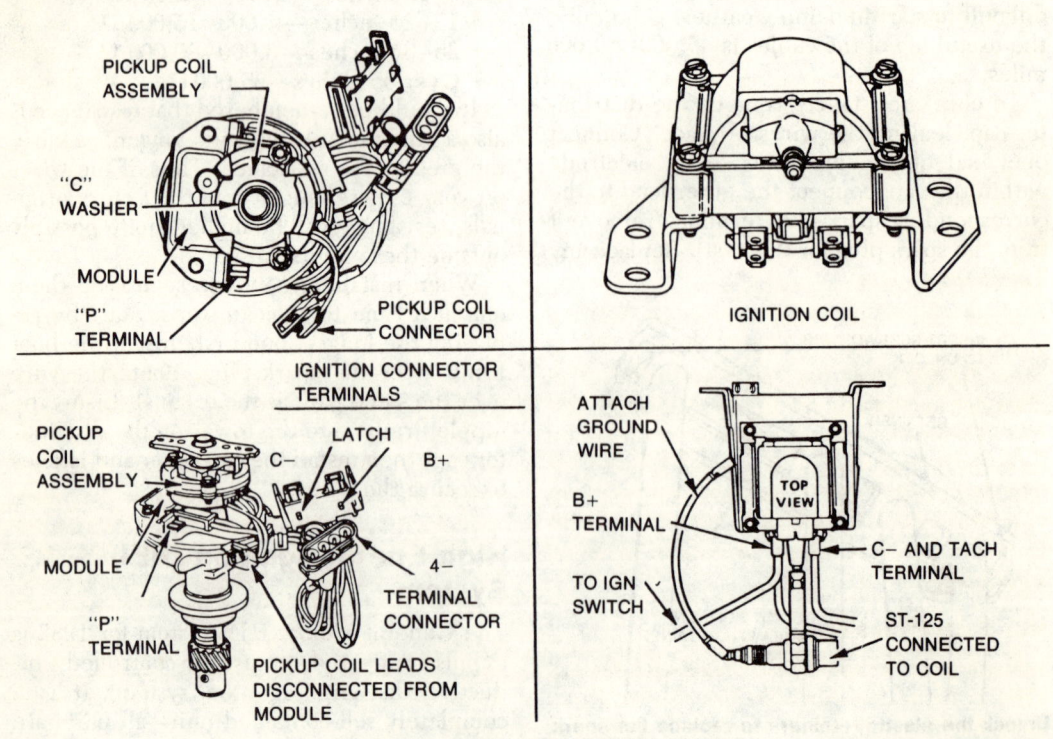

Distributor and ignition coil components

primary circuit. The primary current then decreases, and a high voltage is induced in the ignition coil secondary windings which is then directed through the rotor and high voltage leads (spark plug wires) to fire the spark plugs.

In essence then, the pick-up coil module system simply replaces the conventional breaker points and condenser. The condenser found within the distributor is for radio suppression purposes only and has nothing to do with the ignition process. The module automatically controls the dwell period, increasing it with increasing engine speed. Since dwell is automatically controlled, it cannot be adjusted. The module itself is non-adjustable and non-repairable and must be replaced if found defective.

HEI SYSTEM PRECAUTIONS

Before going on to troubleshooting, it might be a good idea to take note of the following precautions:

Timing Light Use

Inductive pick-up timing lights are the best kind to use with HEI. Timing lights which connect between the spark plug and the spark plug wire occasionally (not always) give false readings.

Spark Plug Wires

The plug wires used with HEI systems are of a different construction than conventional wires. When replacing them, make sure you get the correct wires, since conventional wires won't carry the voltage. Also, handle them carefully to avoid cracking or splitting them and *never* pierce them.

Tachometer Use

Not all tachometers will operate or indicate correctly when used on a HEI system. While some tachometers may give a reading, this does not necessarily mean the reading is correct. In addition, some tachometers hook up differently from others. If you can't figure out whether or not your tachometer will work on your car, check with the tachometer manufacturer. Dwell readings, of course, have no significance at all.

HEI System Testers

Instruments designed specifically for testing HEI systems are available from several tool manufacturers. Some of these will even test the module itself. However, the tests given in the following section will require only an ohmmeter and a voltmeter.

TROUBLESHOOTING THE HEI SYSTEM

The symptoms of a defective component within the HEI system are exactly the same as those you would encounter in a conventional system. Some of these symptoms are:
- Hard or no Starting
- Rough Idle
- Poor Fuel Economy
- Engine misses under load or while accelerating.

HEI Plug Wire Resistance Chart

Wire Length	Minimum	Maximum
0–15 inches	3000 ohms	10,000 ohms
15–25 inches	4000 ohms	15,000 ohms
25–35 inches	6000 ohms	20,000 ohms
Over 35 inches		25,000 ohms

If you suspect a problem in your ignition system, there are certain preliminary checks which you should carry out before you begin to check the electronic portions of the system. First, it is extremely important to make sure the vehicle battery is in good state of charge. A defective or poorly charged battery will cause the various components of the ignition system to read incorrectly when they are being tested. Second, make sure all wiring connections are clean and tight, not only at the battery, but also at the distributor cap, ignition coil, and at the electronic control module.

Since the only change between electronic and conventional ignition systems is in the distributor component area, it is imperative to check the secondary ignition circuit first. If the secondary circuit checks out properly, then the engine condition is probably not the fault of the ignition system. To check the secondary ignition system, perform a simple spark test. Remove one of the plug wires and insert some sort of extension in the plug socket. An old spark plug with the ground electrode removed makes a good extension. Hold the wire and extension about ¼ in. away from the block and crank the engine. If a normal spark occurs, then the problem is most likely *not* in the ignition system. Check for fuel system problems, or fouled spark plugs.

If, however, there is no spark or a weak

TUNE-UP

spark, then further ignition system testing will have to be done. Troubleshooting techniques fall into two categories, depending on the nature of the problem. The categories are (1) Engine cranks, but won't start or (2) Engine runs, but runs rough or cuts out. To begin with, let's consider the first case.

Engine Fails to Start

If the engine won't start, perform a spark test as described earlier. This will narrow the problem area down considerably. If no spark occurs, check for the presence of normal battery voltage at the battery (BAT) terminal on the ignition coil. The ignition switch must be in the "on" position for this test. Either a voltmeter or a test light may be used for this test. Connect the test light wire to ground and the probe end to the BAT terminal at the coil. If the light comes on, you have voltage to the distributor. If the light fails to come on, this indicates an open circuit in the ignition primary wiring leading to the distributor. In this case, you will have to check wiring continuity back to the ignition switch using a test light. If there is battery voltage at the BAT terminal, but no spark at the plugs, then the problem lies within the distributor assembly. Go on to the distributor components test section.

Engine Runs, But Runs Rough or Cuts Out

1. Make sure the plug wires are in good shape first. There should be no obvious cracks or breaks. You can check the plug wires with an ohmmeter, but *do not* pierce the wires with a probe. Check the chart for the correct plug wire resistance.

2. If the plug wires are OK, remove the cap assembly and check for moisture, cracks, chips, or carbon tracks, or any other high voltage leaks or failures. Replace the cap if any defects are found. Make sure the timer wheel rotates when the engine is cranked. If everything is all right so far, go on to the distributor components test section following.

DISTRIBUTOR COMPONENTS TESTING

If the trouble has been narrowed down to the units within the distributor, the following tests can help pinpoint the defective component. An ohmmeter with both high and low ranges should be used. These tests are made with the cap assembly removed and the battery wire disconnected. If a tachometer is

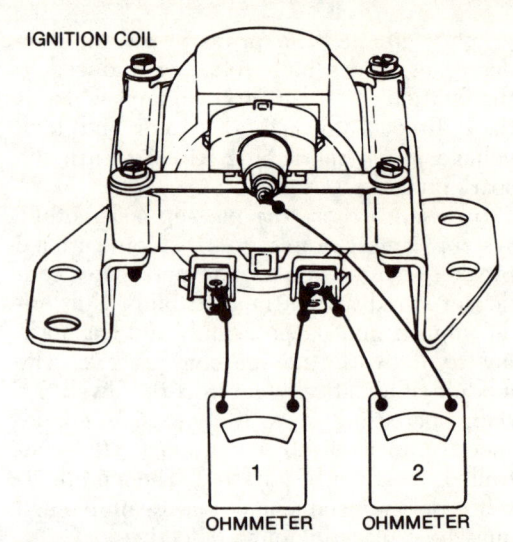

Ohmmeter 1 shows the primary coil resistance connection. Ohmmeter 2 shows the secondary resistance connection

connected to the TACH terminal, disconnect it before making these tests.

1. Connect an ohmmeter between the TACH and BAT terminals on the ignition coil. The primary coil resistance should be less than one ohm.

2. To check the coil secondary resistance, connect an ohmmeter between the high tension terminal and the BAT terminal. Note the reading. Connect the ohmmeter between the high tension terminal and the TACH terminal. Note the reading. The resistance in both cases should be between 6,000 and 30,000 ohms. Be sure to test between the high tension terminal and both the BAT and TACH terminals.

3. Replace the coil *only* if the readings in Step 1 and Step 2 are infinite.

NOTE: *These resistance checks will not disclose shorted coil windings. This condition can only be detected with scope analysis or a suitably designed coil tester. If these instruments are unavailable, replace the coil with a known good coil as a final coil test.*

4. To test the pick-up coil, first disconnect the white and green module leads. Set the ohmmeter on the high scale and connect it between a ground and either the white or green lead. Any resistance measurement *less* than infinity requires replacement of the pick-up coil.

5. Pick-up coil continuity is tested by connecting the ohmmeter (on low range) between the white and green leads. Normal resistance is between 650 and 850 ohms. Move

TUNE-UP 41

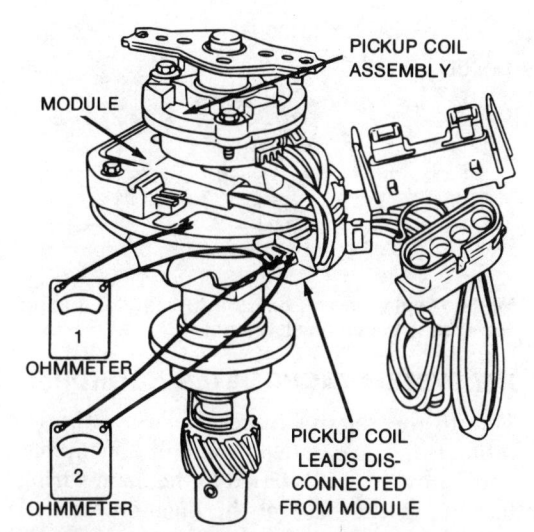

Ohmmeter 1 shows the connections for testing the pick-up coil. Ohmmeter 2 shows the connections for testing the pick-up coil continuity

the vacuum advance arm while performing this test. This will detect any break in coil continuity. Such a condition can cause intermittent misfiring. Replace the pick-up coil if the reading is outside the specified limits.

6. If no defects have been found at this time, and you still have a problem, then the module will have to be checked. If you do not have access to a module tester, the only possible alternative is a substitution test. If the module fails the substitution test, replace it.

HEI SYSTEM MAINTENANCE

Except for periodic checks of the spark plug wires, and an occasional check of the distributor cap for cracks (see Steps 1 and 2 under "Engine Runs, But Runs Rough or Cuts Out" for details), no maintenance is required on the HEI system. No periodic lubrication is necessary; engine oil lubricates the lower bushing, and an oil-filled reservoir lubricates the upper bushing.

COMPONENT REPLACEMENT
Ignition Coil

1. Disconnect the negative battery cable.
2. Raise and support the front of the car.
3. Disconnect the fuel pump outlet pipe to the carburetor and the fuel pump inlet hose.
4. Remove the vacuum pipe bracket retaining nut at the coil and then move the pipe aside for better access to the coil.
5. Remove the fuel pump as detailed in Chapter 4.
6. Tag and disconnect any electrical connections at the coil.
7. Unscrew the mounting bolts and stud and remove the coil.
8. Installation is in the reverse order of removal.

Distributor Cap

1. Disconnect the negative battery cable.
2. Tag and disconnect any wires that may interfere with cap removal.
3. Turn the two retaining latches and lift off the cap.
4. Installation is in the reverse order of removal.

Rotor

1. Disconnect the negative battery cable.
2. Remove the distributor cap.
3. Unscrew the two rotor attaching screws and then lift off the rotor.
4. Installation is in the reverse order of removal.

Pick-Up Coil

1. Disconnect the negative battery cable.
2. Remove the distributor cap and then the rotor.
3. Pop out the thin 'C' washer (waved retaining ring) from the center of the assembly and then carefully lift off the pick-up coil.
4. Installation is in the reverse order of removal.

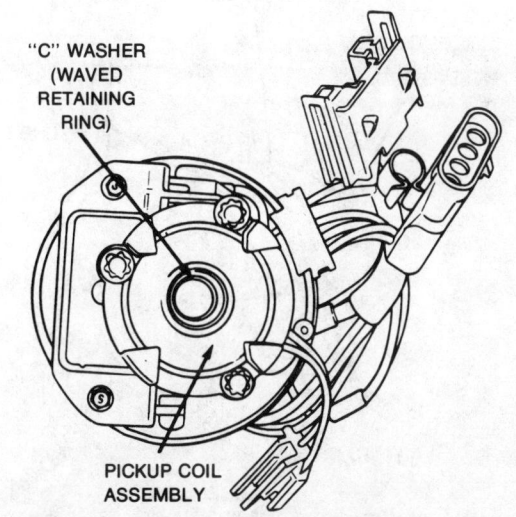

Remove the "C" washer before lifting off the pick-up coil

42 TUNE-UP

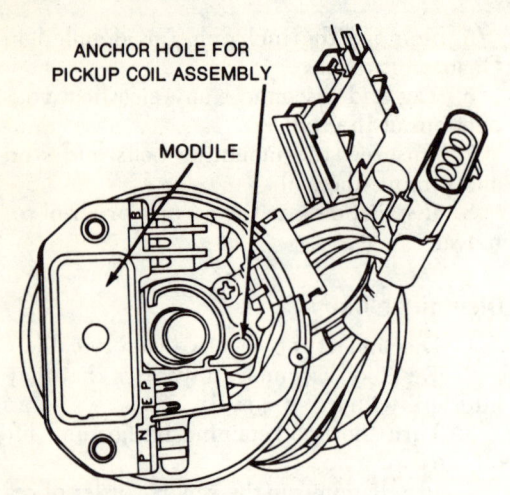

When installing the pick-up coil, make sure that it fits into the anchor hole

Module

1. Remove the distributor cap and rotor as previously described.
2. Disconnect the harness connector and pick-up coil spade connectors from the module. Be careful not to damage the wires when removing the connector.
3. Remove the two screws and module from the distributor housing.
4. Coat the bottom of the new module with dielectric lubricant supplied with the new module. Reverse the above procedure to install.

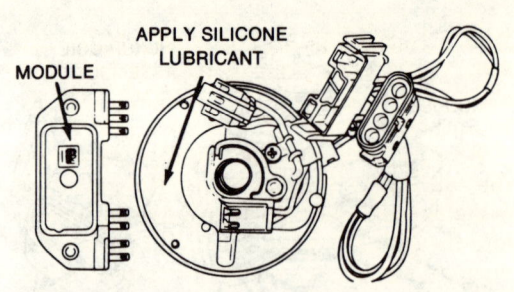

Module replacement; be sure to coat the mating surfaces with silicone lubricant

HEI SYSTEM TACHOMETER HOOKUP

Due to the relative inaccessibility of the ignition coil, a separate tachometer hookup has been provided. It is taped to the main wiring harness in the back of the engine compartment, near the firewall. Connect one tachometer lead to this terminal and the other lead to a suitable ground. On some tachometers, the leads must be connected to the terminal and then to the positive battery terminal.

CAUTION: *Never ground the TACH terminal; serious module and coil damage will result. If there is any doubt as to the correct tachometer hookup, check with the tachometer manufacturer.*

Ignition Timing

Ignition timing is the measurement, in degrees of crankshaft rotation, of the point at

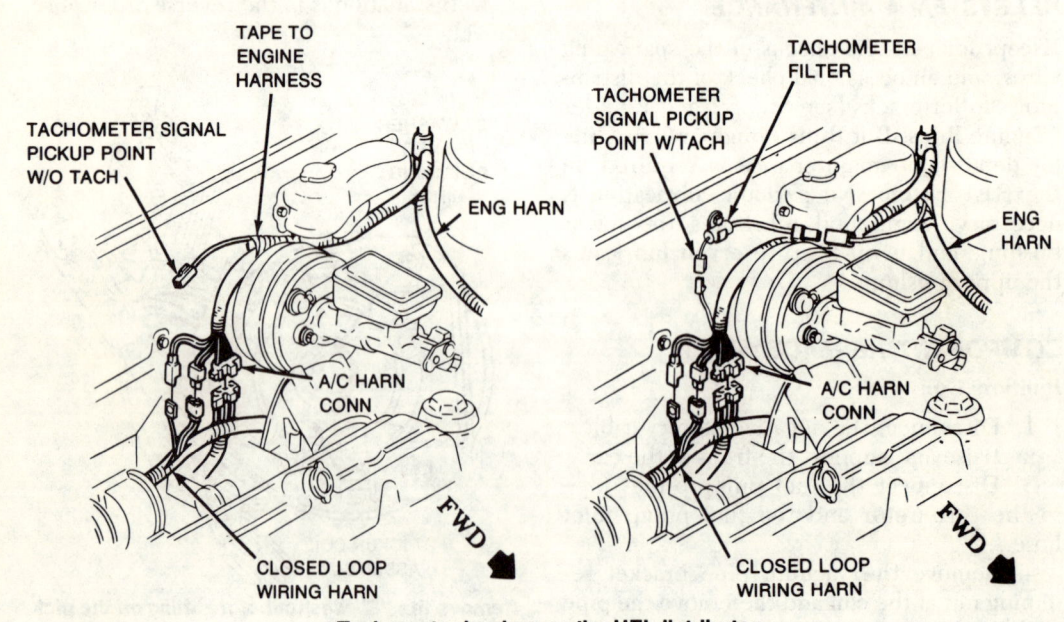

Tachometer hookup on the HEI distributor

TUNE-UP

which the spark plugs fire in each of the cylinders. It is measured in degrees before or after Top Dead Center (TDC) of the compression stroke.

Because it takes a fraction of a second for the spark plug to ignite the mixture in the cylinder, the spark plug must fire a little before the piston reaches TDC. Otherwise, the mixture will not be completely ignited as the piston passes TDC and the full power of the explosion will not be used by the engine.

The timing measurement is given in degrees of crankshaft rotation before the piston reaches TDC (BTDC). If the setting for the ignition timing is 5° BTDC, the spark plug must fire 5° before each piston reaches TDC. This only holds true, however, when the engine is at idle speed.

As the engine speed increases, the pistons go faster. The spark plugs have to ignite the fuel even sooner if it is to be completely ignited when the piston reaches TDC.

If the ignition is set too far advanced (BTDC), the ignition and expansion of the fuel in the cylinder will occur too soon and tend to force the piston down while it is still traveling up. This causes engine ping. If the ignition spark is set too far retarded, after TDC (ATDC), the piston will have already passed TDC and started on its way down when the fuel is ignited. This will cause the piston to be forced down for only a portion of its travel. This will result in poor engine performance and lack of power.

Ignition timing for this engine should be accomplished using the "averaging" method in which the timing of each cylinder can be brought into closer agreement with the base timing specification.

The "averaging" method involves the use of a double notched crankshaft pulley. When timing the engine, the coil wire, instead of the Number 1 plug wire, should be used to trigger the timing light. The notch for the No. 1 cylinder is scribed across all three edges of the double sheave pulley. Another notch located 180 degrees away from the No. 1 cylinder notch is scribed only across the center section of the pulley to make it distinguishable from the No. 1 cylinder notch.

Since the trigger signal for the timing light is picked up at the coil wire, each spark firing results in a flash from the timing light. A slight jiggling of the timing notch may be apparent since each cylinder firing is being displayed. Optimum timing of all cylinders is accomplished by centering the total apparent notch width about the correct timing specification.

There are three basic types of timing light available. The first is a simple neon bulb with two wire connections (one for the spark plug and one for the plug wire, connecting the light in series). This type of light is quite dim,

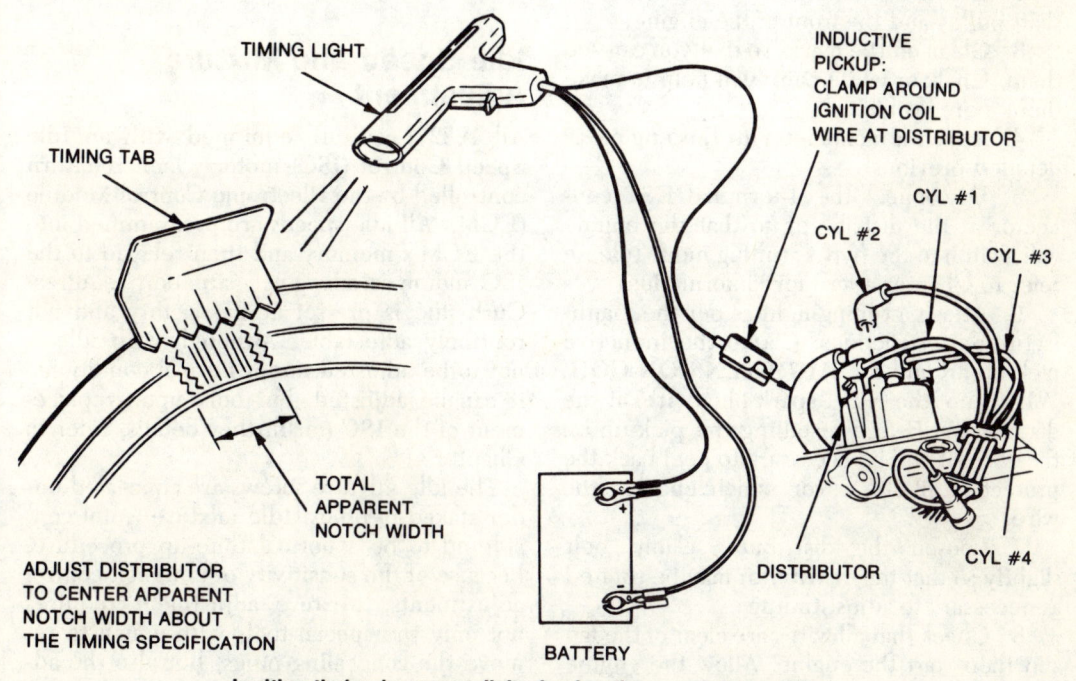

Ignition timing is accomplished using the averaging method

and must be held closely to the marks to be seen, but it is quite inexpensive. The second type of light operates from the car's battery. Two alligator clips connect to the battery terminals, while a third wire connects to the spark plug with an adapter. This type of light is more expensive, but the xenon bulb provides a nice bright flash which can even be seen in sunlight. The third type replaces the battery source with 110 volt house current. Some timing lights have other functions built into them, such as dwell meters, tachometers, or remote starting switches. These are convenient, in that they reduce the tangle of wires under the hood, but may duplicate the functions of tools you already have.

Because your car has electronic ignition, you should use a timing light with an inductive pickup. This pickup simply clamps around the Number 1 spark plug wire (in this case, the coil wire), eliminating the adapter. It is not susceptible to crossfiring or false triggering, which may occur with a conventional light due to the greater voltages produced by HEI.

ADJUSTMENT

1. Refer to the instructions on the emission control sticker inside the engine compartment. Follow all instructions on the label.
2. Locate the timing marks on the crankshaft pulley and the front of the engine.
3. Clean off the marks so that you can see them. Chalk or white paint will help to make them more visible.
4. Attach a tachometer to the engine as detailed previously.
5. Disconnect the 4-terminal EST connector at the distributor so that the engine will switch to the bypass timing mode (please refer to Chapter 4 for more information).
6. Attach a timing light as per the manufacturer's instructions. Clamp the inductive pick-up around the HIGH TENSION COIL WIRE (not the No. 1 spark plug wire) at the distributor. Before installing the pick-up on the wire, it will be necessary to peel back the protective plastic cover which encases the wire.
7. Loosen the distributor clamp bolt slightly so that the distributor may be rotated as necessary to adjust timing.
8. Check that all wires are clear of the fan and then start the engine. Allow the engine to reach normal operating temperature.
9. Aim the timing light at the marks. A slight jiggling of the notch on the pulley may appear due to the fact that each cylinder is being displayed as it fires. The apparent notch 'width' *cannot* be reduced by a timing adjustment.
10. Center the total apparent notch 'width' about the correct timing mark on the indicator by rotating the distributor housing. This will insure that the average cylinder timing is as close to specifications as possible. Once again, the apparent notch 'width' *cannot* be reduced by timing adjustment.
11. Turn off the engine and tighten the distributor lock bolt. Start the engine and recheck the timing. Sometimes the distributor will move a little during the tightening process. If the ignition timing is within 1° of the correct setting, that is close enough; a tolerance of up to 2° is permitted by the manufacturer.
12. Turn off the engine and disconnect the timing light and the tachometer. Reconnect the 4-terminal EST connector.

Valve Adjustment

All models utilize an hydraulic valve lifter system to obtain zero lash. No adjustment is necessary. An initial adjustment is required anytime that the lifters are removed or the valve train is disturbed, this procedure is covered in Chapter 3.

Idle Speed and Mixture Adjustment

All 1982 J-cars are equipped with an Idle Speed Control (ISC) motor which is inturn controlled by the Electronic Control Module (ECM). All idle speeds are programmed into the ECM's memory and then relayed to the ISC motor as any given situation requires. Curb idle is pre-set at the factory and not routinely adjustable. Although curb idle is not to be adjusted under normal conditions, it can be adjusted, but only upon replacement of the ISC (for further details, refer to Chapter 4).

The idle mixture screws are concealed under staked-in plugs. Idle mixture is not considered to be a normal tune-up procedure, because of the sensitivity of emission control adjustments. Mixture adjustment requires not only the special tools with which to remove the concealing plugs, but also the addition of an artificial enrichment substance (generally propane) which must be introduced into the carburetor by means of a finely calibrated metering valve. These tools are not generally available and require a certain amount of expertise to use, therefore, mixture adjustments are purposely not covered in this book. If you suspect that your car's carburetor requires a mixture adjustment, we strongly recommend that the job be referred to a qualified service technician.

Engine and Engine Rebuilding 3

UNDERSTANDING THE ENGINE ELECTRICAL SYSTEM

The engine electrical system can be broken down into three separate and distinct systems—(1) the starting system; (2) the charging system; (3) the ignition system.

Battery and Starting System

The battery is the first link in the chain of mechanisms which work together to provide cranking of the automobile engine. In most modern cars, the battery is a lead-acid electrochemical device consisting of six two-volt (2 V) subsections connected in series so the unit is capable of producing approximately 12 V of electrical pressure. Each subsection, or cell, consists of a series of positive and negative plates held a short distance apart in a solution of sulfuric acid and water. The two types of plates are of dissimilar metals. This causes a chemical reaction to be set up, and it is this reaction which produces current flow from the battery when its positive and negative terminals are connected to an electrical appliance such as a lamp or motor. The continued transfer of electrons would eventually convert the sulfuric acid in the electrolyte to water, and make the two plates identical in chemical composition. As electrical energy is removed from the battery, its voltage output tends to drop. Thus, measuring battery voltage and battery electrolyte composition are two ways of checking the ability of the unit to supply power. During the starting of the engine, electrical energy is removed from the battery. However, if the charging circuit is in good condition and the operating conditions are normal, the power removed from the battery will be replaced by the generator (or alternator) which will force electrons back through the battery, reversing the normal flow, and restoring the battery to its original chemical state.

The battery and starting motor are linked by very heavy electrical cables designed to minimize resistance to the flow of current. Generally, the major power supply cable that leaves the battery goes directly to the starter, while other electrical system needs are supplied by a smaller cable. During starter operation, power flows from the battery to the starter and is grounded through the car's frame and the battery's negative ground strap.

The starting motor is a specially designed, direct current electric motor capable of producing a very great amount of power for its size. One thing that allows the motor to produce a great deal of power is its tremendous rotating speed. It drives the engine through

ENGINE AND ENGINE REBUILDING

a tiny pinion gear (attached to the starter's armature), which drives the very large flywheel ring gear at a greatly reduced speed. Another factor allowing it to produce so much power is that only intermittent operation is required of it. Thus, little allowance for air circulation is required, and the windings can be built into a very small space.

The starter solenoid is a magnetic device which employs the small current supplied by the starting switch circuit of the ignition switch. This magnetic action moves a plunger which mechanically engages the starter and electrically closes the heavy switch which connects it to the battery. The starting switch circuit consists of the starting switch contained within the ignition switch, a transmission neutral safety switch or clutch pedal switch, and the wiring necessary to connect these in series with the starter solenoid or relay.

A pinion, which is a small gear, is mounted to a one-way drive clutch. This clutch is splined to the starter armature shaft. When the ignition switch is moved to the "start" position, the solenoid plunger slides the pinion, toward the flywheel ring gear via a collar and spring. If the teeth on the pinion and flywheel match properly, the pinion will engage the flywheel immediately. If the gear teeth butt one another, the spring will be compressed and will force the gears to mesh as soon as the starter turns far enough to allow them to do so. As the solenoid plunger reaches the end of its travel, it closes the contacts that connect the battery and starter and then the engine is cranked.

As soon as the engine starts, the flywheel ring gear begins turning fast enough to drive the pinion at an extremely high rate of speed. At this point, the one-way clutch begins allowing the pinion to spin faster than the starter shaft so that the starter will not operate at excessive speed. When the ignition switch is released from the starter position, the solenoid is de-energized, and a spring contained within the solenoid assembly pulls the gear out of mesh and interrupts the current flow to the starter.

Some starters employ a separate relay, mounted away from the starter, to switch the motor and solenoid current on and off. The relay thus replaces the solenoid electrical switch, but does not eliminate the need for a solenoid mounted on the starter used to mechanically engage the starter drive gears. The relay is used to reduce the amount of current the starting switch must carry.

The Charging System

The automobile charging system provides electrical power for operation of the vehicle's ignition and starting systems and all the electrical accessories. The battery serves as an electrical surge or storage tank, storing (in chemical form) the energy originally produced by the engine-driven generator. The system also provides a means of regulating generator over-charged and to avoid excessive voltage to the accessories.

The storage battery is a chemical device incorporating parallel lead plates in a tank containing a sulfuric acid-water solution. Adjacent plates are slightly dissimilar, and the chemical reaction of the two dissimilar plates produces electrical energy when the battery is connected to a load such as the starter motor. The chemical reaction is reversible, so that when the generator is producing a voltage (electrical pressure) greater than that produced by the battery, electricity is forced into the battery, and the battery is returned to its fully charged state.

The vehicle's generator is driven mechanically, through V belts, by the engine crankshaft. It consists of two coils of fine wire, one stationary (the "stator"), and one movable (the "rotor"). The rotor may also be known as the "armature," and consists of fine wire wrapped around an iron core which is mounted on a shaft. The electricity which flows through the two coils of wire (provided initially by the battery in some cases) creates an intense magnetic field around both rotor and stator, and the interaction between the two fields creates voltage, allowing the generator to power the accessories and charge the battery.

There are two types of generators; the earlier is the direct current (DC) type. The current produced by the DC generator is generated in the armature and carried off the spinning armature by stationary brushes contacting the commutator. The commutator is a series of smooth metal contact plates on the end of the armature. The commutator plates, which are separated from one another by a very short gap, are connected to the armature circuits so that current will flow in one direction only in the wires carrying the generator output. The generator stator consists of two stationary coils of wire which draw

48 ENGINE AND ENGINE REBUILDING

some of the output current of the generator to form a powerful magnetic field and create the interaction of fields which generates the voltage. The generator field is wired in series with the regulator.

Newer automobiles use alternating current generators or "alternators," because they are more efficient, can be rotated at higher speeds, and have fewer brush problems. In an alternator, the field rotates while all the current produced passes only through the stator windings. The brushes bear against continuous slip rings rather than a commutator. This causes the current produced to periodically reverse the direction of its flow. Diodes (electrical one-way switches) block the flow of current from traveling in the wrong direction. A series of diodes is wired together to permit the alternating flow of the stator to be converted to a pulsating, but unidirectional flow at the alternator output. The alternator's field is wired in series with the voltage regulator.

The regulator consists of several circuits. Each circuit has a core, or magnetic coil of wire, which operates a switch. Each switch is connected to ground through one or more resistors. The coil of wire responds directly to system voltage. When the voltage reaches the required level, the magnetic field created by the winding of wire closes the switch and inserts a resistance into the generator field circuit, thus reducing the output. The contacts of the switch cycle open and closed many times each second to precisely control voltage.

While alternators are self-limiting as far as maximum current is concerned, DC generators employ a current regulating circuit which responds directly to the total amount of current flowing through the generator circuit rather than to the output voltage. The current regulator is similar to the voltage regulator except that all system current must flow through the energizing coil on its way to the various accessories.

SAFETY PRECAUTIONS

Observing these precautions will ensure safe handling of the electrical system components, and will avoid damage to the vehicle's electrical system:

    a. Be *absolutely* sure of the polarity of a booster battery before making connections. Connect the cables positive to positive, and negative to negative. Connect positive cables first and then make the last connection to a ground on the body of the booster vehicle so that arcing cannot ignite hydrogen gas that may have accumulated near the battery. Even momentary connection of a booster battery with the polarity reversed will damage alternator diodes.

    b. Disconnect both vehicle battery cables before attempting to charge a battery.

    c. Never ground the alternator or generator output or battery terminal. Be cautious when using metal tools around a battery to avoid creating a short circuit between the terminals.

    d. Never ground the field circuit between the alternator and regulator.

    e. Never run an alternator or generator without load unless the field circuit is disconnected.

    f. Never attempt to polarize an alternator.

    g. Keep the regulator cover in place when taking voltage and current limiter readings.

    h. Use insulated tools when adjusting the regulator.

    i. Whenever DC generator-to-regulator wires have been disconnected, the generator *must* be repolarized. To do this with an externally grounded, light duty generator, momentarily place a jumper wire between the battery terminal and the generator terminal of the regulator. With an internally grounded heavy duty unit, disconnect the wire to the regulator field terminal and touch the regulator battery terminal with it.

ENGINE ELECTRICAL

Distributor

REMOVAL AND INSTALLATION

1. Disconnect the negative battery cable.
2. Tag and disconnect all wires leading from the distributor cap.
3. Remove the air cleaner housing as previously detailed.
4. Remove the distributor cap.
5. Disconnect the AIR pipe-to-exhaust manifold hose at the air management valve.
6. Unscrew the rear engine lift bracket bolt and nut, lift it off the stud and then position the entire assembly out of the way to facilitate better access to the distributor.
7. Mark the position of the distributor, relative to the engine block and then scribe

ENGINE AND ENGINE REBUILDING 49

a mark on the distributor body indicating the initial position of the rotor.

8. Remove the hold-down nut and clamp from the base of the distributor. Remove the distributor from the engine. The drive gear on the distributor shaft is helical and the shaft will rotate slightly as the distributor is removed. Note and mark the position of the rotor at this second position. *Do not crank the engine while the distributor is removed.*

9. To install the distributor, rotate the shaft until the rotor aligns with the second mark you made (when the shaft stopped moving). Lubricate the drive gear with clean engine oil and install the distributor into the engine. As the distributor is installed, the rotor should move to the first mark that you made. This will ensure proper timing. If the marks do not align properly, remove the distributor and try again.

10. Install the clamp and hold-down nut.
NOTE: *You may wish to use a magnet attached to an extension bar to position the clamp on the stud.*

11. Installation of the remaining components is in the reverse order of removal. Check the ignition timing.

INSTALLATION IF THE ENGINE WAS DISTURBED

If the engine was cranked while the distributor was removed, you will have to place the engine on TDC of the compression stroke to obtain proper ignition timing.

1. Remove the No. 1 spark plug.
2. Place your thumb over the spark plug

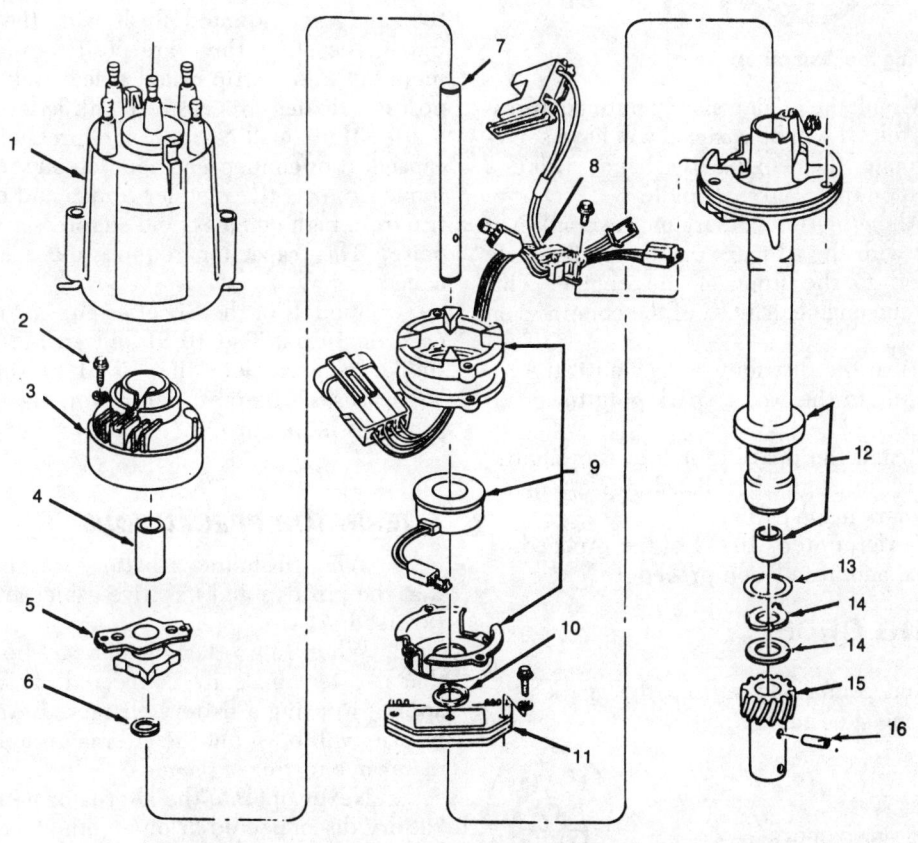

1. Distributor cap
2. Screw
3. Rotor
4. Bushing
5. Distributor shaft
6. Retainer
7. Distributor shaft
8. Wiring harness
9. Pole piece and plate assy. (pick-up coil)
10. Seal
11. Module
12. Housing assembly
13. O-ring
14. Washer
15. Distributor gear
16. Pin

Exploded view of the distributor

ENGINE AND ENGINE REBUILDING

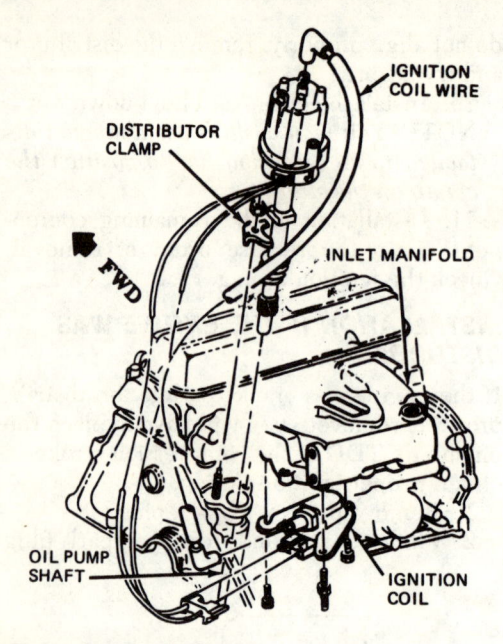

Removing the distributor

hole. Crank the engine slowly until compression is felt. It will be easier if you have someone rotate the engine by hand, using a wrench on the crankshaft pulley.

3. Align the timing mark on the crankshaft pulley with the 0° mark on the timing scale attached to the front of the engine. This places the engine at TDC of the compression stroke.

4. Turn the distributor shaft until the rotor points to the No. 1 spark plug tower on the cap.

5. Install the distributor into the engine. Be sure to align the distributor-to-engine block mark made earlier.

6. Perform Steps 10–11 of the preceeding removal and installation procedure.

FIRING ORDER

To avoid confusion, replace the spark plug wires one at a time.

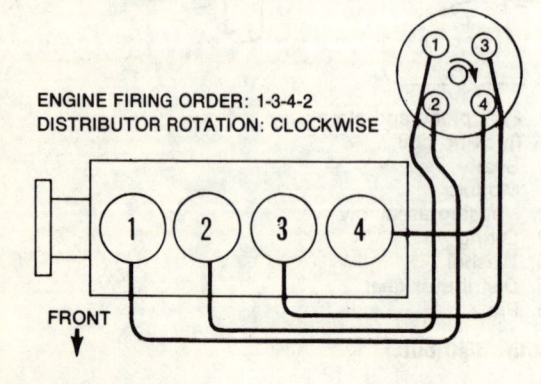

ENGINE FIRING ORDER: 1-3-4-2
DISTRIBUTOR ROTATION: CLOCKWISE

Alternator

The alternating current generator (alternator) supplies a continuous output of electrical energy at all engine speeds. The alternator generates electrical energy for the engine and all electrical components, and recharges the battery by supplying it with current. This unit consists of four main assemblies: two end frame assemblies, a rotor assembly, and a stator assembly. The rotor is supported in the drive end frame by a ball bearing and at the other end by a roller bearing. These bearings are lubricated during manufacture and require no maintenance. There are six diodes in the end frame assembly. Diodes are electrical check valves that change the alternating current supplied from the stator windings to a direct current (DC), delivered to the output (BAT) terminal. Three diodes are negative and are mounted flush with the end frame; the other three are positive and are mounted into a strip called a heat sink. The positive diodes are easily identified as the ones within small cavities or depressions. A capacitor, or condenser, mounted on the end frame protects the rectifier bridge and diode trio from high voltages, and suppresses radio noise. This capacitor requires no maintenance.

Two models of the SI series alternator are used on J-cars. The 10 SI and 15 SI are of similar construction; the 15 SI is slightly larger, uses different stator windings, and produces more current.

ALTERNATOR PRECAUTIONS

1. When installing a battery, make sure that the positive and negative cables are not reversed.

2. When jump-starting the car, be sure that like terminals are connected. This also applies to using a battery charger. Reversed polarity will burn out the alternator and regulator in a matter of seconds.

3. Never operate the alternator with the battery disconnected or on an otherwise uncontrolled open circuit.

4. Do not short across or ground any alternator or regulator terminals.

5. Do not try to polarize the alternator.

6. Do not apply full battery voltage to the field (brown) connector.

7. Always disconnect the battery ground cable before disconnecting the alternator lead.

ENGINE AND ENGINE REBUILDING 51

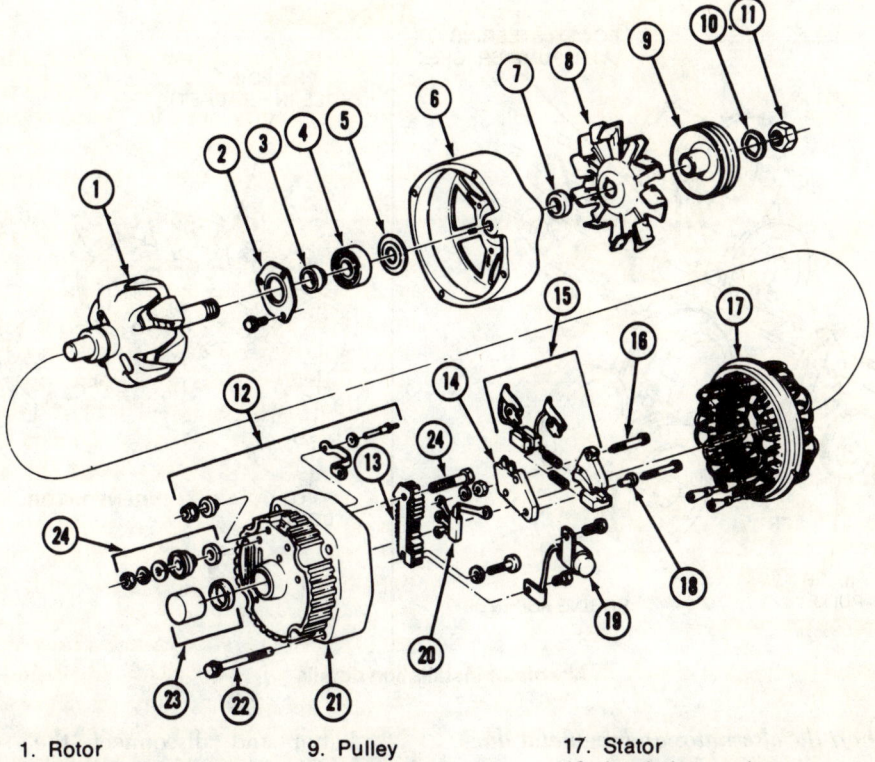

1. Rotor
2. Front bearing retainer
3. Inner collar
4. Bearing
5. Washer
6. Front housing
7. Outer collar
8. Fan
9. Pulley
10. Lockwasher
11. Pulley nut
12. Terminal assembly
13. Rectifier bridge
14. Regulator
15. Brush assembly
16. Screw
17. Stator
18. Insulating washer
19. Capacitor
20. Diode trio
21. Rear housing
22. Through bolt
23. Bearing and seal assembly
24. Terminal assembly

Exploded view of the 10SI alternator (15SI similar)

8. Always disconnect the battery (negative cable first) when charging it.
9. Never subject the alternator to excessive heat or dampness. If you are steamcleaning the engine, cover the alternator.
10. Never use arc-welding equipment on the car with the alternator connected.

REMOVAL AND INSTALLATION

1. Disconnect the negative battery cable at the battery.
CAUTION: *Failure to disconnect the negative cable may result in injury from the positive battery lead at the alternator, and*

Alternator and Regulator Specifications

	Alternator			Regulator					
					Field Relay			Regulator	
Year	Part No. or Manufacturer	Field Current @ 12 V	Output (amps)	Air Gap (in.)	Point Gap (in.)	Volts to Close	Air Gap (in.)	Point Gap (in.)	Volts @ 75°
1982	1100169	4–4.5	63		Integrated with alternator				13.8–14.8
	1101438	4–4.5	70		Integrated with alternator				13.8–14.8

52 ENGINE AND ENGINE REBUILDING

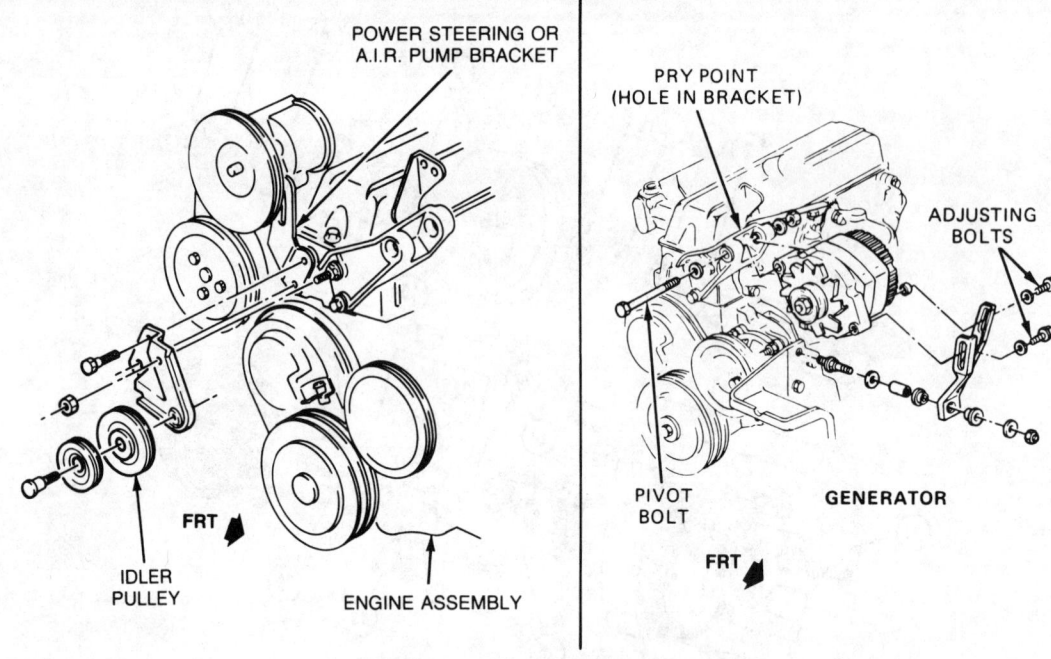

Alternator installation details

may short the alternator and regulator during the removal process.

2. Disconnect and label the two terminal plug and the battery leads from the rear of the alternator.

3. Loosen the mounting bolts. Push the alternator inwards and slip the drive belt off the pulley.

4. Remove the mounting bolts and remove the alternator.

5. To install, place the alternator in its brackets and install the mounting bolts. Do not tighten them yet.

6. Slip the belt back over the pully. Pull outwards on the unit and adjust the belt tension (see Chapter One). Tighten the mounting and adjusting bolts.

7. Install the electrical leads.

8. Install the negative battery cable.

Regulator

A solid state regulator is mounted within the alternator. All regulator components are enclosed in a solid mold. The regulator is non-adjustable and requires no maintenance.

Starter

REMOVAL AND INSTALLATION

1. Disconnect the negative battery cable at the battery.

2. Label and disconnect the solenoid wires and battery cable.

3. Remove the rear motor support bracket. Remove the A/C compressor support rod (if so equipped).

4. Working under the car, remove the two starter-to-engine bolts, and allow the starter to drop down. Note the location and number of any shims. Remove the starter.

5. Installation is the reverse. Tighten the mounting bolts to 25–35 ft. lbs.

STARTER OVERHAUL

Drive Replacement

1. Disconnect the field coil straps from the solenoid.

2. Remove the thru-bolts, and separate the commutator end frame, field frame assembly, drive housing, and armature assembly from each other.

3. Slide the two piece thrust collar off the end of the armature shaft.

4. Slide a suitably sized metal cylinder, such as a standard half-inch pipe coupling, or an old pinion, on the shaft so that the end of the coupling or pinion butts up against the edge of the pinion retainer.

5. Support the lower end of the armature securely on a soft surface, such as a wooden block, and tap the end of the coupling or pin-

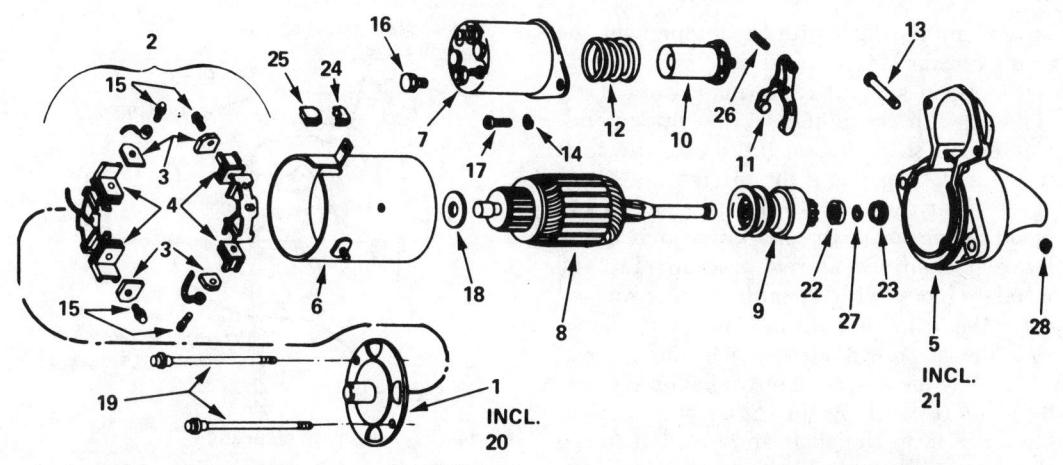

ENGINE AND ENGINE REBUILDING 53

1. Commutator end frame
2. Brush and holder
3. Brush
4. Brush holder
5. Drive end housing
6. Frame and field assembly
7. Solenoid switch
8. Armature
9. Drive assembly
10. Plunger
11. Shift lever
12. Plunger return spring
13. Shift lever shaft
14. Lock washer
15. Brush attaching screw
16. Field lead to switch screw
17. Switch attaching screw
18. Brake washer
19. Through bolt
20. Commutator end bushing
21. Drive end bushing
22. Pinion stop collar
23. Thrust collar
24. Grommet
25. Grommet
26. Plunger pin
27. Pinion stop retainer ring
28. Lever shaft retaining ring

Exploded view of the 5MT starter motor

ion, driving the retainer towards the armature end of the snap ring.

6. Remove the snap ring from the groove in the armature shaft with a pair of pliers. Then, slide the retainer and starter drive from the shaft.

7. To reassemble, lubricate the drive end of the armature shaft with silicone lubricant, and then slide the starter drive onto the shaft with the pinion facing outward. Slide the re-

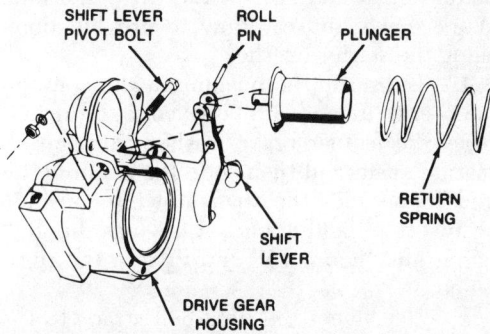

Starter shift lever and drive end housing disassembled

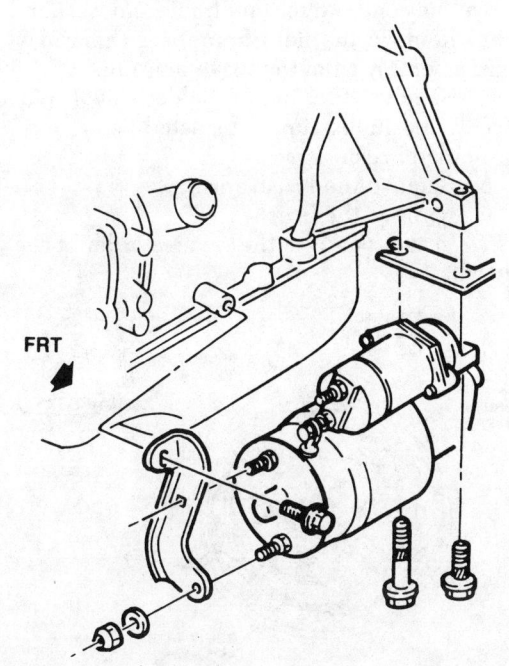

Starter motor mounting

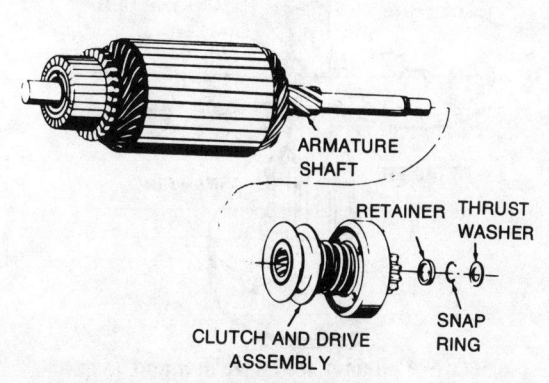

Starter drive assembly details

54 ENGINE AND ENGINE REBUILDING

tainer onto the shaft with the cupped surface facing outward.

8. Again support the armature on a soft surface, with the pinion at the upper end. Center the snap ring on the top of the shaft (use a new snap ring if the original was damaged during removal). Gently place a block of wood flat on top of the snap ring so as not to move it from a centered position. Tap the wooden block with a hammer in order to force the snap ring around the shaft. Then, slide the ring down into the snap ring groove.

9. Lay the armature down flat on the surface you're working on. Slide the retainer close up on to the shaft and position it and the thrust collar next to the snap ring. Using two pairs of pliers on opposite sides of the shaft, squeeze the thrust collar and the retainer together until the snap ring is forced into the retainer.

10. Lube the drive housing bushing with a silicone lubricant. Then, install the armature and clutch assembly into the drive housing, engaging the solenoid shift lever with the clutch, and positioning the front end of armature shaft into the bushing.

11. Apply a sealing compound approved for this application onto the drive housing; then position the field frame around the armature shaft and against the drive housing. Work slowly and carefully to prevent damaging the starter brushes.

12. Lubricate the bushing in the commutator end frame with a silicone lubricant, place the leather brake washer onto the armature shaft, and then slide the commutator end frame over the shaft and into position against the field frame. Line up the bolt holes, and then install and tighten the thrubolts.

13. Reconnect the field coil straps to the "motor" terminal of the solenoid.

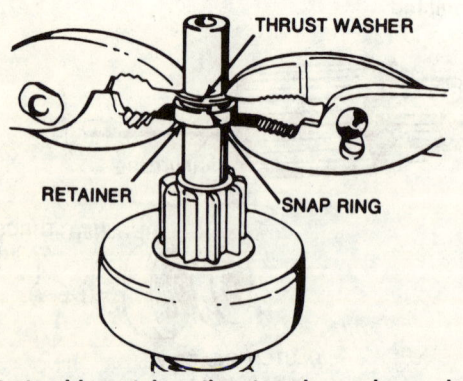

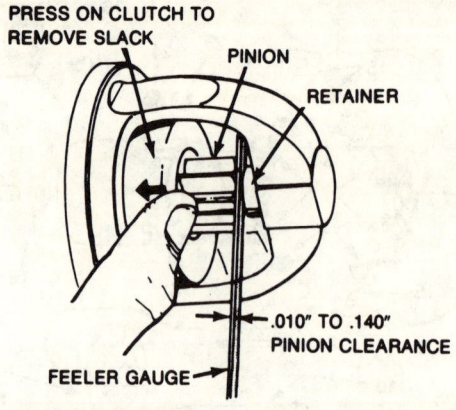

Measuring the pinion clearance

NOTE: *If replacement of the starter drive fails to cure the improper engagement of the starter pinion to the flywheel, there are probably defective parts in the solenoid and/or shift lever. The best procedure would probably be to take the assembly to a shop where a pinion clearance check can be made by energizing the solenoid on a test bench. If the pinion clearance is incorrect, disassemble the solenoid and the shift lever, inspect, and replace worn parts.*

Brush Replacement

1. After removing the starter from the engine, disconnect the field coil from the motor solenoid terminal.

2. Remove the starter thru-bolts and remove the commutator end frame and washer.

3. Remove the field frame and the armature assembly from the drive housing.

4. Remove the brush holder pivot pin which positions one insulated and one grounded brush.

5. Remove the brush springs.

6. Remove the brushes.

7. Installation is in the reverse order of removal.

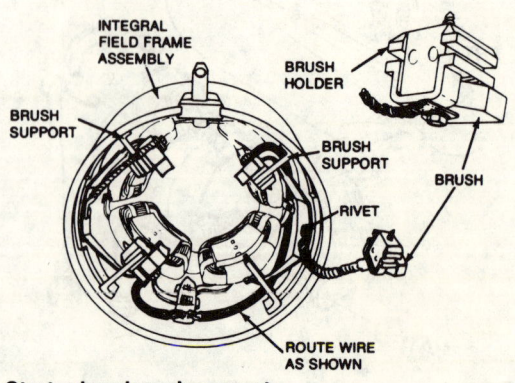

Starter drive retainer, thrust washer and snap ring installation

Starter brush replacement

ENGINE AND ENGINE REBUILDING

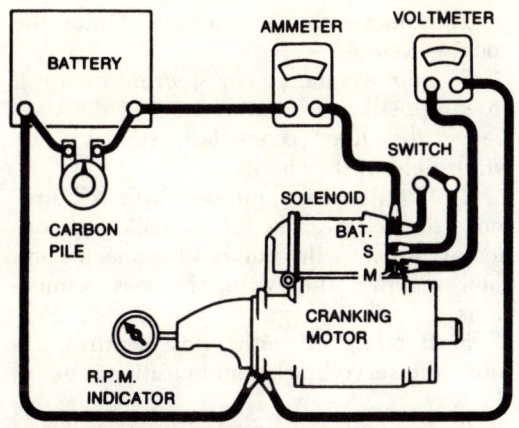

No-load test connections

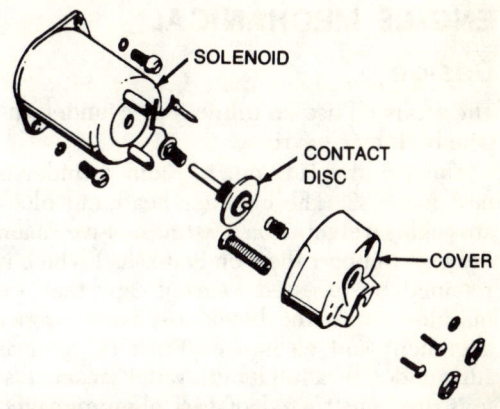

Solenoid switch disassembly

STARTER SOLENOID REMOVAL AND INSTALLATION

1. Remove the screw and washer from the motor connector strap terminal.
2. Remove the two screws which retain the solenoid housing to the end frame assembly.
3. Twist the solenoid clockwise to remove the flange key from the keyway slot in the housing.
4. Remove the solenoid assembly.
5. With the solenoid return spring installed on the plunger, position the solenoid body on the drive housing and turn it counterclockwise to engage the flange key in the keyway slot.
6. Install the two screws which retain the solenoid housing to the end frame.

Battery

Refer to Chapter One for details on battery maintenance.

REMOVAL AND INSTALLATION

1. Disconnect the negative (ground) cable first, then the positive cable. The side terminal cables are retained only by the center bolt.

   CAUTION: *To avoid sparks, always disconnect the negative cable first, and connect it last.*

2. Remove the battery hold-down clamp.
3. Remove the battery.
4. Before installing the battery, clean the battery terminals and the cables thoroughly.
5. Check the battery tray to be sure it is clear of any debris. If it is rusty, it should be wire-brushed clean and given a coat of anti-rust paint, or replaced.
6. Install the battery in the tray, being sure it is centered in the lip.
7. Install the hold-down clamp. Tighten to 6 ft. lbs., which is tight enough to hold the battery in place, but loose enough to prevent the case from cracking.
8. Connect the positive, then the negative battery cables. Installation torque for the cables is 9 ft. lbs. Give the terminals a light external coat of grease after installation to retard corrosion.

   CAUTION: *Make absolutely sure that the battery is connected properly before you turn on the ignition switch. Reversed polarity can burn out the alternator and regulator in a matter of seconds.*

Battery and Starter Specifications

Year	Engine No. Cyl Displacement (cu in.)	Battery Ampere Hour Capacity	Volts	Terminal Grounded	Lock Test Amps	Volts	Torque (ft. lbs.)	No-Load Test Amps	Volts	RPM	Brush Spring Tension (oz)
1982	4-112	315 ①	12	NEG	Not recommended			57-82	9	6,000-12,000	35

① Cranking power in amps @ 0°F

ENGINE AND ENGINE REBUILDING

ENGINE MECHANICAL

Design

The J-cars all use an inline four cylinder engine built by Chevrolet.

The 1.8 litre (112 cu. in.) four cylinder is new for 1982. The cylinder head and block are light weight iron castings. Five main bearings support the iron crankshaft which is retained by recessed bearing caps that are machined with the block to ensure proper alignment and clearance. Each cylinder is surrounded by a full length water jacket. Pistons are constructed of cast aluminum and use two compression rings and one oil control ring. Piston pins are chromium steel and have a floating fit in the pistons while they are press-fit into the connecting rods.

The cylinder head utilizes individual intake and exhaust ports for each cylinder. Valve guides are integral while the rocker arms are retained on individual threaded studs. A ball pivot-type valve train is used. Motion is transmitted from the camshaft through the hydraulic lifter and push rod to the rocker arm. The rocker arm then pivots on its ball, thus transmitting the camshaft motion to the valve.

Because the cylinder head is of the crossflow configuration, the intake manifold is at the back of the engine and the exhaust manifold is at the front. The crossflow design permits better scavenging of gases and more efficient combustion. The intake manifold is cast aluminum and has an integral passage through which coolant circulates, providing faster warm-up and lower exhaust emissions.

Engine Removal and Installation

NOTE: *This procedure will require the use of a special powertrain alignment tool #M6X1X65.*

1. Disconnect the battery cables at the battery, negative cable first.
2. Remove the air cleaner. Drain the cooling system.
3. Remove the power steering pump (if so equipped) and position it out of the way. Leave the lines connected. Remove the windshield washer bottle.
4. If the car is equipped with A/C, remove the relay bracket at the bulkhead connector. Remove the bulkhead connector and then separate the wiring harness connections.
5. If equipped with cruise control, remove the servo bracket and position it out of the way.
6. Tag and disconnect all vacuum hoses and wires.
7. Remove the master cylinder at the vacuum booster.
8. Remove all heater and radiator hoses and position them out of the way.
9. Remove the fan assembly. Remove the horn.
10. Disconnect the carburetor linkage. Raise the front of the car and support it with jack-stands.
11. Disconnect the fuel line at the intake manifold.
12. Remove the air conditioning brace (if so equipped).
13. Remove the exhaust shield. Remove the starter.
14. Disconnect the exhaust pipe at the manifold. Remove the wheels.
15. Disconnect the stabilizer bar from the lower control arms. Remove the ball joints from the steering knuckle.
16. Remove the drive axles at the transaxle and then remove the transaxle strut.
17. If equipped with A/C, remove the inner fender shield. Remove the drive belt, tag and disconnect the wires and then remove the compressor. *Do not disconnect any of the refrigerant lines.*
18. Remove the rear engine mount nuts and plate.
19. If equipped with an automatic transaxle, remove the oil filter.

General Engine Specifications

Year	Engine No. Cyl Displacement (cu in.)	Carburetor Type	Horsepower @ rpm	Torque @ rpm (ft. lbs.)	Bore x Stroke (in.)	Compression Ratio	Oil Pressure @ 2400 rpm
1982	4–112	2BBL	88 @ 5100	100 @ 2800	3.50 x 2.91	9.0:1	45

ENGINE AND ENGINE REBUILDING 57

Valve Specifications

Year	Engine No. Cyl Displacement (cu in.)	Seat Angle (deg)	Face Angle (deg)	Spring Test Pressure (lbs. @ In.)	Spring Installed Height (in.)	Stem to Guide Clearance (in.) Intake	Stem to Guide Clearance (in.) Exhaust	Stem Diameter (in.) Intake	Stem Diameter (in.) Exhaust
1982	4–112	46	45	183 @ 1.33	1.60	0.0011–0.0026	0.0014–0.0031	0.3139–0.3144	0.3129–0.3136

ENGINE AND ENGINE REBUILDING

Crankshaft and Connecting Rod Specifications
All measurements are given in inches

Year	Engine No. Cyl Displacement (cu in.)	Crankshaft Main Brg Journal Dia	Crankshaft Main Brg Oil Clearance	Crankshaft Shaft End-Play	Thrust on No.	Connecting Rod Journal Diameter	Connecting Rod Oil Clearance	Connecting Rod Side Clearance
1982	4–112	2.4936–2.4946	0.0014–0.0026	0.0019–0.0071	4	1.9990–1.9999	0.0009–0.0031	0.0039–0.0240

Camshaft Specifications
All measurements in inches

Year	Engine	Journal Diameter 1	2	3	4	5	Bearing Clearance	Lobe Lift Intake	Lobe Lift Exhaust	Camshaft End Play
1982	4–112	1.8677–1.8696	1.8677–1.8696	1.8677–1.8696	1.8677–1.8696	1.8677–1.8696	0.0010–0.0039	0.2625	0.2625	NA

NA Not available at time of publication

Ring Gap
All measurmtnts are given in inches

Year	Engine	Top Compression	Bottom Compression	Oil Control
1982	4–112	0.0098–0.0196	0.0098–0.0196	None

Ring Side Clearance
All measurements are given in inches

Year	Engine	Top Compression	Bottom Compression	Oil Control
1982	4–112	0.0011–0.0026	0.0011–0.0033	0.0078

Torque Specifications
All readings in ft. lbs.

Year	Engine No. Cyl Displacement (cu in.)	Cylinder Head Bolts	Rod Bearing Bolts	Main Bearing Bolts	Crankshaft Bolt	Flywheel to Crankshaft Bolts	Manifold Intake	Manifold Exhaust
1982	4–112	65–75	34–40	63–74	66–84	45–55	20–25	22–28

ENGINE AND ENGINE REBUILDING

Piston Clearance

All measurements are given in inches

Year	Engine	Piston to Bore Clearance
1982	4-112	0.0007-0.0018

20. Disconnect the speedometer cable and lower the vehicle.
21. If equipped with an automatic transaxle, remove the oil cooler at the transaxle.
22. Remove the front engine mount nuts.
23. Disconnect the clutch cable on the manual transaxle. Disconnect the detent cable on the automatic transaxle.
24. Install an engine lifting device, remove the transaxle mount and bracket. Lift the engine out of the car.

To install:

25. Install the engine mount alignment bolt (M6X1X65) to ensure proper power train alignment.
26. Lower the engine into the car, leaving the lifting device attached.
27. Install the transaxle bracket. Install the mount to the side frame and secure with NEW mount bolts.
28. With the weight not yet on the

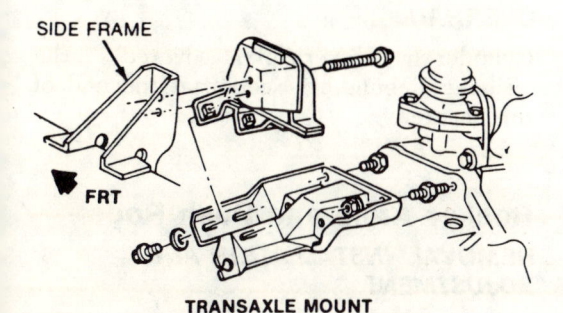

Rear engine mounts

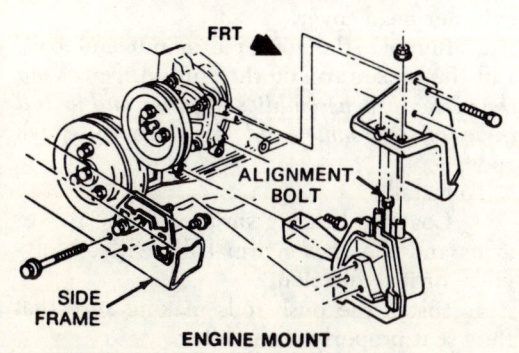

Transaxle and front engine mounts

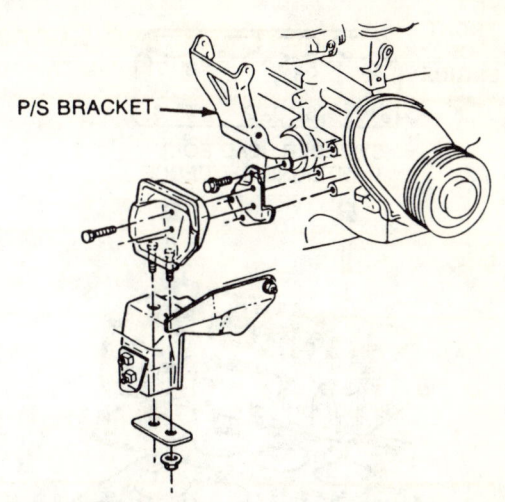

mounts, tighten the transaxle bolts. Tighten the right front mount nuts.
29. Lower the engine fully onto the mounts, remove the lifting device and then raise the front of the car.
30. Installation of the remaining components is in the reverse order of removal. Check the powertrain alignment bolt; if excessive force is required to remove the bolt, loosen the transaxle adjusting bolts and realign the powertrain. Adjust the drive belts and the clutch cable (if equipped with manual transaxle).

Cylinder Head

REMOVAL AND INSTALLATION

NOTE: *The engine should be "overnight" cold before removing the cylinder head.*

1. Disconnect the negative battery cable.
2. Drain the cooling system into a clean container; the coolant can be reused if it is still good.
3. Remove the air cleaner. Raise and support the front of the vehicle.
4. Remove the exhaust shield. Disconnect the exhaust pipe.
5. Remove the heater hose from the intake manifold and then lower the car.
6. Unscrew the mounting bolts and remove the engine lift bracket (includes air management).
7. Remove the distributor. Disconnect the vacuum manifold at the alternator bracket.
8. Tag and disconnect the remaining vacuum lines at the intake manifold and thermostat.

ENGINE AND ENGINE REBUILDING

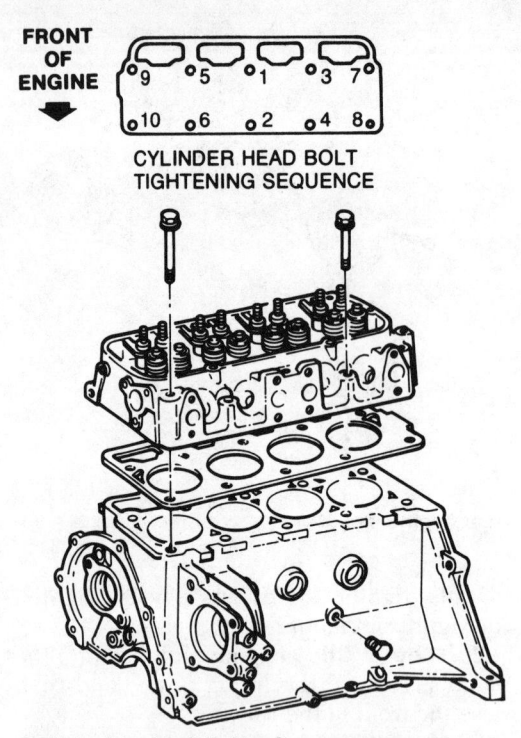

Cylinder head bolt tightening sequence

9. Remove the air management pipe at the exhaust check valve.
10. Disconnect the accelerator linkage at the carburetor and then remove the linkage bracket.
11. Tag and disconnect all necessary wires. Remove the upper radiator hose at the thermostat.
12. Remove the bolt attaching the dipstick tube and hot water bracket.
13. Remove the idler pulley. Remove the A.I.R. and power steering pump drive belts.
14. Remove the A.I.R. bracket-to-intake manifold bolt. If equipped with power steering, remove the air pump pulley, The A.I.R. thru-bolt and the power steering adjusting bracket.
15. Loosen the A.I.R. mounting bracket lower bolt so that the bracket will rotate.
16. Disconnect and plug the fuel line at the carburetor.
17. Remove the alternator. Remove the alternator brace from the head and then remove the upper mounting bracket.
18. Remove the cylinder head cover. Remove the rocker arms and push rods.
19. Remove the cylinder head bolts in the order given in the illustration. Remove the cylinder head with the carburetor, intake and exhaust manifolds still attached.

To install, the gasket surfaces on both the head and the block must be clean of any foreign matter and free of any nicks or heavy scratches. Cylinder bolt threads in the block and the bolt must be clean.

20. Place a new cylinder head gasket in position over the dowel pins on the block. Carefully guide the cylinder head into position.
21. Coat the cylinder bolts with sealing compound and install them finger tight.
22. Using a torque wrench, gradually tighten the bolts in the sequence shown in the illustration to the proper specifications.
23. Installation of the remaining components is in the reverse order of removal.

VALVE GUIDES AND SEATS

Valve guides are integral with the cylinder head. Valves with oversize stems are available; the guides must be reamed oversize to accept these valves. As an alternative, some shops will install replacement valve guides that fit standard size valve stems. Discuss these procedures with your dealer or machine shop.

Valve seats can be reground. This procedure requires special equipment; consult a machine shop or engine rebuilding shop for this service.

OVERHAUL

Cylinder head overhaul is covered in the "Engine Rebuilding" section at the end of this chapter.

Rocker Arms and Push Rods
REMOVAL, INSTALLATION AND ADJUSTMENT

1. Remove the air cleaner. Remove the cylinder head cover.
2. Remove the rocker arm nut and ball. Lift the rocker arm off the stud. *Always keep the rocker arm assemblies together and install them on the same stud.* Remove the push rods.

To install:
3. Coat the bearing surfaces of the rocker arms and the rocker arm balls with "Molykote" or its equivalent.
4. Install the push rods making sure that they seat properly in the lifter.
5. Install the rocker arms, balls and nuts.

ENGINE AND ENGINE REBUILDING   61

NOTE: AT TIME OF INSTALLATION, FLANGES MUST BE FREE OF OIL. A ⅛ BEAD OF SEALANT MUST BE APPLIED TO FLANGES AND SEALANT MUST BE WET TO TOUCH WHEN BOLTS ARE TORQUED.

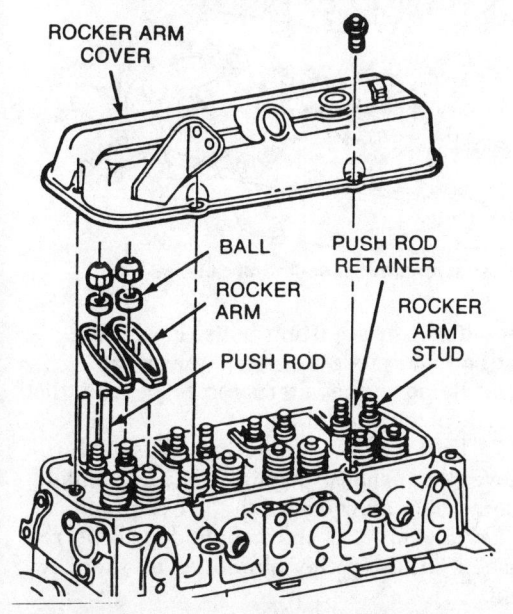

Exploded view of the rocker arm assembly

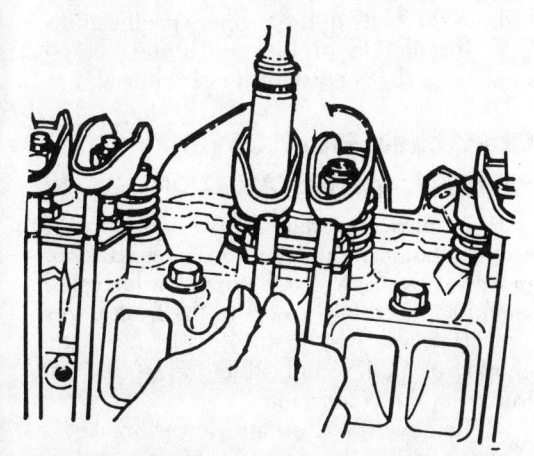

Tighten the rocker arm nut until the pushrod cannot be rotated between your fingers

Tighten the rocker arm nuts until all lash is eliminated.

6. Adjust the valves when the lifter is on the base circle of a camshaft lobe:

a. Crank the engine until the mark on the crankshaft pulley lines up with the '0' mark on the timing tab. Make sure that the engine is in the No. 1 firing position. Place your fingers on the No. 1 rocker arms as the mark on the crank pulley comes near the '0' mark. If the valves are not moving, the engine is in the No. 1 firing position. If the valves move, the engine is in the No. 4 firing position; rotate the engine one complete revolution and it will be in the No. 1 position.

b. When the engine is in the No. 1 firing position, adjust the following valves:
- Exhaust—1, 3
- Intake—1, 2

c. Back the adjusting nut out until lash can be felt at the push rod, then turn the nut until all lash is removed (this can be determined by rotating the push rod while turning the adjusting nut). When all lash has been removed, turn the nut in 1½ additional turns, this will center the lifter plunger.

d. Crank the engine one complete revolution until the timing tab and the '0' mark are again in alignment. Now the engine is in the No. 4 firing position. Adjust the following valves:
- Exhaust—2, 4
- Intake—3, 4

7. Installation of the remaining components is in the reverse order of removal.

Rocker Arm Studs

Cylinder heads use threaded rocker arm studs. Studs that have damaged threads should be replaced with new studs. If the threads in the head are damaged or stripped, the head can be retapped, and a helical-type insert added. If such an insert is not available, the cylinder head will require replacement.

Valve Adjustment

Anytime that the valve train has been disturbed, the valves will require an initial adjustment. This procedure is covered in the "Rocker Arm and Push Rod" section.

Intake Manifold

REMOVAL AND INSTALLATION

1. Disconnect the negative battery cable.
2. Remove the air cleaner. Drain the cooling system.
3. Tag and disconnect all necessary vacuum lines and wires. Remove the idler pulley.
4. Remove the A.I.R. drive belt. If equipped with power steering, remove the drive belt and then remove the pump with

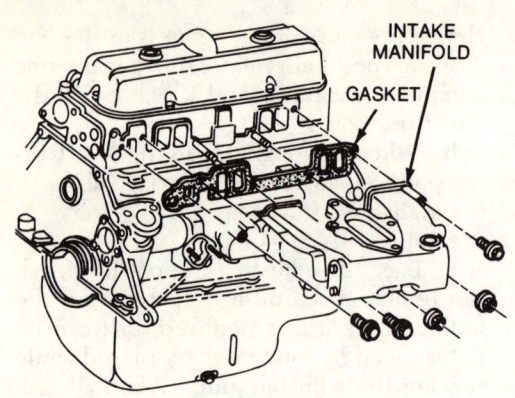

62　ENGINE AND ENGINE REBUILDING

Intake manifold installation details

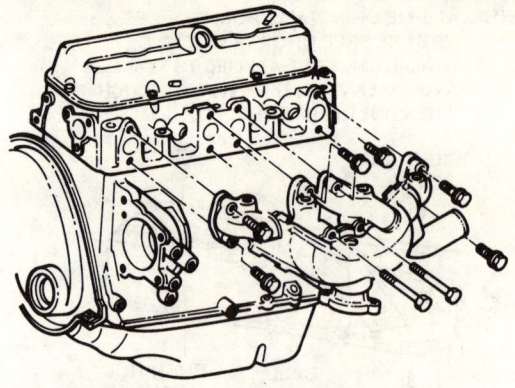

Exhaust manifold installation details

the lines attached. Position the pump out of the way.

5. Remove the A.I.R. bracket-to-intake manifold bolt. Remove the air pump pulley.

6. If equipped with power steering, remove the A.I.R. thru-bolt and then the power steering adjusting bracket.

7. Loosen the lower bolt on the air pump mounting bracket so that the bracket will rotate.

8. Disconnect the fuel line at the carburetor. Disconnect the carburetor linkage and then remove the carburetor.

9. Lift off the Early Fuel Evaporation (EFE) heater grid.

10. Remove the distributor.

11. Remove the mounting bolts and nuts and remove the intake manifold. Make sure to disconnect the heater hose and condenser from the bottom of the intake manifold before you lift it all the way out.

12. Using a new gasket, replace the manifold, tightening the nuts and bolts to specification.

13. Installation of the remaining components is in the reverse order of removal. Adjust all necessary drive belts and check the ignition timing.

Exhaust Manifold
REMOVAL AND INSTALLATION

1. Disconnect the negative battery cable.

2. Remove the air cleaner. Remove the exhaust manifold shield. Raise and support the front of the vehicle.

3. Disconnect the exhaust pipe at the manifold and then lower the vehicle.

4. Disconnect the air management-to-check valve hose and remove the bracket. Disconnect the oxygen sensor lead wire.

5. Remove the alternator belt. Remove

the alternator adjusting bolts, loosen the pivot bolt and pivot the alternator upward.

6. Remove the alternator brace and the A.I.R. pipes bracket bolt.

7. Unscrew the mounting bolts and remove the exhaust manifold. The manifold should be removed with the A.I.R. plumbing as an assembly. If the manifold is to be replaced, transfer the plumbing to the new one.

8. Clean the mating surfaces on the manifold and the head, position the manifold and tighten the bolts to the proper specifications.

9. Installation of the remaining components is in the reverse order of removal.

Crankcase Front Cover
REMOVAL AND INSTALLATION

1. Remove the engine drive belts.

2. Although not absolutely necessary, removal of the right front inner fender splash shield will facilitate access to the front cover.

3. Unscrew the center bolt from the crankshaft pulley and slide the pulley and hub from the crankshaft.

4. Remove the alternator lower bracket.

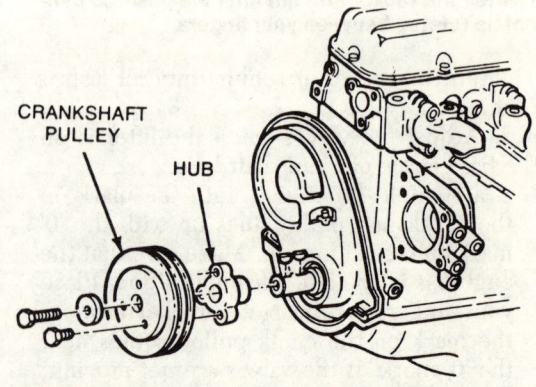

Removing the crankshaft pulley and hub

ENGINE AND ENGINE REBUILDING 63

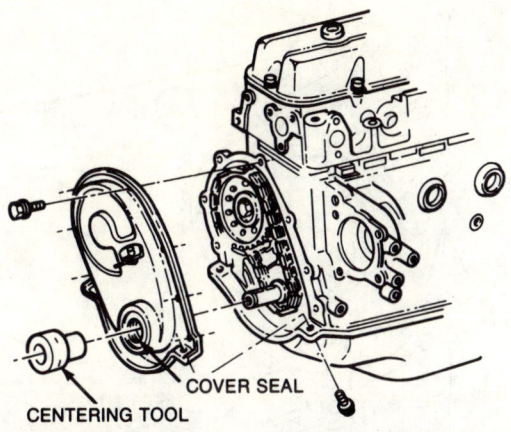

Front cover installation; a centering tool can aid in positioning

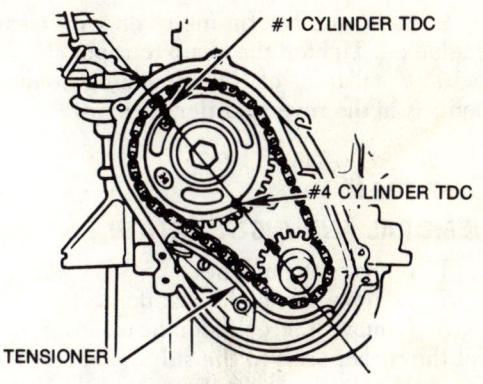

Timing mark alignment

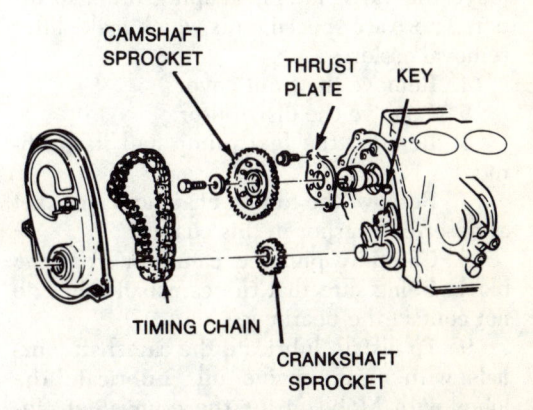

Exploded view of the timing chain and sprockets

5. Remove the oil pan-to-front cover bolts.

6. Remove the front cover-to-block bolts and then remove the front cover. If the front cover is difficult to remove, use a plastic mallet.

7. The surfaces of the block and front cover must be clean and free of oil. Apply a ⅛ in. bead of RTV sealant to the cover. The sealant must be wet to the touch when the bolts are torqued down.

NOTE: *When applying RTV sealant to the front cover, be sure to keep it out of the bolt holes.*

8. Position the front cover on the block using a centering tool (J-23042) and tighten the screws to the proper specifications.

9. Installation of the remaining components is in the reverse order of removal.

TIMING COVER OIL SEAL

The oil seal can be replaced with the cover either on or off the engine. If the cover is on the engine, remove the crankshaft pulley and hub first. Pry out the seal using a large screwdriver, being careful not to distort the seal mating surface. Install the new seal so that the open side or helical side is towards the engine. Press it into place with a seal driver made for the purpose. Install the hub if removed.

Timing Chain and Sprockets

REMOVAL AND INSTALLATION

1. Remove the front cover as previously detailed.

2. Place the No. 1 piston at TDC of the compression stroke so that the marks on the camshaft and crankshaft sprockets are in alignment (see illustration).

3. Loosen the timing chain tensioner nut as far as possible without actually removing it.

4. Remove the camshaft sprocket bolts and remove the sprocket and chain together. If the sprocket does not slide from the camshaft easily, a light blow with a soft mallet at the lower edge of the sprocket will dislodge it.

5. Use a gear puller (J-2288-8-20) and remove the crankshaft sprocket.

6. Press the crankshaft sprocket back onto the crankshaft.

7. Install the timing chain over the camshaft sprocket and then around the crankshaft sprocket. Make sure that the marks on the two sprockets are in alignment (see illustration). Lubricate the thrust surface with Molykote or its equivalent.

8. Align the dowel in the camshaft with the dowel hole in the sprocket and then install the sprocket onto the camshaft. Use the mounting bolts to draw the sprocket onto the camshaft and then tighten them to the proper specifications.

64 ENGINE AND ENGINE REBUILDING

9. Lubricate the timing chain with clean engine oil. Tighten the chain tensioner.
10. Installation of the remaining components is in the reverse order of removal.

Camshaft
REMOVAL AND INSTALLATION

1. Remove the engine.
2. Remove the intake manifold.
3. Remove the cylinder head cover, pivot the rocker arms to the sides, and remove the pushrods, keeping them in order. Remove the valve lifters, keeping them in order. There are special tools which make lifter removal easier.
4. Remove the front cover.
5. Remove the distributor.
6. Remove the fuel pump and its pushrod.
7. Remove the timing chain and sprocket as described earlier in this chapter.
8. Carefully pull the camshaft from the block, being sure that the camshaft lobes do not contact the bearings
9. To install, lubricate the camshaft journals with clean engine oil. Lubricate the lobes with Molykote or the equivalent. Install the camshaft into the engine, being extremely careful not to contact the bearings with the cam lobes.
10. Install the timing chain and sprocket. Install the fuel pump and pushrod. Install the timing cover. Install the distributor.
11. Install the valve lifters. If a new camshaft has been installed, new lifters should be used to ensure durability of the cam lobes.
12. Install the pushrods and rocker arms and the intake manifold. Adjust the valve lash after installing the engine. Install the cylinder head cover.

Pistons and Connecting Rods
REMOVAL AND INSTALLATION

1. Drain the crankcase and remove the oil pan and oil pump, as described later in this chapter.
2. Drain the cooling system and remove the cylinder head.
3. Remove any ridge or deposits from the upper end of the cylinder bores with a ridge reamer. Do this with the piston in the Bottom Dead Center position and a clean rag on top of the piston to collect cuttings.
4. Check the rods and pistons for identification numbers and, if necessary, number them.

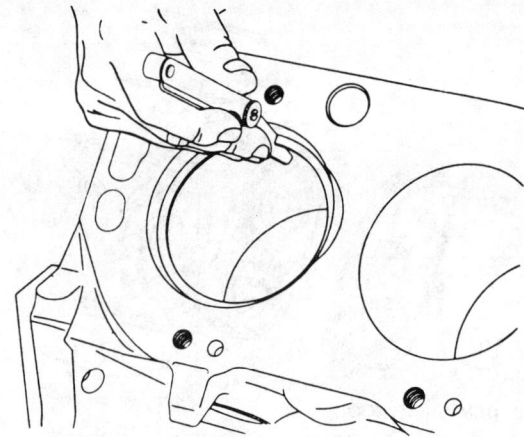

Check the ring end gap with the ring installed in its cylinder

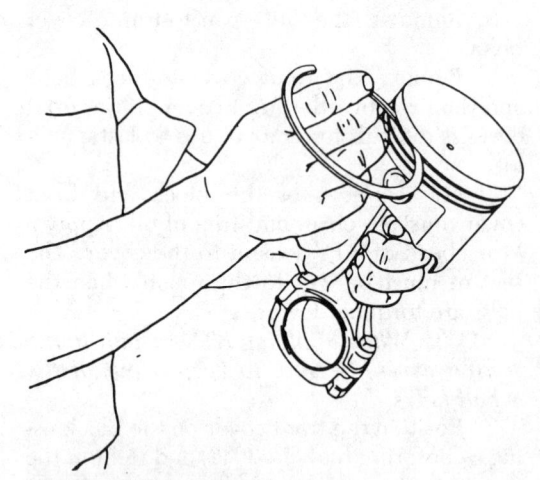

Checking the ring side clearance

5. Remove the connecting rod cap nuts and caps. Push the rods away from the crankshaft and install the caps and nuts loosely to their respective rods.
6. Push the piston and rod assemblies up and out of the cylinders.
7. Before replacing the rings, inspect the cylinder bores. If the cylinder bore is in satisfactory condition, place each ring in its bore in turn and square it in the bore with the head of the piston. Measure the ring end gap. If the gap is incorrect get a new ring. Do not file the end of the ring to obtain the correct gap.
8. Check the ring side clearance by installing the rings in their piston, and inserting a feeler gauge of the correct dimension between the ring and lower land. The gauge should slide freely around the circumference of the ring without binding. Any wear will

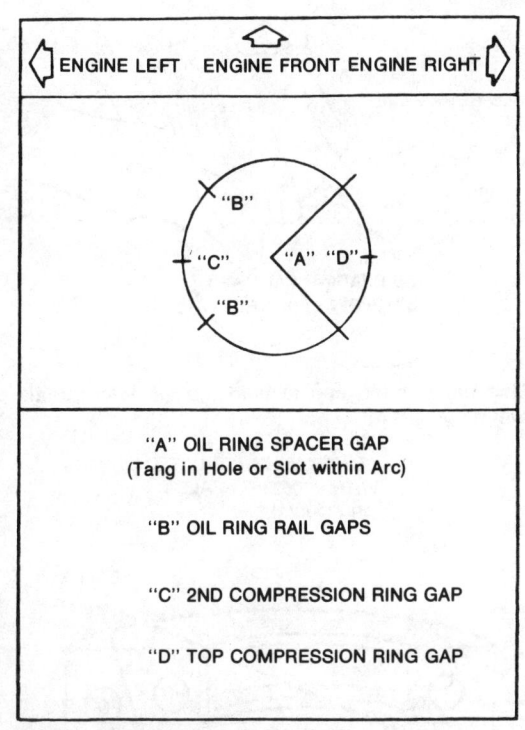

Ring gap locations

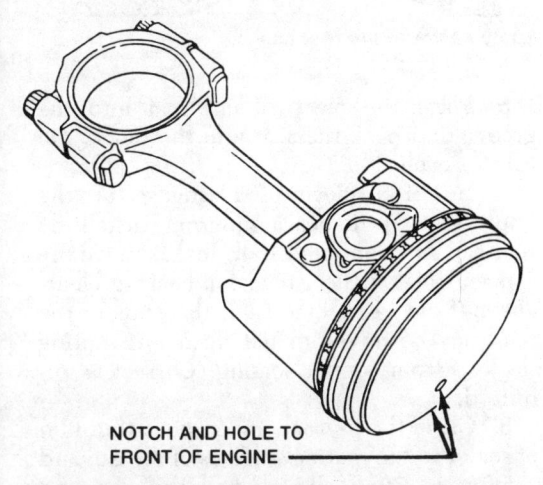

Install the piston with the notch and the hole facing the front of the engine

form a step on the lower land. Replace any pistons having high steps. Before checking the ring side clearance be sure the ring grooves are clean and free of carbon, sludge, or grit.

9. Install piston rings with a ring expander. Compression rings have a mark which must face the top of the piston. The top ring is chrome or molybdenum faced. When installing oil rings, do the following: first, install the oil ring in the ring groove and insert the anti-rotation tang into the oil hole; then, holding the ends of the spacer so they butt up against one another, install the lower steel oil ring rail; repeat this procedure to install the upperrail so that the gap will line up with that of the lower rail; flex the oil ring assembly to make sure it is free—if it binds, the ring groove must be dressed at a narrow point, or a distorted ring must be replaced; install lower compression ring with gap 120 degrees (one third of a circle) away from oil ring gap; install top ring with its gap 180 degrees away from that of the second ring. Be sure to install the piston in its original bore. Install the piston and rod assembly with the notch in the piston facing the front of the engine. Install short lengths of rubber tubing over the connecting rod bolts to prevent damage to the rod journals. Lubricate pistons and rod bearings with light engine oil. Install a ring compressor over the rings on the piston. Lower the piston and rod assembly into the bore until the ring compressor contacts the block. Using the wooden handle of a hammer, push the piston into the bore while guiding the rod onto the journal.

ENGINE LUBRICATION

Oil Pan

REMOVAL AND INSTALLATION

1. Disconnect the negative battery cable.
2. Drain the crankcase. Raise and support the front of the vehicle.
3. Remove the A/C brace if so equipped.
4. Remove the exhaust shield and disconnect the exhaust pipe at the manifold.
5. Remove the starter motor and position it out of the way.
6. Remove the flywheel cover. Remove the oil pan.

NOTE: *Prior to oil pan installation, check that the sealing surfaces on the pan, cylinder block and front cover are clean and free of oil. If installing the old pan, be sure that all old RTV has been removed.*

7. Apply a ⅛ in. bead of RTV sealant to the oil pan sealing surface. Use a new oil pan rear seal and install the pan in place. Tighten the bolts to 9–13 ft. lbs.
8. Installation of the remaining components is in the reverse order of removal.

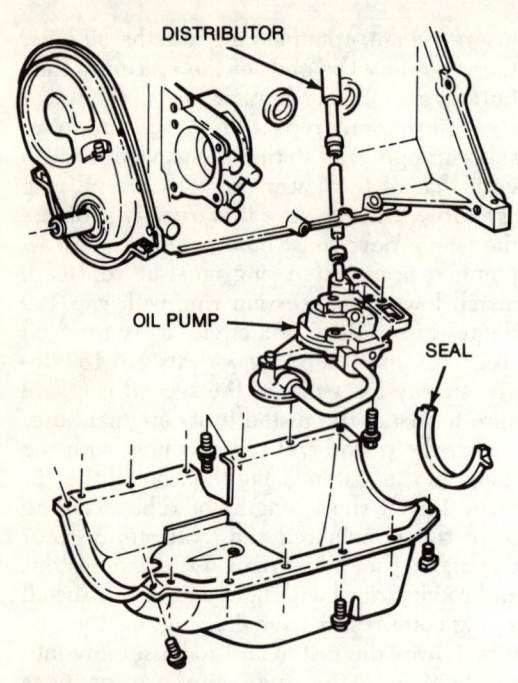

66 ENGINE AND ENGINE REBUILDING

Oil pan and pump installation details

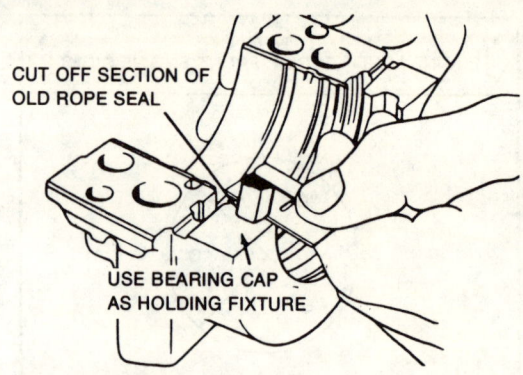

Use the bearing cap to hold the old lower seal while you cut it

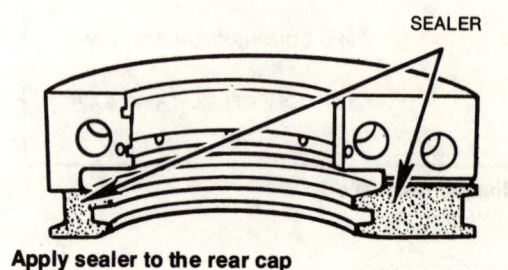

Apply sealer to the rear cap

Rear Main Oil Seal
REMOVAL AND INSTALLATION

1. Remove the oil pan and pump.
2. Remove the rear main bearing cap.
3. Gently pack the upper seal into the groove approximately ¼ inch on each side.
4. Measure the amount the seal was driven in on one side and add 1/16 in. Cut this length from the old lower cap seal. Be sure to get a sharp cut. Repeat for the other side.

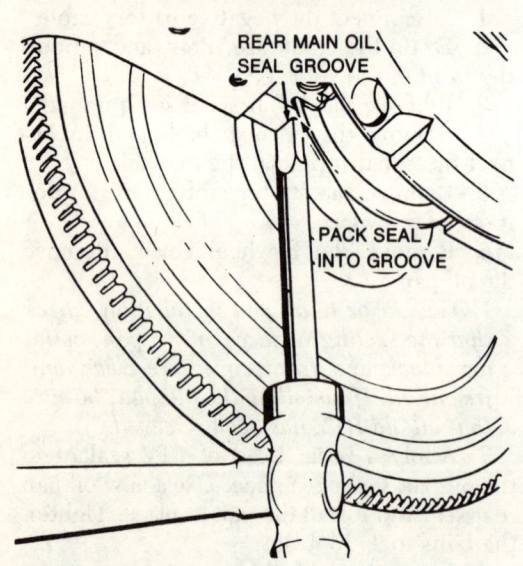

Pack the old upper seal into its groove ¼ in. on each side

5. Place the piece of cut seal into the groove and pack the seal into the block. Do this for each side.
6. Install a piece of Plastigage or the equivalent on the bearing journal. Install the rear cap and tighten to 75 ft. lbs. Remove the cap and check the gauge for bearing clearance. If out of specification, the ends of the seal may be frayed or not flush, preventing the cap from proper seating. Correct as required.
8. Clean the journal, and apply a thin film of sealer to the mating surfaces of the cap and tighten to 70 ft. lbs. Install the pan and pump.

Oil Pump
REMOVAL AND INSTALLATION

1. Remove the engine oil pan.
2. Remove the pump attaching bolts and carefully lower the pump.
3. Install in reverse order. To ensure immediate oil pressure on start-up, the oil pump gear cavity should be packed with petroleum jelly. Installation torque is 26–35 ft. lbs. (35–47 Nm.).

ENGINE AND ENGINE REBUILDING 67

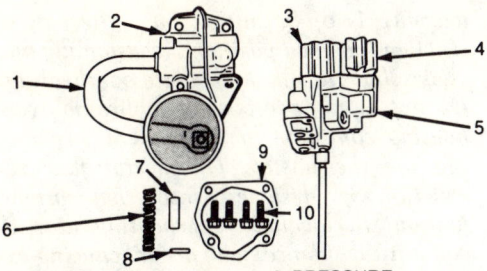

1. PICK UP TUBE AND SCREEN.
2. PUMP COVER.
3. DRIVE GEAR AND SHAFT.
4. IDLER GEAR.
5. PUMP BODY.
6. PRESSURE REGULATOR SPRING.
7. PRESSURE REGULATOR VALVE.
8. RETAINING PIN.
9. GASKET.
10. ATTACHING BOLTS.

Oil pump

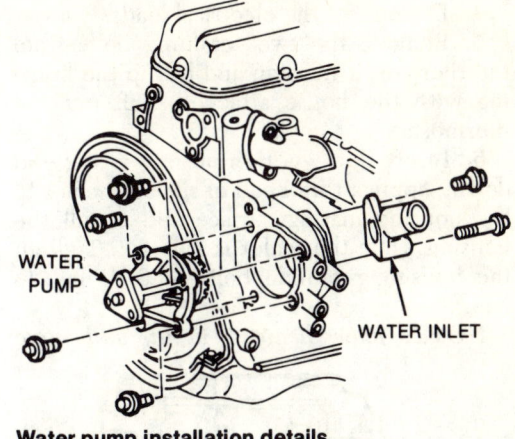

Water pump installation details

ENGINE COOLING

Radiator

REMOVAL AND INSTALLATION

1. Disconnect the negative battery cable.
2. Drain the cooling system.
3. Disconnect the electrical lead at the fan motor.
4. Remove the fan frame-to-radiator support attaching bolts and then remove the fan assembly.
5. Disconnect the upper and lower radiator hoses and the coolant recovery hose from the radiator.
6. Disconnect the transmission oil cooler lines from the radiator and wire them out of the way.
7. Remove the radiator-to-radiator support attaching bolts and clamps. Remove the radiator.
8. Place the radiator in the vehicle so that the bottom is located in the lower mounting pads. Tighten the attaching bolts and clamps.
9. Connect the transmission oil cooler lines and tighten the bolts to 20 ft. lbs. (27 Nm).
10. Installation of the remaining components is in the reverse order of removal.

Water Pump

REMOVAL AND INSTALLATION

1. Disconnect the negative battery cable.
2. Drain the cooling system.
3. Remove all accessory drive belts.
4. Remove the alternator.
5. Unscrew the water pump pulley mounting bolts and then pull off the pulley.

6. Remove the mounting bolts and remove the water pump.
7. Place a ⅛ in. bead of RTV sealant on the water pump sealing surface. While the sealer is still wet, install the pump and tighten the bolts to 13–.18 ft. lbs. (18–24 Nm).
8. Installation of the remaining components is in the reverse order of removal.

Thermostat

REMOVAL AND INSTALLATION

The thermostat is located inside a housing on the back of the cylinder head. It is not necessary to remove the radiator hose from the thermostat housing when removing the thermostat.

1. Disconnect the negative battery cable.
2. Drain the cooling system and remove the air cleaner.
3. Disconnect the A.I.R. pipe at the upper check valve and the bracket at the water outlet.

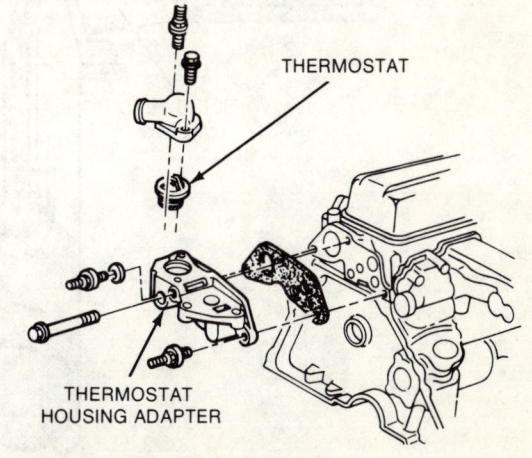

Thermostat installation details

68 ENGINE AND ENGINE REBUILDING

4. Disconnect the electrical lead.

5. Remove the two retaining bolts from the thermostat housing and lift up the housing with the house attached. Lift out the thermostat.

6. Insert the new thermostat, spring end down. Apply a thin bead of silicone sealer to the housing mating surface and install the housing while the sealer is still wet. Tighten the housing retaining bolts to 6 ft. lbs. (8 Nm.).

NOTE: *Poor heater output and slow warmup is often caused by a thermostat stuck in the open position; occasionally one sticks shut causing immediate overheating. Do not attempt to correct a chronic overheating condition by permanently removing the thermostat. Thermostat flow restriction is designed into the system; without it, localized overheating (due to coolant turbulence) may occur, causing expensive troubles.*

7. Installation of the remaining components is in the reverse order of removal.

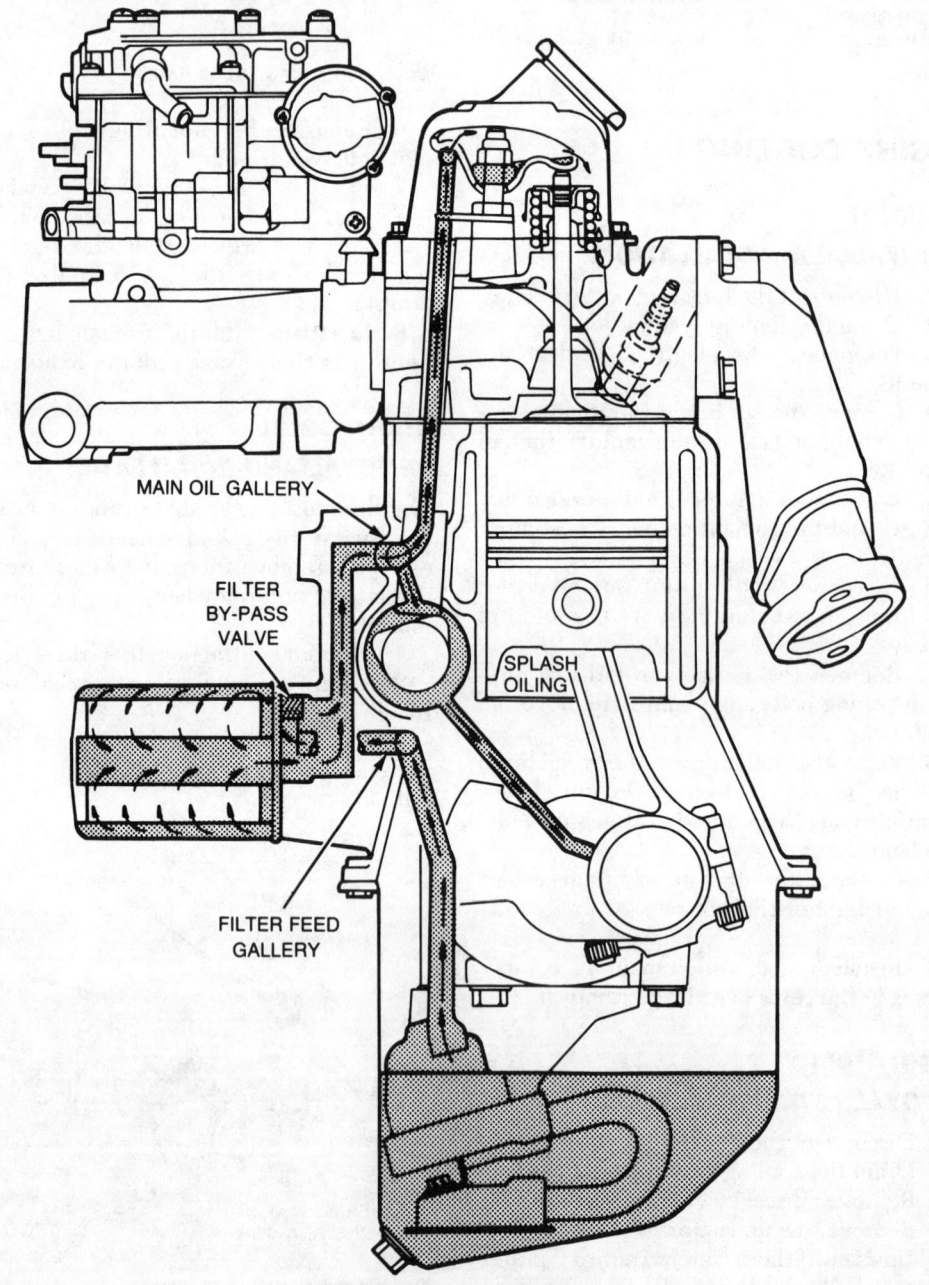

Engine lubrication system

ENGINE REBUILDING

Most procedures involved in rebuilding an engine are fairly standard, regardless of the type of engine involved. This section is a guide accepted rebuilding procedures. Examples of standard rebuilding practices are illustrated and should be used along with specific details concerning your particular engine, found earlier in this chapter.

The procedures given here are those used by any competent rebuilder. Obviously some of the procedures cannot be performed by the do-it-yourself mechanic, but are provided so that you will be familiar with the services that should be offered by rebuilding or machine shops. As an example, in most instances, it is more profitable for the home mechanic to remove the cylinder heads, buy the necessary parts (new valves, seals, keepers, keys, etc.) and deliver these to a machine shop for the necessary work. In this way you will save the money to remove and install the cylinder head and the mark-up on parts.

On the other hand, most of the work involved in rebuilding the lower end is well within the scope of the do-it-yourself mechanic. Only work such as hot-tanking, actually boring the block or Magnafluxing (invisible crack detection) need be sent to a machine shop.

Tools

The tools required for basic engine rebuilding should, with a few exceptions, be those included in a mechanic's tool kit. An accurate torque wrench, and a dial indicator (reading in thousandths) mounted on a universal base should be available. Special tools, where required, are available from the major tool suppliers. The services of a competent automotive machine shop must also be readily available.

Precautions

Aluminum has become increasingly popular for use in engines, due to its low weight and excellent heat transfer characteristics. The following precautions must be observed when handling aluminum (or any other) engine parts:
—Never hot-tank aluminum parts.
—Remove all aluminum parts (identification tags, etc.) from engine parts before hot-tanking (otherwise they will be removed during the process).
—Always coat threads lightly with engine oil or anti-seize compounds before installation, to prevent seizure.
—Never over-torque bolts or spark plugs in aluminum threads. Should stripping occur, threads can be restored using any of a number of thread repair kits available (see next section).

Inspection Techniques

Magnaflux and Zyglo are inspection techniques used to locate material flaws, such as stress cracks. Magnaflux is a magnetic process, applicable only to ferrous materials. The Zyglo process coats the matrial with a fluorescent dye penetrant, and any material may be tested using Zyglo. Specific checks of suspected surface cracks may be made at lower cost and more readily using spot check dye. The dye is sprayed onto the suspected area, wiped off, and the area is then sprayed with a developer. Cracks then will show up brightly.

Overhaul

The section is divided into two parts. The first, Cylinder Head Reconditioning, assumes that the cylinder head is removed from the engine, all manifolds are removed, and the cylinder head is on a workbench. The camshaft should be removed from overhead cam cylinder heads. The second section, Cylinder Block Reconditioning, covers the block, pistons, connecting rods and crankshaft. It is assumed that the engine is mounted on a work stand, and the cylinder head and all accessories are removed.

Procedures are identified as follows:

Unmarked—Basic procedures that must be performed in order to successfully complete the rebuilding process.

Starred (*)—Procedures that should be performed to ensure maximum performance and engine life.

Double starred (**)—Procedures that may be performed to increase engine performance and reliability.

When assembling the engine, any parts that will be in frictional contact must be pre-lubricated, to provide protection on initial start-up. Any product specifically formulated for this purpose may be used. NOTE: *Do not use engine oil.* Where semi-permanent (locked but removable) installation of bolts or nuts is desired, threads should be cleaned and located with Loctite® or a similar product (non-hardening).

ENGINE AND ENGINE REBUILDING

Repairing Damaged Threads

Several methods of repairing damaged threads are available. Heli-Coil® (shown here), Keenserts® and Microdot® are among the most widely used. All involve basically the same principle—drilling out stripped threads, tapping the hole and installing a pre-wound insert—making welding, plugging and oversize fasteners unnecessary.

Two types of thread repair inserts are usually supplied—a standard type for most Inch Coarse, Inch Fine, Metric Coarse and Metric Fine thread sizes and a spark plug type to fit most spark plug port sizes. Consult the individual manufacturer's catalog to determine exact applications. Typical thread repair kits will contain a selection of pre-wound threaded inserts, a tap (corresponding to the outside diameter threads of the insert) and an installation tool. Spark plug inserts usually differ because they require a tap equipped with pilot threads and a combined reamer/tap section. Most manufacturers also supply blister-packed thread repair inserts separately in addition to a master kit containing a variety of taps and inserts plus installation tools.

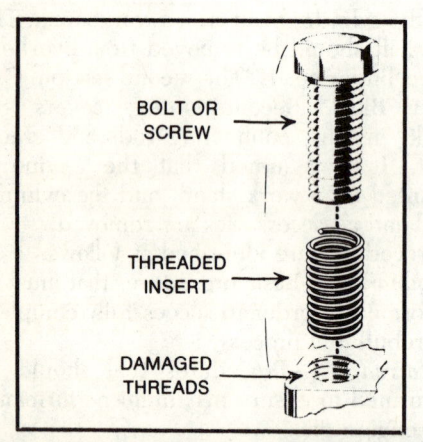

Before effecting a repair to a threaded hole, remove any snapped, broken or damaged bolts or studs. Penetrating oil can be used to free frozen threads; the offending item can be removed with locking pliers or with a screw or stud extractor. After the hole is clear, the thread can be repaired, as follows:

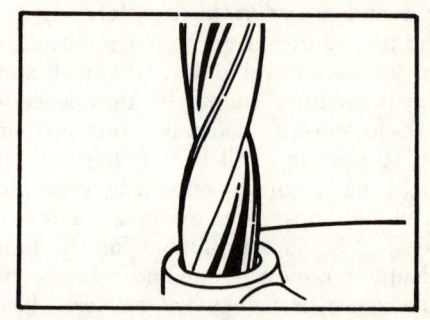

Drill out the damaged threads with specified drill. Drill completely through the hole or to the bottom of a blind hole

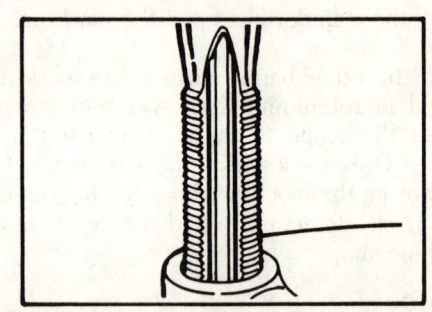

With the tap supplied, tap the hole to receive the thread insert. Keep the tap well oiled and back it out frequently to avoid clogging the threads

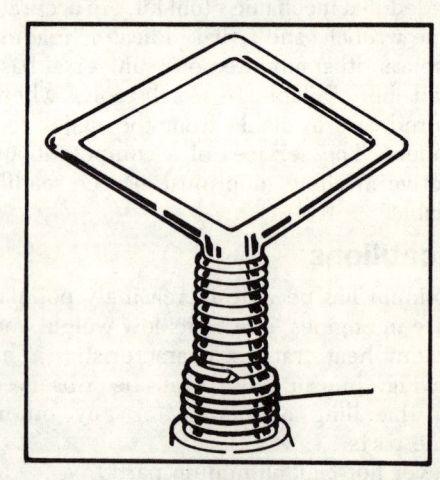

Damaged bolt holes can be repaired with thread repair inserts

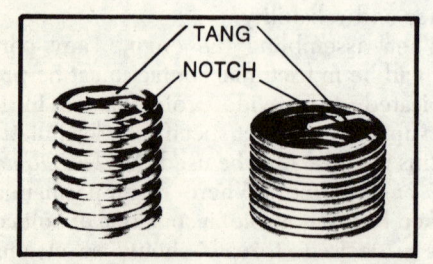

Standard thread repair insert (left) and spark plug thread insert (right)

Screw the threaded insert onto the installation tool until the tang engages the slot. Screw the insert into the tapped hole until it is ¼–½ turn below the top surface. After installation break off the tang with a hammer and punch

ENGINE AND ENGINE REBUILDING 71

Standard Torque Specifications and Fastener Markings

The Newton-metre has been designated the world standard for measuring torque and will gradually replace the foot-pound and kilogram-meter. In the absence of specific torques, the following chart can be used as a guide to the maximum safe torque of a particular size/grade of fastener.

- There is no torque difference for fine or coarse threads.
- Torque values are based on clean, dry threads. Reduce the value by 10% if threads are oiled prior to assembly.
- The torque required for aluminum components or fasteners is considerably less.

U. S. BOLTS

SAE Grade Number	1 or 2			5			6 or 7		

Bolt Markings

Manufacturer's marks may vary—number of lines always 2 less than the grade number.

Usage	Frequent			Frequent			Infrequent		
Bolt Size (inches)—(Thread)	Maximum Torque			Maximum Torque			Maximum Torque		
	Ft-Lb	kgm	Nm	Ft-Lb	kgm	Nm	Ft-Lb	kgm	Nm
¼—20	5	0.7	6.8	8	1.1	10.8	10	1.4	13.5
—28	6	0.8	8.1	10	1.4	13.6			
5/16—18	11	1.5	14.9	17	2.3	23.0	19	2.6	25.8
—24	13	1.8	17.6	19	2.6	25.7			
⅜—16	18	2.5	24.4	31	4.3	42.0	34	4.7	46.0
—24	20	2.75	27.1	35	4.8	47.5			
7/16—14	28	3.8	37.0	49	6.8	66.4	55	7.6	74.5
—20	30	4.2	40.7	55	7.6	74.5			
½—13	39	5.4	52.8	75	10.4	101.7	85	11.75	115.2
—20	41	5.7	55.6	85	11.7	115.2			
9/16—12	51	7.0	69.2	110	15.2	149.1	120	16.6	162.7
—18	55	7.6	74.5	120	16.6	162.7			
⅝—11	83	11.5	112.5	150	20.7	203.3	167	23.0	226.5
—18	95	13.1	128.8	170	23.5	230.5			
¾—10	105	14.5	142.3	270	37.3	366.0	280	38.7	379.6
—16	115	15.9	155.9	295	40.8	400.0			
⅞— 9	160	22.1	216.9	395	54.6	535.5	440	60.9	596.5
—14	175	24.2	237.2	435	60.1	589.7			
1— 8	236	32.5	318.6	590	81.6	799.9	660	91.3	894.8
—14	250	34.6	338.9	660	91.3	849.8			

72 ENGINE AND ENGINE REBUILDING

METRIC BOLTS

NOTE: *Metric bolts are marked with a number indicating the relative strength of the bolt. These numbers have nothing to do with size.*

Description	Torque ft-lbs (Nm)			
Thread size x pitch (mm)	Head mark—4		Head mark—7	
6 x 1.0	2.2–2.9	(3.0–3.9)	3.6–5.8	(4.9–7.8)
8 x 1.25	5.8–8.7	(7.9–12)	9.4–14	(13–19)
10 x 1.25	12–17	(16–23)	20–29	(27–39)
12 x 1.25	21–32	(29–43)	35–53	(47–72)
14 x 1.5	35–52	(48–70)	57–85	(77–110)
16 x 1.5	51–77	(67–100)	90–120	(130–160)
18 x 1.5	74–110	(100–150)	130–170	(180–230)
20 x 1.5	110–140	(150–190)	190–240	(160–320)
22 x 1.5	150–190	(200–260)	250–320	(340–430)
24 x 1.5	190–240	(260–320)	310–410	(420–550)

NOTE: *This engine rebuilding section is a guide to accepted rebuilding procedures. Typical examples of standard rebuilding procedures are illustrated. Use these procedures along with the detailed instructions earlier in this chapter, concerning your particular engine.*

Cylinder Head Reconditioning

Procedure	Method
Remove the cylinder head:	See the engine service procedures earlier in this chapter for details concerning specific engines.
Identify the valves:	Invert the cylinder head, and number the valve faces front to rear, using a permanent felt-tip marker.
Remove the rocker arms:	Remove the rocker arms with shaft(s) or balls and nuts. Wire the sets of rockers, balls and nuts together, and identify according to the corresponding valve.
Remove the valves and springs:	Using an appropriate valve spring compressor (depending on the configuration of the cylinder head), compress the valve springs. Lift out the keepers with needlenose pliers, release the compressor, and remove the valve, spring, and spring retainer. See the engine service procedures earlier in this chapter for details concerning specific engines.
Check the valve stem-to-guide clearance:	Clean the valve stem with lacquer thinner or a similar solvent to remove all gum and varnish. Clean the valve guides using solvent and an expanding wire-type valve guide cleaner. Mount a dial indicator so that the stem is at 90° to the valve stem, as close to the valve guide as possible. Move the valve off its seat, and measure the valve guide-to-stem clearance by rocking the stem back and forth to actuate the dial indicator. Measure the valve stems using a micrometer, and compare to specifications, to determine whether stem or guide wear is responsible for excessive clearance. NOTE: *Consult the Specifications tables earlier in this chapter.*

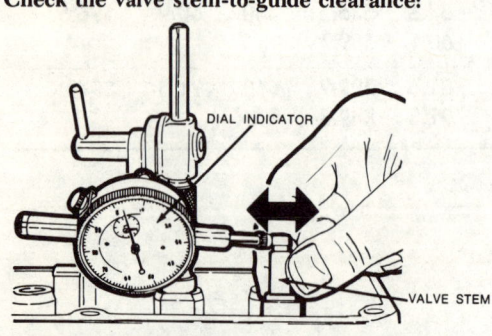

Check the valve stem-to-guide clearance

ENGINE AND ENGINE REBUILDING

Cylinder Head Reconditioning

Procedure	Method
De-carbon the cylinder head and valves: Remove the carbon from the cylinder head with a wire brush and electric drill	Chip carbon away from the valve heads, combustion chambers, and ports, using a chisel made of hardwood. Remove the remaining deposits with a stiff wire brush. NOTE: *Be sure that the deposits are actually removed, rather than burnished.*
Hot-tank the cylinder head (cast iron heads only): CAUTION: *Do not hot-tank aluminum parts.*	Have the cylinder head hot-tanked to remove grease, corrosion, and scale from the water passages. NOTE: *In the case of overhead cam cylinder heads, consult the operator to determine whether the camshaft bearings will be damaged by the caustic solution.*
Degrease the remaining cylinder head parts:	Clean the remaining cylinder head parts in an engine cleaning solvent. Do not remove the protective coating from the springs.
Check the cylinder head for warpage: 1 & 3 CHECK DIAGONALLY 2 CHECK ACROSS CENTER Check the cylinder head for warpage	Place a straight-edge across the gasket surface of the cylinder head. Using feeler gauges, determine the clearance at the center of the straight-edge. If warpage exceeds .003″ in a 6″ span, or .006″ over the total length, the cylinder head must be resurfaced. NOTE: *If warpage exceeds the manufacturer's maximum tolerance for material removal, the cylinder head must be replaced.* When milling the cylinder heads of V-type engines, the intake manifold mounting position is altered, and must be corrected by milling the manifold flange a proportionate amount.
*Knurl the valve guides: Cut-away view of a knurled valve guide	*Valve guides which are not excessively worn or distorted may, in some cases, be knurled rather than replaced. Knurling is a process in which metal is displaced and raised, thereby reducing clearance. Knurling also provides excellent oil control. The possibility of knurling rather than replacing valve guides should be discussed with a machinist.
Replace the valve guides: NOTE: *Valve guides should only be replaced if damaged or if an oversize valve stem is not available.*	See the engine service procedures earlier in this chapter for details concerning specific engines. Depending on the type of cylinder head, valve guides may be pressed, hammered, or shrunk in. In cases where the guides are shrunk into the head, replacement should be left to an equipped machine shop. In other

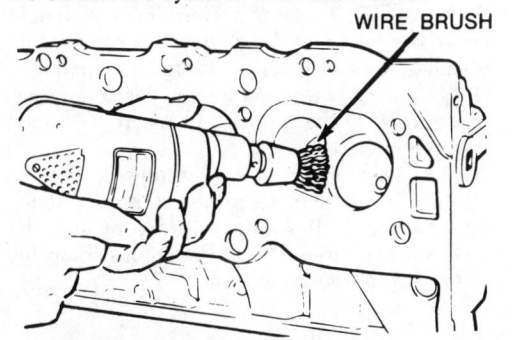

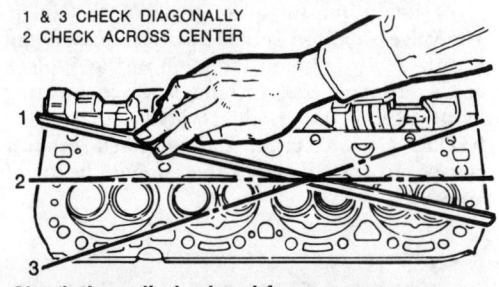

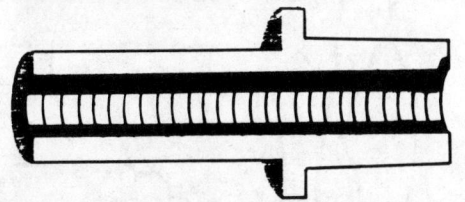

74 ENGINE AND ENGINE REBUILDING

Cylinder Head Reconditioning

Procedure	Method
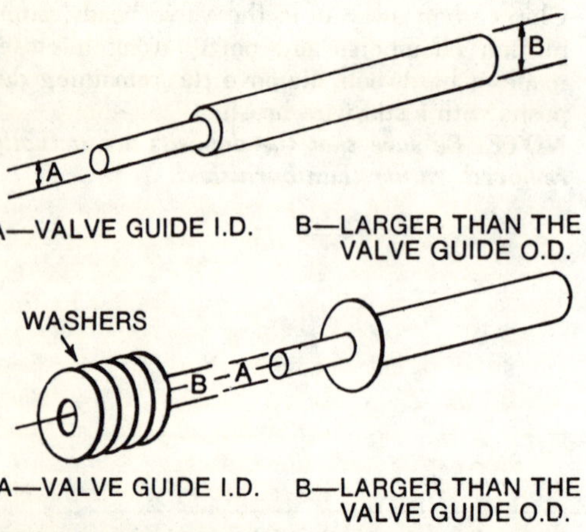 *Valve guide installation tool using washers for installation* (A—VALVE GUIDE I.D., B—LARGER THAN THE VALVE GUIDE O.D., WASHERS)	cases, the guides are replaced using a stepped drift (see illustration). Determine the height above the boss that the guide must extend, and obtain a stack of washers, their I.D. similar to the guide's O.D., of that height. Place the stack of washers on the guide, and insert the guide into the boss. NOTE: *Valve guides are often tapered or beveled for installation.* Using the stepped installation tool (see illustration), press or tap the guides into position. Ream the guides according to the size of the valve stem.
Replace valve seat inserts:	Replacement of valve seat inserts which are worn beyond resurfacing or broken, if feasible, must be done by a machine shop.
Resurface (grind) the valve face: 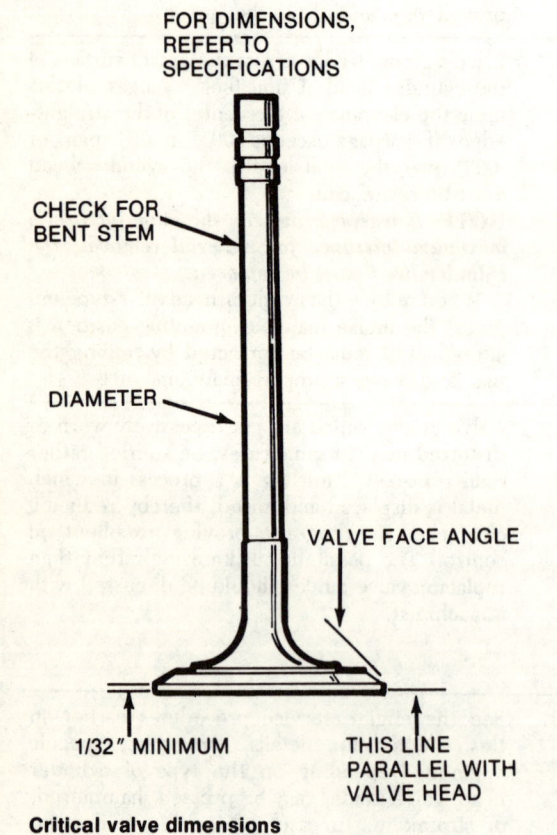 *Critical valve dimensions* (FOR DIMENSIONS, REFER TO SPECIFICATIONS; CHECK FOR BENT STEM; DIAMETER; VALVE FACE ANGLE; 1/32" MINIMUM; THIS LINE PARALLEL WITH VALVE HEAD)	Using a valve grinder, resurface the valves according to specifications given earlier in this chapter. CAUTION: *Valve face angle is not always identical to valve seat angle.* A minimum margin of 1/32" should remain after grinding the valve. The valve stem top should also be squared and resurfaced, by placing the stem in the V-block of the grinder, and turning it while pressing lightly against the grinding wheel. NOTE: *Do not grind sodium filled exhaust valves on a machine. These should be hand lapped.* 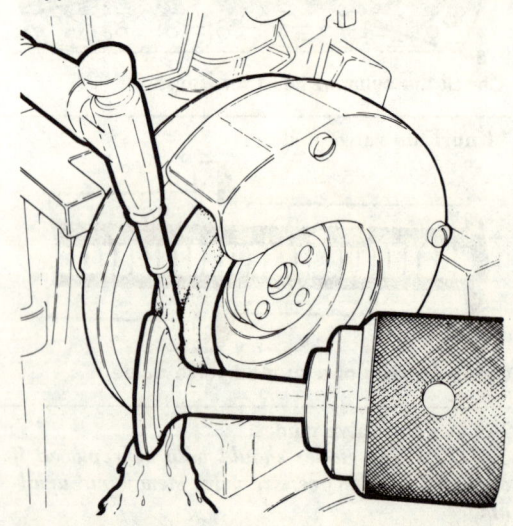 *Valve grinding by machine*

ENGINE AND ENGINE REBUILDING 75

Cylinder Head Reconditioning

Procedure	Method
Resurface the valve seats using reamers of grinder: *Valve seat width and centering* *Reaming the valve seat with a hand reamer*	Select a reamer of the correct seat angle, slightly larger than the diameter of the valve seat, and assemble it with a pilot of the correct size. Install the pilot into the valve guide, and using steady pressure, turn the reamer clockwise. **CAUTION:** *Do not turn the reamer counterclockwise.* Remove only as much material as necessary to clean the seat. Check the concentricity of the seat (following). If the dye method is not used, coat the valve face with Prussian blue dye, install and rotate it on the valve seat. Using the dye marked area as a centering guide, center and narrow the valve seat to specifications with correction cutters. **NOTE:** *When no specifications are available, minimum seat width for exhaust valves should be $5/64''$, intake valves $1/16''$.* After making correction cuts, check the position of the valve seat on the valve face using Prussian blue dye. To resurface the seat with a power grinder, select a pilot of the correct size and coarse stone of the proper angle. Lubricate the pilot and move the stone on and off the valve seat at 2 cycles per second, until all flaws are gone. Finish the seat with a fine stone. If necessary the seat can be corrected or narrowed using correction stones.
Check the valve seat concentricity: *Check the valve seat concentricity with a dial gauge*	Coat the valve face with Prussian blue dye, install the valve, and rotate it on the valve seat. If the entire seat becomes coated, and the valve is known to be concentric, the seat is concentric. *Install the dial gauge pilot into the guide, and rest of the arm on the valve seat. Zero the gauge, and rotate the arm around the seat. Run-out should not exceed .002''.

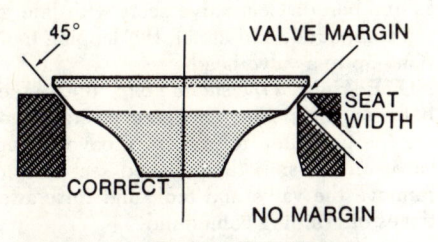

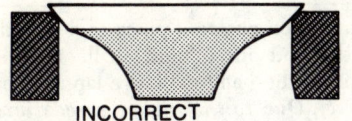

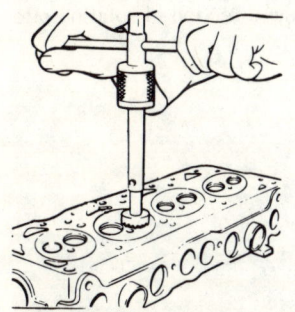

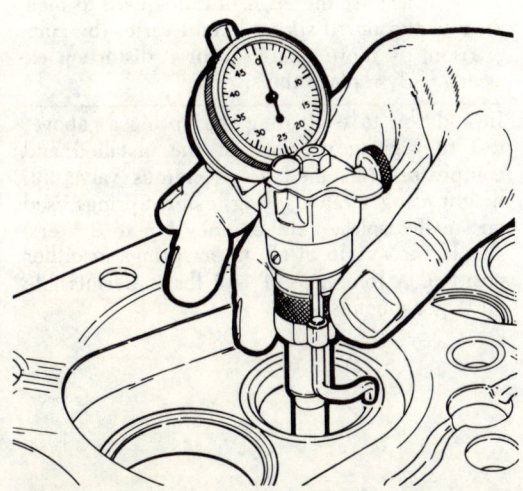

ENGINE AND ENGINE REBUILDING

Cylinder Head Reconditioning

Procedure	Method
*Lap the valves: NOTE: *Valve lapping is done to ensure efficient sealing of resurfaced valves and seats.* *Lapping the valves by hand* *Home-made valve lapping tool*	Invert the cylinder head, lightly lubricate the valve stems, and install the valves in the head as numbered. Coat valve seats with fine grinding compound, and attach the lapping tool suction cup to a valve head. NOTE: *Moisten the suction cup.* Rotate the tool between the palms, changing position and lifting the tool often to prevent grooving. Lap the valve until a smooth, polished seat is evident. Remove the valve and tool, and rinse away all traces of grinding compound. **Fasten a suction cup to a piece of drill rod, and mount the rod in a hand drill. Proceed as above, using the hand drill as a lapping tool. CAUTION: *Due to the higher speeds involved when using the hand drill, care must be exercised to avoid grooving the seat.* Lift the tool and change direction of rotation often.
Check the valve springs: *Check the valve spring free length and squareness* *Check the valve spring test pressure*	Place the spring on a flat surface next to a square. Measure the height of the spring, and rotate it against the edge of the square to measure distortion. If spring height varies (by comparison) by more than $1/16''$ or if distortion exceeds $1/16''$, replace the spring. **In addition to evaluating the spring as above, test the spring pressure at the installed and compressed (installed height minus valve lift) height using a valve spring tester. Springs used on small displacement engines (up to 3 liters) should be ∓ 1 lb of all other springs in either position. A tolerance of ∓ 5 lbs is permissible on larger engines.

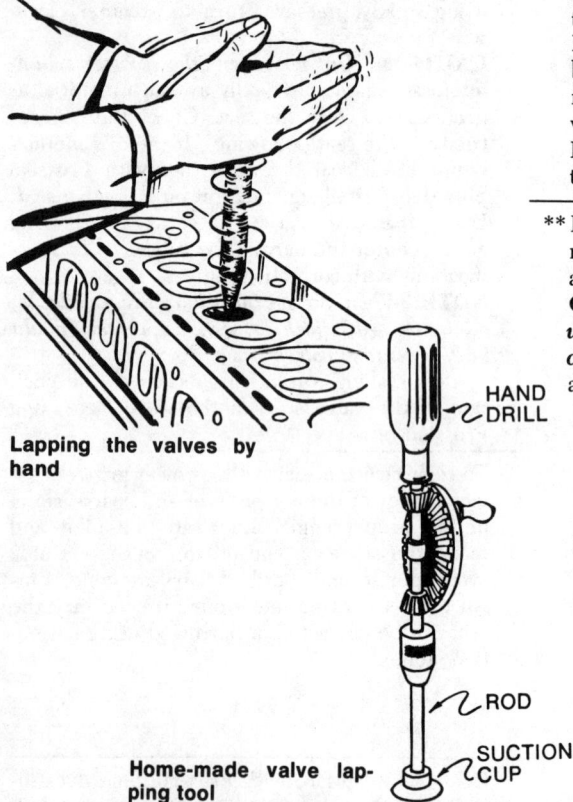

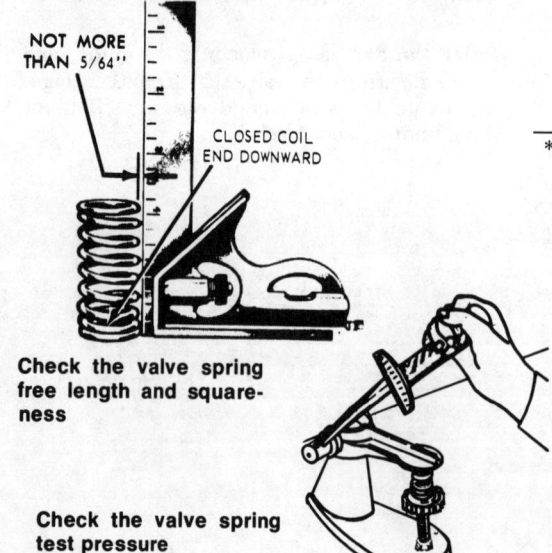

ENGINE AND ENGINE REBUILDING

Cylinder Head Reconditioning

Procedure	Method
*Install valve stem seals: RETAINER SPRING VALVE SEAL **Install valve stem seals**	*Due to the pressure differential that exists at the ends of the intake valve guides (atmospheric pressure above, manifold vacuum below), oil is drawn through the valve guides into the intake port. This has been alleviated somewhat since the addition of positive crankcase ventilation, which lowers the pressure above the guides. Several types of valve stem seals are available to reduce blow-by. Certain seals simply slip over the stem and guide boss, while others require that the boss be machined. Recently, Teflon guide seals have become popular. Consult a parts supplier or machinist concerning availability and suggested usages. NOTE: *When installing seals, ensure that a small amount of oil is able to pass the seal to lubricate the valve guides; otherwise, excessive wear may result.*
Install the valves:	See the engine service procedures earlier in this chapter for details concerning specific engines. Lubricate the valve stems, and install the valves in the cylinder head as numbered. Lubricate and position the seals (if used) and the valve springs. Install the spring retainers, compress the springs, and insert the keys using needlenose pliers or a tool designed for this purpose. NOTE: *Retain the keys with wheel bearing grease during installation.*
Check valve spring installed height: **Valve spring installed height (A)** GRIND OUT THIS PORTION **Measure the valve spring installed height (A) with a modified steel rule**	Measure the distance between the spring pad the lower edge of the spring retainer, and compare to specifications. If the installed height is incorrect, add shim washers between the spring pad and the spring. CAUTION: *Use only washers designed for this purpose.*

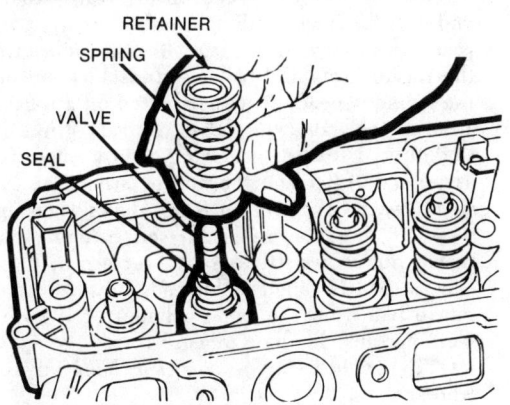

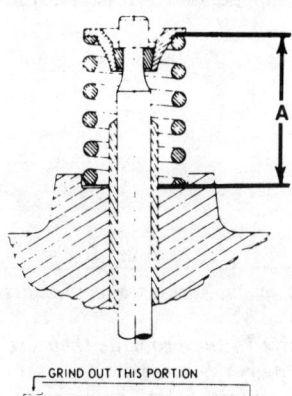

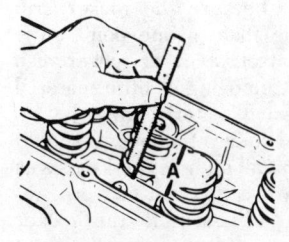

ENGINE AND ENGINE REBUILDING

Cylinder Head Reconditioning

Procedure	Method
Inspect the rocker arms, balls, studs, and nuts: *Stress cracks in the rocker nuts*	Visually inspect the rocker arms, balls, studs, and nuts for cracks, galling, burning, scoring, or wear. If all parts are intact, liberally lubricate the rocker arms and balls, and install them on the cylinder head. If wear is noted on a rocker arm at the point of valve contact, grind it smooth and square, removing as little material as possible. Replace the rocker arm if excessively worn. If a rocker stud shows signs of wear, it must be replaced (see below). If a rocker nut shows stress cracks, replace it. If an exhaust ball is galled or burned, substitute the intake ball from the same cylinder (if it is intact), and install a new intake ball. **NOTE:** *Avoid using new rocker balls on exhaust valves.*
Replace rocker studs: *Extracting a pressed-in rocker stud* *Ream the stud bore for oversize rocker studs*	In order to remove a threaded stud, lock two nuts on the stud, and unscrew the stud using the lower nut. Coat the lower threads of the new stud with Loctite, and install. Two alternative methods are available for replacing pressed in studs. Remove the damaged stud using a stack of washers and a nut (see illustration). In the first, the boss is reamed .005–.006" oversize, and an oversize stud pressed in. Control the stud extension over the boss using washers, in the same manner as valve guides. Before installing the stud, coat it with white lead and grease. To retain the stud more positively drill a hole through the stud and boss, and install a roll pin. In the second method, the boss is tapped, and a threaded stud installed.
Inspect the rocker shaft(s) and rocker arms: *Check the rocker arm-to-rocker shaft contact area*	Remove the rocker arms, springs and washers from rocker shaft. **NOTE:** *Lay out parts in the order as they are removed.* Inspect rocker arms for pitting or wear on the valve contact point, or excessive bushing wear. Bushings need only be replaced if wear is excessive, because the rocker arm normally contacts the shaft at one point only. Grind the valve contact point of rocker arm smooth if necessary, removing as little material as possible. If excessive material must be removed to smooth and square the arm, it should be replaced. Clean out all oil holes and passages in rocker shaft. If shaft is grooved or worn, replace it. Lubricate and assemble the rocker shaft.

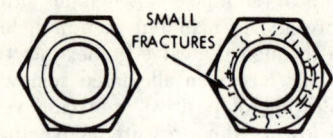

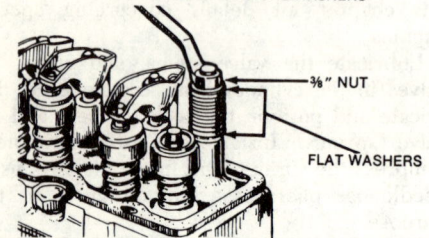

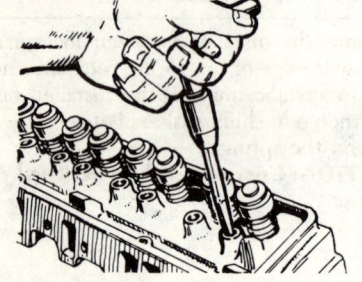

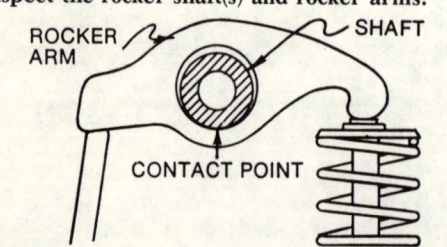

ENGINE AND ENGINE REBUILDING

Cylinder Head Reconditioning

Procedure	Method
Inspect the pushrods:	Remove the pushrods, and, if hollow, clean out the oil passages using fine wire. Roll each pushrod over a piece of clean glass. If a distinct clicking sound is heard as the pushrod rolls, the rod is bent, and must be replaced.
	*The length of all pushrods must be equal. Measure the length of the pushrods, compare to specifications, and replace as necessary.
*Inspect the valve lifters: 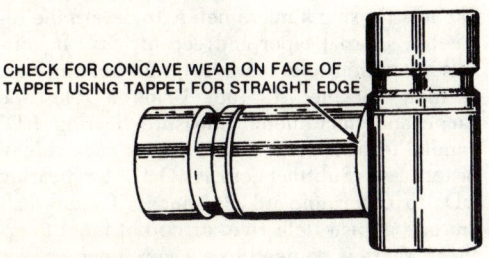 CHECK FOR CONCAVE WEAR ON FACE OF TAPPET USING TAPPET FOR STRAIGHT EDGE **Check the lifter face for squareness**	Remove lifters from their bores, and remove gum and varnish, using solvent. Clean walls of lifter bores. Check lifters for concave wear as illustrated. If face is worn concave, replace lifter, and carefully inspect the camshaft. Lightly lubricate lifter and insert it into its bore. If play is excessive, an oversize lifter must be installed (where possible). Consult a machinist concerning feasibility. If play is satisfactory, remove, lubricate, and reinstall the lifter.
*Testing hydraulic lifter leak down:	Submerge lifter in a container of kerosene. Chuck a used pushrod or its equivalent into a drill press. Position container of kerosene so pushrod acts on the lifter plunger. Pump lifter with the drill press, until resistance increases. Pump several more times to bleed any air out of lifter. Apply very firm, constant pressure to the lifter, and observe rate at which fluid bleeds out of lifter. If the fluid bleeds very quickly (less than 15 seconds), lifter is defective. If the time exceeds 60 seconds, lifter is sticking. In either case, recondition or replace lifter. If lifter is operating properly (leak down time 15–60 seconds), lubricate and install it.

Cylinder Block Reconditioning

Procedure	Method
Checking the main bearing clearance: 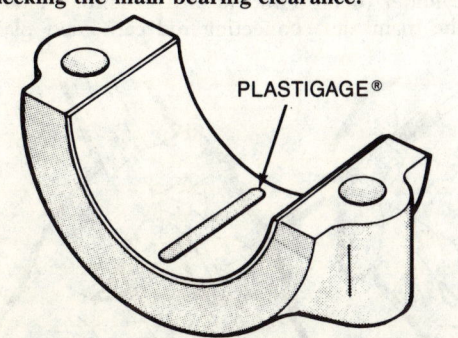 PLASTIGAGE® **Plastigage® installed on the lower bearing shell**	Invert engine, and remove cap from the bearing to be checked. Using a clean, dry rag, thoroughly clean all oil from crankshaft journal and bearing insert. NOTE: *Plastigage® is soluble in oil; therefore, oil on the journal or bearing could result in erroneous readings.* Place a piece of Plastigage along the full length of journal, reinstall cap, and torque to specifications. NOTE: Specifications are given in the engine specifications earlier in this chapter. Remove bearing cap, and determine bearing clearance by comparing width of Plastigage to the scale on Plastigage envelope. Journal taper is determined by comparing width of the Plas-

ENGINE AND ENGINE REBUILDING

Cylinder Block Reconditioning

Procedure	Method
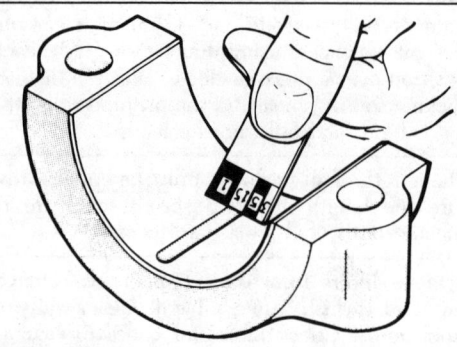 **Measure Plastigage® to determine main bearing clearance**	tigage strip near its ends. Rotate crankshaft 90° and retest, to determine journal eccentricity. **NOTE:** *Do not rotate crankshaft with Plastigage installed.* If bearing insert and journal appear intact, and are within tolerances, no further main bearing service is required. If bearing or journal appear defective, cause of failure should be determined before replacement.
	*Remove crankshaft from block (see below). Measure the main bearing journals at each end twice (90° apart) using a micrometer, to determine diameter, journal taper and eccentricity. If journals are within tolerances, reinstall bearing caps at their specified torque. Using a telescope gauge and micrometer, measure bearing I.D. parallel to piston axis and at 30° on each side of piston axis. Subtract journal O.D. for bearing I.D. to determine oil clearance. If crankshaft journals appear defective, or do not meet tolerances, there is no need to measure bearings; for the crankshaft will require grinding and/or undersize bearings will be required. If bearing appears defective, cause for failure should be determined prior to replacement.
Check the connecting rod bearing clearance:	Connecting rod bearing clearance is checked in the same manner as main bearing clearance, using Plastigage. Before removing the crankshaft, connecting rod side clearance also should be measured and recorded.
	*Checking connecting rod bearing clearance, using a micrometer, is identical to checking main bearing clearance. If no other service is required, the piston and rod assemblies need not be removed.
Remove the crankshaft:	Using a punch, mark the corresponding main bearing caps and saddles according to position (i.e., one punch on the front main cap and saddle, two on the second, three on the third, etc.). Using number stamps, identify the corresponding connecting rods and caps, according to cylinder (if no numbers are present). Remove the main and connecting rod caps, and place
Match the connecting rod to the cylinder with a number stamp	**Match the connecting rod and cap with scribe marks**

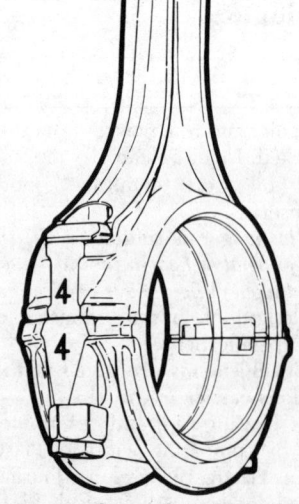

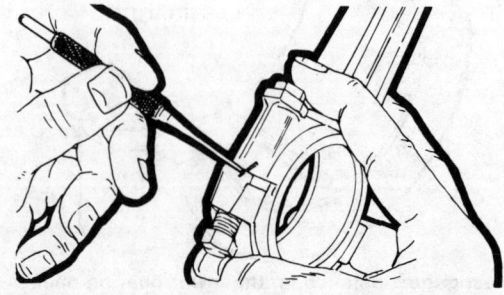

ENGINE AND ENGINE REBUILDING

Cylinder Block Reconditioning

Procedure	Method
	sleeves of plastic tubing or vacuum hose over the connecting rod bolts, to protect the journals as the crankshaft is removed. Lift the crankshaft out of the block.
Remove the ridge from the top of the cylinder: *Cylinder bore ridge*	In order to facilitate removal of the piston and connecting rod, the ridge at the top of the cylinder (unworn area; see illustration) must be removed. Place the piston at the bottom of the bore, and cover it with a rag. Cut the ridge away using a ridge reamer, exercising extreme care to avoid cutting too deeply. Remove the rag, and remove cuttings that remain on the piston. **CAUTION:** *If the ridge is not removed, and new rings are installed, damage to rings will result.*
Remove the piston and connecting rod: *Push the piston out with a hammer handle*	Invert the engine, and push the pistons and connecting rods out of the cylinders. If necessary, tap the connecting rod boss with a wooden hammer handle, to force the piston out. **CAUTION:** *Do not attempt to force the piston past the cylinder ridge* (see above).
Service the crankshaft:	Ensure that all oil holes and passages in the crankshaft are open and free of sludge. If necessary, have the crankshaft ground to the largest possible undersize.
	** Have the crankshaft Magnafluxed, to locate stress cracks. Consult a machinist concerning additional service procedures, such as surface hardening (e.g., nitriding, Tuftriding) to improve wear characteristics, cross drilling and chamfering the oil holes to improve lubrication, and balancing.
Removing freeze plugs:	Drill a small hole in the middle of the freeze plugs. Thread a large sheet metal screw into the hole and remove the plug with a slide hammer.
Remove the oil gallery plugs:	Threaded plugs should be removed using an appropriate (usually square) wrench. To remove soft, pressed in plugs, drill a hole in the plug, and thread in a sheet metal screw. Pull the plug out by the screw using pliers.

82 ENGINE AND ENGINE REBUILDING

Cylinder Block Reconditioning

Procedure	Method
Hot-tank the block: NOTE: *Do not hot-tank aluminum parts.*	Have the block hot-tanked to remove grease, corrosion, and scale from the water jackets. NOTE: *Consult the operator to determine whether the camshaft bearings will be damaged during the hot-tank process.*

Check the block for cracks:	Visually inspect the block for cracks or chips. The most common locations are as follows:
	    Adjacent to freeze plugs.
	    Between the cylinders and water jackets.
	    Adjacent to the main bearing saddles.
	    At the extreme bottom of the cylinders.
	Check only suspected cracks using spot check dye (see introduction). If a crack is located, consult a machinist concerning possible repairs.

	** Magnaflux the block to locate hidden cracks. If cracks are located, consult a machinist about feasibility of repair.
Install the oil gallery plugs and freeze plugs:	Coat freeze plugs with sealer and tap into position using a piece of pipe, slightly smaller than the plug, as a driver. To ensure retention, stake the edges of the plugs. Coat threaded oil gallery plugs with sealer and install. Drive replacement soft plugs into block using a large drift as a driver.
	* Rather than reinstalling lead plugs, drill and tap the holes, and install threaded plugs.
Check the bore diameter and surface:	Visually inspect the cylinder bores for roughness, scoring, or scuffing. If evident, the cylinder bore must be bored or honed oversize to eliminate imperfections, and the smallest possible oversize piston used. The new pistons should be given to the machinist with the block, so that the cylinders can be bored or honed exactly to the piston size (plus clearance). If no flaws are evident, measure the bore diameter using a telescope gauge and micrometer, or dial gauge, parallel and perpendicular to the engine centerline, at the top (below the ridge) and bottom of the bore. Subtract the bottom measurements from the top to determine taper, and the parallel to

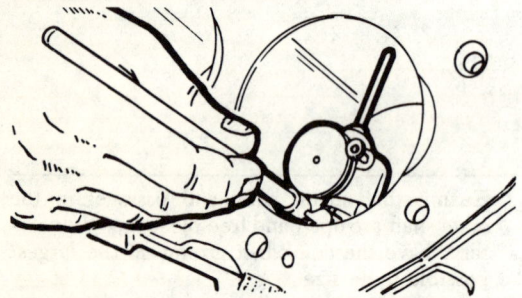

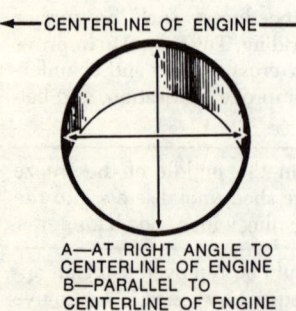

Measure the cylinder bore with a dial gauge

Cylinder bore measuring points
A—AT RIGHT ANGLE TO CENTERLINE OF ENGINE
B—PARALLEL TO CENTERLINE OF ENGINE

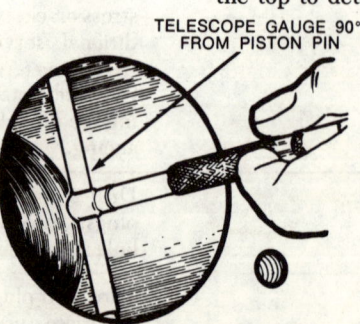

Measure the cylinder bore with a telescope gauge

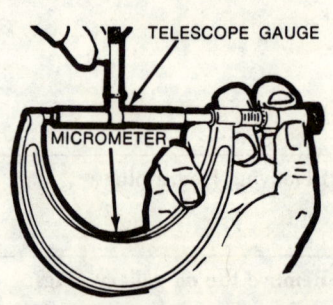

TELESCOPE GAUGE 90° FROM PISTON PIN

Measure the telescope gauge with a micrometer to determine the cylinder bore

TELESCOPE GAUGE
MICROMETER

ENGINE AND ENGINE REBUILDING

Cylinder Block Reconditioning

Procedure	Method
	the centerline measurements from the perpendicular measurements to determine eccentricity. If the measurements are not within specifications, the cylinder must be bored or honed, and an oversize piston installed. If the measurements are within specifications the cylinder may be used as is, with only finish honing (see below). **NOTE:** *Prior to submitting the block for boring, perform the following operation(s).*
Check the cylinder block bearing alignment: *Check the main bearing saddle alignment*	Remove the upper bearing inserts. Place a straightedge in the bearing saddles along the centerline of the crankshaft. If clearance exists between the straightedge and the center saddle, the block must be alignbored.
*Check the deck height:	The deck height is the distance from the crankshaft centerline to the block deck. To measure, invert the engine, and install the crankshaft, retaining it with the center main cap. Measure the distance from the crankshaft journal to the block deck, parallel to the cylinder centerline. Measure the diameter of the end (front and rear) main journals, parallel to the centerline of the cylinders, divide the diameter in half, and subtract it from the previous measurement. The results of the front and rear measurements should be identical. If the difference exceeds .005", the deck height should be corrected. **NOTE:** *Block deck height and warpage should be corrected at the same time.*
Check the block deck for warpage:	Using a straightedge and feeler gauges, check the block deck for warpage in the same manner that the cylinder head is checked (see Cylinder Head Reconditioning). If warpage exceeds specifications, have the deck resurfaced. **NOTE:** *In certain cases a specification for total material removal (cylinder head and block deck) is provided. This specification must not be exceeded.*
Clean and inspect the pistons and connecting rods: RING EXPANDER *Remove the piston rings*	Using a ring expander, remove the rings from the piston. Remove the retaining rings (if so equipped) and remove piston pin. **NOTE:** *If the piston pin must be pressed out, determine the proper method and use the proper tools; otherwise the piston will distort.* Clean the ring grooves using an appropriate tool, exercising care to avoid cutting too deeply. Thoroughly clean all carbon and varnish from the piston with solvent. **CAUTION:** *Do not use a wire brush or caustic solvent on pistons.* Inspect the pistons for scuffing, scoring, cracks, pitting, or excessive ring

ENGINE AND ENGINE REBUILDING

Cylinder Block Reconditioning

Procedure	Method
Clean the piston ring grooves (RING GROOVE CLEANER)	groove wear. If wear is evident, the piston must be replaced. Check the connecting rod length by measuring the rod from the inside of the large end to the inside of the small end using calipers (see illustration). All connecting rods should be equal length. Replace any rod that differs from the others in the engine.
Check the connecting rod length (arrow)	*Have the connecting rod alignment checked in an alignment fixture by a machinist. Replace any twisted or bent rods. *Magnaflux the connecting rods to locate stress cracks. If cracks are found, replace the connecting rod.
Fit the pistons to the cylinders: **Measure the piston prior to fitting** (90°)	Using a telescope gauge and micrometer, or a dial gauge, measure the cylinder bore diameter perpendicular to the piston pin, 2½" below the deck. Measure the piston perpendicular to its pin on the skirt. The difference between the two measurements is the piston clearance. If the clearance is within specifications or slightly below (after boring or honing), finish honing is all that is required. If the clearance is excessive, try to obtain a slightly larger piston to bring clearance within specifications. Where this is not possible, obtain the first oversize piston, and hone (or if necessary, bore) the cylinder to size.
Assemble the pistons and connecting rods: **Install the piston pin lock-rings (if used)**	Inspect piston pin, connecting rod small end bushing, and piston bore for galling, scoring, or excessive wear. If evident, replace defective part(s). Measure the I.D. of the piston boss and connecting rod small end, and the O.D. of the piston pin. If within specifications, assemble piston pin and rod. **CAUTION:** *If piston pin must be pressed in, determine the proper method and use the proper tools; otherwise the piston will distort.* Install the lock rings; ensure that they seat properly. If the parts are not within specifications, determine the service method for the type of engine. In some cases, piston and pin are serviced as an assembly when either is defective. Others specify reaming the piston and connecting rods for an oversize pin. If the connecting rod bushing is worn, it may in many cases be replaced. Reaming the piston and replacing the rod bushing are machine shop operations.

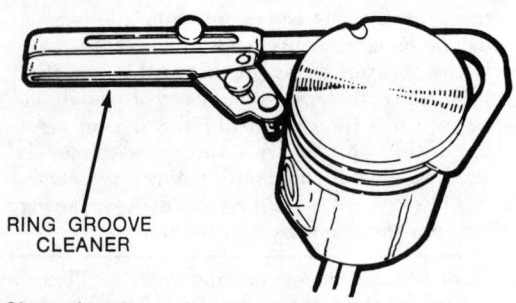

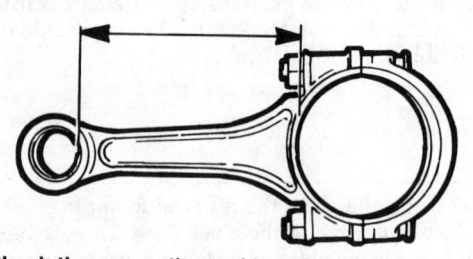

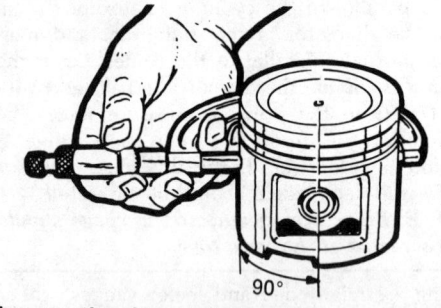

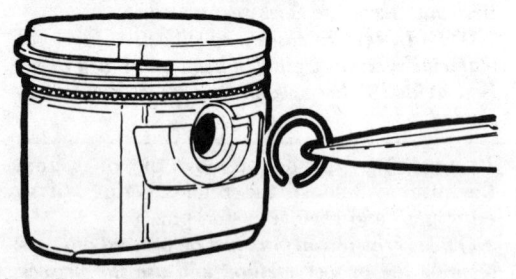

ENGINE AND ENGINE REBUILDING 85

Cylinder Block Reconditioning

Procedure	Method
Clean and inspect the camshaft: **Check the camshaft for straightness**	Degrease the camshaft, using solvent, and clean out all oil holes. Visually inspect cam lobes and bearing journals for excessive wear. If a lobe is questionable, check all lobes as indicated below. If a journal or lobe is worn, the camshaft must be reground or replaced. NOTE: *If a journal is worn, there is a good chance that the bushings are worn.* If lobes and journals appear intact, place the front and rear journals in V-blocks, and rest a dial indicator on the center journal. Rotate the camshaft to check straightness. If deviation exceeds .001″, replace the camshaft. *Check the camshaft lobes with a micrometer, by measuring the lobes from the nose to base and again at 90° (see illustration). The lift is determined by subtracting the second measurement from the first. If all exhaust lobes and all intake lobes are not identical, the camshaft must be reground or replaced. **Camshaft lobe measurement**
Replace the camshaft bearings: **Camshaft bearing removal and installation tool (OHV engines only)**	If excessive wear is indicated, or if the engine is being completely rebuilt, camshaft bearings should be replaced as follows: Drive the camshaft rear plug from the block. Assemble the removal puller with its shoulder on the bearing to be removed. Gradually tighten the puller nut until bearing is removed. Remove remaining bearings, leaving the front and rear for last. To remove front and rear bearings, reverse position of the tool, so as to pull the bearings in toward the center of the block. Leave the tool in this position, pilot the new front and rear bearings on the installer, and pull them into position: Return the tool to its original position and pull remaining bearings into position. NOTE: *Ensure that oil holes align when installing bearings.* Replace camshaft rear plug, and stake it into position to aid retention.
Finish hone the cylinders:	Chuck a flexible drive hone into a power drill, and insert it into the cylinder. Start the hone, and remove it up and down in the cylinder at a rate which will produce approximately a 60° cross-hatch pattern. NOTE: *Do not extend the hone below the cylinder bore.* After developing the pattern, remove

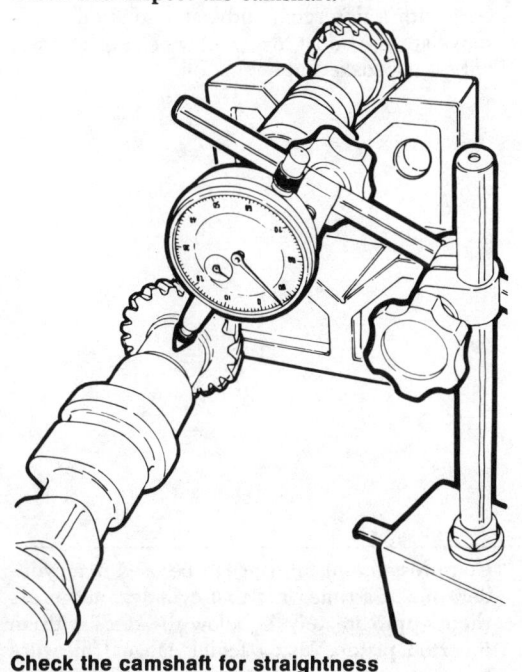

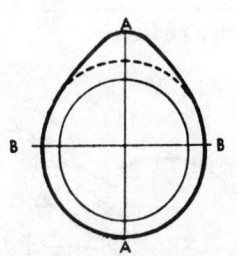

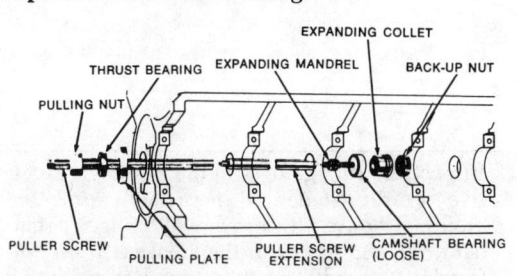

86 ENGINE AND ENGINE REBUILDING

Cylinder Block Reconditioning

Procedure	Method
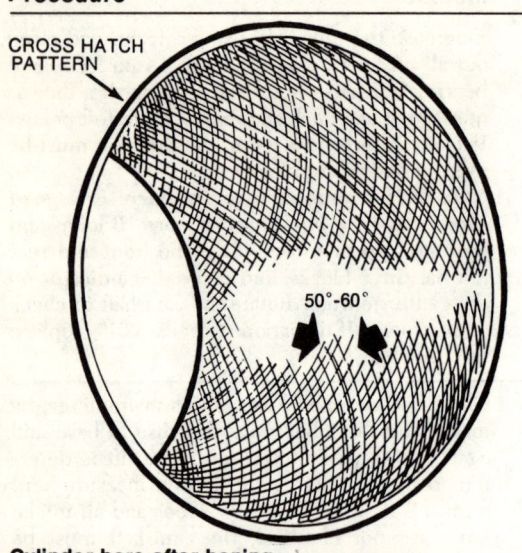 **Cylinder bore after honing** (CROSS HATCH PATTERN, 50°–60°)	the hone and recheck piston fit. Wash the cylinders with a detergent and water solution to remove abrasive dust, dry, and wipe several times with a rag soaked in engine oil.
Check piston ring end-gap: 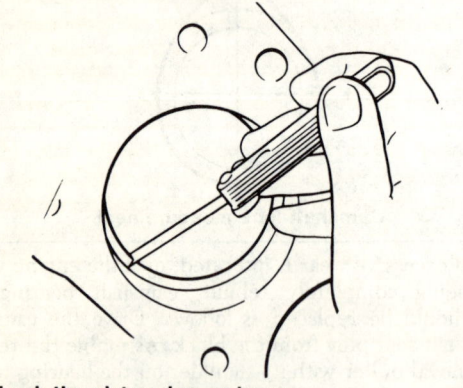 Check the piston ring end gap	Compress the piston rings to be used in a cylinder, one at a time, into that cylinder, and press them approximately 1″ below the deck with an inverted piston. Using feeler gauges, measure the ring end-gap, and compare to specifications. Pull the ring out of the cylinder and file the ends with a fine file to obtain proper clearance. **CAUTION:** *If inadequate ring end-gap is utilized, ring breakage will result.*
Install the piston rings: 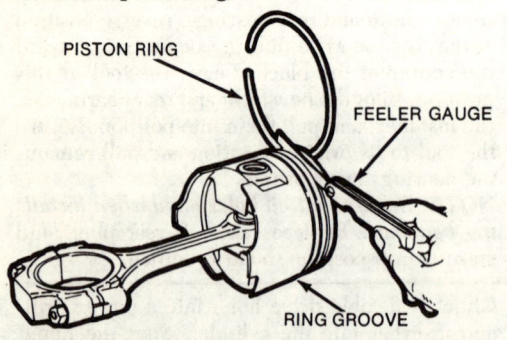 PISTON RING, FEELER GAUGE, RING GROOVE Check the piston ring side clearance	Inspect the ring grooves in the piston for excessive wear or taper. If necessary, recut the groove(s) for use with an overwidth ring or a standard ring and spacer. If the groove is worn uniformly, overwidth rings, or standard rings and spacers may be installed without recutting. Roll the outside of the ring around the groove to check for burrs or deposits. If any are found, remove with a fine file. Hold the ring in the groove, and measure side clearance. If necessary, correct as indicated above. **NOTE:** *Always install any additional spacers above the piston ring.* The ring groove must be deep enough to allow the ring to seat below the lands (see illustration). In many cases, a "go-no-go" depth gauge will be provided with the piston rings. Shallow grooves may be corrected by recutting, while deep grooves require some type of filler or expander

ENGINE AND ENGINE REBUILDING

Cylinder Block Reconditioning

Procedure	Method
	behind the piston. Consult the piston ring supplier concerning the suggested method. Install the rings on the piston, lowest ring first, using a ring expander. NOTE: *Position the rings as specified by the manufacturer.* Consult the engine service procedures earlier in this chapter for details concerning specific engines.
Install the camshaft:	Liberally lubricate the camshaft lobes and journals, and install the camshaft. CAUTION: *Exercise extreme care to avoid damaging the bearings when inserting the camshaft.* Install and tighten the camshaft thrust plate retaining bolts. See the engine service procedures earlier in this chapter for details concerning specific engines.
Check camshaft end-play (OHV engines only): Check the camshaft end-play with a feeler gauge DIAL INDICATOR CAMSHAFT Check the camshaft end-play with a dial indicator	Using feeler gauges, determine whether the clearance between the camshaft boss (or gear) and backing plate is within specifications. Install shims behind the thrust plate, or reposition the camshaft gear and retest endplay. In some cases, adjustment is by replacing the thrust plate. See the engine service procedures earlier in this chapter for details concerning specific engines. * Mount a dial indicator stand so that the stem of the dial indicator rests on the nose of the camshaft, parallel to the camshaft axis. Push the camshaft as far in as possible and zero the gauge. Move the camshaft outward to determine the amount of camshaft endplay. If the endplay is not within tolerance, install shims behind the thrust plate, or reposition the camshaft gear and retest. See the engine service procedures earlier in this chapter for details concerning specific engines.
Install the rear main seal:	See the engine service procedures earlier in this chapter for details concerning specific engines.
Install the crankshaft: INSTALLING BEARING SHELL REMOVING BEARING SHELL Remove or install the upper bearing insert using a roll-out pin	Thoroughly clean the main bearing saddles and caps. Place the upper halves of the bearing inserts on the saddles and press into position. NOTE: *Ensure that the oil holes align.* Press the corresponding bearing inserts into the main bearing caps. Lubricate the upper main bearings, and lay the crankshaft in position. Place a strip of Plastigage on each of the crankshaft journals, install the main caps, and torque to specifications. Remove the main caps, and compare the Plastigage to the scale on the Plastigage envelope. If clearances are within tolerances, remove the Plastigage, turn the crankshaft 90°, wipe off all oil and retest. If all clearances are correct,

ENGINE AND ENGINE REBUILDING

Cylinder Block Reconditioning

Procedure	Method
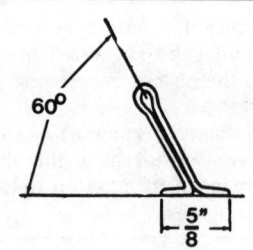 **Home-made bearing roll-out pin** (60°, 5/8")	remove all Plastigage, thoroughly lubricate the main caps and bearing journals, and install the main caps. If clearances are not within tolerance, the upper bearing inserts may be removed, without removing the crankshaft, using a bearing roll out pin (see illustration). Roll in a bearing that will provide proper clearance, and retest. Torque all main caps, excluding the thrust bearing cap, to specifications. Tighten the thrust bearing cap finger tight. To properly align the thrust bearing, pry the crankshaft the extent of its axial travel several times, the last movement held toward the front of the engine, and torque the thrust bearing cap to specifications. Determine the crankshaft end-play (see below), and bring within tolerance with thrust washers.

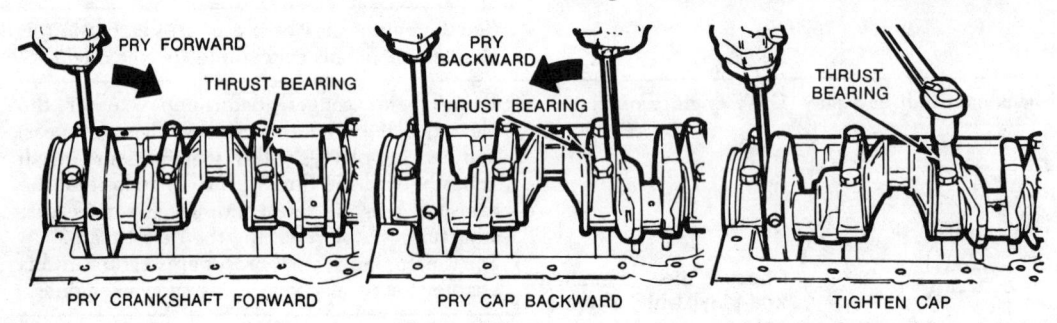

Aligning the thrust bearing (PRY CRANKSHAFT FORWARD / PRY CAP BACKWARD / TIGHTEN CAP)

Measure crankshaft end-play:	Mount a dial indicator stand on the front of the block, with the dial indicator stem resting on the nose of the crankshaft, parallel to the crankshaft axis. Pry the crankshaft the extent of its travel rearward, and zero the indicator. Pry the crankshaft forward and record crankshaft end-play. *NOTE: Crankshaft end-play also may be measured at the thrust bearing, using feeler gauges (see illustration).*

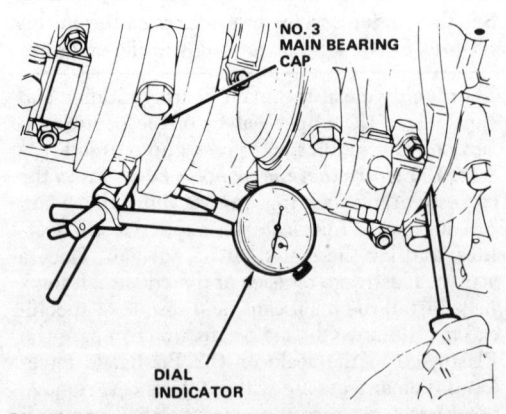

Check the crankshaft end-play with a dial indicator

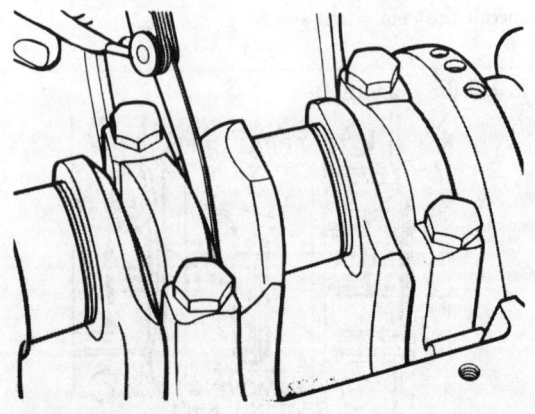

Check the crankshaft end-play with a feeler gauge

ENGINE AND ENGINE REBUILDING

Cylinder Block Reconditioning

Procedure	Method
Install the pistons: *Use lengths of vacuum hose or rubber tubing to protect the crankshaft journals and cylinder walls during piston installation* *Install the piston using a ring compressor*	Press the upper connecting rod bearing halves into the connecting rods, and the lower halves into the connecting rod caps. Position the piston ring gaps according to specifications (see car section), and lubricate the pistons. Install a ring compresser on a piston, and press two long (8″) pieces of plastic tubing over the rod bolts. Using the tubes as a guide, press the pistons into the bores and onto the crankshaft with a wooden hammer handle. After seating the rod on the crankshaft journal, remove the tubes and install the cap finger tight. Install the remaining pistons in the same manner. Invert the engine and check the bearing clearance at two points (90° apart) on each journal with Plastigage. **NOTE:** *Do not turn the crankshaft with Plastigage installed.* If clearance is within tolerances, remove *all* Plastigage, thoroughly lubricate the journals, and torque the rod caps to specifications. If clearance is not within specifications, install different thickness bearing inserts and recheck. **CAUTION:** *Never shim or file the connecting rods or caps.* Always install plastic tube sleeves over the rod bolts when the caps are not installed, to protect the crankshaft journals.
Check connecting rod side clearance: *Check the connecting rod side clearance with a feeler gauge*	Determine the clearance between the sides of the connecting rods and the crankshaft using feeler gauges. If clearance is below the minimum tolerance, the rod may be machined to provide adequate clearance. If clearance is excessive, substitute an unworn rod, and recheck. If clearance is still outside specifications, the crankshaft must be welded and reground, or replaced.
Inspect the timing chain (or belt):	Visually inspect the timing chain for broken or loose links, and replace the chain if any are found. If the chain will flex sideways, it must be replaced. Install the timing chain as specified. Be sure the timing belt is not stretched, frayed or broken. **NOTE:** *If the original timing chain is to be reused, install it in its original position.*

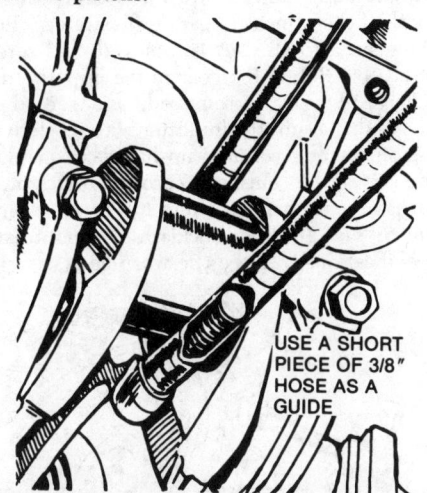

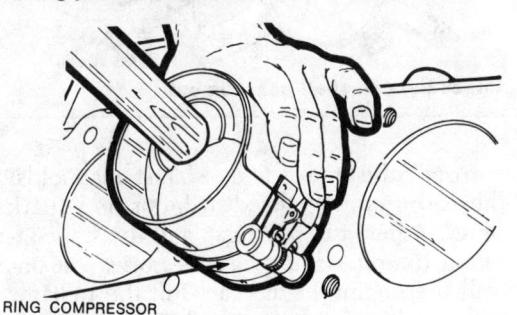

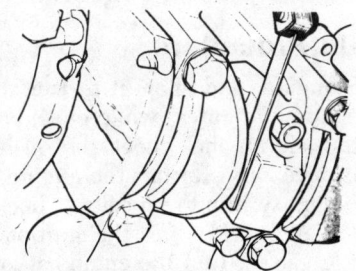

ENGINE AND ENGINE REBUILDING

Cylinder Block Reconditioning

Procedure	Method
Check timing gear backlash and runout (OHV engines):	Mount a dial indicator with its stem resting on a tooth of the camshaft gear (as illustrated). Rotate the gear until all slack is removed, and zero the indicator. Rotate the gear in the opposite direction until slack is removed, and record gear backlash. Mount the indicator with its stem resting on the edge of the camshaft gear, parallel to the axis of the camshaft. Zero the indicator, and turn the camshaft gear one full turn, recording the runout. If either backlash or runout exceed specifications, replace the worn gear(s).

Check the camshaft gear backlash

Check the camshaft gear run-out

Completing the Rebuilding Process

Follow the above procedures, complete the rebuilding process as follows:

Fill the oil pump with oil, to prevent cavitating (sucking air) on initial engine start up. Install the oil pump and the pickup tube on the engine. Coat the oil pan gasket as necessary, and install the gasket and the oil pan. Mount the flywheel and the crankshaft vibration damper or pulley on the crankshaft.

NOTE: *Always use new bolts when installing the flywheel.* Inspect the clutch shaft pilot bushing in the crankshaft. If the bushing is excessively worn, remove it with an expanding puller and a slide hammer, and tap a new bushing into place.

Position the engine, cylinder head side up. Lubricate the lifters, and install them into their bores. Install the cylinder head, and torque it as specified. Insert the pushrods and install the rocker shaft(s) or position the rocker arms on the pushrods. Adjust the valves.

Install the intake and exhaust manifolds, the carburetor(s), the distributor and spark plugs. Adjust the point gap and the static ignition timing. Mount all accessories and install the engine in the car. Fill the radiator with coolant, and the crankcase with high quality engine oil.

Break-in Procedure

Start the engine, and allow it to run at low speed for a few minutes, while checking for leaks. Stop the engine, check the oil level, and fill as necessary. Restart the engine, and fill the cooling system to capacity. Check the point dwell angle and adjust the ignition timing and the valves. Run the engine at low to medium speed (800–2500 rpm) for approximately ½ hour, and retorque the cylinder head bolts. Road test the car, and check again for leaks.

Follow the manufacturer's recommended engine break-in procedure and maintenance schedule for new engines.

Emission Controls and Fuel System

EMISSION CONTROLS

There are three sources of automotive pollutants: crankcase fumes, exhaust gases, and gasoline evaporation. The pollutants formed from these substances fall into three categories: unburnt hydrocarbons (HC), carbon monoxide (CO), and oxides of nitrogen (NO_x). The equipment that is used to limit these pollutants is commonly called emission control equipment.

Positive Crankcase Ventilation System

All J-cars are equipped with a positive crankcase ventilation (PCV) system to control crankcase blow-by vapors. The system functions as follows:

When the engine is running, a small portion of the gases which are formed in the combustion chamber leak by the piston rings and enter the crankcase. Since these gases are under pressure, they tend to escape from the crankcase and enter the atmosphere. If these gases are allowed to remain in the crankcase for any period of time, they contaminate the engine oil and cause sludge to build up in the crankcase. If the gases are allowed to escape into the atmosphere, they pollute the air with unburned hydrocarbons. The job of the crankcase emission control equipment is to recycle these gases back into the engine combustion chamber where they are reburned.

The crankcase (blow-by) gases are recycled in the following way: as the engine is running, clean, filtered air is drawn through the air filter and into the crankcase. As the air passes through the crankcase, it picks up the combustion gases and carries them out of the crankcase, through the oil separator, through the PCV valve, and into the induction system. As they enter the intake manifold, they are drawn into the combustion chamber where they are reburned.

The most critical component in the system is the PCV valve. This valve controls the amount of gases which are recycled into the

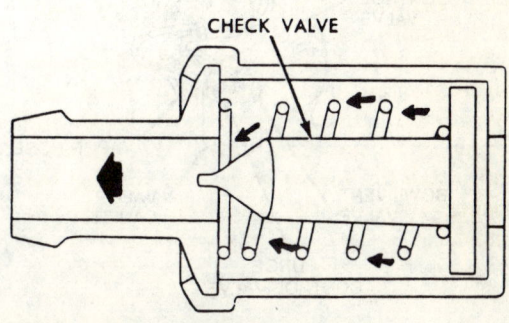

Cross section of a PCV valve

EMISSION CONTROLS AND FUEL SYSTEM

combustion chamber. At low engine speeds, the valve is partially closed, limiting the flow of gases into the intake manifold. As engine speed increases, the valve opens to admit greater quantities of gases into the intake manifold. If the valve should become blocked or plugged, the gases will be prevented from escaping from the crankcase by the normal route. Since these gases are under pressure, they will find their own way out of the crankcase. This alternate route is usually a weak oil seal or gasket in the engine. As the gas escapes by the gasket, it also creates an oil leak. Besides causing oil leaks, a clogged PCV valve also allows these gases to remain in the crankcase for an extended period of time, promoting the formation of sludge in the engine.

SERVICE

Inspect the PCV system hose and connections at each tune-up and replace any deteriorated hoses. Check the PCV valve at every tune-up and replace it at 30,000 mile intervals. Replacement procedures are in Chapter One.

Evaporative Emission Control System

The basic Evaporative Emission Control System (EEC) used on all J-cars is the carbon canister storage method. The system is used to reduce emissions of fuel vapors from the car's fuel system. Evaporated fuel vapors are stored for burning during combustion rather than being vented into the atmosphere when the engine is not running. To accomplish this, the fuel tank and the carburetor float bowl are vented through a vapor canister containing activated charcoal. The system utilizes a sealed fuel tank with a dome that collects fuel vapors and allows them to pass on into a line connected with the vapor canister. In addition, the vapors that form above the float chamber in the carburetor also pass into a line connected with the canister. The canister absorbs these vapors in a bed of activated charcoal and retains them until the canister is purged or cleared by air drawn through the filter at its bottom. The absorbing occurs when the car is not running, while the purging or cleaning occurs when the car is running. The amount of vapor being drawn into the engine at any given time is too small to have an effect on either fuel economy or engine performance.

The Electronic Control Module (ECM) controls the vacuum to the canister purge valve by using an electrically operated solenoid valve. When the system is in the 'Open Loop' mode, the solenoid valve is energized and blocks all vacuum to the canister purge valve. When the system is in the 'Closed Loop' mode, the solenoid valve is de-energized and vacuum is then supplied to operate the purge valve. This releases the fuel va-

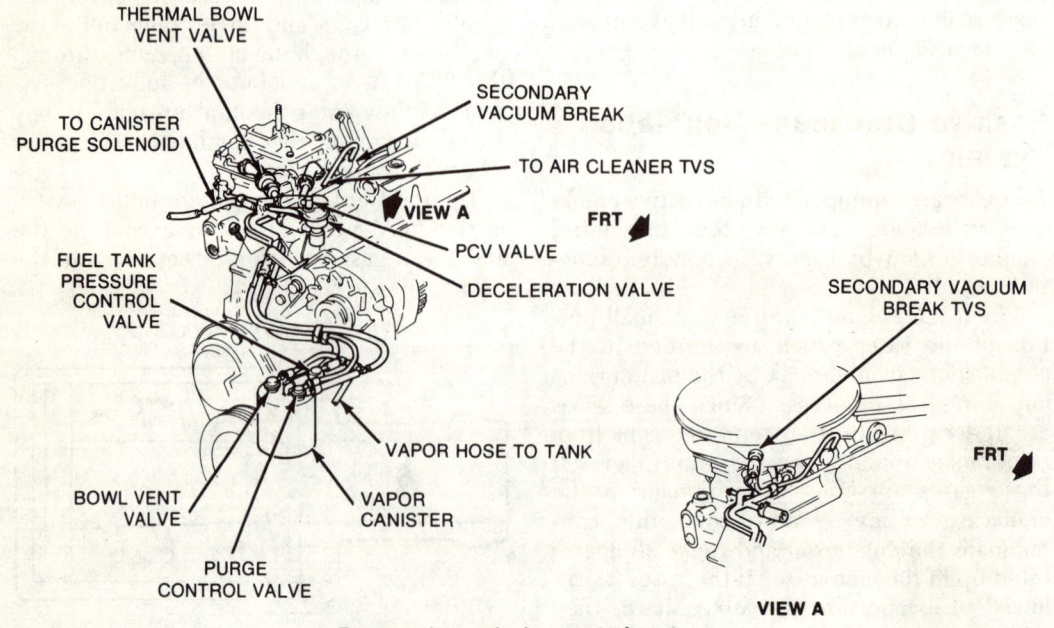

Evaporative emission control system

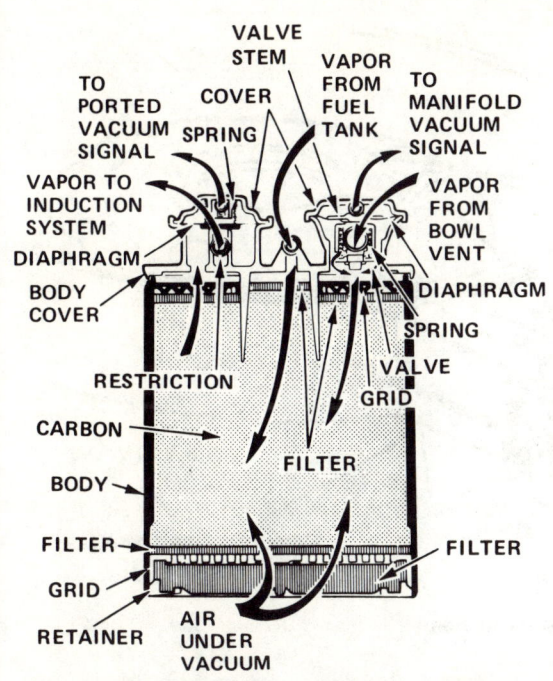

EMISSION CONTROLS AND FUEL SYSTEM

Cross section of the vapor canister

Vapor canister removal and installation details

FILTER REPLACEMENT

1. Remove the vapor canister.
2. Pull the filter out from the bottom of the canister.
3. Install a new filter and then replace the canister.

pors, collected in the canister, into the induction system.

It is extremely important that only vapors be transferred to the engine. To avoid the possibility of liquid fuel being drawn into the system, the following features are included as part of the total system:

• A fuel tank overfill protector is provided to assure adequate room for expansion of liquid fuel volume with temperature changes.

• A one point fuel tank venting system is provided on all models to assure that the tank will be vented under any normal car attitude. This is accomplished by the use of a domed tank.

• A pressure-vacuum relief valve is located in the fuel cap.

VAPOR CANISTER REMOVAL AND INSTALLATION

1. Loosen the screw holding the canister retaining bracket.
2. If equipped with A/C, loosen the attachments holding the accumulator and pipe assembly.
3. Rotate the canister retaining bracket and remove the canister.
4. Tag and disconnect the hoses leading from the canister.
5. Installation is in the reverse order of removal.

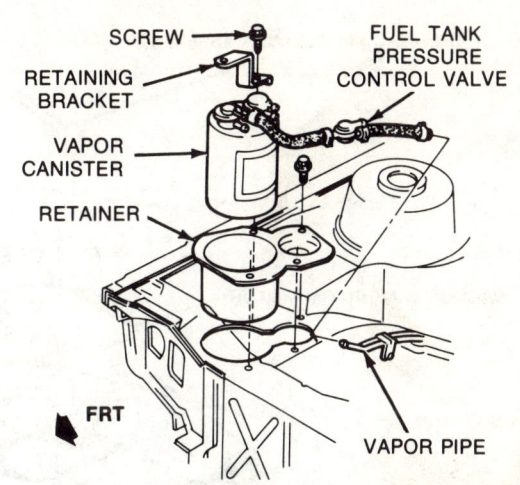

Exhaust Emission Controls

Exhaust emission control systems constitute the largest body of emission control devices installed on the J-car. Included in this category are: Thermostatic Air Cleaner (THERMAC); Air Management System; Early Fuel Evaporation System (EFE); Exhaust Gas Recirculation (EGR); Computer Command Control System (CCC); Deceleration Valve; Mixture Control Solenoid (M/C); Throttle Position Sensor (TPS); Idle Speed Control (ISC); Electronic Spark Timing (EST); Transmission Converter Clutch (TCC); Catalytic Converter and the Oxygen Sensor System. A brief description of each system and any applicable service procedures follows.

Thermostatic Air Cleaner (THERMAC)

All engines use the THERMAC system. This system is designed to warm the air entering the carburetor when underhood temperatures are low, and to maintain a controlled air temperature into the carburetor at all times. By allowing preheated air to enter the carburetor, the amount of time the choke is on is reduced, resulting in better fuel economy and lower emissions. Engine warm-up time is also reduced.

94 EMISSION CONTROLS AND FUEL SYSTEM

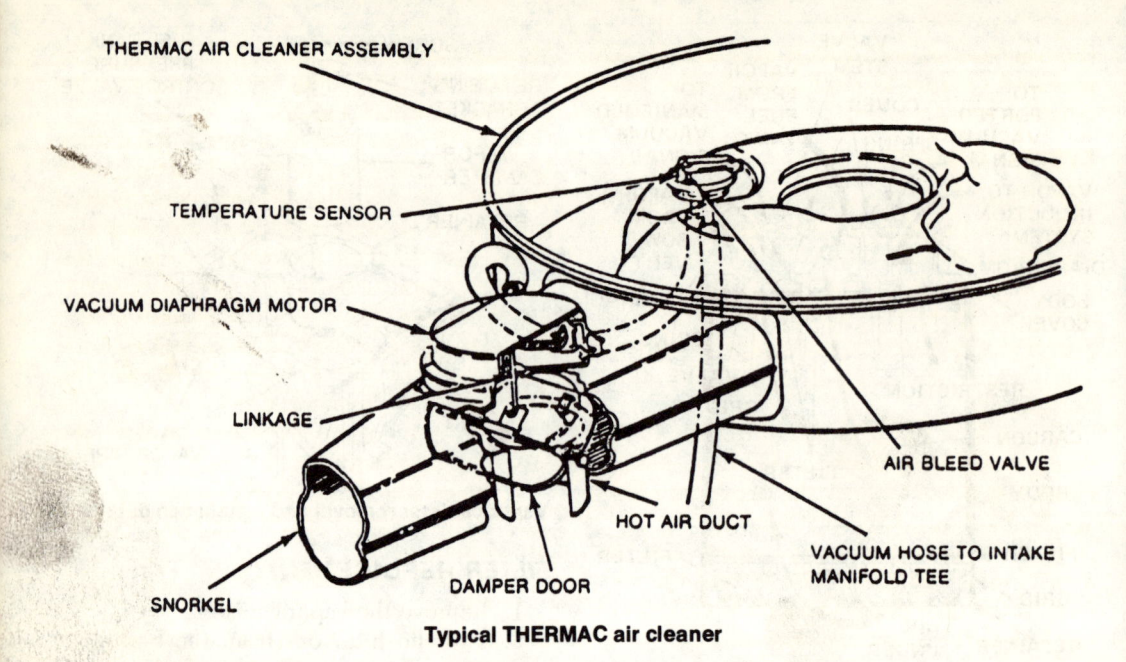

Typical THERMAC air cleaner

The THERMAC system is composed of the air cleaner body, a filter, sensor unit, vacuum diaphragm, damper door, and associated hoses and connections. Heat radiating from the exhaust manifold is trapped by a heat stove and is ducted to the air cleaner to supply heated air to the carburetor. A movable door in the air cleaner case snorkel allows air to be drawn in from the heat stove (cold operation). The door position is controlled by

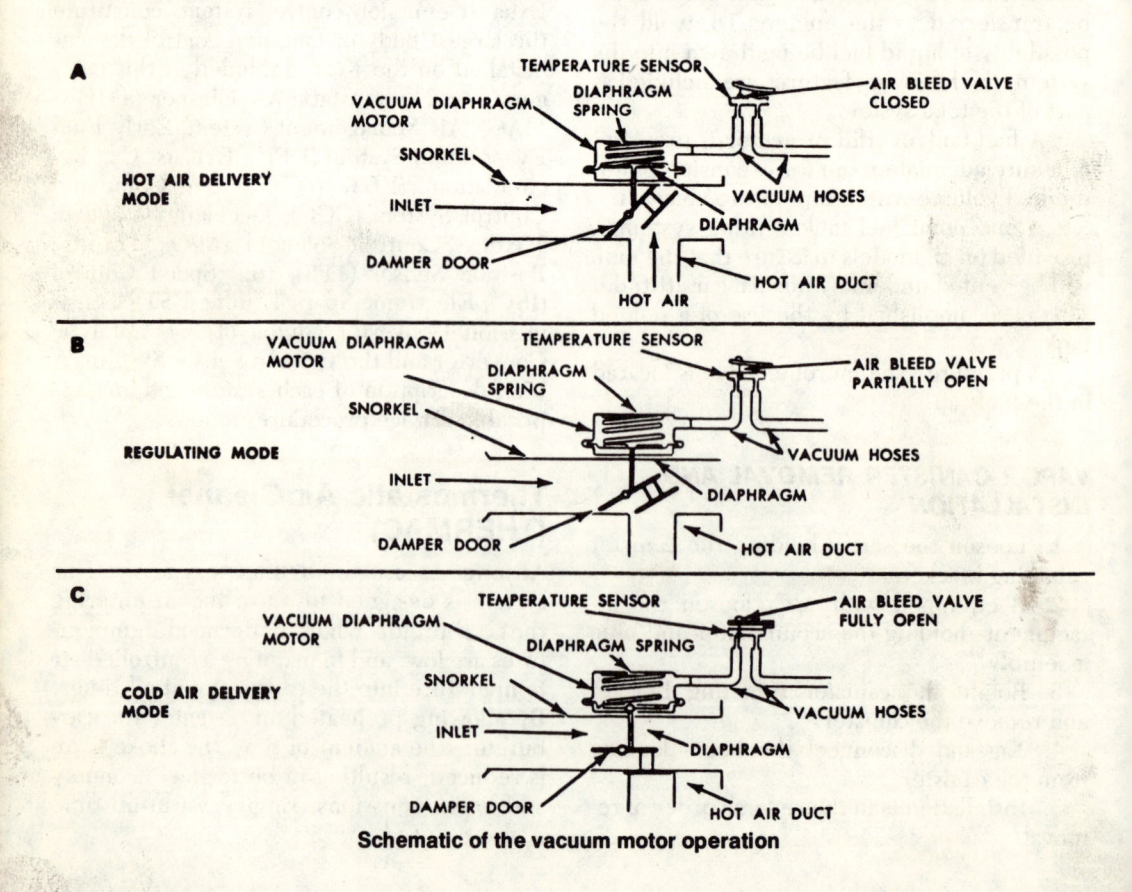

Schematic of the vacuum motor operation

EMISSION CONTROLS AND FUEL SYSTEM

the vacuum motor, which receives intake manifold vacuum as modulated by the temperature sensor.

SYSTEM CHECKS

1. Check the vacuum hoses for leaks, kinks, breaks, or improper connections and correct any defects.
2. With the engine off, check the position of the damper door within the snorkel. A mirror can be used to make this job easier. The damper door should be open to admit outside air.
3. Apply at least 7 in. Hg of vacuum to the damper diaphragm unit. The door should close. If it doesn't, check the diaphragm linkage for binding and correct hookup.
4. With the vacuum still applied and the door closed, clamp the tube to trap the vacuum. If the door doesn't remain closed, there is a leak in the diaphragm assembly.

Air Management System

The AIR management system, is used to provide additional oxygen to continue the combustion process after the exhaust gases leave the combustion chamber. Air is injected into either the exhaust port(s), the exhaust manifold(s) or the catalytic converter by an engine driven air pump. The system is in operation at all times and will bypass air only momentarily during deceleration and at high speeds. The bypass function is performed by the Air Management Valve, while the check valve protects the air pump by preventing any backflow of exhaust gases.

The AIR management system helps reduce HC and CO content in the exhaust gases by injecting air into the exhaust ports during cold engine operation. This air injection also helps the catalytic converter to reach the proper temperature quicker during warm-up. When the engine is warm (Closed Loop), the AIR system injects air into the beds of a three-way converter to lower the HC and the CO content in the exhaust.

The Air Management system utilizes the following components:

1. An engine driven AIR pump
2. AIR management valves (Air Control, Air Switching)
3. Air flow and control hoses
4. Check valves
5. A dual-bed, three-way catalytic converter.

The belt driven, vane-type air pump is located at the front of the engine and supplies clean air to the AIR system for purposes already stated. When the engine is cold, the Electronic Control Module (ECM) energizes an AIR control solenoid. This allows air to flow to the AIR switching valve. The AIR switching valve is then energized to direct air to the exhaust ports.

When the engine is warm, the ECM de-energizes the AIR switching valve, thus di-

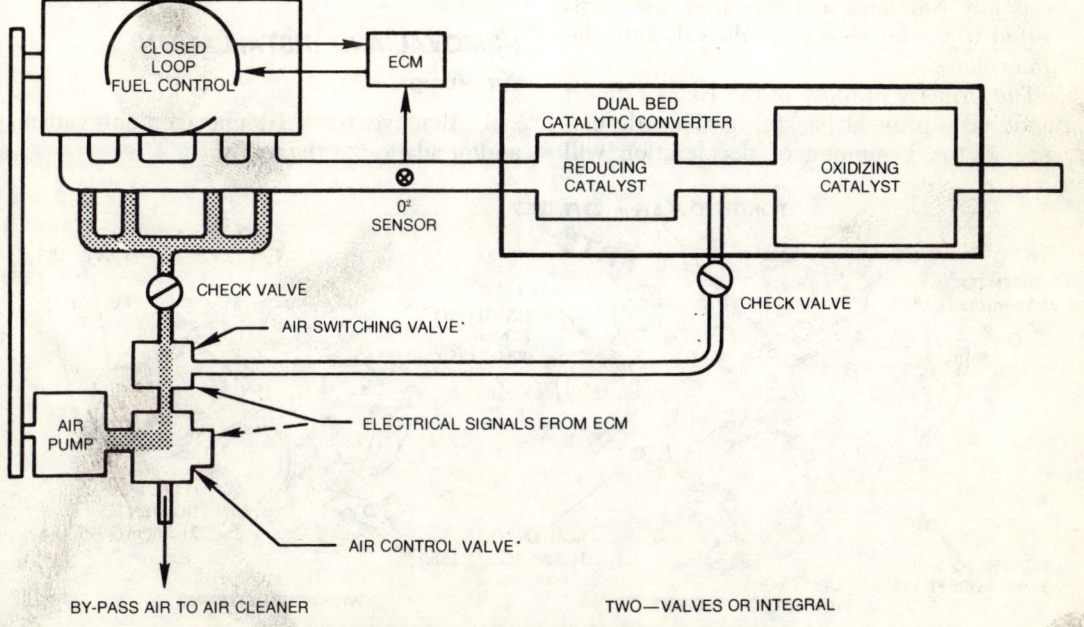

Air management system operation—cold engine

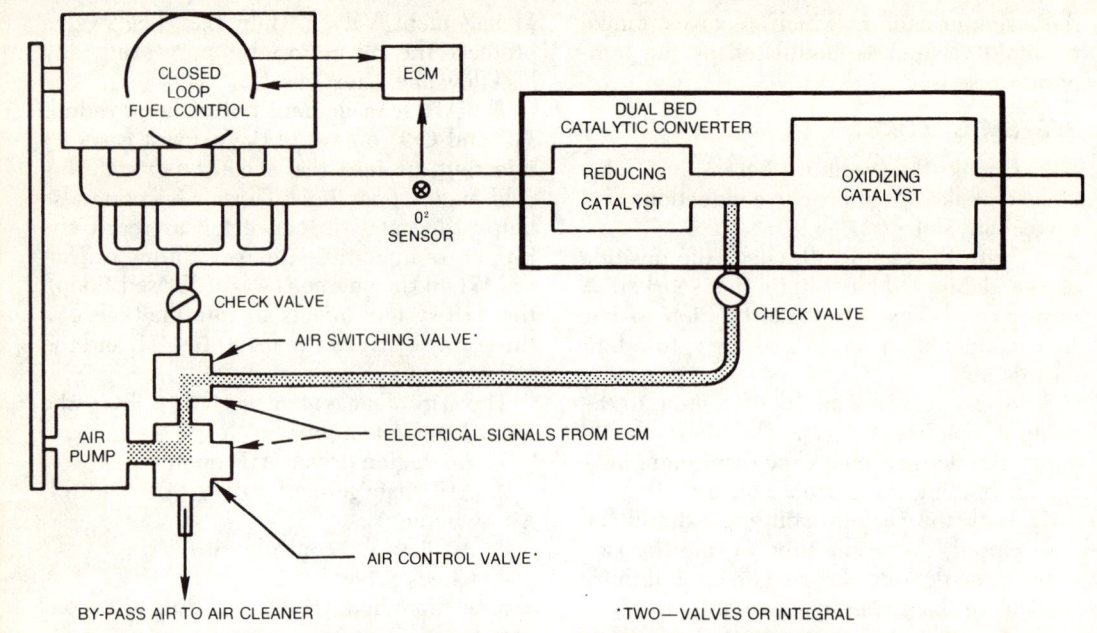

96 EMISSION CONTROLS AND FUEL SYSTEM

Air management system operation—warm engine

recting the air between the beds of the catalytic converter. This provides additional oxygen for the oxidizing catalyst in the second bed to decrease HC and CO, while at the same time keeping oxygen levels low in the first bed, enabling the reducing catalyst to effectively decrease the levels of NO_x.

If the AIR control valve detects a rapid increase in manifold vacuum (deceleration), certain operating modes (wide open throttle, etc.) or if the ECM self-diagnostic system detects any problem in the system, air is diverted to the air cleaner or directly into the atmosphere.

The primary purpose of the ECM's divert mode is to prevent backfiring. Throttle closure at the beginning of deceleration will temporarily create air/fuel mixtures which are too rich to burn completely. These mixtures become burnable when they reach the exhaust if combined with the injection air. The next firing of the engine will ignite this mixture causing an exhaust backfire. Momentary diverting of the injection air from the exhaust prevents this.

The AIR management system check valves and hoses should be checked periodically for any leaks, cracks or deterioration.

REMOVAL AND INSTALLATION
Air Pump

1. Remove the AIR management valves and/or adapter at the pump.

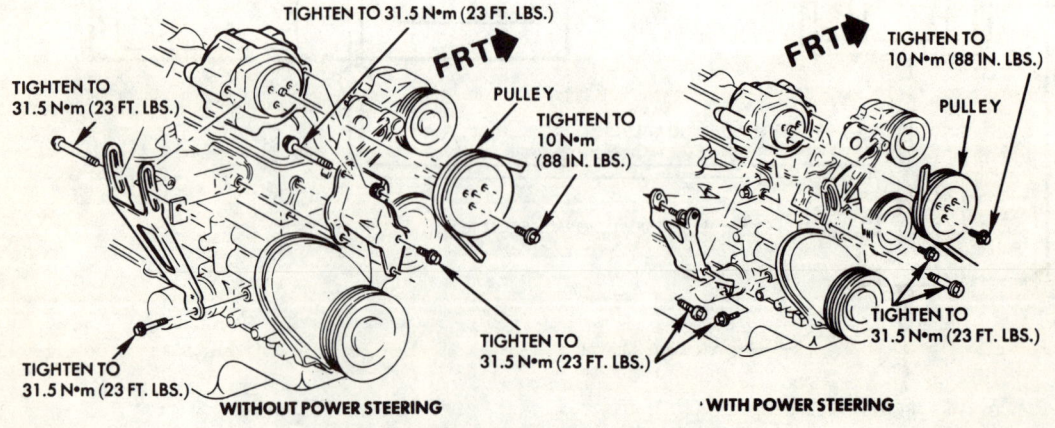

Air pump removal and installation details

EMISSION CONTROLS AND FUEL SYSTEM

2. Loosen the air pump adjustment bolt and remove the drive belt.

3. Unscrew the pump mounting bolts and then remove the pump pulley.

4. Unscrew the pump mounting bolts and then remove the pump.

5. Installation is in the reverse order of removal. Be sure to adjust the drive belt tension after installing it.

Check Valve

1. Release the clamp and disconnect the air hoses from the valve.

2. Unscrew the check valve from the air injection pipe.

3. Installation is in the reverse order of removal.

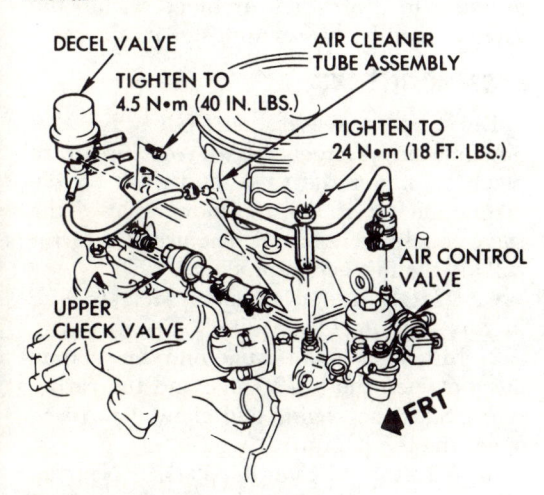

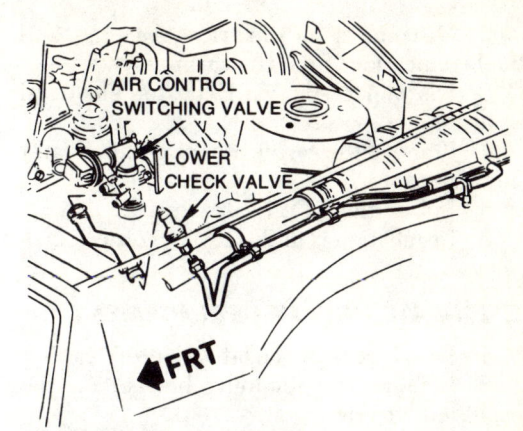

Lower check valve and hoses

Upper check valve and hoses

Air Management Valve

1. Disconnect the negative battery cable.
2. Remove the air cleaner.
3. Tag and disconnect the vacuum hose from the valve.
4. Tag and disconnect the air outlet hoses from the valve.
5. Bend back the lock tabs and then remove the bolts holding the elbow to the valve.
6. Tag and disconnect any electrical connections at the valve and then remove the valve from the elbow.
7. Installation is in the reverse order of removal.

Early Fuel Evaporation (EFE)

All models are equipped with this system to reduce engine warm-up time, improve driveability and reduce emissions. The system is electric and uses a ceramic heater grid located underneath the primary bore of the carburetor as part of the carburetor insulator/gasket. When the ignition switch is turned on and the engine coolant temperature is low, voltage is applied to the EFE relay by the ECM. The EFE relay inturn energizes the heater grid. When the coolant temperature increases, the ECM de-energizes the relay which will then "shut off" the EFE heater.

REMOVAL AND INSTALLATION

1. Remove the air cleaner and disconnect the negative battery cable.

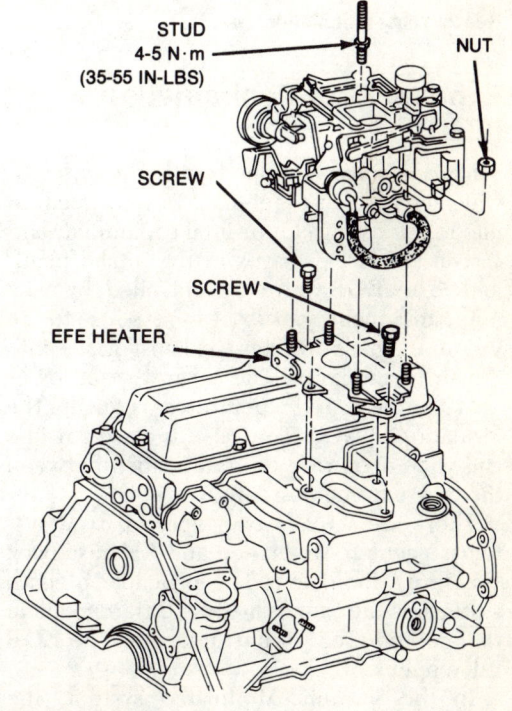

EFE heater grid

98 EMISSION CONTROLS AND FUEL SYSTEM

2. Disconnect all electrical, vacuum and fuel connections from the carburetor.
3. Disconnect the EFE heater electrical lead.
4. Remove the carburetor as detailed later in this chapter.
5. Lift off the EFE heater grid.
6. Installation is in the reverse order of removal.

EFE HEATER RELAY REPLACEMENT

1. Disconnect the negative battery cable.
2. Remove the retaining bracket on the right fender skirt.
3. Tag and disconnect all electrical connections.
4. Unscrew the retaining bolts and remove the relay.
5. Installation is in the reverse order of removal.

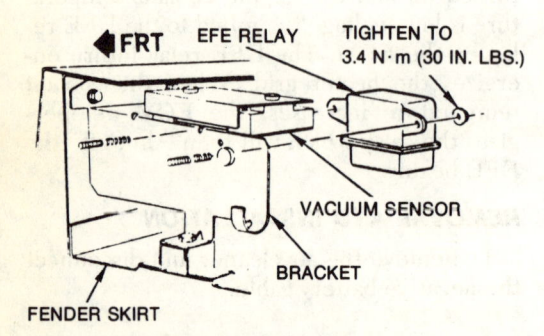

Heater relay installation details

Exhaust Gas Recirculation (EGR)

All models are equipped with this system, which consists of a metering valve, a vacuum line to the carburetor or intake manifold, and cast-in exhaust passages in the intake manifold. The EGR valve is controlled by vacuum, and opens and closes in response to the vacuum signals to admit exhaust gases into the air/fuel mixture. The exhaust gases lower peak combustion temperatures, reducing the formation of NO_x. The valve is closed at idle and wide open throttle, but is open between the two extreme positions.

There are actually two types of EGR systems: Vacuum Modulated and Exhaust Back Pressure Modulated. The principle of both systems is the same; the only difference is in the method used to control how far the EGR valve opens.

In the Vacuum Modulated system, the amount of exhaust gas admitted into the intake manifold depends on a ported vacuum signal. A ported vacuum signal is one taken from the carburetor above the throttle plates; thus, the vacuum signal (amount of vacuum) is dependent on how far the throttle plates are opened. When the throttle is closed (idle or deceleration) there is no vacuum signal. Thus, the EGR valve is closed, and no exhaust gas enters the intake manifold. As the throttle is opened, a vacuum is produced, which opens the EGR valve, admitting exhaust gas into the intake manifold.

In the Exhaust Back Pressure Modulated system, a transducer is installed in the EGR valve body. The vacuum is still ported vacuum, but the transducer uses exhaust gas pressure to control an air bleed within the valve to modify this vacuum signal.

SYSTEM CHECKS

1. Check to see if the EGR valve diaphragm moves freely. Use your finger to reach up under the valve and push on the diaphragm. If it doesn't move freely, the valve should be replaced. The use of a mirror will aid the inspection process.
CAUTION: *If the engine is hot, wear a glove to protect your hand.*
2. Install a vacuum gauge into the vacuum line between the EGR valve and the carburetor. Start the engine and allow it to reach operating temperature.
3. With the car in either Park or Neutral, increase the engine speed until at least 5 in. Hg. is showing on the gauge.
4. Remove the vacuum hose from the EGR valve. The diaphragm should move downward (valve closed). The engine speed should increase.
5. Install the vacuum hose and watch for the EGR valve to open (diaphragm moving upward). The engine speed should decrease to its former level, indicating exhaust recirculation.

If the diaphragm doesn't move:
1. Check engine vacuum; it should be at least 5 in. Hg. with the throttle open and engine running.
2. Check to see that the engine is at normal operating temperature.
3. Check for vacuum at the EGR hose. If no vacuum is present, check the hose for leaks, breaks, kinks, improper connections, etc., and replace as necessary.

If the diaphragm moves, but the engine speed doesn't change, check the EGR passages in the intake manifold for blockage.

EMISSION CONTROLS AND FUEL SYSTEM 99

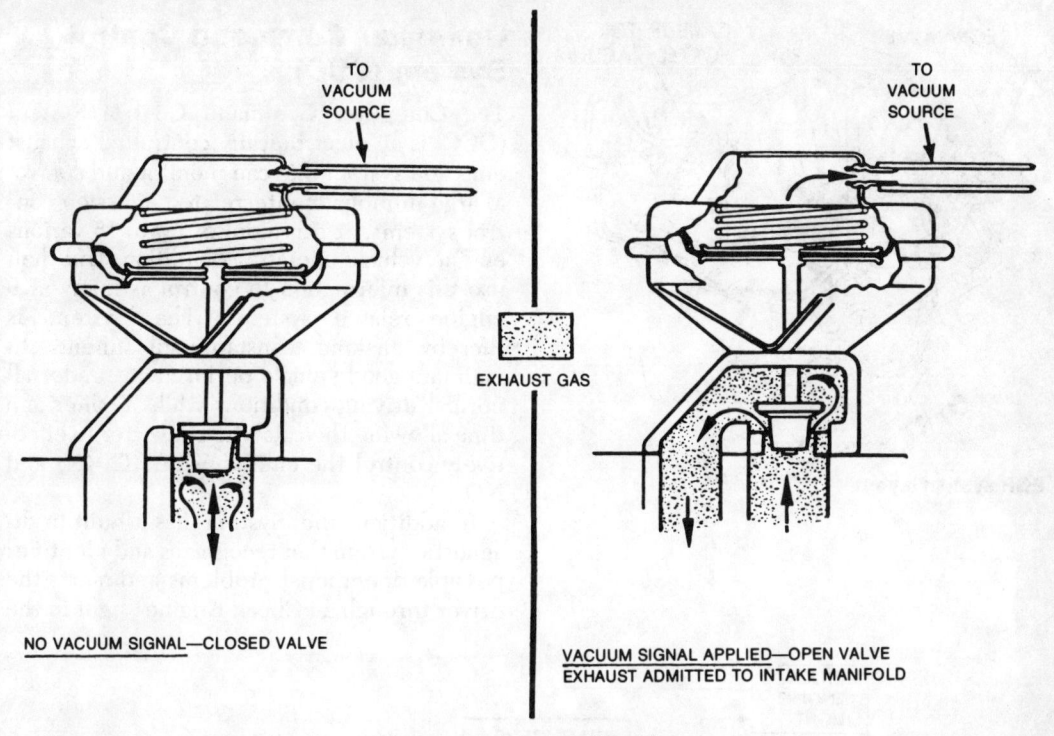

NO VACUUM SIGNAL—CLOSED VALVE

VACUUM SIGNAL APPLIED—OPEN VALVE
EXHAUST ADMITTED TO INTAKE MANIFOLD

Vacuum modulated EGR valve

REMOVAL AND INSTALLATION

1. Disconnect the vacuum hose.
2. Remove the bolts or nuts holding the EGR valve to the engine.
3. Remove the valve.
4. Clean the mounting surfaces before replacing the valve. Install the valve onto the manifold, using a new gasket. Be sure to install the spacer, if used. Connect the vacuum hose and check the valve operation.

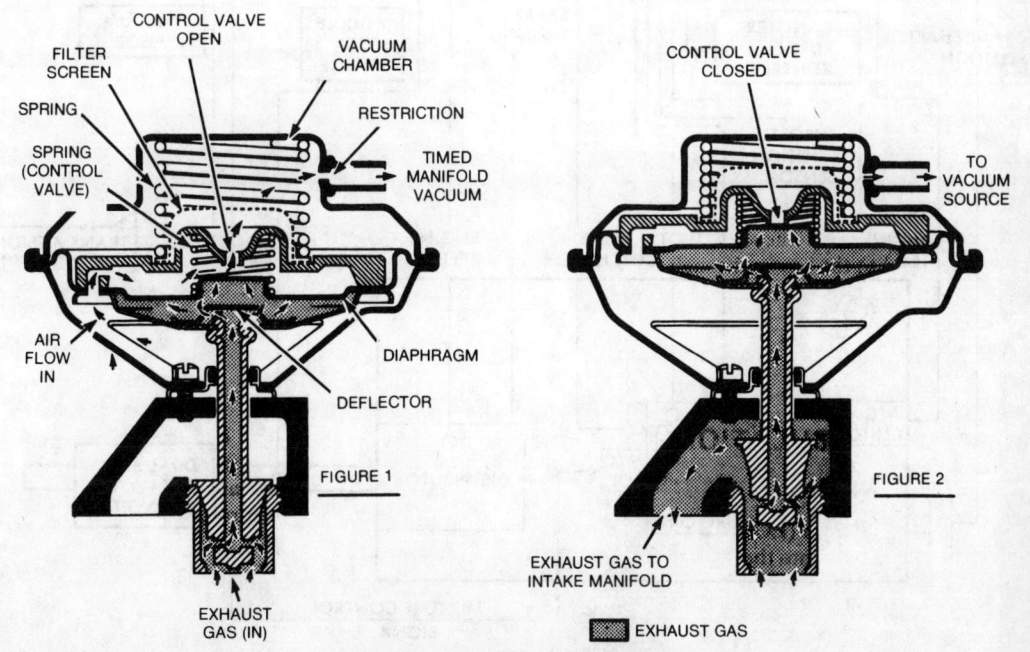

Exhaust gas modulated EGR valve

100 EMISSION CONTROLS AND FUEL SYSTEM

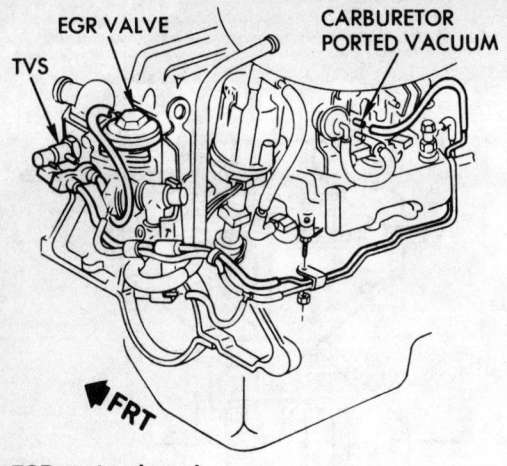

EGR system layout

Computer Command Control System (CCC)

The Computer Command Control System (CCC) is an electronically controlled exhaust emission system that can monitor and control a large number of interrelated emission control systems. It can monitor up to 15 various engine/vehicle operating conditions and then use this information to control as many as 9 engine related systems. The 'System' is thereby making constant adjustments to maintain good vehicle performance under all normal driving conditions while at the same time allowing the catalytic converter to effectively control the emissions of HC, CO and NO_x.

In addition, the 'System' has a built in diagnostic system that recognizes and identifies possible operational problems and alerts the driver through a "Check Engine" light in the

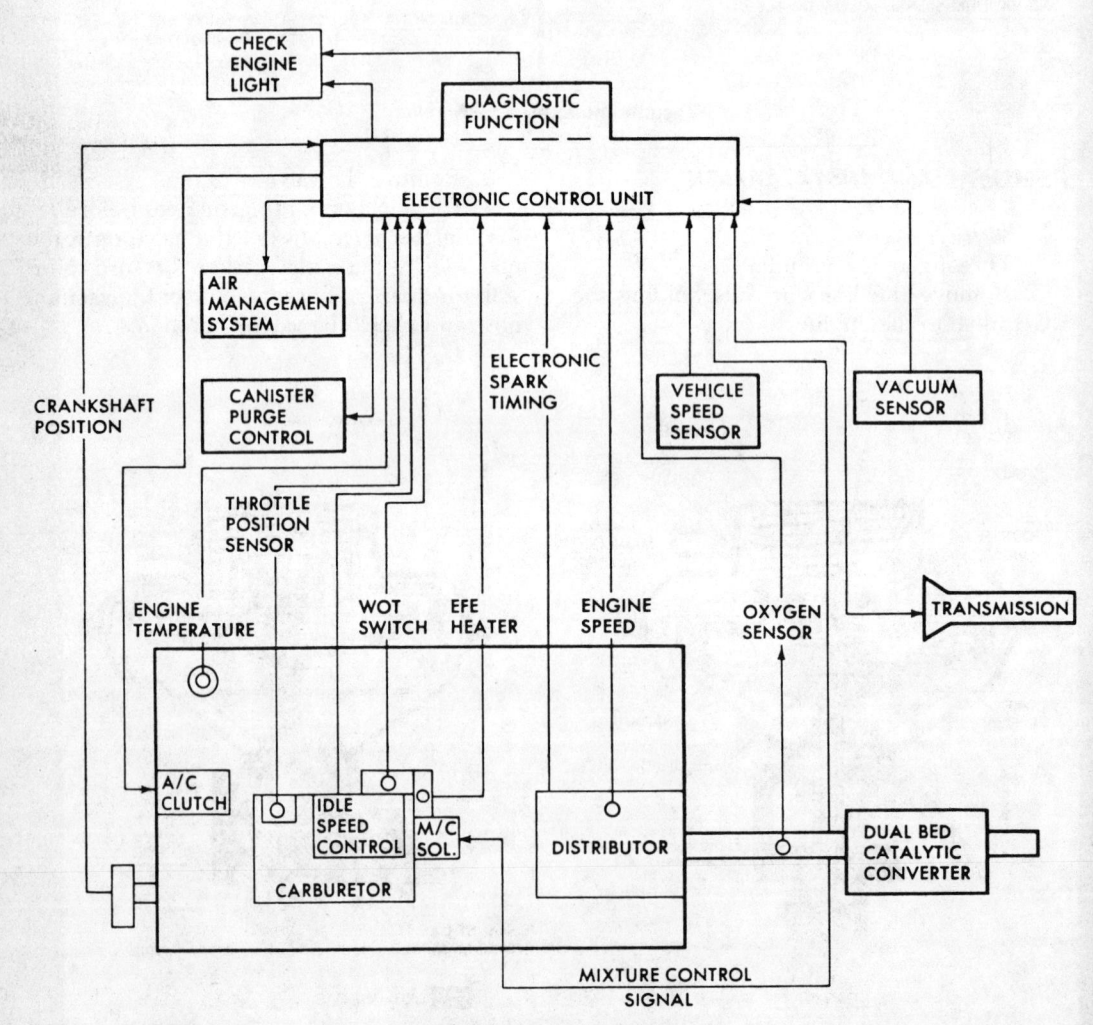

CCC system schematic

CHILTON'S
FUEL ECONOMY & TUNE-UP TIPS

Tune-Up • Spark Plug Diagnosis • Emission Controls
Fuel System • Cooling System • Tires and Wheels
General Maintenance

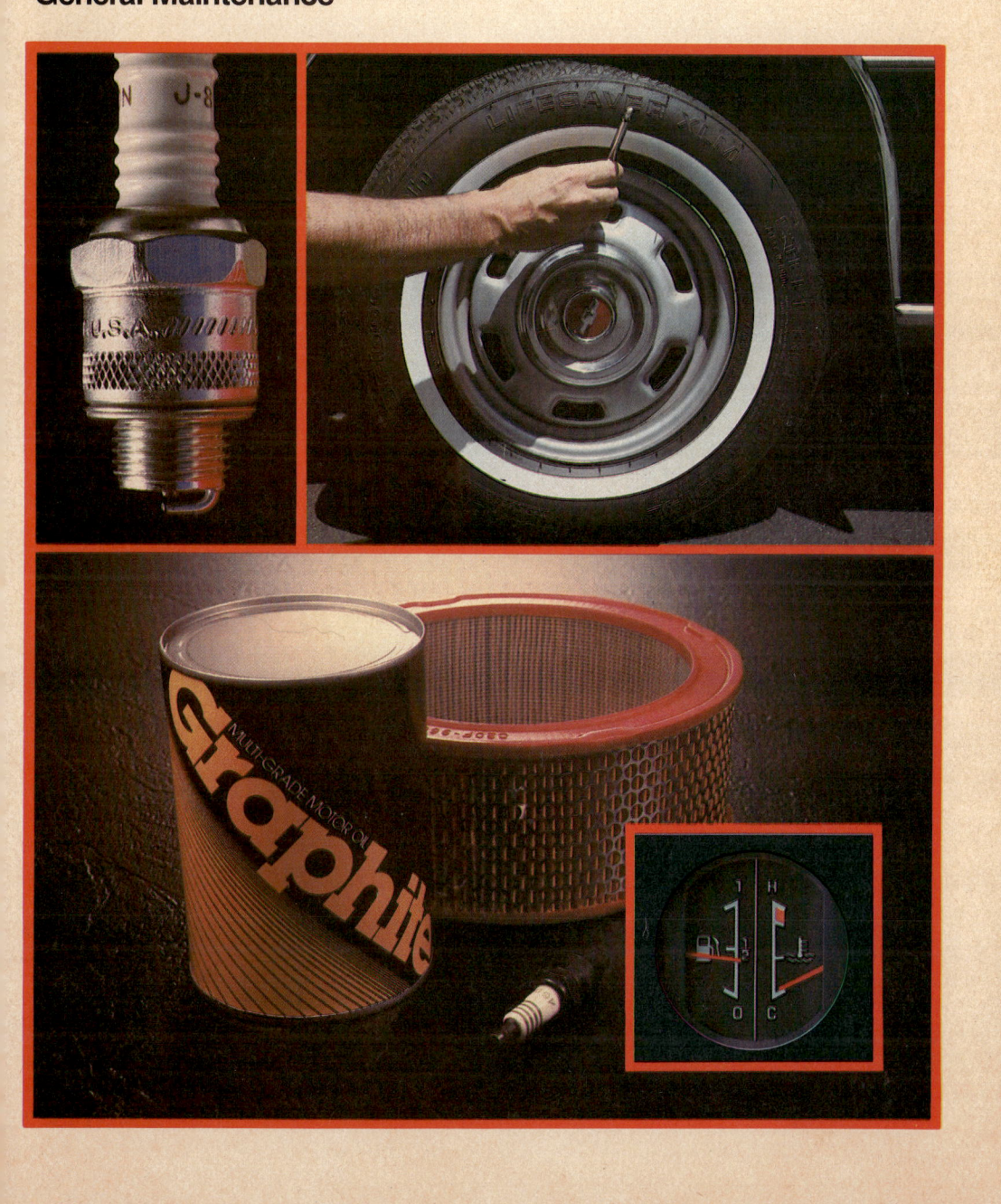

55 WAYS TO IMPROVE FUEL ECONOMY

CHILTON'S FUEL ECONOMY & TUNE-UP TIPS

Fuel economy is important to everyone, no matter what kind of vehicle you drive. The maintenance-minded motorist can save both money and fuel using these tips and the periodic maintenance and tune-up procedures in this Repair and Tune-Up Guide.

There are more than 130,000,000 cars and trucks registered for private use in the United States. Each travels an average of 10-12,000 miles per year, and, in total they consume close to 70 billion gallons of fuel each year. This represents nearly $2/3$ of the oil imported by the United States each year. The Federal government's goal is to reduce consumption 10% by 1985. A variety of methods are either already in use or under serious consideration, and they all affect your driving and the cars you will drive. In addition to "down-sizing", the auto industry is using or investigating the use of electronic fuel delivery, electronic engine controls and alternative engines for use in smaller and lighter vehicles, among other alternatives to meet the federally mandated Corporate Average Fuel Economy (CAFE) of 27.5 mpg by 1985. The government, for its part, is considering rationing, mandatory driving curtailments and tax increases on motor vehicle fuel in an effort to reduce consumption. The government's goal of a 10% reduction could be realized — and further government regulation avoided — if every private vehicle could use just 1 less gallon of fuel per week.

How Much Can You Save?

Tests have proven that almost anyone can make at least a 10% reduction in fuel consumption through regular maintenance and tune-ups. When a major manufacturer of spark plugs sur-

---

TUNE-UP

1. Check the cylinder compression to be sure the engine will really benefit from a tune-up and that it is capable of producing good fuel economy. A tune-up will be wasted on an engine in poor mechanical condition.

2. Replace spark plugs regularly. New spark plugs alone can increase fuel economy 3%.

3. Be sure the spark plugs are the correct type (heat range) for your vehicle. See the Tune-Up Specifications.

Heat range refers to the spark plug's ability to conduct heat away from the firing end. It must conduct the heat away in an even pattern to avoid becoming a source of pre-ignition, yet it must also operate hot enough to burn off conductive deposits that could cause misfiring.

The heat range is usually indicated by a number on the spark plug, part of the manufacturer's designation for each individual spark plug. The numbers in bold-face indicate the heat range in each manufacturer's identification system.

Manufacturer	Typical Designation
AC	R **45** TS
Bosch (old)	WA **145** T30
Bosch (new)	HR **8** Y
Champion	RBL **15** Y
Fram/Autolite	**415**
Mopar	P-**62** PR
Motorcraft	BRF-**42**
NGK	BP **5** ES-15
Nippondenso	W **16** EP
Prestolite	14GR **5** 2A

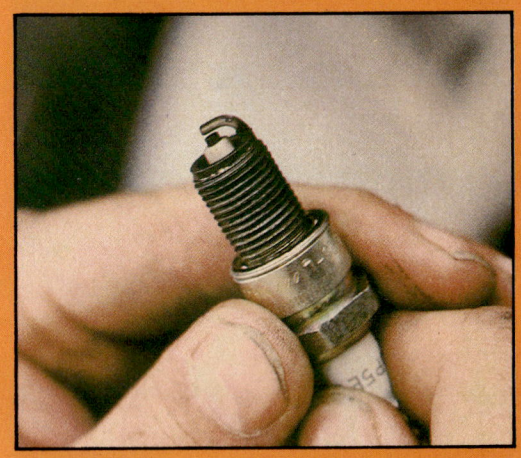

Periodically, check the spark plugs to be sure they are firing efficiently. They are excellent indicators of the internal condition of your engine.

On AC, Bosch (new), Champion, Fram/Autolite, Mopar, Motorcraft and Prestolite, a higher number indicates a hotter plug. On Bosch (old), NGK and Nippondenso, a higher number indicates a colder plug.

4. Make sure the spark plugs are properly gapped. See the Tune-Up Specifications in this book.

5. Be sure the spark plugs are firing efficiently. The illustrations on the next 2 pages show you how to "read" the firing end of the spark plug.

6. Check the ignition timing and set it to specifications. Tests show that almost all cars

veyed over 6,000 cars nationwide, they found that a tune-up, on cars that needed one, increased fuel economy over 11%. Replacing worn plugs alone, accounted for a 3% increase. The same test also revealed that 8 out of every 10 vehicles will have some maintenance deficiency that will directly affect fuel economy, emissions or performance. Most of this mileage-robbing neglect could be prevented with regular maintenance.

Modern engines require that all of the functioning systems operate properly for maximum efficiency. A malfunction anywhere wastes fuel. You can keep your vehicle running as efficiently and economically as possible, by being aware of your vehicles operating and performance characteristics. If your vehicle suddenly develops performance or fuel economy problems it could be due to one or more of the following:

PROBLEM	POSSIBLE CAUSE
Engine Idles Rough	Ignition timing, idle mixture, vacuum leak or something amiss in the emission control system.
Hesitates on Acceleration	Dirty carburetor or fuel filter, improper accelerator pump setting, ignition timing or fouled spark plugs.
Starts Hard or Fails to Start	Worn spark plugs, improperly set automatic choke, ice (or water) in fuel system.
Stalls Frequently	Automatic choke improperly adjusted and possible dirty air filter or fuel filter.
Performs Sluggishly	Worn spark plugs, dirty fuel or air filter, ignition timing or automatic choke out of adjustment.

Check spark plug wires on conventional point type ignition for cracks by bending them in a loop around your finger.

Be sure that spark plug wires leading to adjacent cylinders do not run too close together. (Photo courtesy Champion Spark Plug Co.)

have incorrect ignition timing by more than 2°.

7. If your vehicle does not have electronic ignition, check the points, rotor and cap as specified.

8. Check the spark plug wires (used with conventional point-type ignitions) for cracks and burned or broken insulation by bending them in a loop around your finger. Cracked wires decrease fuel efficiency by failing to deliver full voltage to the spark plugs. One misfiring spark plug can cost you as much as 2 mpg.

9. Check the routing of the plug wires. Misfiring can be the result of spark plug leads to adjacent cylinders running parallel to each other and too close together. One wire tends to pick up voltage from the other causing it to fire "out of time".

10. Check all electrical and ignition circuits for voltage drop and resistance.

11. Check the distributor mechanical and/or vacuum advance mechanisms for proper functioning. The vacuum advance can be checked by twisting the distributor plate in the opposite direction of rotation. It should spring back when released.

12. Check and adjust the valve clearance on engines with mechanical lifters. The clearance should be slightly loose rather than too tight.

SPARK PLUG DIAGNOSIS

Normal

APPEARANCE: This plug is typical of one operating normally. The insulator nose varies from a light tan to grayish color with slight electrode wear. The presence of slight deposits is normal on used plugs and will have no adverse effect on engine performance. The spark plug heat range is correct for the engine and the engine is running normally.
CAUSE: Properly running engine.
RECOMMENDATION: Before reinstalling this plug, the electrodes should be cleaned and filed square. Set the gap to specifications. If the plug has been in service for more than 10-12,000 miles, the entire set should probably be replaced with a fresh set of the same heat range.

Oil Deposits

APPEARANCE: The firing end of the plug is covered with a wet, oily coating.
CAUSE: The problem is poor oil control. On high mileage engines, oil is leaking past the rings or valve guides into the combustion chamber. A common cause is also a plugged PCV valve, and a ruptured fuel pump diaphragm can also cause this condition. Oil fouled plugs such as these are often found in new or recently overhauled engines, before normal oil control is achieved, and can be cleaned and reinstalled.
RECOMMENDATION: A hotter spark plug may temporarily relieve the problem, but the engine is probably in need of work.

Incorrect Heat Range

APPEARANCE: The effects of high temperature on a spark plug are indicated by clean white, often blistered insulator. This can also be accompanied by excessive wear of the electrode, and the absence of deposits.
CAUSE: Check for the correct spark plug heat range. A plug which is too hot for the engine can result in overheating. A car operated mostly at high speeds can require a colder plug. Also check ignition timing, cooling system level, fuel mixture and leaking intake manifold.
RECOMMENDATION: If all ignition and engine adjustments are known to be correct, and no other malfunction exists, install spark plugs one heat range colder.

Carbon Deposits

APPEARANCE: Carbon fouling is easily identified by the presence of dry, soft, black, sooty deposits.
CAUSE: Changing the heat range can often lead to carbon fouling, as can prolonged slow, stop-and-start driving. If the heat range is correct, carbon fouling can be attributed to a rich fuel mixture, sticking choke, clogged air cleaner, worn breaker points, retarded timing or low compression. If only one or two plugs are carbon fouled, check for corroded or cracked wires on the affected plugs. Also look for cracks in the distributor cap between the towers of affected cylinders.
RECOMMENDATION: After the problem is corrected, these plugs can be cleaned and reinstalled if not worn severely.

Photos Courtesy Champion Spark Plug Co.

MMT Fouled

APPEARANCE: Spark plugs fouled by MMT (Methycyclopentadienyl Maganese Tricarbonyl) have reddish, rusty appearance on the insulator and side electrode.
CAUSE: MMT is an anti-knock additive in gasoline used to replace lead. During the combustion process, the MMT leaves a reddish deposit on the insulator and side electrode.
RECOMMENDATION: No engine malfunction is indicated and the deposits will not affect plug performance any more than lead deposits (see Ash Deposits). MMT fouled plugs can be cleaned, regapped and reinstalled.

High Speed Glazing

APPEARANCE: Glazing appears as shiny coating on the plug, either yellow or tan in color.
CAUSE: During hard, fast acceleration, plug temperatures rise suddenly. Deposits from normal combustion have no chance to fluff-off; instead, they melt on the insulator forming an electrically conductive coating which causes misfiring.
RECOMMENDATION: Glazed plugs are not easily cleaned. They should be replaced with a fresh set of plugs of the correct heat range. If the condition recurs, using plugs with a heat range one step colder may cure the problem.

Ash (Lead) Deposits

APPEARANCE: Ash deposits are characterized by light brown or white colored deposits crusted on the side or center electrodes. In some cases it may give the plug a rusty appearance.
CAUSE: Ash deposits are normally derived from oil or fuel additives burned during normal combustion. Normally they are harmless, though excessive amounts can cause misfiring. If deposits are excessive in short mileage, the valve guides may be worn.
RECOMMENDATION: Ash-fouled plugs can be cleaned, gapped and reinstalled.

Detonation

APPEARANCE: Detonation is usually characterized by a broken plug insulator.
CAUSE: A portion of the fuel charge will begin to burn spontaneously, from the increased heat following ignition. The explosion that results applies extreme pressure to engine components, frequently damaging spark plugs and pistons.
   Detonation can result by over-advanced ignition timing, inferior gasoline (low octane) lean air/fuel mixture, poor carburetion, engine lugging or an increase in compression ratio due to combustion chamber deposits or engine modification.
RECOMMENDATION: Replace the plugs after correcting the problem.

Photos Courtesy Fram Corporation

EMISSION CONTROLS

13. Be aware of the general condition of the emission control system. It contributes to reduced pollution and should be serviced regularly to maintain efficient engine operation.

14. Check all vacuum lines for dried, cracked or brittle conditions. Something as simple as a leaking vacuum hose can cause poor performance and loss of economy.

15. Avoid tampering with the emission control system. Attempting to improve fuel econ-

FUEL SYSTEM

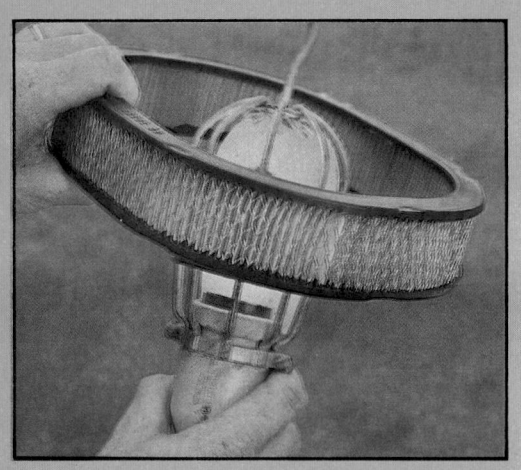

Check the air filter with a light behind it. If you can see light through the filter it can be reused.

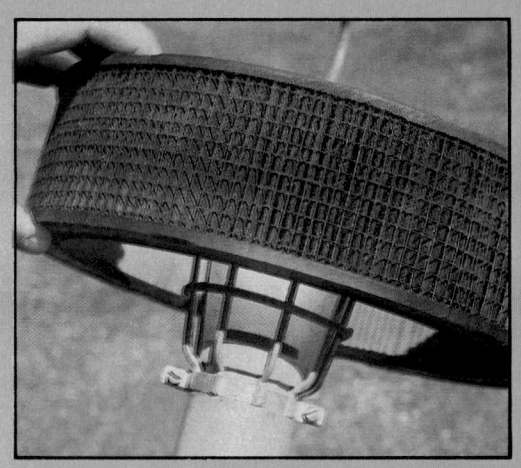

Extremely clogged filters should be discarded and replaced with a new one.

18. Replace the air filter regularly. A dirty air filter richens the air/fuel mixture and can increase fuel consumption as much as 10%. Tests show that ⅓ of all vehicles have air filters in need of replacement.

19. Replace the fuel filter at least as often as recommended.

20. Set the idle speed and carburetor mixture to specifications.

21. Check the automatic choke. A sticking or malfunctioning choke wastes gas.

22. During the summer months, adjust the automatic choke for a leaner mixture which will produce faster engine warm-ups.

COOLING SYSTEM

29. Be sure all accessory drive belts are in good condition. Check for cracks or wear.

30. Adjust all accessory drive belts to proper tension.

31. Check all hoses for swollen areas, worn spots, or loose clamps.

32. Check coolant level in the radiator or expansion tank.

33. Be sure the thermostat is operating properly. A stuck thermostat delays engine warm-up and a cold engine uses nearly twice as much fuel as a warm engine.

34. Drain and replace the engine coolant at least as often as recommended. Rust and scale

TIRES & WHEELS

38. Check the tire pressure often with a pencil type gauge. Tests by a major tire manufacturer show that 90% of all vehicles have at least 1 tire improperly inflated. Better mileage can be achieved by over-inflating tires, but never exceed the maximum inflation pressure on the side of the tire.

39. If possible, install radial tires. Radial tires deliver as much as ½ mpg more than bias belted tires.

40. Avoid installing super-wide tires. They only create extra rolling resistance and decrease fuel mileage. Stick to the manufacturer's recommendations.

41. Have the wheels properly balanced.

omy by tampering with emission controls is more likely to worsen fuel economy than improve it. Emission control changes on modern engines are not readily reversible.

16. Clean (or replace) the EGR valve and lines as recommended.

17. Be sure that all vacuum lines and hoses are reconnected properly after working under the hood. An unconnected or misrouted vacuum line can wreak havoc with engine performance.

23. Check for fuel leaks at the carburetor, fuel pump, fuel lines and fuel tank. Be sure all lines and connections are tight.

24. Periodically check the tightness of the carburetor and intake manifold attaching nuts and bolts. These are a common place for vacuum leaks to occur.

25. Clean the carburetor periodically and lubricate the linkage.

26. The condition of the tailpipe can be an excellent indicator of proper engine combustion. After a long drive at highway speeds, the inside of the tailpipe should be a light grey in color. Black or soot on the insides indicates an overly rich mixture.

27. Check the fuel pump pressure. The fuel pump may be supplying more fuel than the engine needs.

28. Use the proper grade of gasoline for your engine. Don't try to compensate for knocking or "pinging" by advancing the ignition timing. This practice will only increase plug temperature and the chances of detonation or pre-ignition with relatively little performance gain.

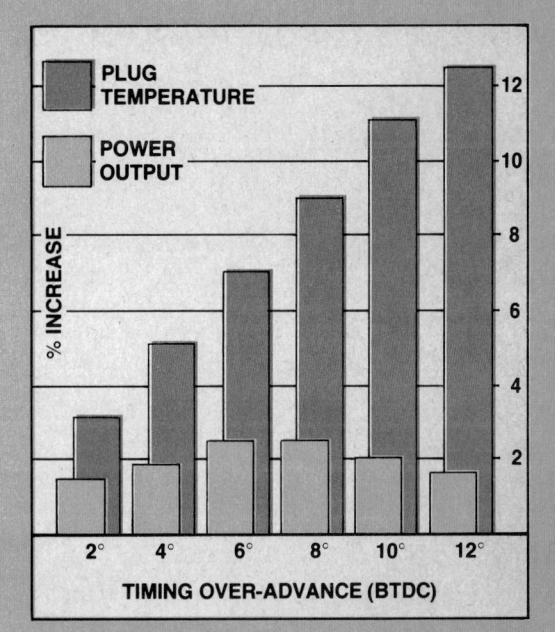

Increasing ignition timing past the specified setting results in a drastic increase in spark plug temperature with increased chance of detonation or preignition. Performance increase is considerably less. (Photo courtesy Champion Spark Plug Co.)

that form in the engine should be flushed out to allow the engine to operate at peak efficiency.

35. Clean the radiator of debris that can decrease cooling efficiency.

36. Install a flex-type or electric cooling fan, if you don't have a clutch type fan. Flex fans use curved plastic blades to push more air at low speeds when more cooling is needed; at high speeds the blades flatten out for less resistance. Electric fans only run when the engine temperature reaches a predetermined level.

37. Check the radiator cap for a worn or cracked gasket. If the cap does not seal properly, the cooling system will not function properly.

42. Be sure the front end is correctly aligned. A misaligned front end actually has wheels going in different directions. The increased drag can reduce fuel economy by .3 mpg.

43. Correctly adjust the wheel bearings. Wheel bearings that are adjusted too tight increase rolling resistance.

Check tire pressures regularly with a reliable pocket type gauge. Be sure to check the pressure on a cold tire.

GENERAL MAINTENANCE

Check the fluid levels (particularly engine oil) on a regular basis. Be sure to check the oil for grit, water or other contamination.

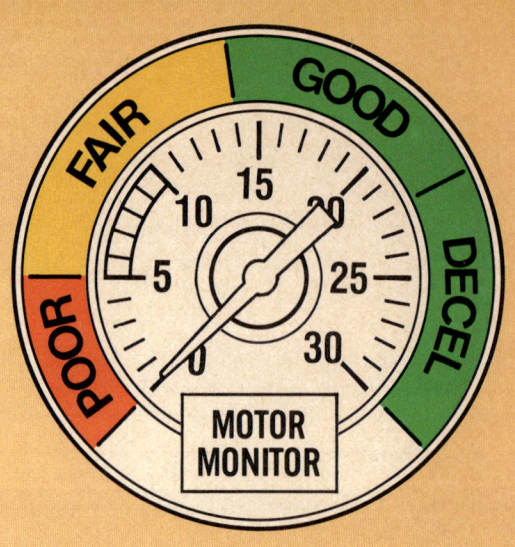

A vacuum gauge is another excellent indicator of internal engine condition and can also be installed in the dash as a mileage indicator.

44. Periodically check the fluid levels in the engine, power steering pump, master cylinder, automatic transmission and drive axle.

45. Change the oil at the recommended interval and change the filter at every oil change. Dirty oil is thick and causes extra friction between moving parts, cutting efficiency and increasing wear. A worn engine requires more frequent tune-ups and gets progressively worse fuel economy. In general, use the lightest viscosity oil for the driving conditions you will encounter.

46. Use the recommended viscosity fluids in the transmission and axle.

47. Be sure the battery is fully charged for fast starts. A slow starting engine wastes fuel.

48. Be sure battery terminals are clean and tight.

49. Check the battery electrolyte level and add distilled water if necessary.

50. Check the exhaust system for crushed pipes, blockages and leaks.

51. Adjust the brakes. Dragging brakes or brakes that are not releasing create increased drag on the engine.

52. Install a vacuum gauge or miles-per-gallon gauge. These gauges visually indicate engine vacuum in the intake manifold. High vacuum = good mileage and low vacuum = poorer mileage. The gauge can also be an excellent indicator of internal engine conditions.

53. Be sure the clutch is properly adjusted. A slipping clutch wastes fuel.

54. Check and periodically lubricate the heat control valve in the exhaust manifold. A sticking or inoperative valve prevents engine warm-up and wastes gas.

55. Keep accurate records to check fuel economy over a period of time. A sudden drop in fuel economy may signal a need for tune-up or other maintenance.

© 1980 Chilton Book Company, Radnor, PA 19089

EMISSION CONTROLS AND FUEL SYSTEM

instrument panel. The light will remain 'On' until the problem is corrected. The 'System' also has built in back-up systems that in most cases of an operational problem will allow for the continued operation of the vehicle in a near normal manner until the repairs can be made.

The CCC system has some components in common with the old G.M. C-4 system, although they are not interchangeable. These components include the Electronic Control Module (ECM), which controls many more functions than does its predecessor, an oxygen sensor system, an electronically controlled variable-mixture carburetor, a three-way catalytic converter, throttle position and coolant sensors, a Barometric Pressure Sensor (BARO), a Manifold Absolute Pressure Sensor (MAP) and a "Check Engine" light in the instrument panel.

Components unique to the CCC system include the Air Injection Reaction (AIR) management system, a charcoal canister purge solenoid, EGR valve controls, a vehicle speed sensor (in the instrument panel), a transmission converter clutch solenoid (only on models with automatic transmission), idle speed control and Electronic Spark Timing (EST).

The ECM, in addition to monitering sensors and sending out a control signal to the carburetors, also controls the following components or sub-systems: charcoal canister purge control, the AIR system, idle speed, automatic transmission converter lockup, distributor ignition timing, the EGR valve, and the air conditioner converter clutch.

The EGR valve control solenoid is activated by the ECM in a fashion similar to that of the charcoal canister purge solenoid described earlier in this chapter. When the engine is cold, the ECM energizes the solenoid, which blocks the vacuum signal to the EGR valve. When the engine is warm, the ECM de-energizes the solenoid and the vacuum signal is allowed to reach and then activate the EGR valve.

The idle speed control adjusts the idle speed to all particular engine load conditions and will lower the idle under no-load or low-load conditions in order to conserve fuel.

BASIC TROUBLESHOOTING

NOTE: *The following explains how to activate the Trouble Code signal light in the instrument cluster. This is not a full fledged CCC system troubleshooting and isolation procedure.*

Before suspecting the CCC system, or any of its components as being faulty, check the ignition system (distributor, timing, spark plugs and wires). Check the engine compression, the air cleaner and any of the emission control components that are not controlled by the ECM. Also check the intake manifold, the vacuum hoses and hose connectors for any leaks. Check the carburetor mounting bolts for tightness.

The following symptoms could indicate a possible problem area with the CCC system:

1. Detonation;
2. Stalling or rough idling when the engine is cold;
3. Stalling or rough idling when the engine is hot;
4. Missing;
5. Hesitation;
6. Surging;
7. Poor gasoline mileage;
8. Sluggish or spongy performance;
9. Hard starting when engine is cold;
10. Hard starting when the engine is hot;
11. Objectionable exhaust odors;
12. Engine cuts out;
13. Improper idle speed.

As a bulb and system check, the "Check Engine" light will come on when the ignition switch is turned to the 'ON' position but the engine is not started.

The "Check Engine" light will also produce the trouble code/codes by a series of flashes which translate as follows: When the diagnostic test terminal under the instrument panel is grounded, with the ignition in the 'ON' position and the engine not running, the "Check Engine" light will flash once, pause, and then flash twice in rapid succession. This is a Code 12, which indicates that the diagnostic system is working. After a long pause, the Code 12 will repeat itself two more times. This whole cycle will then repeat itself until the engine is started or the ignition switch is turned 'OFF'.

When the engine is started, the "Check Engine" light will remain on for a few seconds and then turn off. If the "Check Engine" light remains on, the self-diagnostic system has detected a problem. If the test terminal is then grounded, the trouble code will flash (3) three times. If more than one problem is found to be in existence, each trouble code will flash (3) three times and then change to the next one. Trouble codes

EMISSION CONTROLS AND FUEL SYSTEM

will flash in numerical order (lowest code number to highest). The trouble code series will repeat themselves for as long as the test terminal remains grounded.

A trouble code indicates a problem with a given circuit. For example, trouble code 14 indicates a problem in the cooling sensor circuit. This includes the coolant sensor, its electrical harness and the Electronic Control Module (ECM).

Since the self-diagnostic system cannot diagnose every possible fault in the system, the absence of a trouble code does not necessarily mean that the system is trouble-free. To determine whether or not a problem with the system exists that does not activate a trouble code, a system performance check must be made. This job should be left to a qualified service technician.

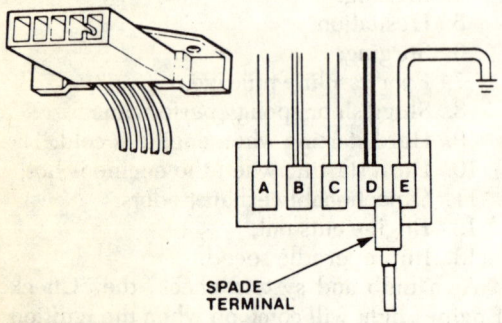

Test terminal and ground location

In the case of an intermittent fault in the system, the "Check Engine" light will go out when the fault goes away, but the trouble code will remain in the memory of the ECM. Therefore, if a trouble code can be obtained even though the "Check Engine" light is not on, it must still be evaluated. It must be determined if the fault is intermittent or if the engine must be operating under certain conditions (acceleration, deceleration, etc.) before the "Check Engine" light will come on. In some cases, certain trouble codes will not be recorded in the ECM until the engine has been operated at part throttle for at least 5 to 18 minutes.

On the CCC system, a trouble code will be stored until the terminal 'R' at the ECM has been disconnected from the battery for at least 10 seconds.

ACTIVATING THE TROUBLE CODE

On the CCC system, locate the test terminal under the instrument panel (see illus-

Trouble Code Identification Chart

NOTE: *Always ground the test terminal AFTER the engine is running.*

Trouble Code	Refers To:
12	No reference pulses to the ECM. This is not stored in the memory and will only flash when the fault is present (not to be confused with the Code 12 discussed earlier).
13	Oxygen sensor circuit. The engine must run for at least 5 min. before this code will set.
14	Shorted coolant circuit. The engine must run at least 2 min. before this code will set.
15	Open coolant sensor circuit. The engine must run at least 5 min. before this code will set.
21	Throttle position sensor circuit. The engine must run up to 25 sec., below 800 rpm, before this code will set.
23	Open or grounded carburetor solenoid circuit.
24	Vehicle Speed Sensor (VSS) circuit. The engine must run for at least 5 min. at road speed for this code to set.
32	Altitude Compensator circuit.
34	Vacuum sensor circuit. The engine must run up to 5 min., below 800 rpm, before this code will set.
35	Idle speed control switch circuit shorted. Over ½ throttle for at least 2 sec.
41	No distributor reference pulses to the ECM at specified engine vacuum. This code will store in memory
42	Electronic Spark Timing (EST) bypass circuit grounded.

EMISSION CONTROLS AND FUEL SYSTEM

Trouble Code Identification Chart (cont.)

Trouble Code	Refers To
44	Lean oxygen sensor indication. The engine must run at least 5 min., in closed loop, at part throttle and road load for this code to set.
45	Rich system indication. The engine must run at least 5 min., in closed loop, at part throttle and road load for this code to set.
44 & 45	(at same time) Faulty oxygen sensor circuit.
51	Faulty calibration unit (PROM) or installation. It takes 30 sec. for this code to set.
54	Shorted M/C solenoid circuit and/or faulty ECM.
55	Grounded Vref (terminal 21), faulty oxygen sensor or ECM.

tration). Use a jumper wire and ground only the lead.

NOTE: *Ground the test terminal according to the instructions given previously in the "Basic Troubleshooting" section.*

Deceleration Valve

The purpose of the decleration valve is to prevent backfiring in the exhaust system during deceleration. The normal position of the valve is closed. When deceleration causes a sudden vacuum increase in the vacuum signal lines, the pressure differential on the diaphragm will overcome the closing force of the spring, opening the valve and bleeding air into the intake manifold.

Air trapped in the chamber above the vacuum diaphragm will bleed at a calibrated rate through the delay valve portion of the integral 'check and delay valve', reducing the vacuum acting on the diaphragm. When the vacuum load on the diaphragm and the spring load equalize, the valve assembly will close, shutting off the air flow into the intake manifold.

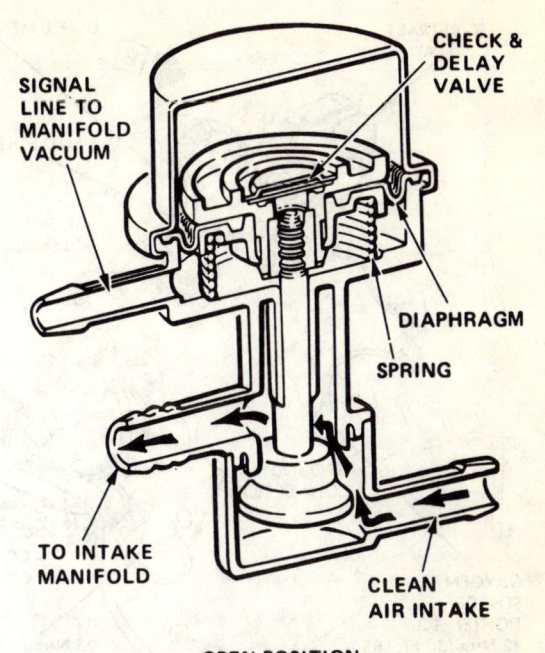

OPEN POSITION
Cross section of the deceleration valve

The check valve portion of the 'check and delay valve' provides quick balancing of chamber pressure when a sudden decrease in vacuum is caused by acceleration rather than deceleration.

Mixture Control Solenoid (M/C)

The fuel flow through the carburetor idle main metering circuits is controlled by a mixture control (M/C) solenoid located in the carburetor. The M/C solenoid changes the air/fuel mixture to the engine by controlling the fuel flow through the carburetor. The ECM controls the solenoid by providing a ground. When the solenoid is energized, the fuel flow through the carburetor is reduced, providing a leaner mixture. When the ECM removes the ground, the solenoid is de-energized, increasing the fuel flow and providing a richer mixture. The M/C solenoid is energized and de-energized at a rate of 10 times per second.

Throttle Position Sensor (TPS)

The throttle position sensor is mounted in the carburetor body and is used to supply throttle position information to the ECM. The ECM memory stores an average of op-

104 EMISSION CONTROLS AND FUEL SYSTEM

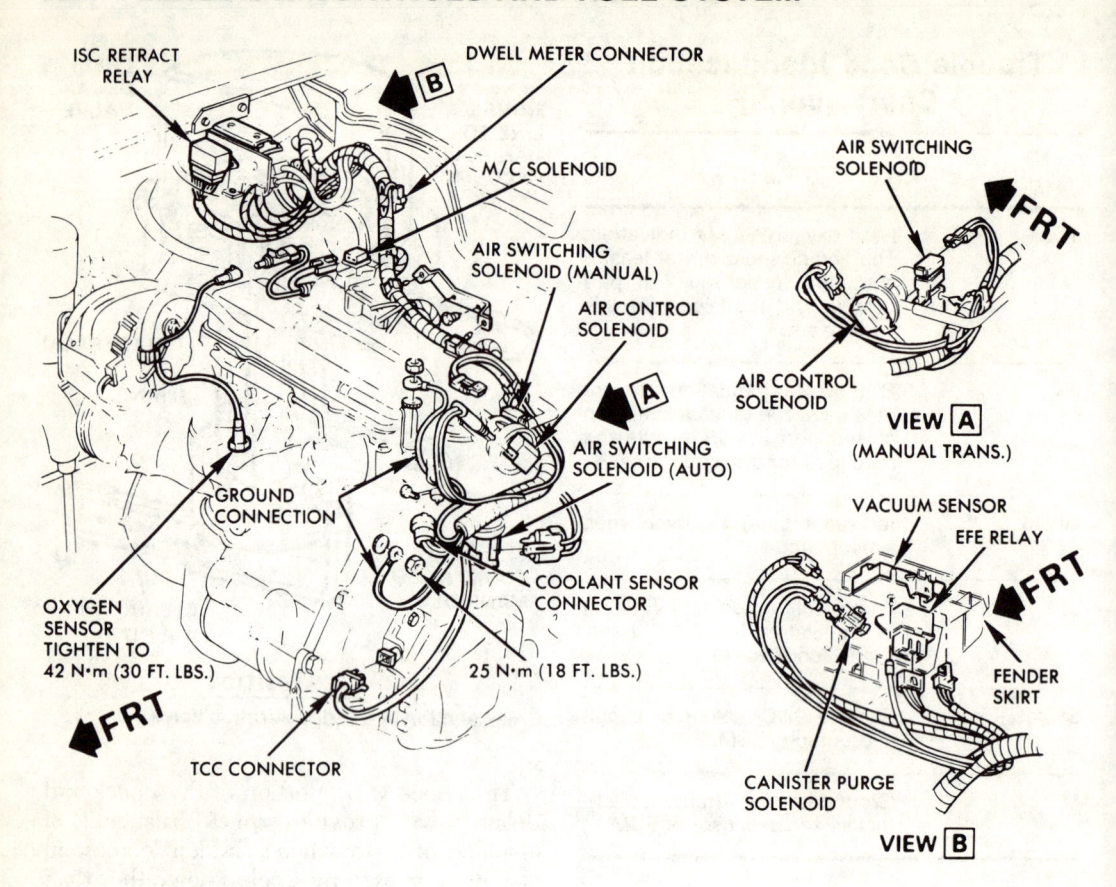

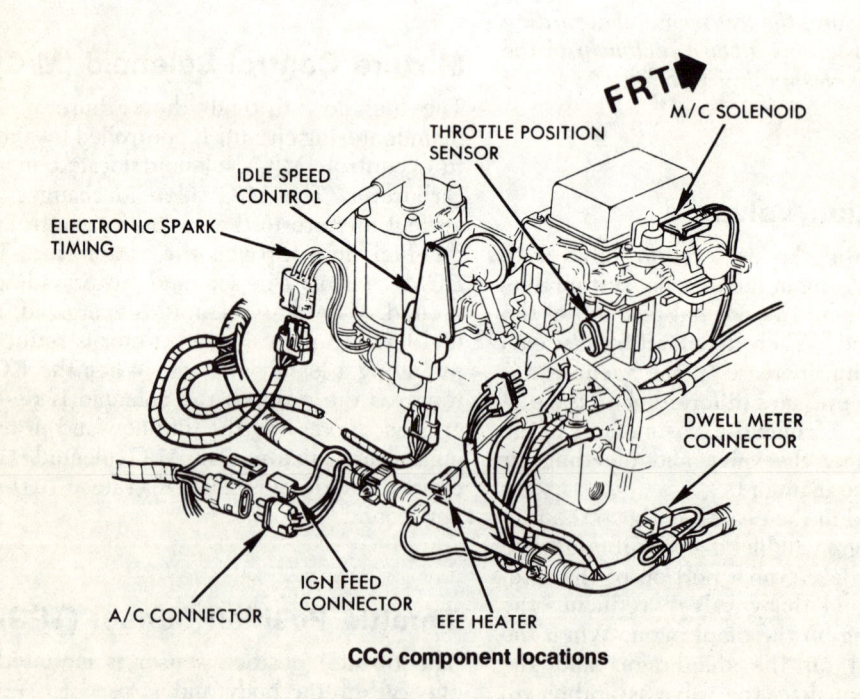

CCC component locations

EMISSION CONTROLS AND FUEL SYSTEM 105

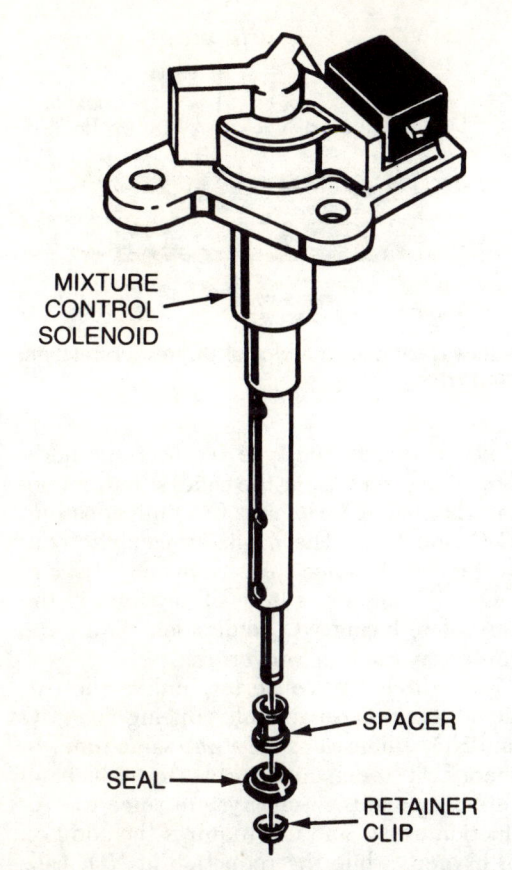

The mixture control (M/C) solenoid is located in the carburetor

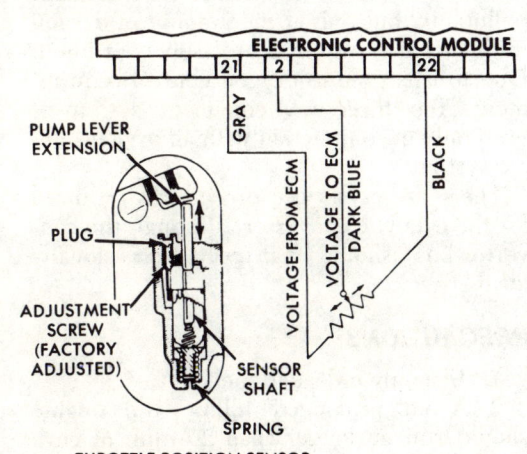

Throttle position sensor

erating conditions with the ideal air/fuel ratios for each of those conditions. When the ECM receives a signal that indicates throttle position change, it immediately shifts to the last remembered set of operating conditions that resulted in an ideal air/fuel ratio control. The memory is continually being updated during normal operations.

Idle Speed Control (ISC)

The idle speed control does just what its name implies—it controls the idle. The ISC is used to maintain low engine speeds while at the same time preventing stalling due to engine load changes. The system consists of a motor assembly mounted on the carburetor which moves the throttle lever so as to open or close the throttle blades.

The whole operation is controlled by the ECM. The ECM moniters engine load to determine the proper idle speed. To prevent stalling, it moniters the air conditioning compressor switch, the transmission, the park/neutral switch and the ISC throttle switch. The ECM processes all this information and then uses it to control the ISC motor which in turn will vary the idle speed as necessary.

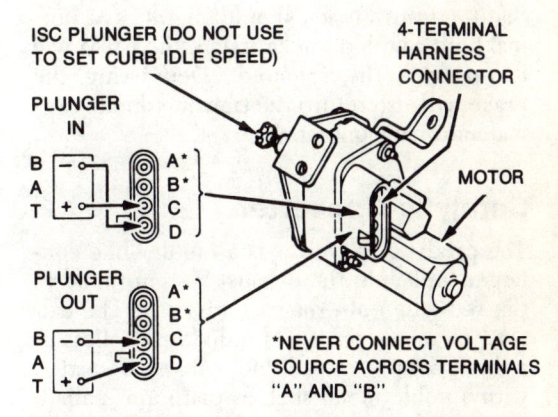

The idle speed control motor (ISC) is mounted on the carburetor

Electronic Spark Timing (EST)

All models use EST. The EST distributor, as described in an earlier chapter, contains no vacuum or centrifugal advance mechanism and uses a seven terminal HEI module. It has four wires going to a four terminal connector in addition to the connectors normally found on HEI distributors. A reference pulse, indicating engine rpm is sent to the ECM. The ECM determines the proper spark advance for the engine operating conditions and then sends an 'EST' pulse back to the distributor.

Under most normal operating conditions, the ECM will control the spark advance. However, under certain operating conditions such as cranking or when setting base timing, the distributor is capable of operating without ECM control. This condition is called BYPASS and is determined by the BYPASS

106 EMISSION CONTROLS AND FUEL SYSTEM

lead which runs from the ECM to the distributor. When the BYPASS lead is at the proper voltage (5), the ECM will control the spark. If the lead is grounded or open circuited, the HEI module itself will control the spark. Disconnecting the 4-terminal EST connector will also cause the engine to operate in the BYPASS mode.

Transmission Converter Clutch (TCC)

All models with an automatic transmission use TCC. The ECM controls the converter by means of a solenoid mounted in the transmission. When the vehicle speed reaches a certain level, the ECM energizes the solenoid and allows the torque converter to mechanically couple the transmission to the engine. When the operating conditions indicate that the transmission should operate as a normal fluid coupled transmission, the ECM will de-energize the solenoid. Depressing the brake will also return the transmission to normal automatic operation.

Catalytic Converter

The catalytic converter is a muffler-like container built into the exhaust system to aid in the reduction of exhaust emissions. The catalyst element consists of individual pellets or a honeycomb monolithic substrate coated with a noble metal such as platinum, palladium, rhodium or a combination. When the exhaust gases come into contact with the catalyst, a chemical reaction occurs which will reduce the pollutants into harmless substances like water and carbon dioxide.

There are essentially two types of catalytic converters: an oxidizing type and a three-way

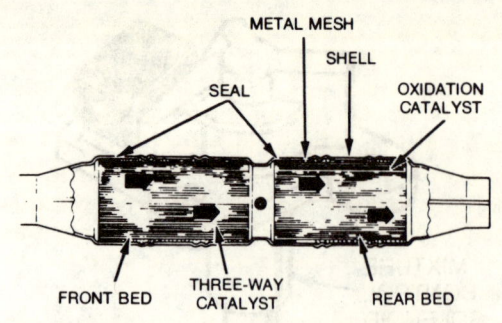

Cutaway view of the typical three-way catalytic converter

type. The oxidizing type requires the addition of oxygen to spur the catalyst into reducing the engine's HC and CO emissions into H_2O and CO_2. The oxidizing catalytic converter, while effectively reducing HC and CO emissions, does little, if anything in the way of reducing NO_x emissions. Thus, the three-way catalytic converter.

The three-way converter, unlike the oxidizing type, is capable of reducing HC, CO and NO_x emmissions; all at the same time. In theory, it seems impossible to reduce all three pollutants in one system since the reduction of HC and CO requires the addition of oxygen, while the reduction of NO_x calls for the removal of oxygen. In actuality, the three-way system really can reduce all three pollutants, but only if the amount of oxygen in the exhaust system is precisely controlled. Due to this precise oxygen control requirement, the three-way converter system is used only in conjunction with an oxygen sensor system.

There are no service procedures required for the catalytic converter, although the converter body should be inspected occasionally for damage.

PRECAUTIONS

1. Use only unleaded fuel.
2. Avoid prolonged idling; the engine should run no longer than 20 min. at curb idle and no longer than 10 min. at fast idle.
3. Do not disconnect any of the spark plug leads while the engine is running.
4. Make engine compression checks as quickly as possible.

CATALYST TESTING

At the present time there is no known way to reliably test catalytic converter operation in the field. The only reliable test is a 12 hour

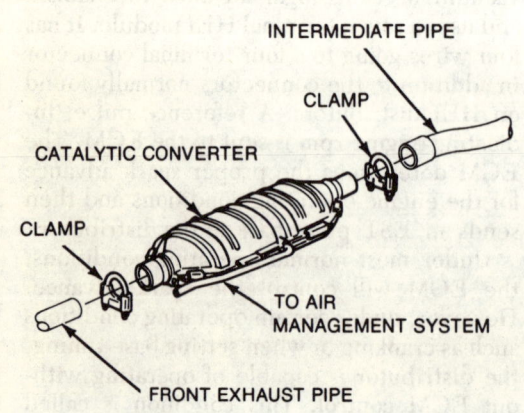

The catalytic converter is upstream of the muffler

EMISSION CONTROLS AND FUEL SYSTEM 107

and 40 min. "soak" test (CVS) which must be done in a laboratory.

An infrared HC/CO tester is not sensitive enough to measure the higher tailpipe emissions from a failing converter. Thus, a bad converter may allow enough emissions to escape so that the car is no longer in compliance with Federal or state standards, but will still not cause the needle on a tester to move off zero.

The chemical reactions which occur inside a catalytic converter generate a great deal of heat. Most converter problems can be traced to fuel or ignition system problems which cause unusually high emissions. As a result of the increased intensity of the chemical reactions, the converter literally burns itself up.

A completely failed converter might cause a tester to show a slight reading. As a result, it is occasionally possible to detect one of these.

As long as you avoid severe overheating and the use of leaded fuels it is reasonably safe to assume that the converter is working properly. If you are in doubt, take the car to a diagnostic center that has a tester.

Oxygen Sensor

An oxygen sensor is used on all models. The sensor protrudes into the exhaust stream and monitors the oxygen content of the exhaust gases. The difference between the oxygen content of the exhaust gases and that of the outside air generates a voltage signal to the ECM. The ECM monitors this voltage and, depending upon the value of the signal received, issues a command to adjust for a rich or a lean condition.

No attempt should ever be made to measure the voltage output of the sensor. The current drain of any conventional voltmeter would be such that it would permanently damage the sensor. No jumpers, test leads or any other electrical connections should ever be made to the sensor. Use these tools ONLY on the ECM side of the wiring harness connector AFTER disconnecting it from the sensor.

REMOVAL AND INSTALLATION

The oxygen sensor must be replaced every 30,000 miles (48,000 km.). The sensor may be difficult to remove when the engine temperature is below 120°F (48°C). Excessive removal force may damage the threads in the exhaust manifold or pipe; follow the removal procedure carefully.

1. Locate the oxygen sensor. It protrudes from the center of the exhaust manifold at the front of the engine compartment (it looks somewhat like a spark plug).

Oxygen sensor

EMISSION CONTROLS AND FUEL SYSTEM

2. Disconnect the electrical connector from the oxygen sensor.

3. Spray a commercial heat riser solvent onto the sensor threads and allow it to soak in for at least five minutes.

4. Carefully unscrew and remove the sensor.

5. To install, first coat the new sensor's threads with G.M. anti-seize compound No. 5613695 or the equivalent. This is *not* a conventional anti-seize paste. The use of a regular compound may electrically insulate the sensor, rendering it inoperative. You must coat the threads with an electrically conductive anti-seize compound.

6. Installation torque is 30 ft. lbs. (42 Nm.). Do not overtighten.

7. Reconnect the electrical connector. Be careful not to damage the electrical pigtail. Check the sensor boot for proper fit and installation.

FUEL SYSTEM

Fuel Pump

A mechanical fuel pump is used on the J-cars. It is of the diaphragm-type and because of the design is serviced by replacement only. No adjustments or repairs are possible. The pump is operated by an eccentric on the camshaft.

TESTING THE FUEL PUMP

To determine if the pump is in good condition, tests for both volume and pressure should be performed. The tests are made with the pump installed, and the engine at normal operating temperature and idle speed. Never replace a fuel pump without first performing these simple tests.

Be sure that the fuel filter has been changed at the specified interval. If in doubt, install a new filter first.

Pressure Test

1. Disconnect the fuel line at the carburetor and connect a fuel pump pressure gauge. Fill the carburetor float bowl with gasoline.

2. Start the engine and check the pressure with the engine at idle. If the pump has a vapor return hose, squeeze it off so that an accurate reading can be obtained. Pressure should not be below 4.5 psi.

3. If the pressure is incorrect, replace the pump. If it is ok, go on to the volume test.

Volume Test

4. Disconnect the pressure gauge. Run the fuel line into a graduated container.

5. Run the engine at idle until one pint of gasoline has been pumped. One pint should be delivered in 30 seconds or less. There is normally enough fuel in the carburetor float bowl to perform this test, but refill it if necessary.

6. If the delivery rate is below the minimum, check the lines for restrictions or leaks, then replace the pump.

REMOVAL AND INSTALLATION

The fuel pump is located at the center rear of the engine.

1. Disconnect the negative cable at the battery. Raise and support the car.

2. Disconnect the inlet hose from the pump. Disconnect the vapor return hose, if equipped.

3. Loosen the fuel line at the carburetor, then disconnect the outlet pipe from the pump.

4. Remove the two mounting bolts and remove the pump from the engine.

5. To install, place a new gasket on the pump and install the pump on the engine. Tighten the two mounting bolts alternately and evenly.

6. Install the pump outlet pipe. This is easier if the pipe is disconnected from the carburetor. Tighten the fitting while backing up the pump nut with another wrench. Install the pipe at the carburetor.

7. Install the inlet and vapor hoses. Lower the car, connect the negative battery cable, start the engine, and check for leaks.

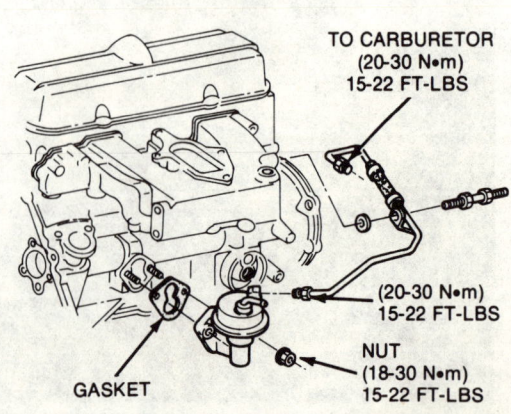

TO CARBURETOR
(20-30 N•m)
15-22 FT-LBS

(20-30 N•m)
15-22 FT-LBS

NUT
(18-30 N•m)
15-22 FT-LBS

GASKET

Fuel pump installation details

EMISSION CONTROLS AND FUEL SYSTEM

Carburetor

The Rochester E2SE is used on all 1982 J-cars. It is a two barrel, two stage carburetor of downdraft design used in conjunction with the Computer Command Control system of fuel control. The carburetor has special design features for optimum air/fuel mixture control during all ranges of engine operation.

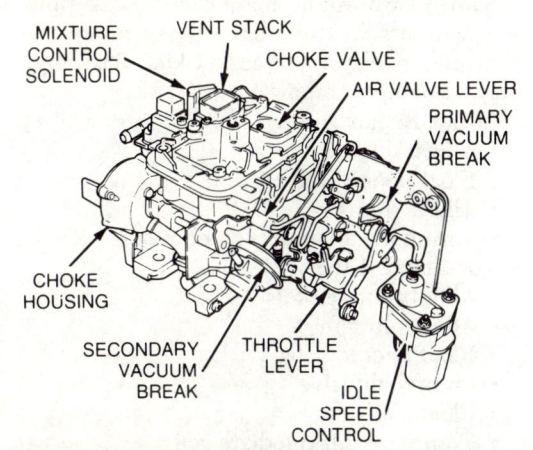

Rochester E2SE carburetor

MODEL IDENTIFICATION

General Motors Rochester carburetors are identified by their model code. The first number indicates the number of barrels, while one of the last letters indicates the type of choke used. These are V for the manifold mounted choke coil, C for the choke coil mounted in the carburetor body, and E for electric choke, also mounted on the carburetor. Model codes ending in A indicate an altitude-compensating carburetor.

REMOVAL AND INSTALLATION

1. Remove the air cleaner and gasket.
2. Disconnect the fuel pipe and all vacuum lines.
3. Tag and disconnect all electrical connections.
4. Disconnect the downshift cable.
5. If equipped with cruise control, disconnect the linkage.
6. Unscrew the carburetor mounting bolts and remove the carburetor.
7. Before installing the carburetor, fill the float bowl with gasoline to reduce the battery strain and the possibility of backfiring when the engine is started again.
8. Inspect the EFE heater for damage. Be sure that the throttle body and EFE mating surfaces are clean.
9. Install the carburetor and tighten the nuts alternately to the proper specifications.
10. Installation of the remaining components is in the reverse order of removal.

OVERHAUL

Efficient carburetion depends greatly on careful cleaning and inspection during overhaul, since dirt, gum, water, or varnish in or on the carburetor parts are often responsible for poor performance.

Overhaul your carburetor in a clean, dust-free area. Carefully disassemble the carburetor, referring often to the exploded views and directions packaged with the rebuilding kit. Keep all similar and look-alike parts segregated during disassembly and cleaning to avoid accidental interchange during assembly. Make a note of all jet sizes.

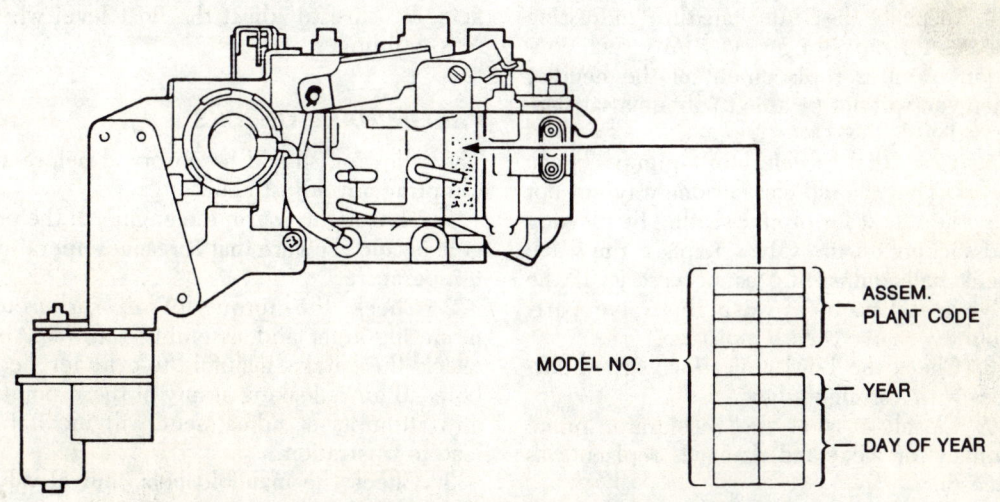

The carburetor identification number is stamped on the float bowl

When the carburetor is disassembled, wash all parts (except diaphragms, electric choke units, pump plunger, and any other plastic, leather, fiber, or rubber parts) in clean carburetor solvent. Do not leave parts in the solvent any longer than is necessary to sufficiently loosen the deposits. Excessive cleaning may remove the special finish from the float bowl and choke valve bodies, leaving these parts unfit for service. Rinse all parts in clean solvent and blow them dry with compressed air or allow them to air dry. Wipe clean all cork, plastic, leather, and fiber parts with a clean, lint-free cloth.

Blow out all passages and jets with compressed air and be sure that there are no restrictions or blockages. Never use wire or similar tools to clean jets, fuel passages, or air bleeds. Clean all jets and valves separately to avoid accidental interchange.

Check all parts for wear or damage. If wear or damage is found, replace the defective parts. Especially check the following:

1. Check the float needle and seat for wear. If wear is found, replace the complete assembly.

2. Check the float hinge pin for wear and the float(s) for dents or distortion. Replace the float if fuel has leaked into it.

3. Check the throttle and choke shaft bores for wear or an out-of-round condition. Damage or wear to the throttle arm, shaft, or shaft bore will often require replacement of the throttle body. These parts require a close tolerance of fit; wear may allow air leakage, which could affect starting and idling.

NOTE: *Throttle shafts and bushings are not included in overhaul kits. They can be purchased separately.*

4. Inspect the idle mixture adjusting needles for burrs or grooves. Any such condition requires replacement of the needle, since you will not be able to obtain a satisfactory idle.

5. Test the accelerator pump check valves. They should pass air one way but not the other. Test for proper seating by blowing and sucking on the valve. Replace the valve check ball and spring as necessary. If the valve is satisfactory, wash the valve parts again to remove breath moisture.

6. Check the bowl cover for warped surfaces with a straightedge.

7. Closely inspect the accelerator pump plunger for wear and damage, replacing as necessary.

8. After the carburetor is assembled, check the choke valve for freedom of operation.

Carburetor overhaul kits are recommended for each overhaul. These kits contain all gaskets and new parts to replace those which deteriorate most rapidly. Failure to replace all parts supplied with the kit (especially gaskets) can result in poor performance later.

Some carburetor manufacturers supply overhaul kits for three basic types: minor repair; major repair; and gasket kits. Basically, they contain the following:

Minor Repair Kits:
- All gaskets
- Float needle valve
- All diagrams
- Spring for the pump diaphragm

Major Repair Kits:
- All jets and gaskets
- All diaphragms
- Float needle valve
- Pump ball valve
- Float
- Complete intermediate rod
- Intermediate pump lever
- Some cover hold-down screws and washers

Gasket Kits:
- All gaskets

After cleaning and checking all components, reassemble the carburetor, using new parts and referring to the exploded view. When reassembling, make sure that all screws and jets are tight in their seats, but do not overtighten as the tips will be distorted. Tighten all screws gradually, in rotation. Do not tighten needle valves into their seats; uneven jetting will result. Always use new gaskets. Be sure to adjust the float level when reassembling.

PRELIMINARY CHECKS

The following should be observed before attempting any adjustments.

1. Thoroughly warm the engine. If the engine is cold, be sure that it reaches operating temperature.

2. Check the torque of all carburetor mounting nuts and assembly screws. Also check the intake manifold-to-cylinder head bolts. If air is leaking at any of these points, any attempts at adjustment will inevitably lead to frustration.

3. Check the manifold heat control valve (if used) to be sure that it is free.

EMISSION CONTROLS AND FUEL SYSTEM

4. Check and adjust the choke as necessary.

5. Adjust the idle speed and mixture. If the mixture screws are capped, don't adjust them unless all other causes of rough idle have been eliminated. If any adjustments are performed that might possibly change the idle speed or mixture, adjust the idle and mixture again when you are finished.

Before you make any carburetor adjustments make sure that the engine is in tune. Many problems which are thought to be carburetor-related can be traced to an engine which is simply out-of-tune. Any trouble in these areas will have symptoms like those of carburetor problems.

FLOAT ADJUSTMENT

1. Remove the air horn from the throttle body.
2. Use your fingers to hold the retainer in place, and to push the float down into light contact with the needle.
3. Measure the distance from the toe of the float (furthest from the hinge) to the top of the carburetor (gasket removed).
4. To adjust, remove the float and gently bend the arm to specification. After adjustment, check the float alignment in the chamber.

PUMP ADJUSTMENT

E2SE carburetors have a non-adjustable pump lever. No adjustments are either necessary or possible.

FAST IDLE ADJUSTMENT

1. Set the ignition timing and curb idle speed, and disconnect and plug hoses as directed on the emission control decal.
2. Place the fast idle screw on the highest step of the cam.
3. Start the engine and adjust the engine speed to specification with the fast idle screw.

CHOKE COIL LEVER ADJUSTMENT

1. Remove the three retaining screws and remove the choke cover and coil. On models with a riveted choke cover, drill out the three rivets and remove the cover and choke coil.

NOTE: *A choke stat cover retainer kit is required for reassembly.*

2. Place the fast idle screw on the high step of the cam.
3. Close the choke by pushing in on the intermediate choke lever.
4. Insert a drill or gauge of the specified size into the hole in the choke housing. The

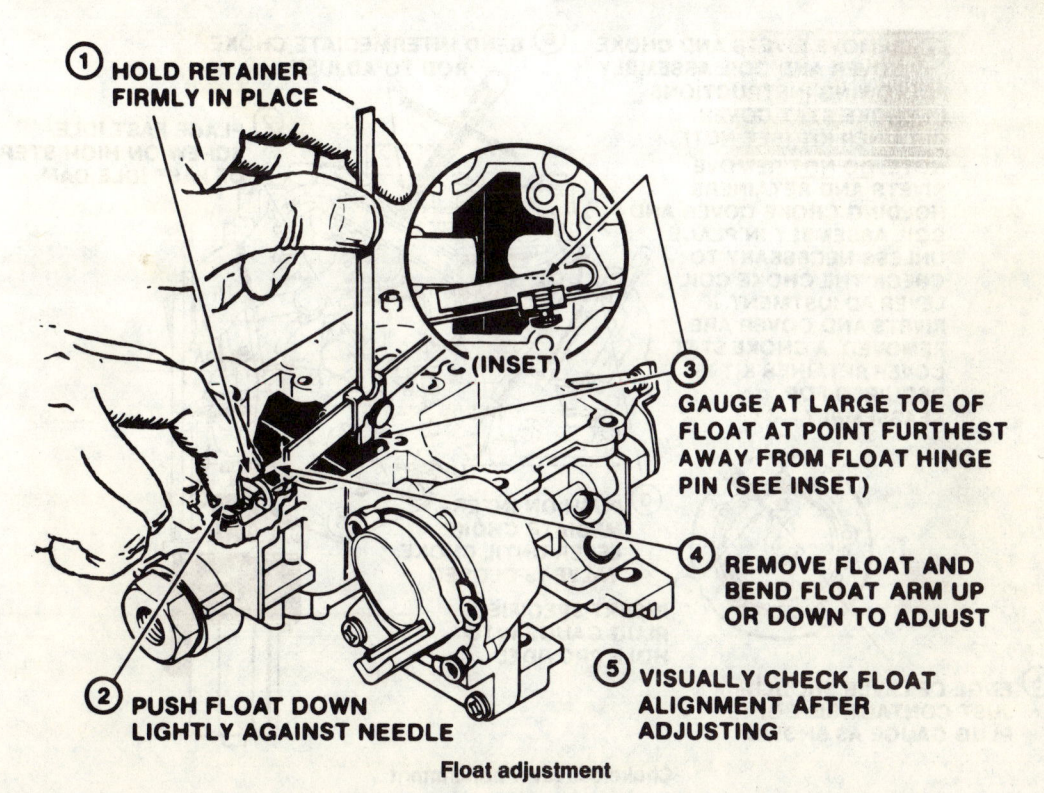

① HOLD RETAINER FIRMLY IN PLACE

(INSET)

③ GAUGE AT LARGE TOE OF FLOAT AT POINT FURTHEST AWAY FROM FLOAT HINGE PIN (SEE INSET)

④ REMOVE FLOAT AND BEND FLOAT ARM UP OR DOWN TO ADJUST

② PUSH FLOAT DOWN LIGHTLY AGAINST NEEDLE

⑤ VISUALLY CHECK FLOAT ALIGNMENT AFTER ADJUSTING

Float adjustment

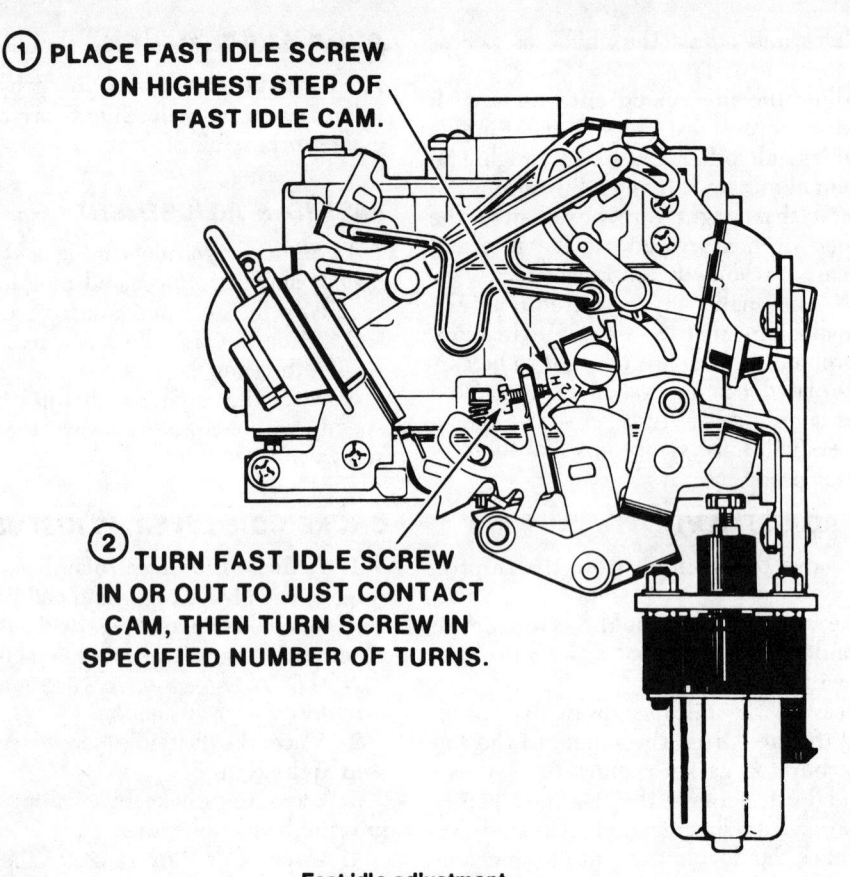

112 EMISSION CONTROLS AND FUEL SYSTEM

① PLACE FAST IDLE SCREW ON HIGHEST STEP OF FAST IDLE CAM.

② TURN FAST IDLE SCREW IN OR OUT TO JUST CONTACT CAM, THEN TURN SCREW IN SPECIFIED NUMBER OF TURNS.

Fast idle adjustment

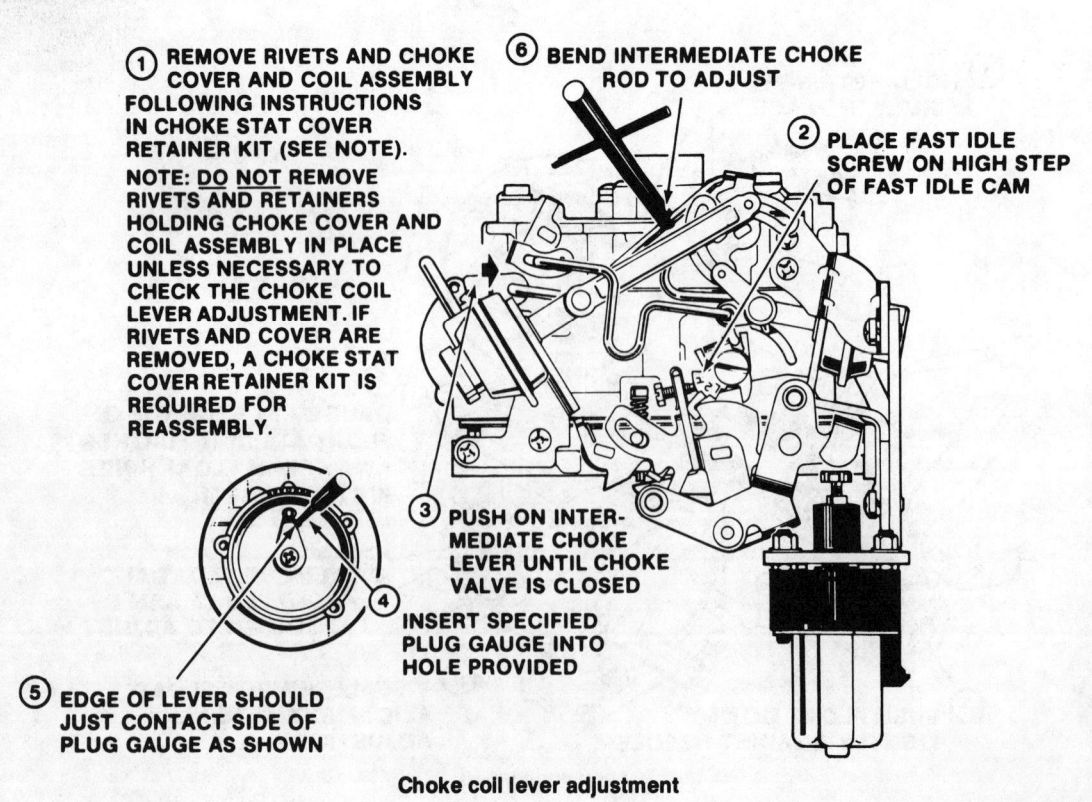

① REMOVE RIVETS AND CHOKE COVER AND COIL ASSEMBLY FOLLOWING INSTRUCTIONS IN CHOKE STAT COVER RETAINER KIT (SEE NOTE).
NOTE: DO NOT REMOVE RIVETS AND RETAINERS HOLDING CHOKE COVER AND COIL ASSEMBLY IN PLACE UNLESS NECESSARY TO CHECK THE CHOKE COIL LEVER ADJUSTMENT. IF RIVETS AND COVER ARE REMOVED, A CHOKE STAT COVER RETAINER KIT IS REQUIRED FOR REASSEMBLY.

⑥ BEND INTERMEDIATE CHOKE ROD TO ADJUST

② PLACE FAST IDLE SCREW ON HIGH STEP OF FAST IDLE CAM

③ PUSH ON INTERMEDIATE CHOKE LEVER UNTIL CHOKE VALVE IS CLOSED

④ INSERT SPECIFIED PLUG GAUGE INTO HOLE PROVIDED

⑤ EDGE OF LEVER SHOULD JUST CONTACT SIDE OF PLUG GAUGE AS SHOWN

Choke coil lever adjustment

EMISSION CONTROLS AND FUEL SYSTEM

choke lever in the housing should be up against the side of the gauge.

5. If the lever does not just touch the gauge, bend the intermediate choke rod to adjust.

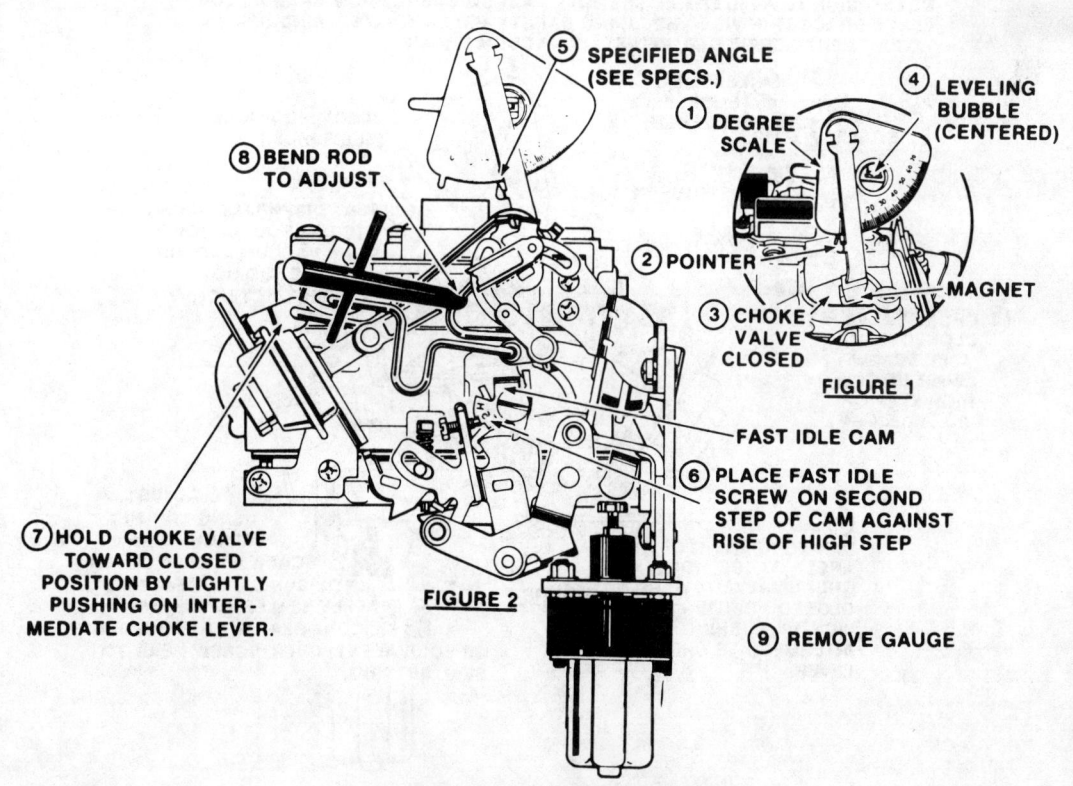

FAST IDLE CAM (CHOKE ROD) ADJUSTMENT

NOTE: *A special angle gauge should be used. If it is not available, an inch measurement can be made.*

1. Adjust the choke coil lever and fast idle first.
2. Rotate the degree scale until it is zeroed.
3. Close the choke and install the degree scale onto the choke plate. Center the leveling bubble.
4. Rotate the scale so that the specified degree is opposite the scale pointer.
5. Place the fast idle screw on the second step of the cam (against the high step). Close the choke by pushing in the intermediate lever.
6. Bend the fast idle cam rod at the U to adjust the angle to specifications.

AIR VALVE ROD ADJUSTMENT

1. Seat the vacuum diaphragm with an outside vacuum source. Tape over the purge bleed hole if present.
2. Close the air valve.
3. Insert the specified gauge between the rod and the end of the slot in the plunger.
4. Bend the rod to adjust the clearance.

PRIMARY SIDE VACUUM BREAK ADJUSTMENT

1. Follow Steps 1–4 of the "Fast Idle Cam Adjustment."
2. Seat the choke vacuum diaphragm with an outside vacuum source.
3. Push in on the intermediate choke lever to close the choke valve, and hold closed during adjustment.
4. Adjust by using a ⅛ in. Hex wrench to turn the screw in the rear cover until the bubble is centered.
5. After adjusting, apply RTV silicone sealant over the screw to seal the setting.

SECONDARY VACUUM BREAK ADJUSTMENT

1. Follow Steps 1–4 of the "Fast Idle Cam Adjustment."

Fast idle cam (choke rod) adjustment

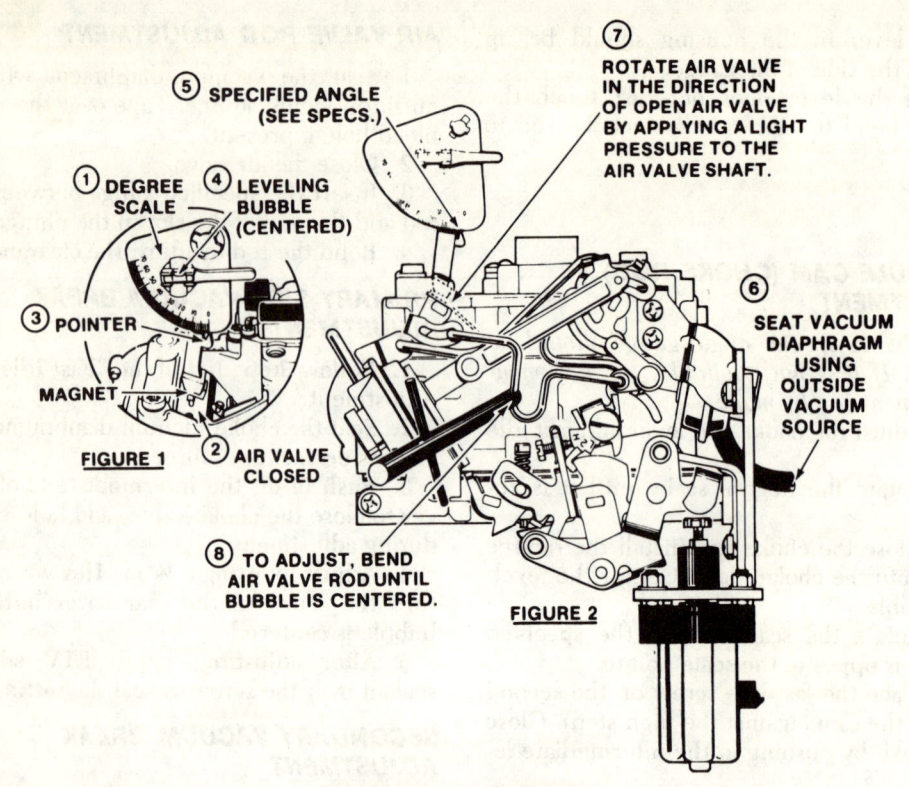

114 EMISSION CONTROLS AND FUEL SYSTEM

FIGURE 1
① DEGREE SCALE
② AIR VALVE CLOSED
③ POINTER / MAGNET
④ LEVELING BUBBLE (CENTERED)
⑤ SPECIFIED ANGLE (SEE SPECS.)

FIGURE 2
⑥ SEAT VACUUM DIAPHRAGM USING OUTSIDE VACUUM SOURCE
⑦ ROTATE AIR VALVE IN THE DIRECTION OF OPEN AIR VALVE BY APPLYING A LIGHT PRESSURE TO THE AIR VALVE SHAFT.
⑧ TO ADJUST, BEND AIR VALVE ROD UNTIL BUBBLE IS CENTERED.

Air valve rod adjustment

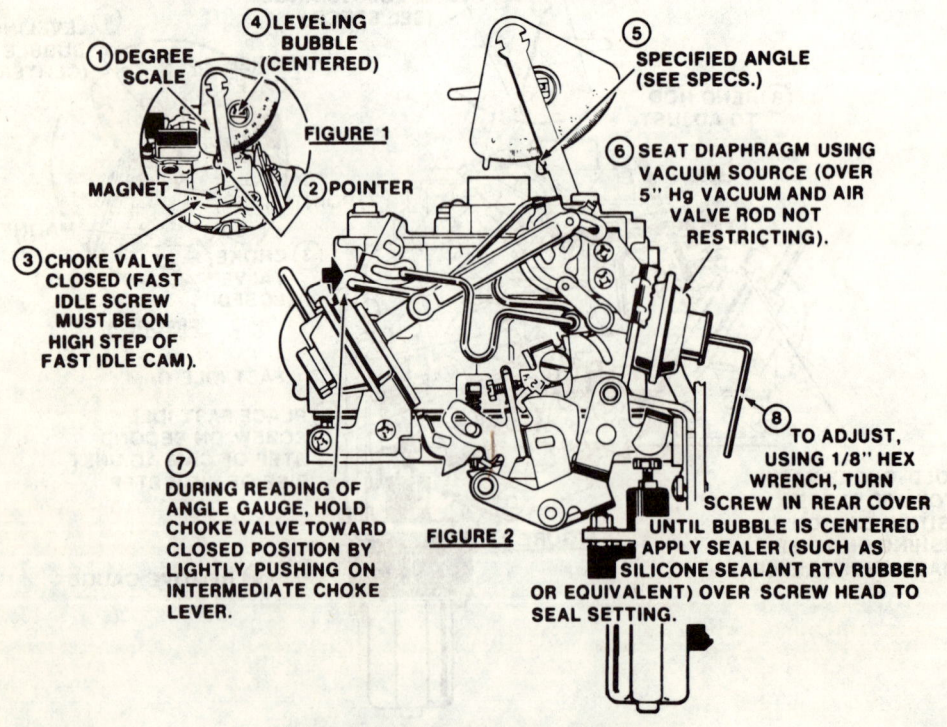

NOTE: PRIOR TO ADJUSTMENT, REMOVE VACUUM BREAK FROM CARBURETOR. PLACE BRACKET IN VICE AND, USING SAFETY PRECAUTIONS, GRIND OFF ADJUSTMENT SCREW CAP. REINSTALL VACUUM BREAK.

FIGURE 1
① DEGREE SCALE
② POINTER
③ CHOKE VALVE CLOSED (FAST IDLE SCREW MUST BE ON HIGH STEP OF FAST IDLE CAM).
④ LEVELING BUBBLE (CENTERED)
MAGNET

FIGURE 2
⑤ SPECIFIED ANGLE (SEE SPECS.)
⑥ SEAT DIAPHRAGM USING VACUUM SOURCE (OVER 5" Hg VACUUM AND AIR VALVE ROD NOT RESTRICTING).
⑦ DURING READING OF ANGLE GAUGE, HOLD CHOKE VALVE TOWARD CLOSED POSITION BY LIGHTLY PUSHING ON INTERMEDIATE CHOKE LEVER.
⑧ TO ADJUST, USING 1/8" HEX WRENCH, TURN SCREW IN REAR COVER UNTIL BUBBLE IS CENTERED APPLY SEALER (SUCH AS SILICONE SEALANT RTV RUBBER OR EQUIVALENT) OVER SCREW HEAD TO SEAL SETTING.

Primary side vacuum break adjustment

EMISSION CONTROLS AND FUEL SYSTEM 115

NOTE: PRIOR TO ADJUSTMENT, REMOVE VACUUM BREAK FROM CARBURETOR. PLACE BRACKET IN VICE AND, USING SAFETY PRECAUTIONS, GRIND OFF ADJUSTMENT SCREW CAP. REINSTALL VACUUM BREAK.

① ADJUSTMENT SCREW ACCESS (CAP REMOVED)
FIGURE 1

⑥ SPECIFIED ANGLE (SEE SPECS.)

② DEGREE SCALE

⑤ LEVELING BUBBLE (CENTERED)

MAGNET
FIGURE 2
③ POINTER

⑧ DURING READING OF ANGLE GAUGE, HOLD CHOKE VALVE TOWARD CLOSED POSITION BY LIGHTLY PUSHING ON INTERMEDIATE CHOKE LEVER. MAKE SURE VACUUM DIAPHRAGM IS SEATED (OVER 5" Hg APPLIED TO VACUUM BREAK).

④ CHOKE VALVE CLOSED (FAST IDLE SCREW MUST BE ON HIGH STEP OF FAST IDLE CAM).

⑨ TO ADJUST, USING 1/8" HEX WRENCH, TURN SCREW IN REAR COVER UNTIL BUBBLE IS CENTERED.

AFTER ADJUSTMENT, APPLY SEALER (SUCH AS SILICONE SEALANT RTV RUBBER OR EQUIVALENT) OVER SCREW HEAD TO SEAL SETTING.

FIGURE 3

⑦ SEAT DIAPHRAGM USING VACUUM SOURCE.

Secondary vacuum break adjustment

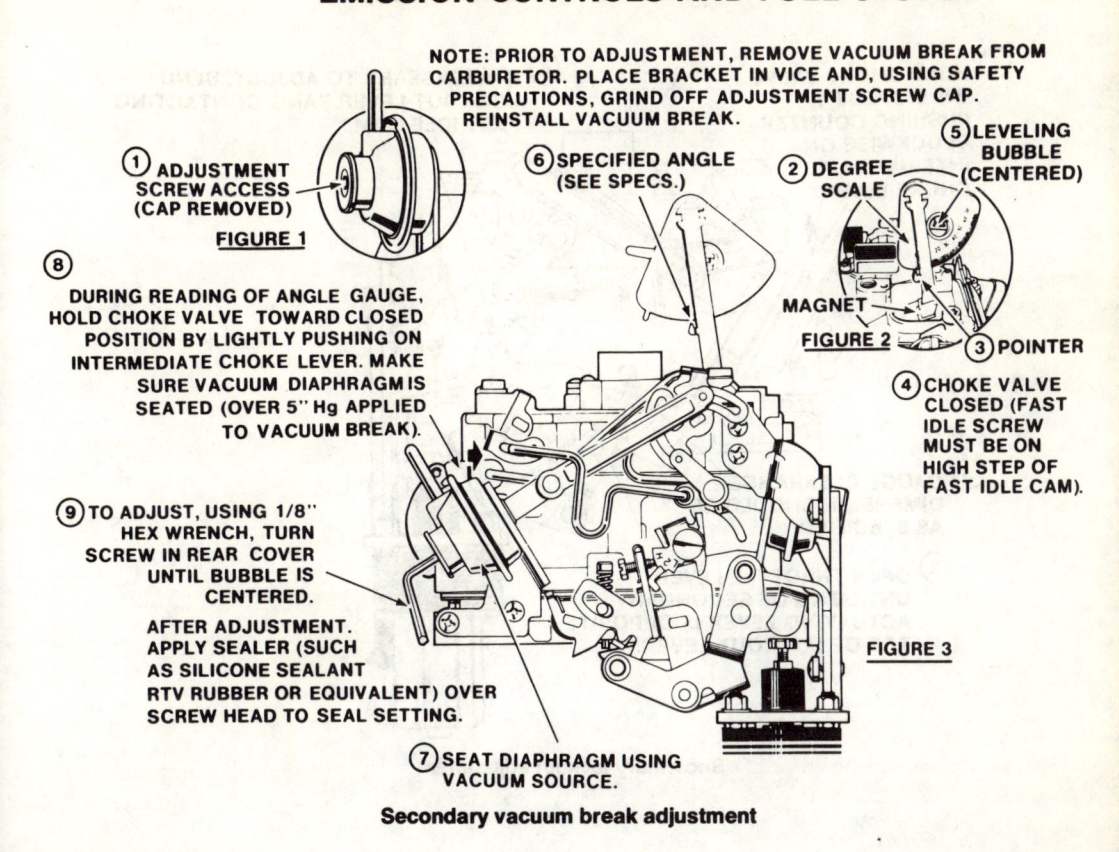

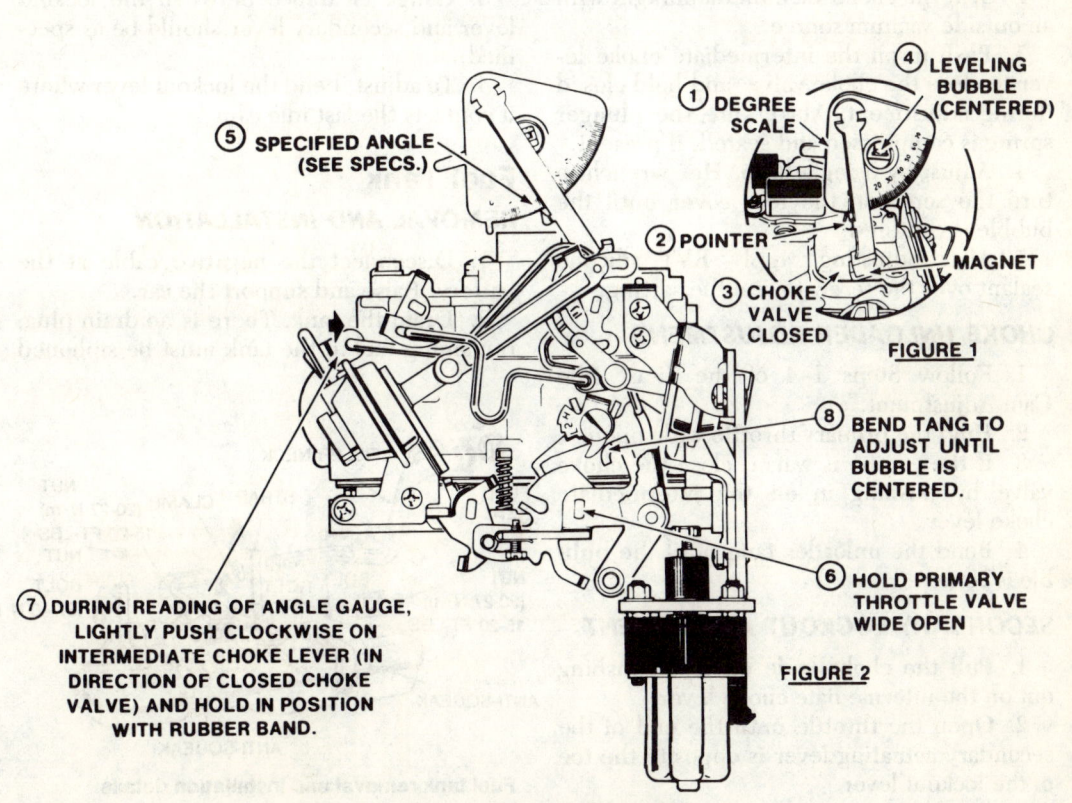

⑤ SPECIFIED ANGLE (SEE SPECS.)

① DEGREE SCALE

④ LEVELING BUBBLE (CENTERED)

② POINTER

MAGNET

③ CHOKE VALVE CLOSED
FIGURE 1

⑧ BEND TANG TO ADJUST UNTIL BUBBLE IS CENTERED.

⑥ HOLD PRIMARY THROTTLE VALVE WIDE OPEN

⑦ DURING READING OF ANGLE GAUGE, LIGHTLY PUSH CLOCKWISE ON INTERMEDIATE CHOKE LEVER (IN DIRECTION OF CLOSED CHOKE VALVE) AND HOLD IN POSITION WITH RUBBER BAND.

FIGURE 2

Choke unloader adjustment

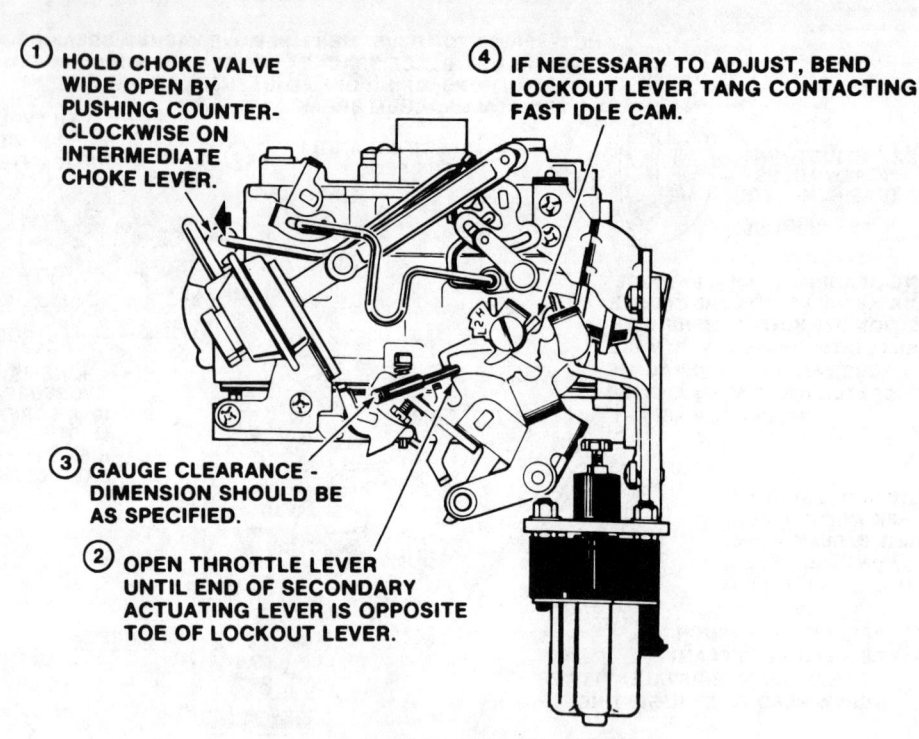

116 EMISSION CONTROLS AND FUEL SYSTEM

Secondary lockout adjustment

2. Seat the choke vacuum diaphragm with an outside vacuum source.
3. Push in on the intermediate choke lever to close the choke valve, and hold closed during adjustment. Make sure the plunger spring is compressed and seated, if present.
4. Adjust by using a ⅛ in. Hex wrench to turn the screw in the rear cover until the bubble is centered.
5. After adjusting, apply RVT silicone sealant over the screw to seal the setting.

CHOKE UNLOADER ADJUSTMENT

1. Follow Steps 1–4 of the "Fast Idle Cam Adjustment."
2. Hold the primary throttle wide open.
3. If the engine is warm, close the choke valve by pushing in on the intermediate choke lever.
4. Bend the unloader tang until the bubble is centered.

SECONDARY LOCKOUT ADJUSTMENT

1. Pull the choke wide open by pushing out on the intermediate choke lever.
2. Open the throttle until the end of the secondary actuating lever is opposite the toe of the lockout lever.
3. Gauge clearance between the lockout lever and secondary lever should be as specified.
4. To adjust, bend the lockout lever where it contacts the fast idle cam.

Fuel Tank

REMOVAL AND INSTALLATION

1. Disconnect the negative cable at the battery. Raise and support the car.
2. Drain the tank. There is no drain plug; remaining fuel in the tank must be siphoned

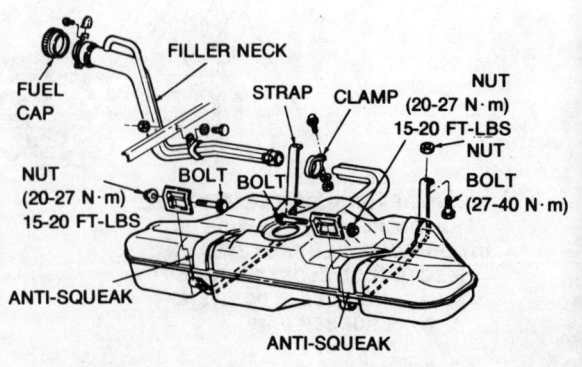

Fuel tank removal and installation details

EMISSION CONTROLS AND FUEL SYSTEM

E2SE Carburetor Specifications

Year	Carburetor Identification	Float Level (in.)	Fast Idle (rpm)	Choke Coil Lever (in.)	Fast Idle Cam (deg.)	Air Valve Rod (deg.)	Primary Vacuum Break (deg/in.)	Choke Setting (notches)	Secondary Vacuum Break (deg/in.)	Choke Unloader (deg/in.)	Secondary Lockout (in.)
1982	17081600	5/16	①	.085	24	1	20/.110	①	27/.157	35/.220	.012
	17081601	5/16	①	.085	24	1	20/.110	①	27/.157	35/.220	.012
	17081607	5/16	①	.085	24	1	20/.110	①	27/.157	35/.220	.012
	17081700	5/16	①	.085	24	1	20/.110	①	27/.157	35/.220	.012
	17081701	5/16	①	.085	24	1	20/.110	①	27/.157	35/.220	.012

① See underhood emissions sticker

through the fuel feed line (the line to the fuel pump), because of the restrictor in the filler neck.

3. Disconnect the hose and the vapor return hose from the level sending unit fittings.

4. Remove the ground wire screw.

5. Unplug the level sending unit electrical connector.

6. Disconnect the vent hose.

7. Unbolt the support straps, and lower and remove the tank. Installation is the reverse.

Chassis Electrical

HEATER

Blower Motor

REMOVAL AND INSTALLATION

1. Disconnect the negative battery cable.
2. Disconnect the electrical connections at the blower motor and blower resistor.
3. Remove the plastic water shield from the right side of the cowl.
4. Remove the blower motor retaining screws and then pull the blower motor and cage out.
5. Hold the blower motor cage and remove the cage retaining nut from the blower motor shaft.

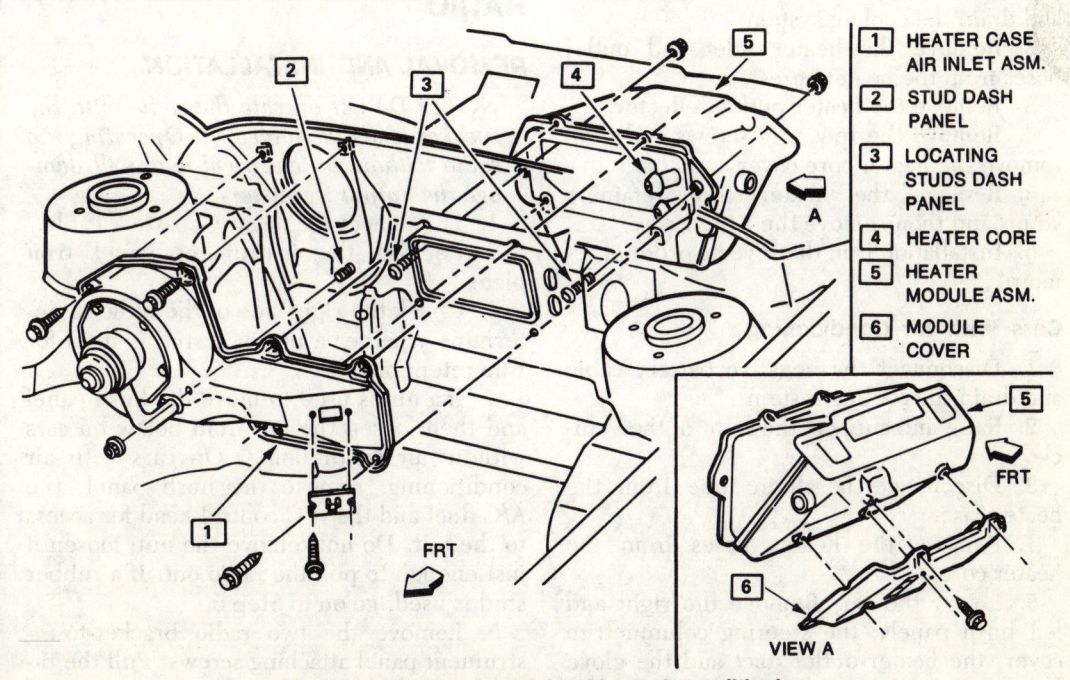

1	HEATER CASE AIR INLET ASM.
2	STUD DASH PANEL
3	LOCATING STUDS DASH PANEL
4	HEATER CORE
5	HEATER MODULE ASM.
6	MODULE COVER

Heater assembly on models without air conditioning

120 CHASSIS ELECTRICAL

1 HEATER & EVAPORATOR
2 DRAIN TUBE
3 BLOWER ASSEMBLY

NOTICE: WHEN REMOVING THE HEATER & EVAPORATOR ASSEMBLY, PULL ASSEMBLY STRAIGHT TOWARD INTERIOR OF CAR UNTIL PLASTIC DRAIN TUBE CLEARS COWL. IF ASSEMBLY IS TILTED IN ANY DIRECTION BEFORE THE TUBE CLEARS THE COWL, THE TUBE MAY BREAK.

Heater assembly on models with air conditioning

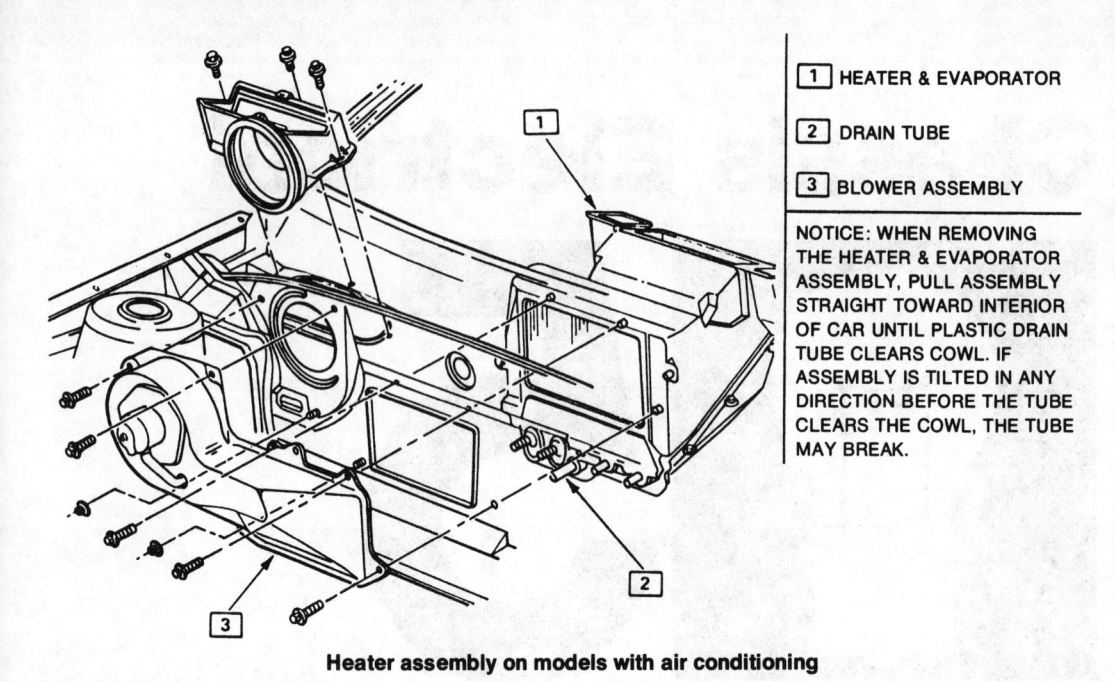

6. Remove the blower motor and cage.
7. Installation is in the reverse order of removal.

Heater Core

REMOVAL AND INSTALLATION

Cars Without Air Conditioning

1. Disconnect the negative battery cable and drain the cooling system.
2. Remove the heater inlet and outlet hoses from the heater core.
3. Remove the heater outlet deflector.
4. Remove the retaining screws and then remove the heater core cover.
5. Remove the heater core retaining straps and then remove the heater core.
6. Installation is in the reverse order of removal.

Cars With Air Conditioning

1. Disconnect the negative battery cable and drain the cooling system.
2. Raise and support the front of the vehicle.
3. Disconnect the drain tube from the heater case.
4. Remove the heater hoses from the heater core.
5. Lower the car. Remove the right and left hush panels, the steering column trim cover, the heater outlet duct and the glove box.

6. Remove the heater core cover. Be sure to pull the cover straight to the rear so as not to damage the drain tube.
7. Remove the heater core clamps and then remove the core.
8. Installation is in the reverse order of removal.

RADIO

REMOVAL AND INSTALLATION

NOTE: *Do not operate the radio with the speaker leads disconnected. Operating the radio without an electrical load will damage the output transistors.*

1. Disconnect the negative battery cable.
2. Remove the instrument panel trim plate.
3. Check the right side of the radio to determine whether a nut or a stud is used for side retention.
4. If a nut is used, remove the hush panel and then loosen the nut from below on cars without air conditioning. On cars with air conditioning, remove the hush panel, the A/C duct and the A/C control head for access to the nut. Do not remove the nut; loosen it just enough to pull the radio out. If a rubber stud is used, go on to Step 5.
5. Remove the two radio bracket-to-instrument panel attaching screws. Pull the radio forward far enough to disconnect the wir-

CHASSIS ELECTRICAL   121

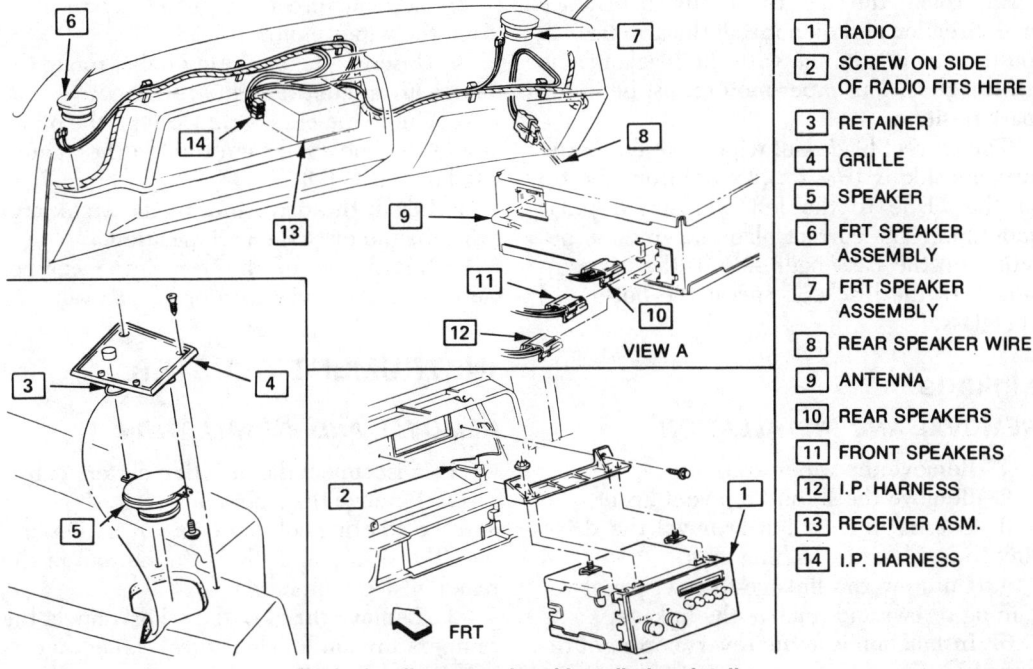

1	RADIO
2	SCREW ON SIDE OF RADIO FITS HERE
3	RETAINER
4	GRILLE
5	SPEAKER
6	FRT SPEAKER ASSEMBLY
7	FRT SPEAKER ASSEMBLY
8	REAR SPEAKER WIRE
9	ANTENNA
10	REAR SPEAKERS
11	FRONT SPEAKERS
12	I.P. HARNESS
13	RECEIVER ASM.
14	I.P. HARNESS

Typical radio removal and installation details

ing and antenna and then remove the radio.

6. Installation is in the reverse order of removal.

WINDSHIELD WIPERS

Blade and Arm

REPLACEMENT

Wiper blade replacement procedures are detailed in Chapter 1.

Removal of the wiper arms requires the use of a special tool, G.M. J8966 or its equivalent. Versions of this tool are generally available in auto parts stores.

1. Insert the tool under the wiper arm and lever the arm off the shaft.

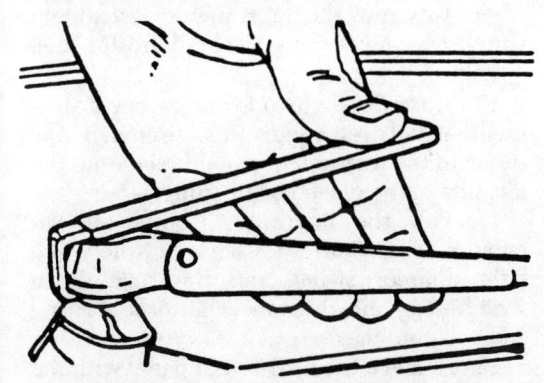

Remove the wiper arm with the special tool

2. Disconnect the washer hose from the arm (if so equipped). Remove the arm.

3. Installation is in the reverse order of removal.

The proper park position is at the top of the blackout line on the glass. If the wiper arms and blades were in the proper position prior to removal, adjustment should not be required.

ADJUSTMENT

The only adjustment for the wiper arms is to remove an arm from the transmission

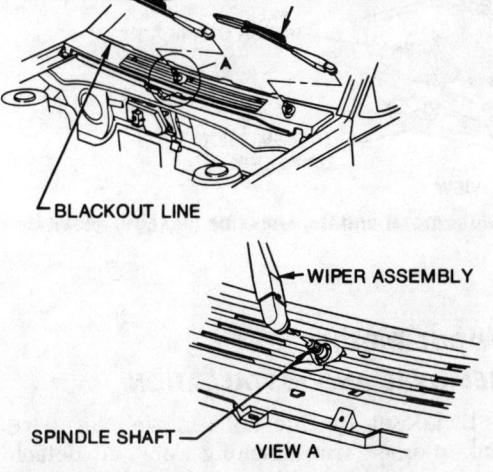

Windshield wiper arm installation details

CHASSIS ELECTRICAL

shaft, rotate the arm the required distance and direction and then install the arm back in position so it is in line with the blackout line on the glass. The wiper motor must be in the park position.

The correct blade-out wipe position on the driver's side is $1^3/_{32}$ in. (28mm) from the tip of the blade to the left windshield pillar moulding. The correct blade-down wipe position on the passenger side of the car is in line with the blackout line at the bottom of the glass.

Linkage

REMOVAL AND INSTALLATION

1. Remove the wiper arms.
2. Remove the shroud top vent grille.
3. Loosen (but do not remove) the drive link-to-crank arm attaching nuts.
4. Unscrew the linkage-to-cowl panel retaining screws and remove the linkage.
5. Installation is in the reverse order of removal.

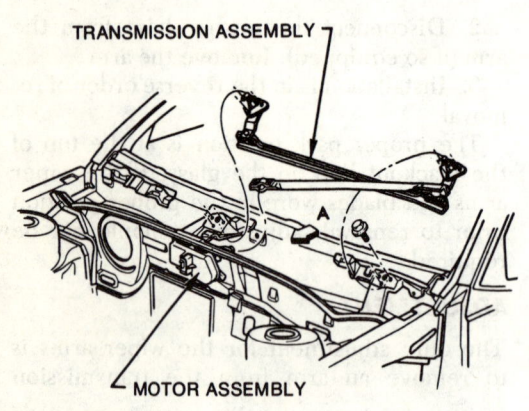

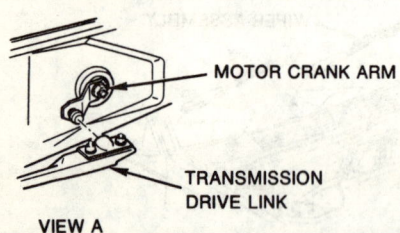

Wiper motor and transmission (linkage) assembly

Wiper Motor

REMOVAL AND INSTALLATION

1. Loosen (but do not remove) the drive link-to-crank arm attaching nuts and detach the drive link from the motor crank arm.

2. Tag and disconnect all electrical leads from the wiper motor.
3. Unscrew the mounting bolts, rotate the motor up and outward and remove it.
4. Guide the crank arm through the opening in the body and then tighten the mounting bolts to 4–6 ft. lbs.
5. Install the drive link to the crank arm with the motor in the park position.
6. Installation of the remaining components is in the reverse order of removal.

INSTRUMENT CLUSTER

REMOVAL AND INSTALLATION

1. Disconnect the negative battery cable.
2. Remove the right and left hush panels and the steering column trim cover. Disconnect the vent panels from the bottom of the panel (if so equipped).
3. Remove the glove box. Disconnect the temperature and mode control cables on cars without air conditioning. On cars with air conditioning, remove the lower A/C duct.
4. Remove the three steering column retaining bolts (two at the instrument panel pad and one at the cowl) and lower the steering column.
5. Remove the lower right hand trim plate. Disconnect the cigar lighter and accessory switches.
6. Pull the heater or A/C control head out far enough to disconnect any wiring or vacuum harnesses, then remove the head.
7. Disconnect the front end and engine harnesses from the bulkhead connector in the engine compartment and then remove the bulkhead connector from the cowl (2 screws).
8. Loosen the set screw and remove the hood release handle. Unscrew the retaining nut and pull the hood release cable loose.
9. Unscrew the four upper instrument panel retaining screws (in the defroster duct openings).
10. Unscrew the two lower corner instrument panel retaining nuts. Remove the screw to the instrument panel brace from the left side of the glove box opening.
11. Pull the instrument panel out far enough to disconnect the ignition, the headlight dimmer switch and the turn signal switch. Tag and disconnect all other wiring and vacuum lines.
12. Remove the instrument panel with the wiring harness intact.

CHASSIS ELECTRICAL 123

1	DASH PANEL
2	WELD NUTS
3	CENTER REINF.
4	PAD ASM.
5	SNAP-IN CLIPS
6	R.H. LOWER I.P. TRIM PLATE
7	L.H. LOWER I.P. TRIM PLATE
8	I.P. TRIM PLATE
9	TORX SCREW
10	HUSH PANEL
11	STEERING COLUMN TRIM COVER

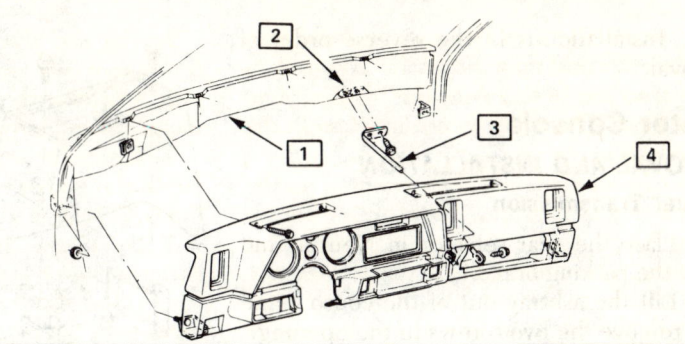

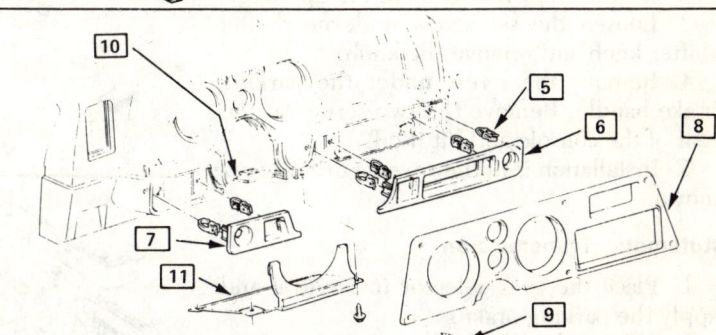

Instrument panel and trim plate removal and installation details

1	ASH TRAY	5	REAR MOUNTING BRACKET	9	ASH TRAY
2	BOOT	6	CENTER MOUNTING BRACKET	10	TRIMPLATE
3	CONSOLE ASM.	7	FRONT MOUNTING BRACKET	11	REAR ASH TRAY ASSEMBLY
4	PUSH-IN NUT	8	FLOOR PANEL		

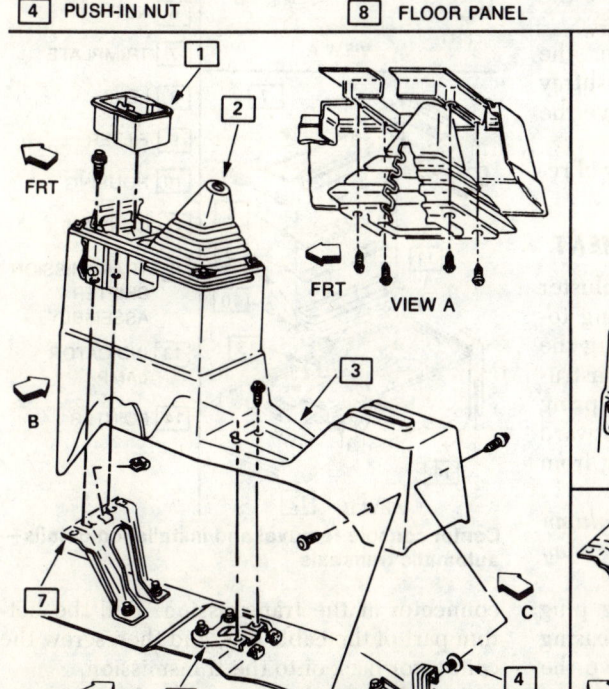

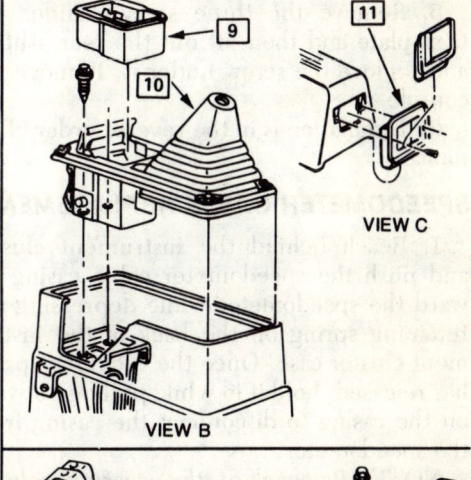

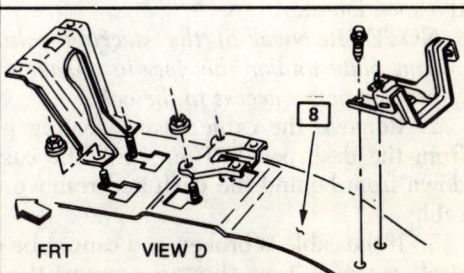

Center console removal and installation details—manual transaxle

CHASSIS ELECTRICAL

13. Installation is in the reverse order of removal.

Center Console
REMOVAL AND INSTALLATION
Manual Transmission

1. Place the gear selector in Neutral and apply the parking brake.
2. Lift the ashtray out of the console and then remove the two screws in the opening.
3. Loosen the set screw underneath the shifter knob and remove the knob.
4. Remove the screw under the parking brake handle. Remove the two screws at the rear of the console and lift it off.
5. Installation is in the reverse order of removal.

Automatic Transmission

1. Place the gear selector in Neutral and apply the parking brake.
2. Lift out the ashtray from the front of the console and remove the two screws from the opening.
3. Gently pry the emblem out of the center of the shift knob and remove the snap ring that secures the knob. Remove the knob.
4. Lift the trim plate assembly out by pulling the front end up first. Disconnect the wiring harness.
5. Remove the three screws under the trim plate and then lift out the rear ashtray and remove the screw under it. Remove the console.
6. Installation is in the reverse order of removal.

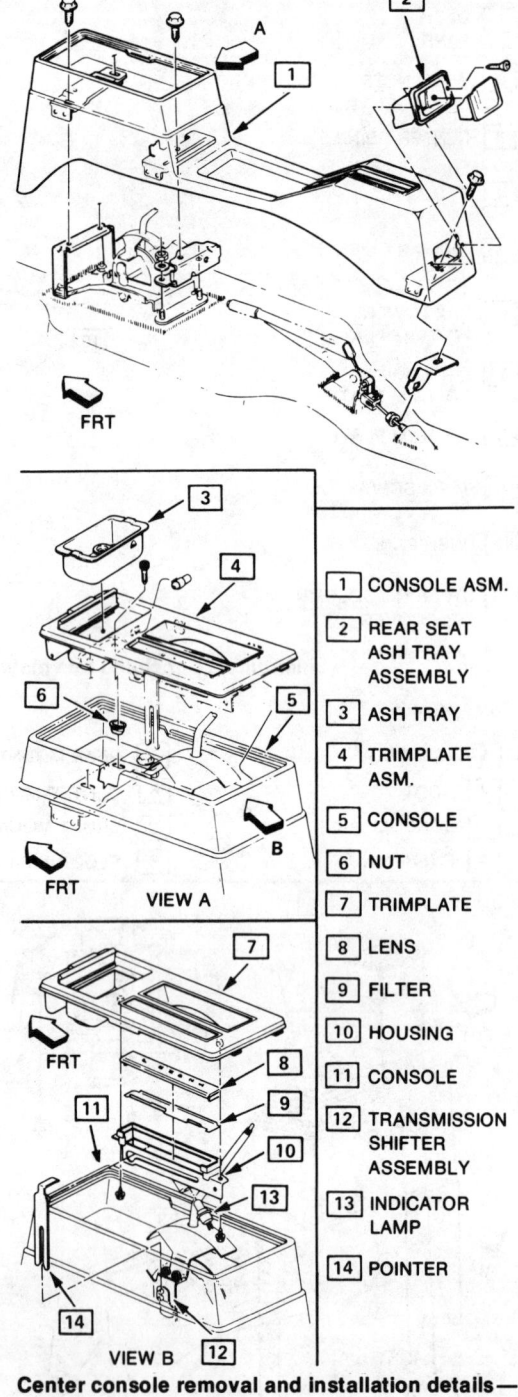

SPEEDOMETER CABLE REPLACEMENT

1. Reach behind the instrument cluster and push the speedometer cable casing toward the speedometer while depressing the retaining spring on the back of the instrument cluster case. Once the retaining spring has released, hold it while pulling outward on the casing to disconnect the casing from the speedometer.
   NOTE: *Removal of the steering column trim plate and/or the speedo cluster may provide better access to the cable.*
2. Remove the cable casing sealing plug from the dash panel. Then, pull the casing down from behind the dash and remove the cable.
3. If the cable is broken and cannot be entirely removed from the top, support the car securely, and then unscrew the cable casing connector at the transmission. Pull the bottom part of the cable out, and then screw the connector back onto the transmission.
4. Lubricate the new cable. Insert it into the casing until it bottoms. Push inward while rotating it until the square portion at the bottom engages with the coupling in the

1	CONSOLE ASM.
2	REAR SEAT ASH TRAY ASSEMBLY
3	ASH TRAY
4	TRIMPLATE ASM.
5	CONSOLE
6	NUT
7	TRIMPLATE
8	LENS
9	FILTER
10	HOUSING
11	CONSOLE
12	TRANSMISSION SHIFTER ASSEMBLY
13	INDICATOR LAMP
14	POINTER

Center console removal and installation details—automatic transaxle

CHASSIS ELECTRICAL 125

1	DASH PANEL	5	CLUSTER ASM.
2	CLUSER ASM.	6	TRANSDUCER
3	TRANS	7	TRANSMISSION
4	DASH PANEL		

Speedometer cable routing

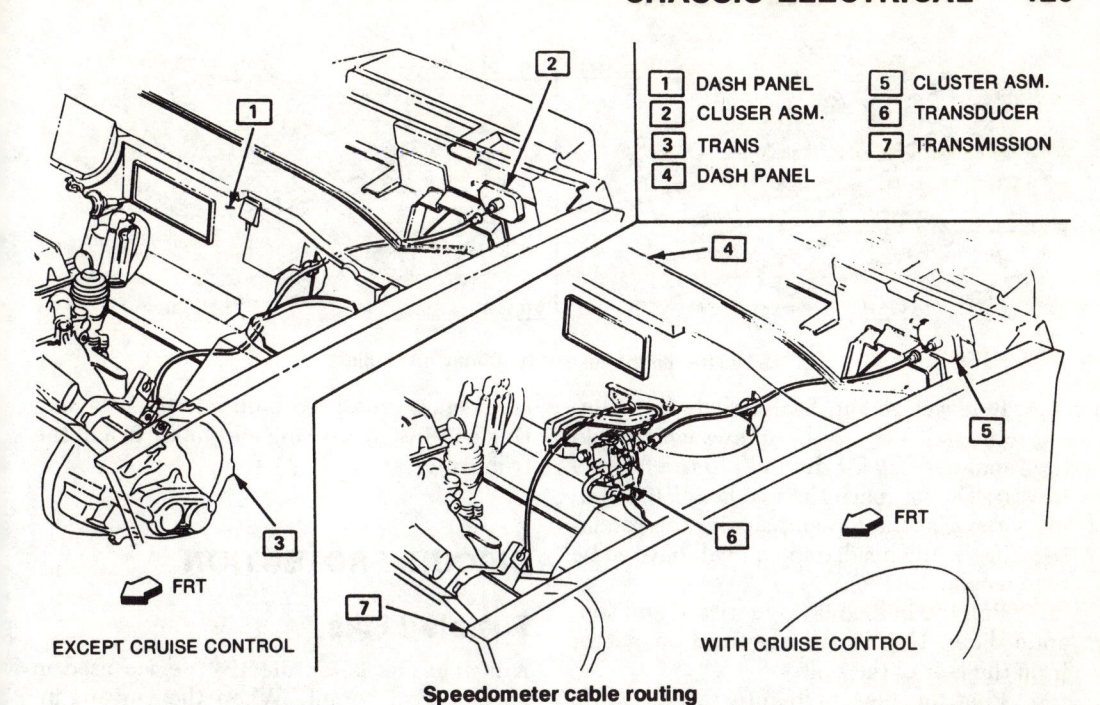

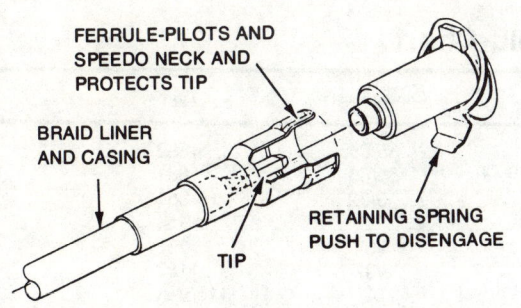

Speedometer cable disengagement at the speedometer

transmission, permitting the cable to move in another inch or so. Then, reconnect the cable casing to the speedometer and install the sealing plug into the dash panel.

Ignition Switch

The ignition switch removal and installation procedure is given in Chapter 7, under "steering", because the steering wheel must be removed for access to the ignition switch.

LIGHTING

Headlights

REMOVAL AND INSTALLATION

1. Remove the headlamp trim panel (grille panel) attaching screws.

NOTE: *The trim panel retaining screws on the Cavalier are under the hood, on top of the front support (see illustration).*

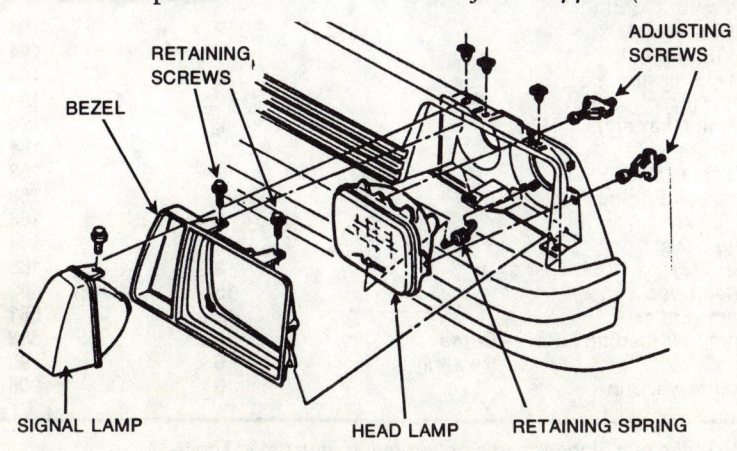

Cavalier headlight assembly

126 CHASSIS ELECTRICAL

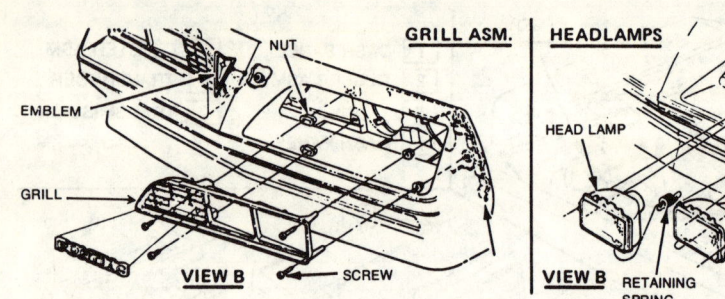

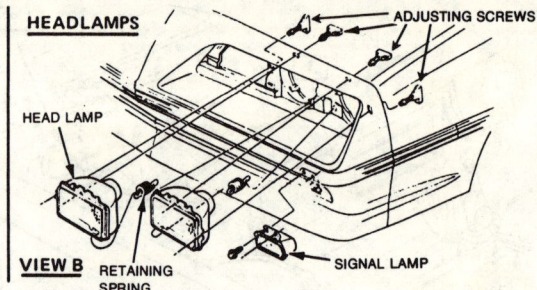

J2000 headlight assembly (Cimarron similar)

2. Remove the four headlamp bulb retaining screws. These are the screws which hold the retaining ring for the bulb to the front of the car. Do not touch the two headlamp aiming screws, at the top and side of the retaining ring, or the headlamp aim will have to be readjusted.

3. Pull the bulb and ring forward and separate them. Unplug the electrical connector from the rear of the bulb.

4. Plug the new bulb into the electrical connector. Install the bulb into the retaining ring and install the ring and bulb. Install the trim panel.

CIRCUIT PROTECTION

Fusible Links

A fusible link is a protective device used in an electrical circuit. When the current in-

Light Bulb Chart

Application	Candle Power	Type
Headlamp—Lo Beam	55/65	4652
High Beam	55/65	4651
Halogen High Beam (opt)	3/32	H4651
Side Marker	2	154
Tail and Stop Light (exc. wgn.)	3/32	1157
Tail, Stop & Turn (wgn.)	3/32	1157
Turn Signal (exc. wgn.)	32	1156NA
Rear Side Marker	2	1157
Luggage Compart. Light (exc. wgn.)	15	1103
(wgn.)	12	561
License Plate Light	N/A	194
Back-Up Light	32	1156
Instrument Cluster Lights—Stud.	2	194
Gauges	3	168
Heater/A/C Control	N/A	168
Indicator Lights		
High Beam	2	194
Turn Signal	2	194
Oil Pressure	2	194
Temp.	2	194
Volts (battery)	2	194
Brake	2	194
Fasten Belts	3	168
Check Engine	3	168
Choke	3	168
Radio Dial	2	194
Ash Tray	3	168
Underhood	15	93
Dome Lamp	12	561
Dome W/Reading Lamp—Dome	6	562
Reading	6	90
Courtesy Lamp	6	906

NOTE: *Do not use bulbs of a higher candle power rating than listed above.*
NOTE: *Certain models may differ, always check with Owner's Manual if possible.*

CHASSIS ELECTRICAL

Fusible links before and after a short circuit

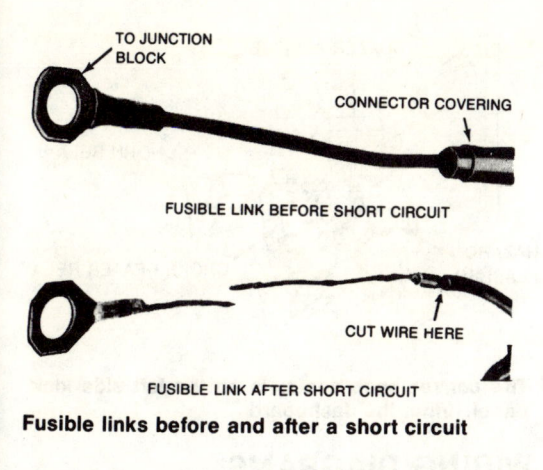

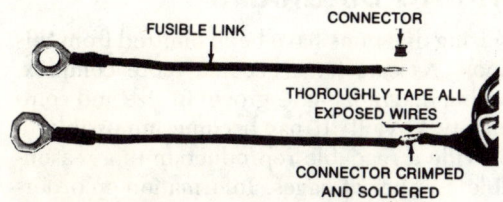

New fusible links are spliced to the wire

creases beyond a certain amperage, the fusible metal of the wire link melts, thus breaking the electrical circuit and preventing further damage to other components and wiring. Whenever a fusible link is melted because of a short circuit, correct the cause before installing a new one.

To replace a fusible link, cut off the burned link beyond the original splice. Replace the link with a new one of the same rating. If the splice has two wires, two repair links are required, one for each wire. Connect the new fusible link to the wires, then crimp securely.

CAUTION: *Use only replacements of the same electrical capacity as the original, available from your dealer. Replacements of a different electrical value will not provide adequate system protection.*

Fuses

Fuses protect all the major electrical systems in the car. In case of an electrical overload, the fuse melts, breaking the circuit and stopping the flow of electricity.

If a fuse blows, the cause should be investigated and corrected before the installation of a new fuse. This, however, is easier to say than to do. Because each fuse protects a limited number of components, your job is narrowed down somewhat. Begin your investigation by looking for obvious fraying, loose connections, breaks in insulation, etc. Use

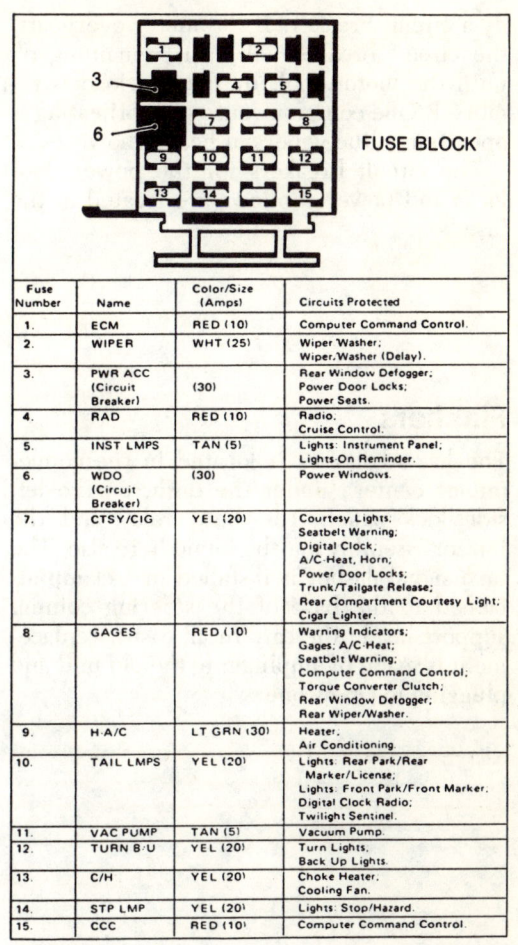

FUSE BLOCK

Fuse Number	Name	Color/Size (Amps)	Circuits Protected
1.	ECM	RED (10)	Computer Command Control.
2.	WIPER	WHT (25)	Wiper Washer; Wiper/Washer (Delay).
3.	PWR ACC (Circuit Breaker)	(30)	Rear Window Defogger; Power Door Locks; Power Seats.
4.	RAD	RED (10)	Radio. Cruise Control.
5.	INST LMPS	TAN (5)	Lights: Instrument Panel; Lights-On Reminder.
6.	WDO (Circuit Breaker)	(30)	Power Windows.
7.	CTSY/CIG	YEL (20)	Courtesy Lights; Seatbelt Warning; Digital Clock; A/C-Heat, Horn; Power Door Locks; Trunk/Tailgate Release; Rear Compartment Courtesy Light; Cigar Lighter.
8.	GAGES	RED (10)	Warning Indicators; Gages; A/C-Heat; Seatbelt Warning; Computer Command Control; Torque Converter Clutch; Rear Window Defogger; Rear Wiper/Washer.
9.	H-A/C	LT GRN (30)	Heater. Air Conditioning.
10.	TAIL LMPS	YEL (20)	Lights: Rear Park/Rear Marker/License; Lights: Front Park/Front Marker; Digital Clock Radio; Twilight Sentinel.
11.	VAC PUMP	TAN (5)	Vacuum Pump.
12.	TURN B-U	YEL (20)	Turn Lights; Back Up Lights.
13.	C/H	YEL (20)	Choke Heater. Cooling Fan.
14.	STP LMP	YEL (20)	Lights: Stop/Hazard.
15.	CCC	RED (10)	Computer Command Control.

The fuse box is under the left side of the instrument panel

the techniques outlined at the beginning of this chapter. Electrical problems are almost always a real headache to solve, but if you are patient and persistent, and approach the problem logically (that is, don't start replacing electrical components randomly), you will eventually find the solution.

The amperage of each fuse and the circuit it protects are marked on the fusebox, which is located under the left side (driver's side) of the instrument panel and pulls down for easy access.

Circuit Breakers

The headlights are protected by a circuit breaker in the headlamp switch. If the circuit breaker trips, the headlights will either flash on and off, or stay off altogether. The circuit breaker resets automatically after the overload is removed.

The windshield wipers are also protected

128 CHASSIS ELECTRICAL

by a circuit breaker. If the motor overheats, the circuit breaker will trip, remaining off until the motor cools or the overload is removed. One common cause of overheating is operation of the wipers in heavy snow.

The circuit breakers for the power door locks and power windows are located in the fuse box.

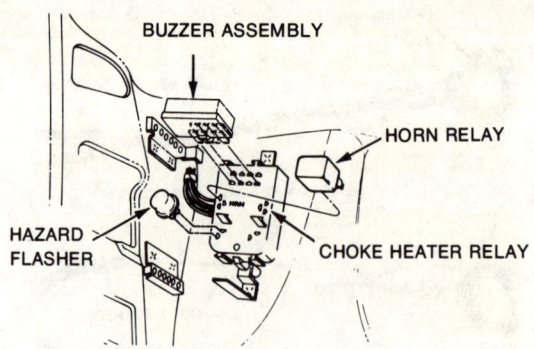

The convenience center is on the left side kick panel, under the dashboard

Flashers

The hazard flasher is located in the convenience center', under the dash, on the left side kick panel. The horn relay and the buzzer assembly may be found here also. The turn signal flasher is installed in a clamp attached to the base of the steering column support inside the car. In all cases, replacement is made by unplugging the old unit and plugging in a new one.

WIRING DIAGRAMS

Wiring diagrams have been omitted from this book. As cars have become more complex, wiring diagrams have grown in size and complexity as well. It has become impossible to provide a readable reproduction in a reasonable number of pages. Information on ordering wiring diagrams from the vehicle manufacturer can be found in the owner's manual.

Clutch and Transaxle 6

MANUAL TRANSAXLE

"Transaxle" is the term used to identify a unit which combines the transmission and drive axle into one component. The J-cars use a model MT-125 manual transaxle as standard equipment. All forward gears in this design are in constant mesh. Final drive from the transmission is taken from the output gear, which is an integral part of the output shaft; the output gear transfers power to the differential ring gear and differential assembly. The differential is of conventional design.

Because of the complexity of the transaxle, no overhaul procedures are given in this book. However, removal and installation, adjustment, and halfshaft removal, installation and overhaul are covered.

REMOVAL AND INSTALLATION

1. Disconnect the negative battery cable.
2. Install an engine holding bar so that one end is supported on the cowl tray over the wiper motor and the other end rests on the radiator support. Use padding and be careful not to damage the paint or body work with the bar. Attach a lifting hook to the engine lift ring and to the bar and raise the engine enough to take the pressure off the motor mounts.

NOTE: *If a lifting bar and hook is not available, a chain hoist can be used, however, during the procedure the vehicle must be raised, at which time the chain hoist must be adjusted to keep tension on the engine/transaxle assembly.*

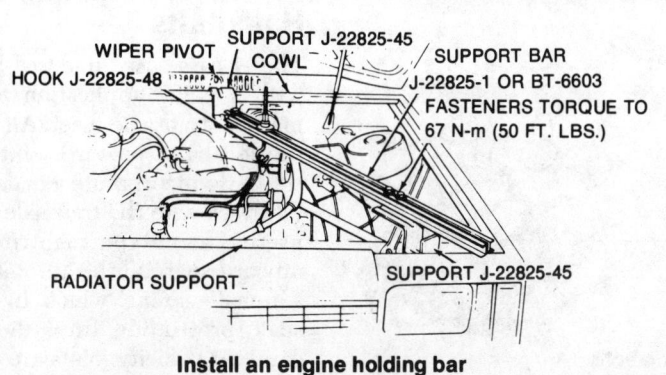

Install an engine holding bar

CLUTCH AND TRANSAXLE

3. Remove the heater hose clamp at the transaxle mount bracket. Disconnect the electrical connector and remove the horn assembly.

4. Remove the transaxle mount attaching bolts. Discard the bolts attaching the mount to the side frame: *New bolts must be used at installation.*

5. Disconnect the clutch cable from the clutch release lever. Remove the transaxle mount bracket attaching bolts and nuts.

6. Disconnect the shift cables and retaining clips at the transaxle. Disconnect the ground cables at the transaxle mounting stud.

7. Remove the four upper transaxle-to-engine mounting bolts.

8. Raise the vehicle and support it on stands. Remove the left front wheel.

9. Remove the left front inner splash shield. Remove the transaxle strut and bracket.

10. Remove the clutch housing cover bolts.

11. Disconnect the speedometer cable at the transaxle.

12. Disconnect the stabilizer bar at the left suspension support and control arm.

13. Disconnect the ball joint from the steering knuckle.

14. Remove the left suspension support attaching bolts and remove the support and control arm as an assembly.

15. Install boot protectors and disengage the drive axles at the transaxle. Remove the left side shaft from the transaxle.

16. Position a jack under the transaxle case, remove the lower two transaxle-to-engine mounting bolts and remove the transaxle by sliding it towards the driver's side, away from the engine. Carefully lower the jack, guiding the right shaft out the transaxle.

17. When installing the transaxle, guide the right drive axle into its bore as the transaxle is being raised. The right drive axle CANNOT be readily installed after the transaxle is connected to the engine. Installation of the remaining components is in the reverse order of removal with the following notes: Tighten the transaxle-to-engine mounting bolts to 55 ft. lbs. Tighten the suspension support-to-body attaching bolts to 75 ft. lbs. and the clutch housing cover bolts to 10 ft. lbs. Using new bolts, install and tighten the transaxle mount-to-side frame to 40 ft. lbs. When installing the bolts attaching the mount-to-transaxle bracket, check the alignment bolt at the engine mount. If excessive effort is required to remove the alignment bolt, realign the powertrain components and tighten the bolts to 40 ft. lbs., and then remove the alignment bolt.

SHIFT LINKAGE ADJUSTMENT

1. Disconnect the negative battery cable.

2. Place the transaxle in first gear, then loosen the shift cable attaching pins at the transaxle levers on the transaxle case.

3. Remove the shifter boot and retainer.

4. Install a No. 22 ($5/32$ in.) drill bit into the alignment hole at the side of the shifter assembly. Install a yoke clip between the shifter tower and carrier.

5. Remove the lash from the transaxle by rotating the upright select lever (lever D) while tightening the cable attaching pin nut.

6. Remove the drill bit and yoke at the shifter assembly, install the shifter boot and retainer and connect the negative battery cable.

7. Road test the vehicle to check for good gate feel during shifting. Fine tune the adjustment as necessary.

Halfshafts

The J-cars use unequal-length halfshafts, with specific application for automatic and manual transaxle use. All halfshafts except the left-hand inboard joint of the automatic transaxle incorporate a male spline; the shafts interlock with the transaxle gears through the use of barrel-type snap rings. The left-hand inboard shaft on the automatic transaxle uses a female spline which installs over a stub shaft protruding from the transaxle. Four constant velocity joints are used, two on each

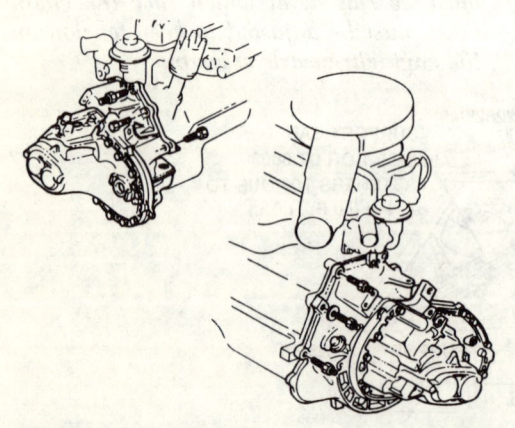

Engine-to-transaxle bolts

CLUTCH AND TRANSAXLE 131

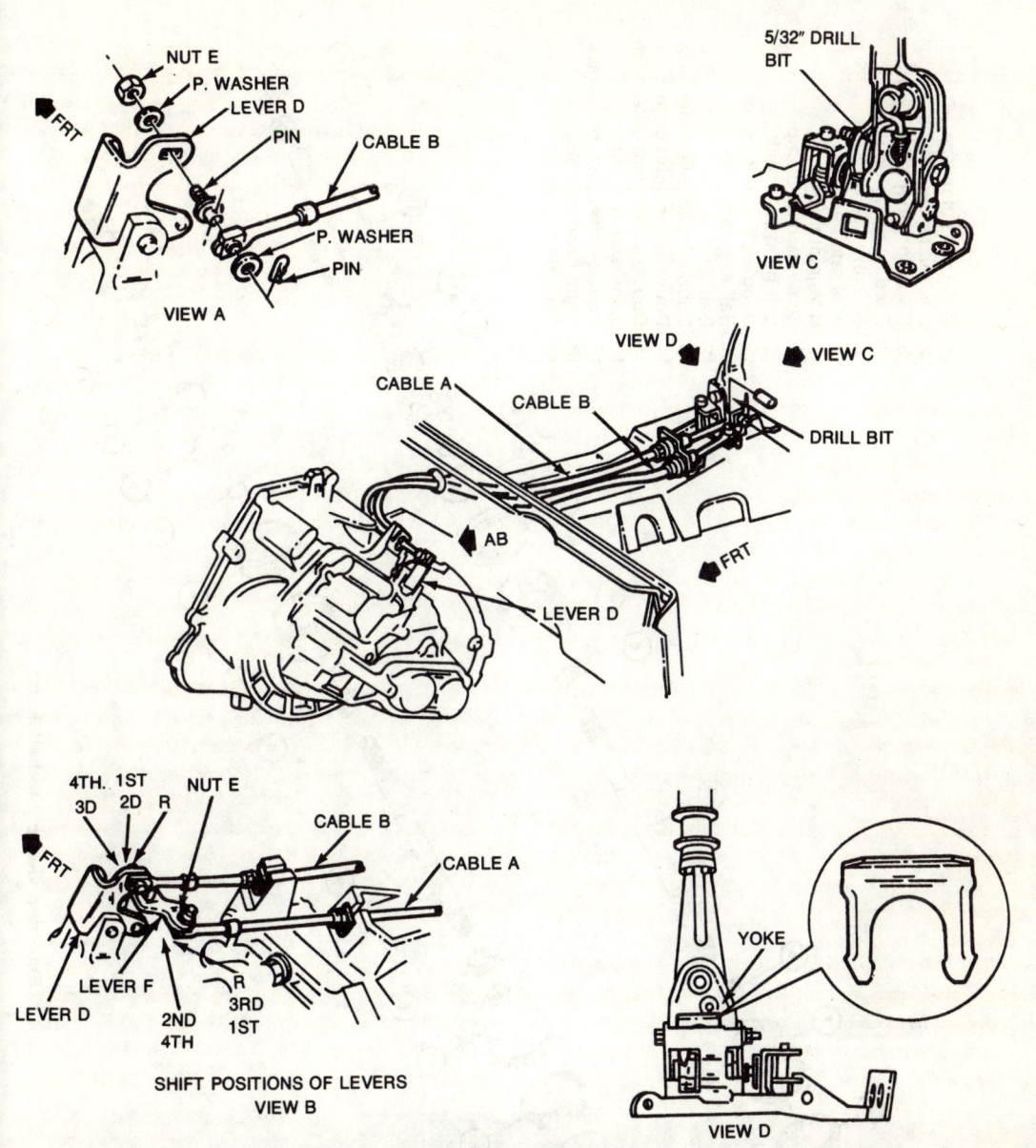

Shift linkage adjustment

shaft. The inner joints are of the double offset design; the outer joints are Rzeppa-type.

REMOVAL AND INSTALLATION

1. Remove the hub nut.
2. Raise the front of the car. Remove the wheel and tire.
3. Install an axle shaft boot seal protector, G.M. special tool no. J-28712 or the equivalent, onto the seal.
4. Disconnect the brake hose clip from the MacPherson strut, but do not disconnect the hose from the caliper. Remove the brake caliper from the spindle, and hang the caliper out of the way by a length of wire. *Do not allow the caliper to hang by the brake hose.*
5. Mark the camber alignment cam bolt for reassembly. Remove the cam bolt and the upper attaching bolt from the strut and spindle.
6. Pull the steering knuckle assembly from the strut bracket.
7. Using G.M. special tool J-28468 or the equivalent, remove the axle shaft from the transaxle.
8. Using G.M. special tool J-28733 or the equivalent spindle remover, remove the axle shaft from the hub and bearing assembly.

132 CLUTCH AND TRANSAXLE

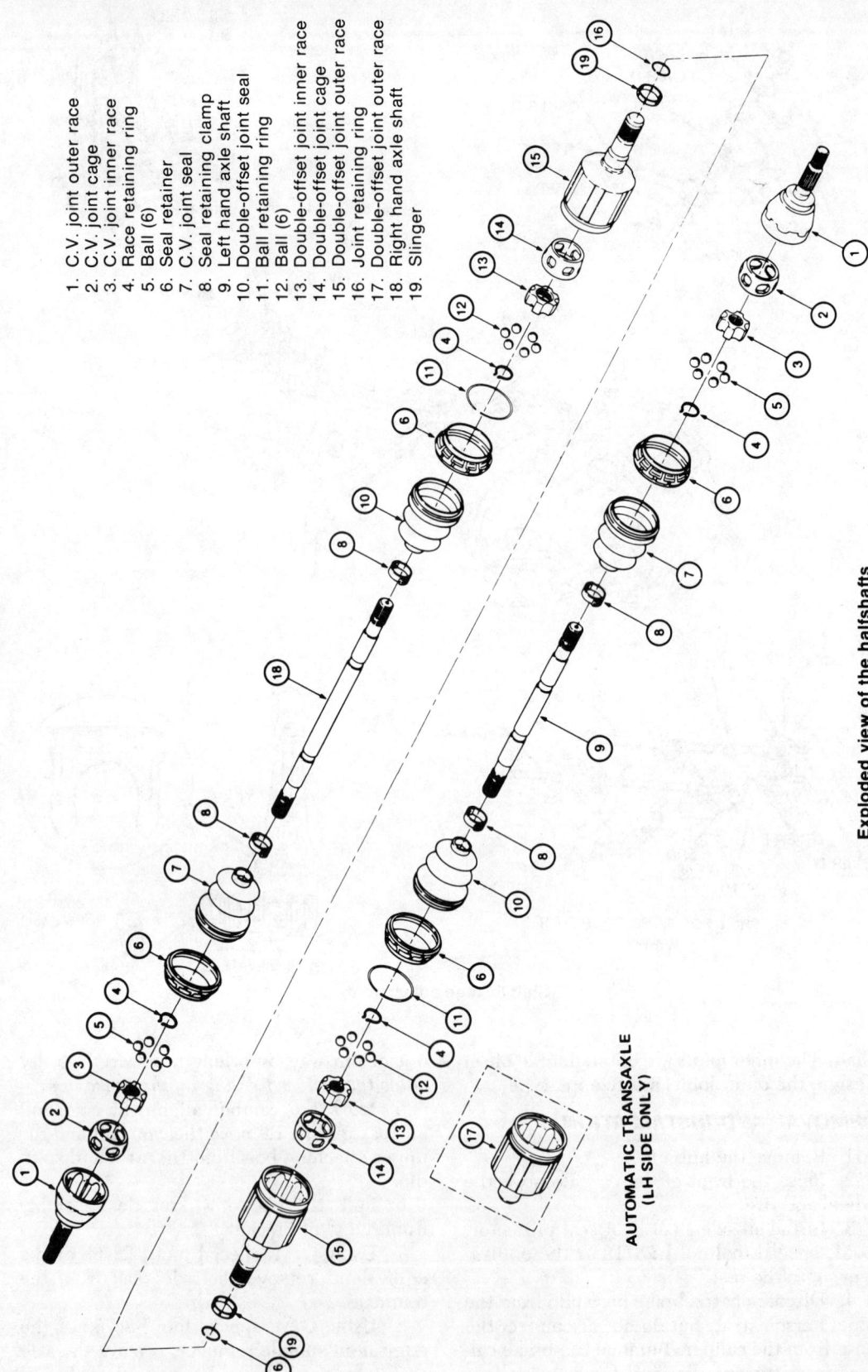

1. C.V. joint outer race
2. C.V. joint cage
3. C.V. joint inner race
4. Race retaining ring
5. Ball (6)
6. Seal retainer
7. C.V. joint seal
8. Seal retaining clamp
9. Left hand axle shaft
10. Double-offset joint seal
11. Ball retaining ring
12. Ball (6)
13. Double-offset joint inner race
14. Double-offset joint cage
15. Double-offset joint outer race
16. Joint retaining ring
17. Double-offset joint outer race
18. Right hand axle shaft
19. Slinger

AUTOMATIC TRANSAXLE (LH SIDE ONLY)

Exploded view of the halfshafts

CLUTCH AND TRANSAXLE

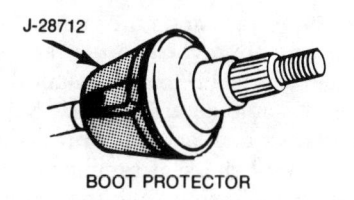

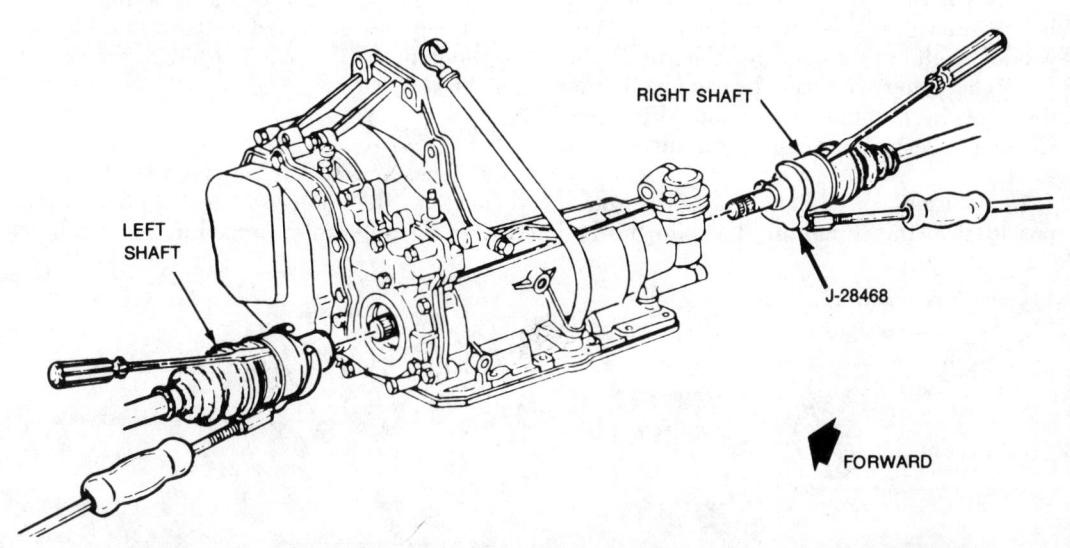

Halfshaft removal; the special tools are attached to slide hammers in this diagram

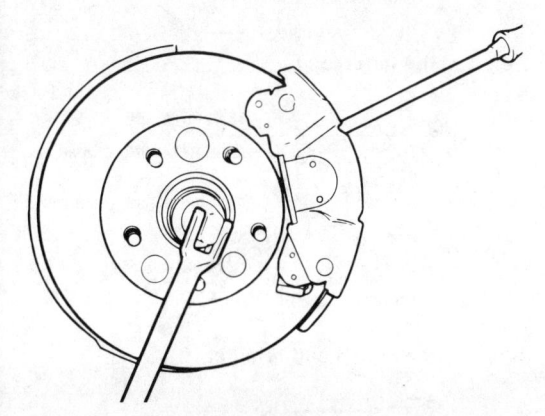

Insert a drift into the caliper when tightening the hub nut

To install:
1. If a new drive axle is to be installed, a new knuckle seal should be installed first.
2. Loosely install the drive axle into the transaxle and steering knuckle.
3. Loosely attach the steering knuckle to the suspension strut.
4. Install the brake caliper. Tighten the bolts to 30 ft. lbs. (40 Nm.).
5. The drive axle is an interference fit in the steering knuckle. Press the axle into place, then install the hub nut. When the shaft begins to turn with the hub, insert a drift through the caliper into one of the cooling slots in the rotor to keep it from turning. Tighten the hub nut to 70 ft. lbs. (100 Nm.) to completely seat the shaft.
6. Load the hub assembly by lowering it onto a jackstand. Align the camber cam bolt marks made during removal, install the bolt and tighten to 140 ft. lbs. (190 Nm). Tighten the upper nut to the same value.
7. Install the axle shaft all the way into the transaxle using a screwdriver inserted into the groove provided on the inner retainer. Tap the screwdriver until the shaft seats in the transaxle.
8. Connect the brake hose clip to the strut. Install the tire and wheel, lower the car, and tighten the hub nut to 225 ft. lbs. (305 Nm).

CONSTANT VELOCITY JOINT OVERHAUL
Outer Joint
1. Remove the axle shaft.
2. Cut off the seal retaining clamp. Using a brass drift and a hammer, lightly tap the seal retainer from the outside toward the inside of the shaft to remove from the joint.
3. Use a pair of snap ring pliers to spread

134 CLUTCH AND TRANSAXLE

the retaining ring apart. Pull the axle shaft from the joint.

4. Using a brass drift and a hammer, lightly tap on the inner race cage until it has tilted sufficiently to remove one of the balls. Remove the other balls in the same manner.

5. Pivot the cage 90° and, with the cage ball windows aligned with the outer joint windows, lift out the cage and the inner race.

6. The inner race can be removed from the cage by pivoting it 90° and lifting out. Clean all parts thoroughly and inspect for wear.

7. To install, put a light coat of the grease provided in the rebuilding kit onto the ball grooves of the inner race and outer joint. Install the parts in the reverse order of removal. To install the seal retainer, install the axle shaft assembly into an arbor press. Support the seal retainer on blocks, and press the axle shaft down until the seal retainer seats on the outer joint. When assembling, apply half the grease provided in the rebuilding kit to the joint; fill the seal (boot) with the rest of the grease.

Inner Joint

1. The joint seal is removed in the same manner as the outer joint seal. Follow Steps 1–3 of the outer joint procedure.

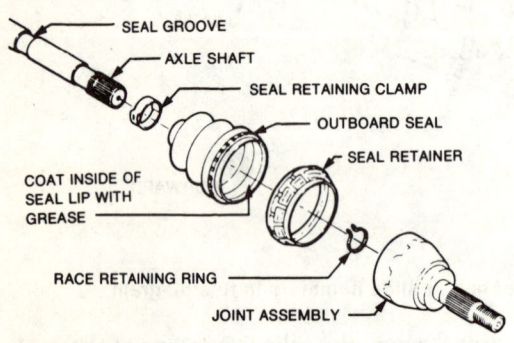

Detail of the outer joint

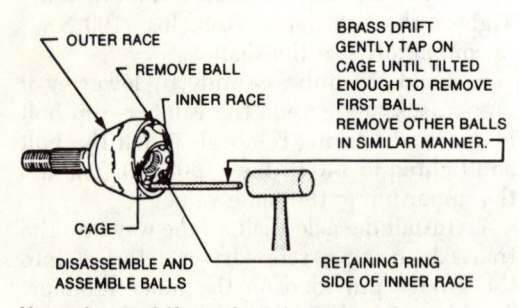

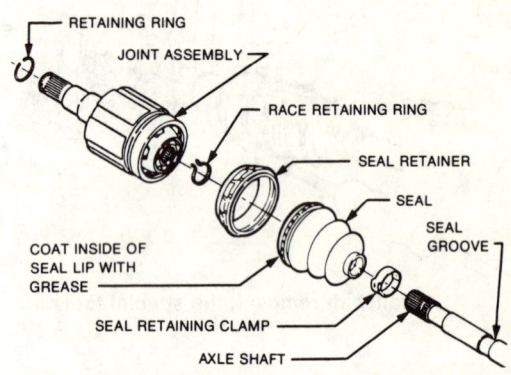

Detail of the inner joint

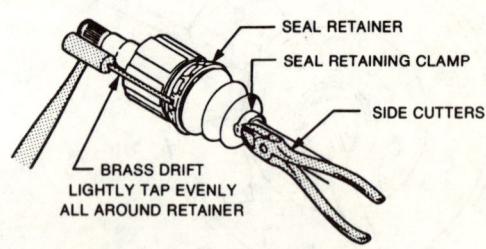

Use a brass drift to pivot the cage

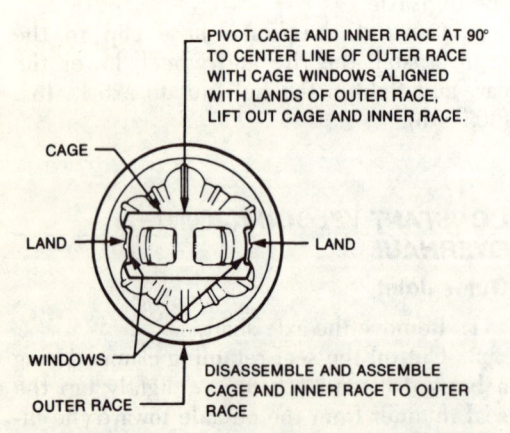

Remove the clamp and retainer

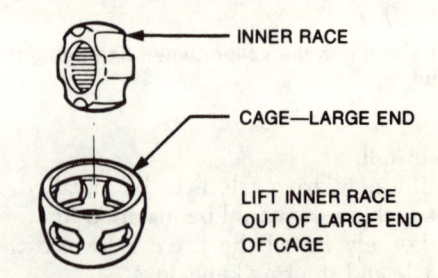

The inner race and cage can be removed from the outer race when pivoted 90°

The inner race exits from the large end of the cage

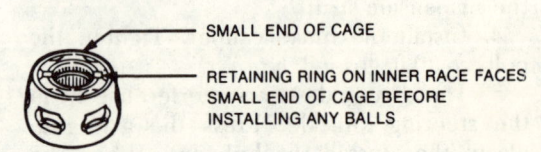

Inner race installed in the cage

CLUTCH AND TRANSAXLE

2. To disassemble the inner joint, remove the ball retaining ring from the joint. Pull the cage and inner race from the joint. The balls will come out with the race.

3. Center the inner race lobes in the cage windows, pivot the race 90°, and lift the race from the cage.

4. Assembly of the joint is the reverse. The inner joint seal retainer must be pressed onto the joint. See Step 7 of the outer joint procedure.

CLUTCH

ADJUSTMENT

The J-cars have a self-adjusting clutch mechanism located on the clutch pedal, eliminating the need for periodic free play adjustments. The self-adjusting mechanism should be inspected periodically as follows:

1. Depress the clutch pedal and look for the pawl on the self-adjusting mechanism to firmly engage the teeth on the ratchet.
2. Release the clutch. The pawl should be lifted off of the teeth by the metal stop on the bracket.

NEUTRAL START SWITCH

A neutral start switch is located on the clutch pedal assembly; the switch prevents the engine from starting unless the clutch is depressed. If the switch is faulty, it can be unbolted and replaced without removing the pedal assembly from the car. No adjustments for the switch are provided.

CLUTCH REMOVAL AND INSTALLATION

1. Remove the transaxle.
2. Mark the pressure plate assembly and the flywheel so that they can be assembled in the same position. They were balanced as an assembly at the factory.
3. Loosen the attaching bolts one turn at a time until spring tension is relieved.
4. Support the pressure plate and remove the bolts. Remove the pressure plate and clutch disc. Do not disassemble the pressure plate assembly; replace it if defective.
5. Inspect the flywheel, clutch disc, pressure plate, throwout bearing and the clutch fork and pivot shaft assembly for wear. Replace the parts as required. If the flywheel shows any signs of overheating, or if it is badly grooved or scored, it should be refaced or replaced.
6. Clean the pressure plate and flywheel mating surfaces thoroughly. Position the clutch disc and pressure plate into the installed position, and support with a dummy shaft or clutch aligning tool. The clutch plate is assembled with the damper springs offset toward the transaxle. One side of the factory-

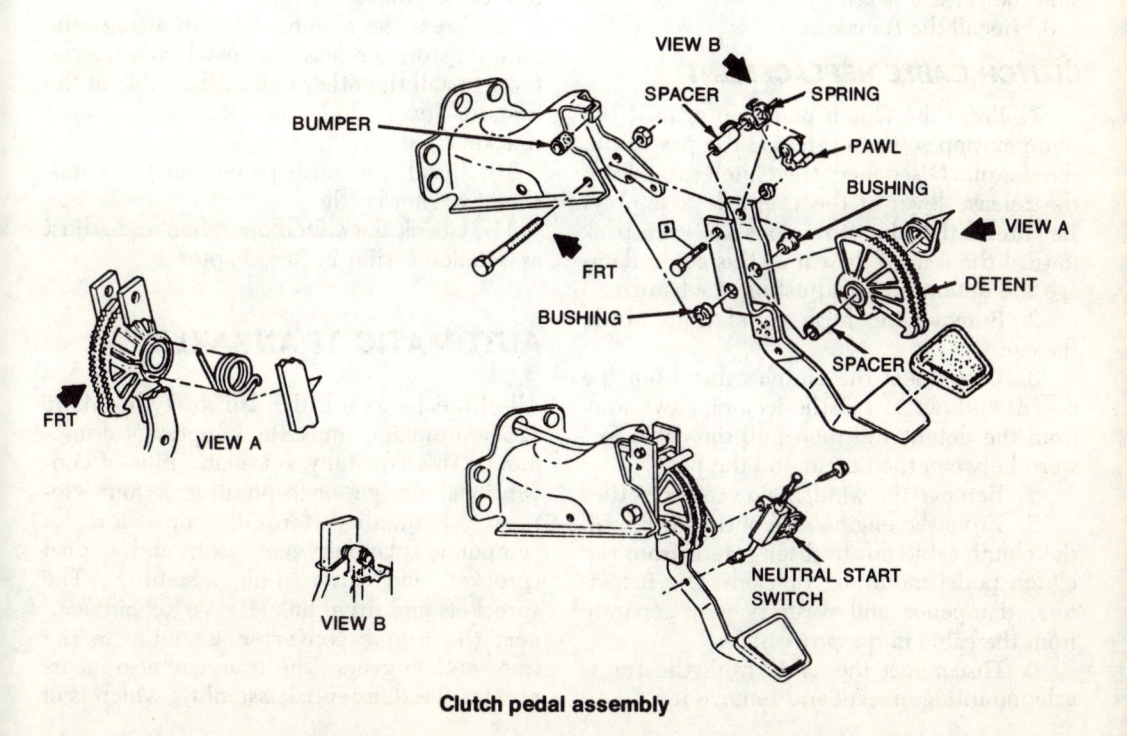

Clutch pedal assembly

CLUTCH AND TRANSAXLE

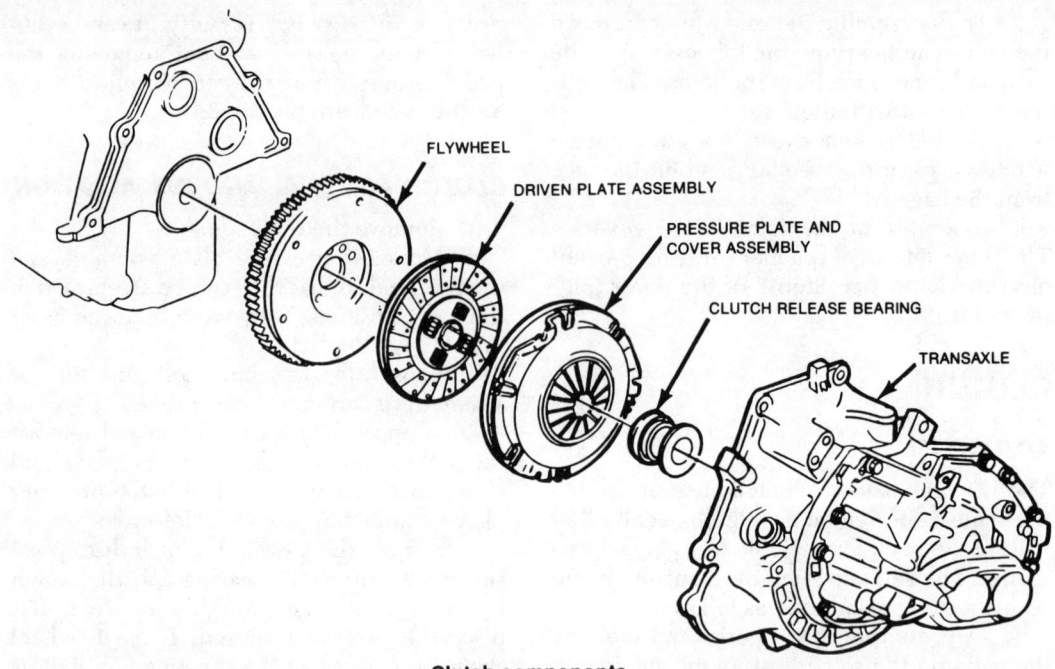

Clutch components

supplied clutch disc is stamped "Flywheel Side."

7. Install the pressure plate-to-flywheel bolts. Tighten them gradually in a criss-cross pattern.

8. Lubricate the outside groove and the inside recess of the release bearing with high temperature grease. Wipe off any excess. Install the release bearing.

9. Install the transaxle.

CLUTCH CABLE REPLACEMENT

1. Press the clutch pedal up against the bumper stop so as to releaase the pawl from the detent. Disconnect the clutch cable from the release lever at the transaxle assembly. Be careful that the cable does not snap back toward the rear of the car as this could damage the detent in the adjusting mechanism.

2. Remove the hush panel from inside the car.

3. Disconnect the clutch cable from the detent end tangs. Lift the locking pawl away from the detent and then pull the cable forward between the detent and the pawl.

4. Remove the windshield washer bottle.

5. From the engine side of the cowl, pull the clutch cable out to disengage it from the clutch pedal mounting bracket. The insulators, dampener and washers may separate from the cable in the process.

6. Disconnect the cable from the transaxle mounting bracket and remove it.

7. Install the cable into both insulators, damper and washer. Lubricate the rear insulator with tire mounting lube or the like to ease installation into the pedal mounting bracket.

8. From inside the car, attach the end of the cable to the detent. Be sure to route the cable underneath the pawl and into the detent cable groove.

9. Press the clutch pedal up against the bumper stop to release the pawl from the detent. Install the other end of the cable at the release lever and the transaxle mount bracket.

10. Install the hush panel and the windshield washer bottle.

11. Check the clutch operation and adjust as detailed earlier in this chapter.

AUTOMATIC TRANSAXLE

All of the J-cars use the Turbo Hydra-Matic 125C automatic transaxle as optional equipment. This is a fully automatic unit of conventional design, incorporating a four element hydraulic torque converter, a compound planetary gear set, and a dual sprocket and drive link assembly. The sprockets and drive link (Hy-Vo® chain) connect the torque converter assembly to the transmission gears. The transaxle also incorporates the differential assembly, which is of

CLUTCH AND TRANSAXLE 137

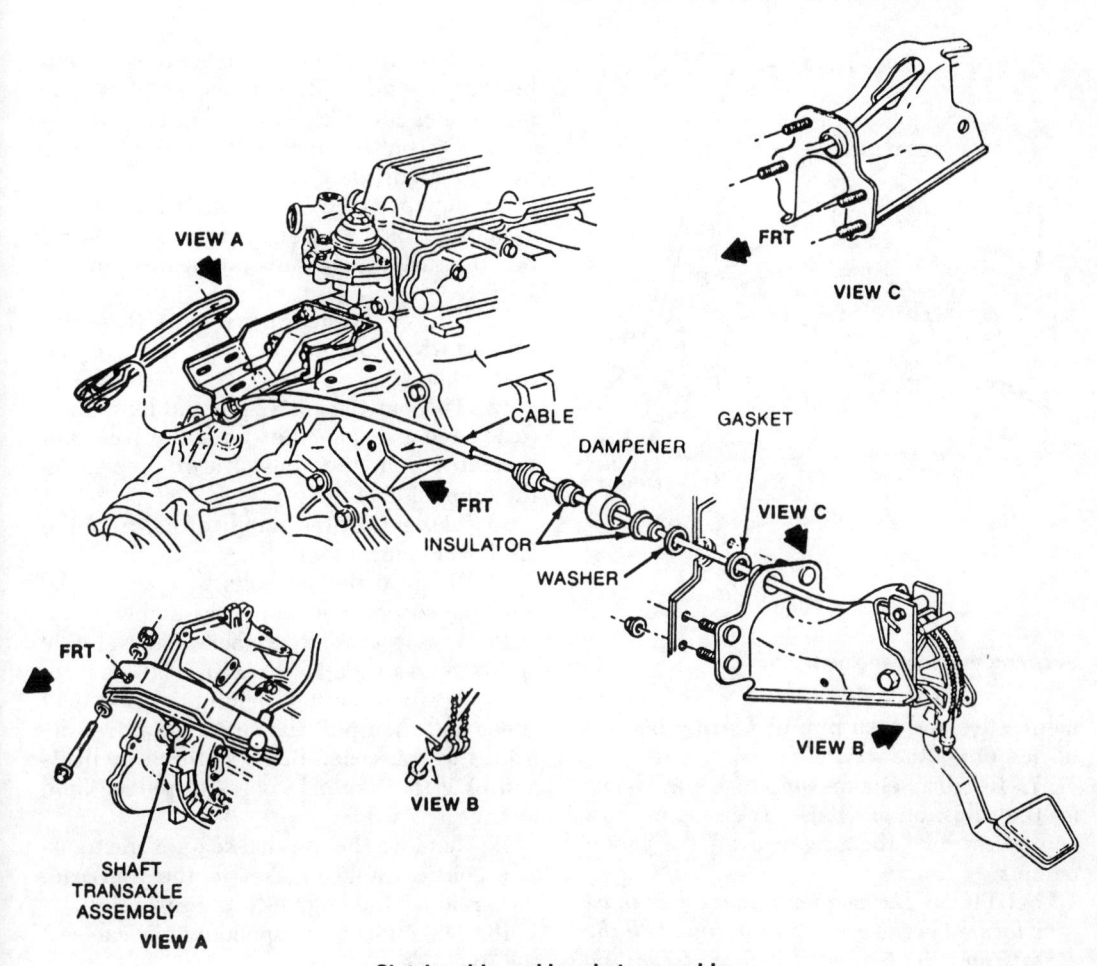

Clutch cable and bracket assembly

conventional design. Power is transmitted from the transmission to the final drive and differential assembly through helical cut gears.

No overhaul procedures are given in this book because of the complexity of the transaxle. Transaxle removal and installation, adjustment, and halfshaft removal, installation, and overhaul procedures are covered.

ADJUSTMENTS

The only adjustment required on the TH-M 125C transaxle is the shift linkage (cable) adjustment. The neutral start switch and throttle valve are self-adjusting. The transaxle has only one band, with no provision for periodic adjustment. Pan removal, fluid and filter changes are covered in Chapter One.

SHIFT LINKAGE ADJUSTMENT

1. Place the shift lever inside the car into Neutral.
2. Disconnect the shift cable from the transaxle lever. Place the transaxle lever in Neutral, by moving the lever clockwise to the Low (L) detent, then counterclockwise through the Second (S) and Drive (D) detents to the Neutral detent.
3. Attach the shift cable to the pin on the transaxle lever. Check the shift operation.

REMOVAL AND INSTALLATION

1. Disconnect the negative battery cable where it attaches to the transaxle.
2. Insert a ¼ x 2 in. bolt into the hole in the right front motor mount to prevent any mislocation during the transaxle removal.
3. Remove the air cleaner. Disconnect the T.V. cable at the carburetor.
4. Unscrew the bolt securing the T.V. cable to the transaxle. Pull up on the cable cover at the transaxle until the cable can be seen. Disconnect the cable from the transaxle rod.
5. Remove the wiring harness retaining bolt at the top of the transaxle.
6. Remove the hose from the air manage-

138 CLUTCH AND TRANSAXLE

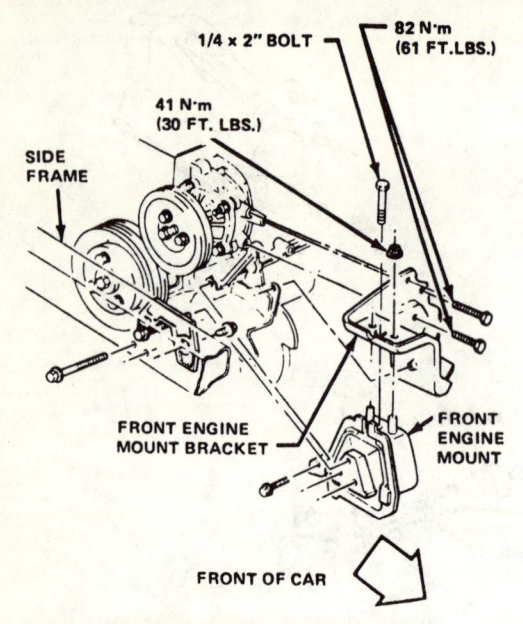

Securing the front engine mount

ment valve and then pull the wiring harness up and out of the way.

7. Install an engine support bar as shown in the illustration. Raise the engine just enough to take the pressure off the motor mounts.

> CAUTION: *The engine support bar must be located in the center of the cowl and the bolts must be tightened before attempting to support the engine.*

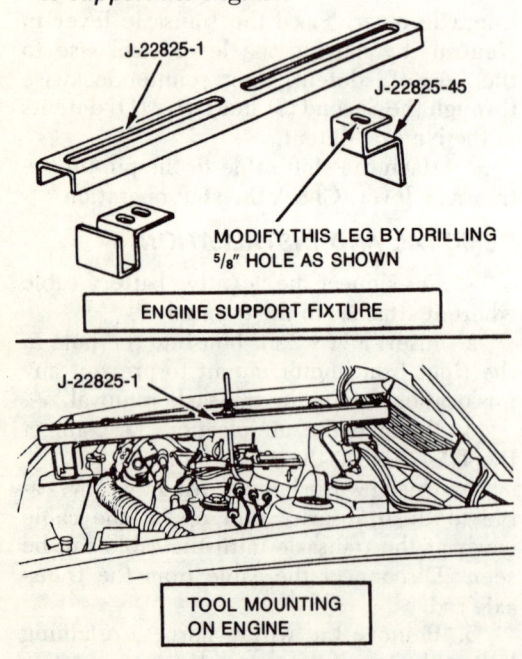

You must hold the engine with the engine support bar

8. Remove the transaxle mount and bracket assembly. It may be necessary to raise the engine slightly to aid in removal.

9. Disconnect the shift control linkage from the transaxle.

10. Remove the top transaxle-to-engine mounting bolts. Loosen, but do not remove, the transaxle-to-engine bolt nearest to the starter.

11. Unlock the steering column. Raise and support the front of the car. Remove the front wheels.

12. Pull out the cotter pin and loosen the castellated ball joint nut until the ball joint separates from the control arm. Repeat on the other side of the car.

13. Disconnect the stabilizer bar from the left lower control arm.

14. Remove the six bolts that secure the left front suspension support assembly.

15. Connect an axle shaft removal tool (J-28468) to a slide hammer (J-23907).

16. Position the tool behind the axle shaft cones and then pull the cones out and away from the transaxle. Remove the axle shafts and plug the transaxle bores to reduce fluid leakage.

17. Remove the nut that secures the transaxle control cable bracket to the transaxle, then remove the engine-to-transaxle stud.

18. Disconnect the speedometer cable at the transaxle.

19. Disconnect the transaxle strut (stabilizer) at the transaxle.

20. Remove the four retaining screws and remove the torque converter shield.

21. Remove the three bolts securing the torque converter to the flex plate.

22. Disconnect and plug the oil cooler lines at the transaxle. Remove the starter.

23. Remove the screws that hold the

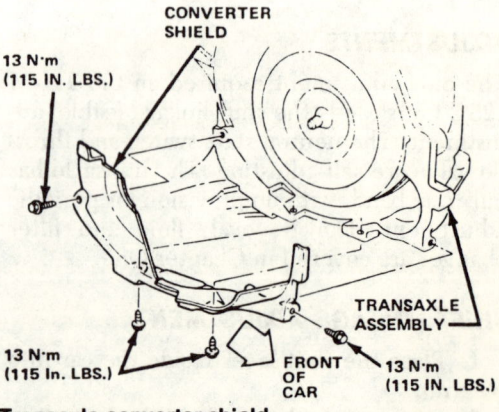

Transaxle converter shield

CLUTCH AND TRANSAXLE 139

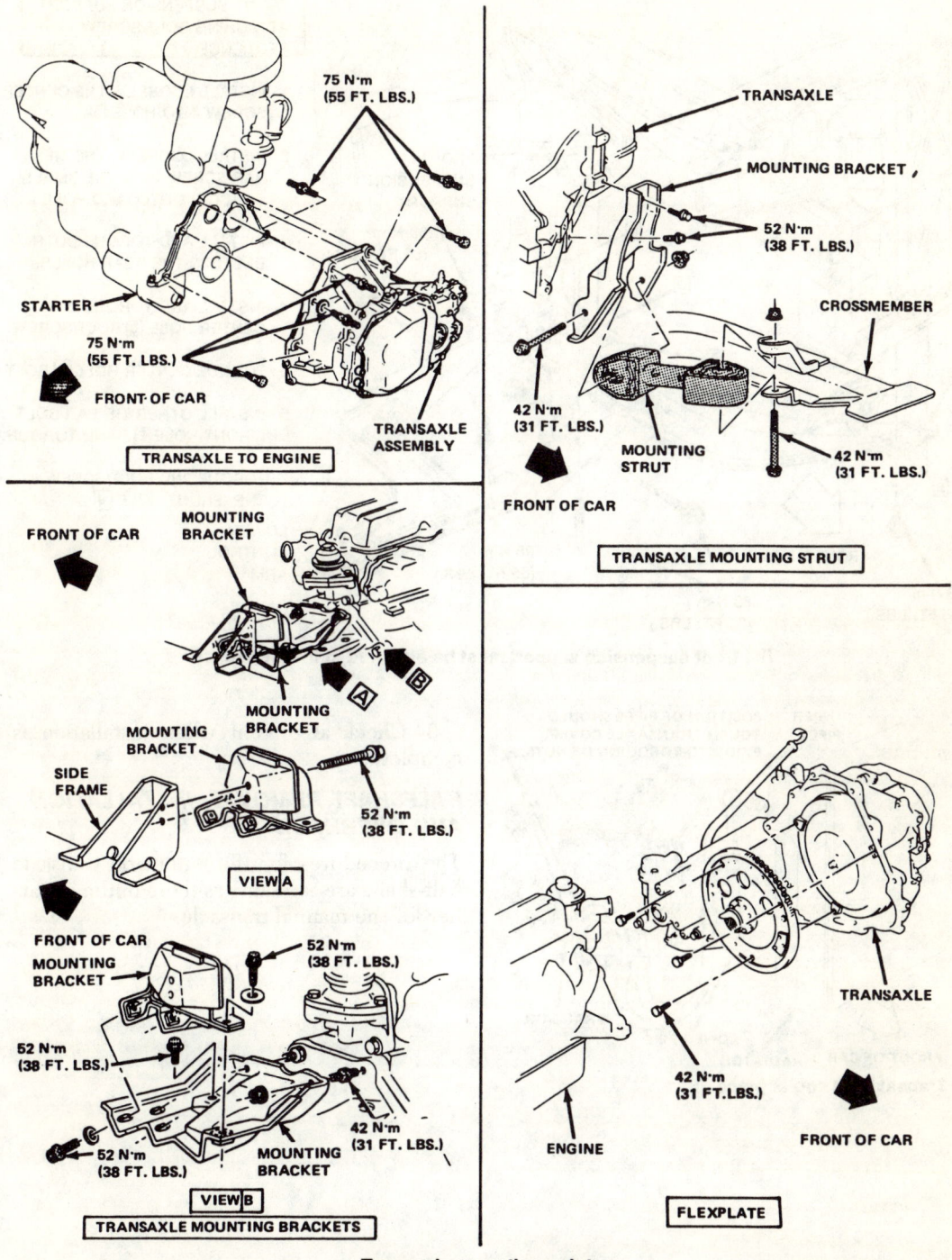

Transaxle mounting points

brake and fuel line brackets to the left side of the underbody. This will allow the lines to be moved slightly for clearance during transaxle removal.

24. Remove the bolt that was loosened in Step 10.

25. Remove the transaxle to the left.

Installation is in the reverse order of removal. Please note the following:

1. Reinstall both axle shafts AFTER the transaxle is in position.

2. When installing the front suspension support assembly you must follow the tightening sequence shown in the illustration.

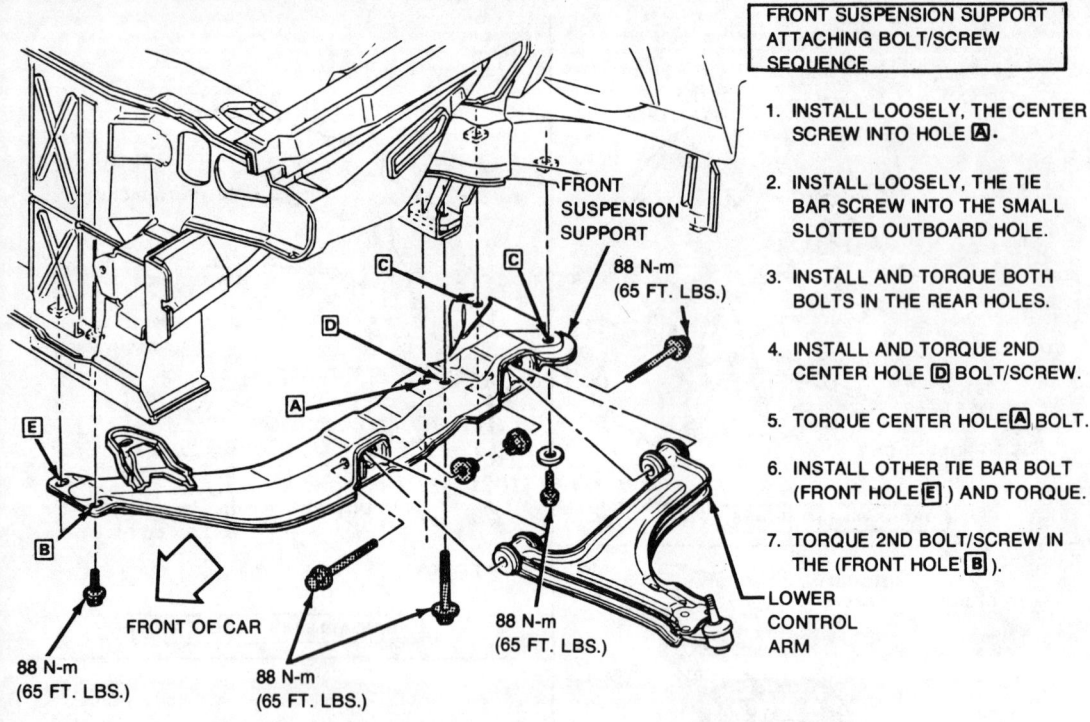

140   CLUTCH AND TRANSAXLE

FRONT SUSPENSION SUPPORT ATTACHING BOLT/SCREW SEQUENCE

1. INSTALL LOOSELY, THE CENTER SCREW INTO HOLE **A**.
2. INSTALL LOOSELY, THE TIE BAR SCREW INTO THE SMALL SLOTTED OUTBOARD HOLE.
3. INSTALL AND TORQUE BOTH BOLTS IN THE REAR HOLES.
4. INSTALL AND TORQUE 2ND CENTER HOLE **D** BOLT/SCREW.
5. TORQUE CENTER HOLE **A** BOLT.
6. INSTALL OTHER TIE BAR BOLT (FRONT HOLE **E**) AND TORQUE.
7. TORQUE 2ND BOLT/SCREW IN THE (FRONT HOLE **B**).

88 N-m (65 FT. LBS.)
88 N-m (65 FT. LBS.)
88 N-m (65 FT. LBS.)
88 N-m (65 FT. LBS.)

FRONT OF CAR
FRONT SUSPENSION SUPPORT
LOWER CONTROL ARM

The front suspension support must be attached in this sequence

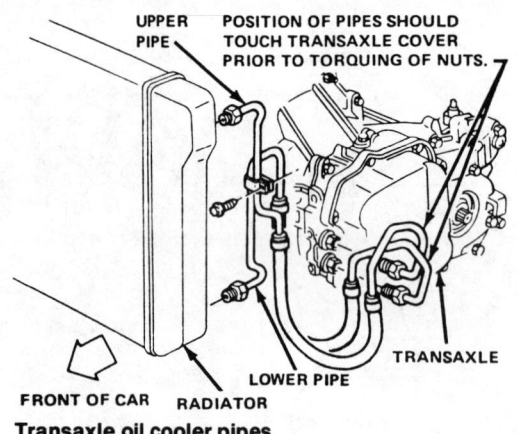

UPPER PIPE
POSITION OF PIPES SHOULD TOUCH TRANSAXLE COVER PRIOR TO TORQUING OF NUTS.
LOWER PIPE
RADIATOR
TRANSAXLE
FRONT OF CAR

Transaxle oil cooler pipes

3. Check alignment when installation is complete.

HALFSHAFT REMOVAL, INSTALLATION AND OVERHAUL

The procedures for the automatic transaxle half-shafts are the same as those outlined earlier for the manual transaxle.

Suspension and Steering

7

FRONT SUSPENSION

The J-cars use a MacPherson strut front suspension design. A MacPherson strut combines the functions of a shock absorber and an upper suspension member (upper arm) into one unit. The strut is surrounded by a coil spring, which provides normal front suspension functions.

The strut bolts to the body shell at its upper end, and to the steering knuckle at the lower end. The strut pivots with the steering knuckle by means of a sealed mounting assembly at the upper end which contains a preloaded, non-adjustable bearing.

The steering knuckle is connected to the chassis at the lower end by a conventional lower control arm, and pivots in the arm in a preloaded ball joint of standard design. The knuckle is fastened to the ball joint stud by means of a castellated nut and cotter pin.

Advantages of the MacPherson strut design, aside from its relative simplicity, include reduced weight and friction, minimal intrusion into the engine and passenger compartments, and ease of service.

Springs and Shock Absorbers
TESTING

The function of the shock absorber is to dampen harsh spring movement and provide a means of dissipating the motion of the wheels so that the shocks encountered by the wheels are not totally transmitted to the body and, therefore, to you and your passengers. As the wheel moves up and down, the shock absorber shortens and lengthens, thereby imposing a restraint on movement by its hydraulic action.

A good way to see if your shock absorbers are functioning correctly is to push one corner of the car until it is moving up and down for almost the full suspension travel, then release it and watch its recovery. If the car bounces slightly about one more time and then comes to a rest, the shock is alright. If the car continues to bounce excessively, the shocks will probably require replacement.

MacPherson Struts
REMOVAL AND INSTALLATION

The struts are precious parts and retain the springs under tremendous pressure even when removed from the car. For these reasons, several expensive special tools and substantial specialized knowledge are required to safely and effectively work on these parts. We recommend that if spring or shock absorber repair work is required, you remove the strut or struts involved and take them to

142　SUSPENSION AND STEERING

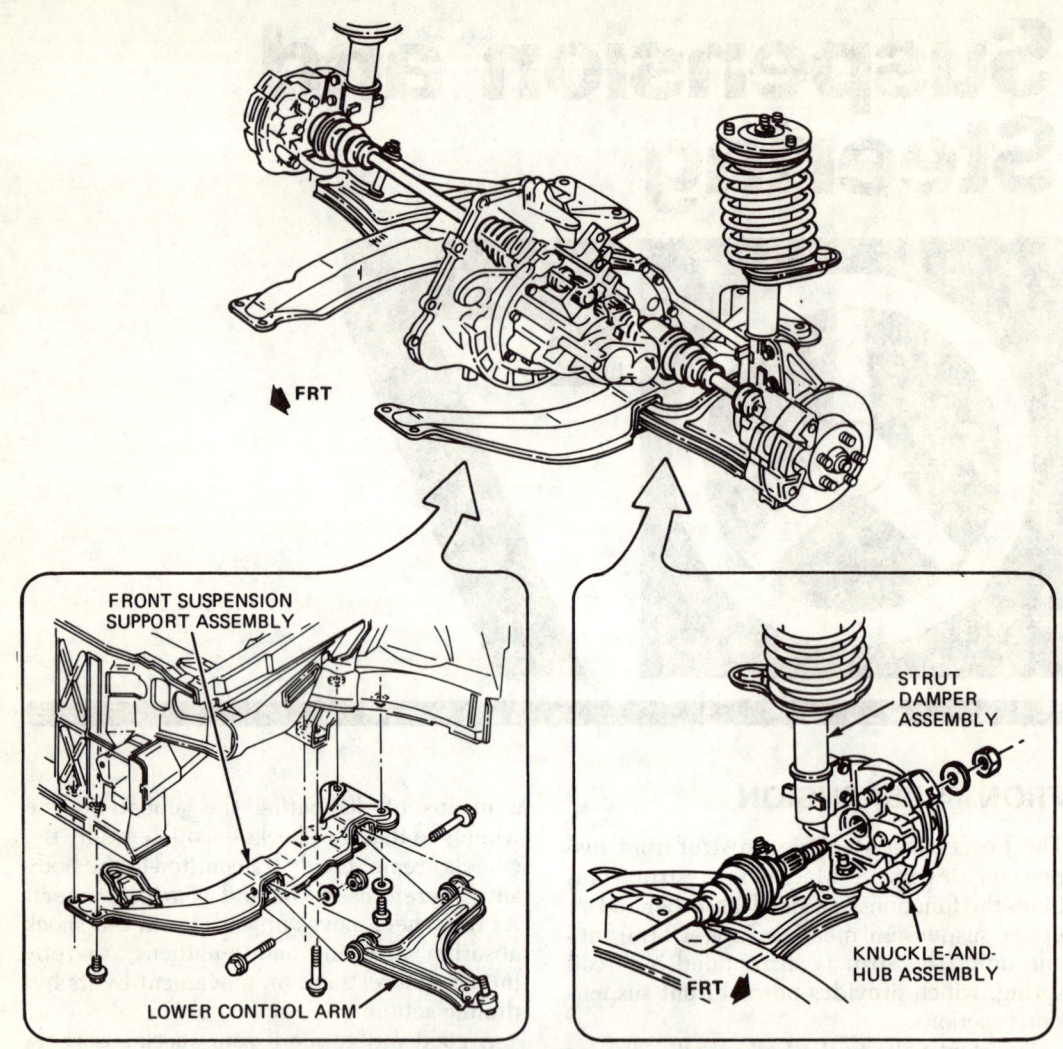

The J-cars use MacPherson strut front suspension

a repair facility which is fully equipped and familiar with the car.

1. Working under the hood, pry off the shock cover and then unscrew the upper strut-to-body nuts.
2. Loosen the wheel nuts, raise and support the car and then remove the wheel and tire.
3. Install a drive axle protective cover (J28712).
4. Use a two-armed puller and press the tie rod out of the strut bracket.
5. Remove both strut-to-steering knuckle bolts and carefully lift out the strut.
6. Installation is in the reverse order of removal. Be sure that the flat sides of the strut-to-knuckle bolt heads are horizontal (see illustration).

STRUT MODIFICATION

This modification is made only if a camber adjustment is anticipated.

1. Place the strut in a vise. This step is not absolutely necessary; filing can be accomplished by disconnecting the strut from the steering knuckle.
2. File the holes in the outer flanges so as to enlarge the bottom holes until they match the slots already in the inner flanges.
3. Camber adjustment procedures are detailed later in this chapter.

Coil Springs

REMOVAL AND INSTALLATION

WARNING: *The coil springs are retained under considerable pressure. They can ex-*

SUSPENSION AND STEERING   143

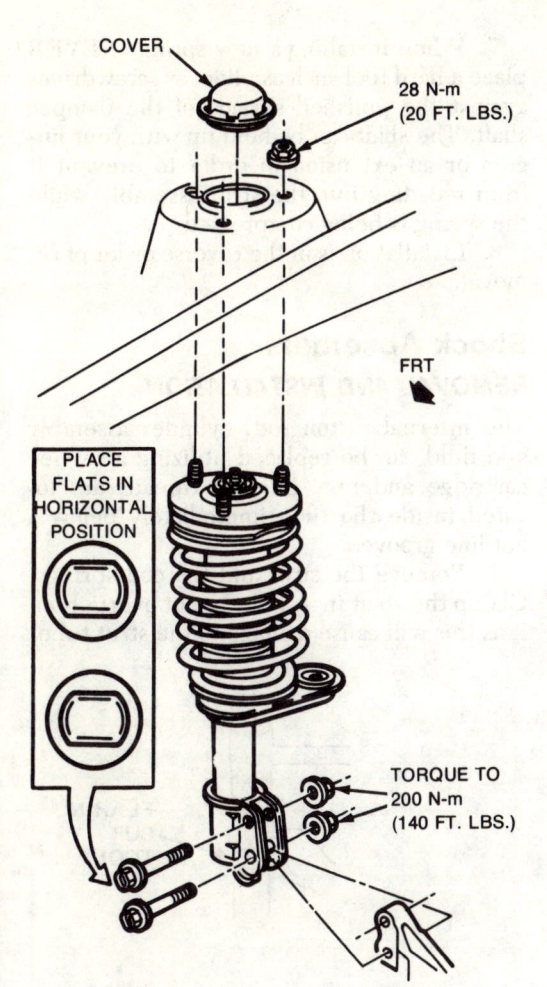

Strut assembly removal and installation details

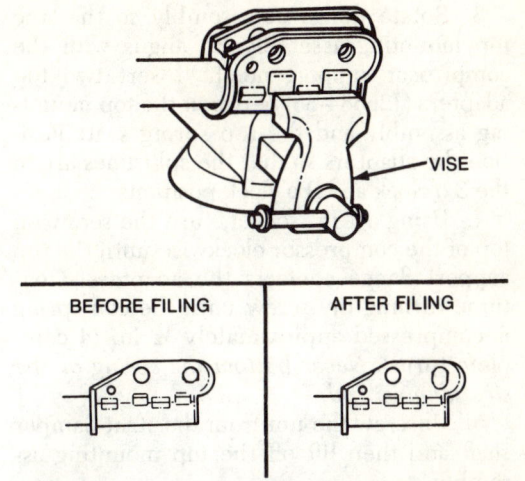

Modifying the strut mounting holes for camber adjustment

ert enough force to cause serious injury. Exercise extreme caution when disassembling the strut for coil spring removal.

This procedure requires the use of a spring compressor and several other special tools. It cannot be performed without them. If you do not have access to these tools, DO NOT attempt to disassemble the strut.

1. Remove the strut assembly.
2. Clamp the spring compressor (J26584) in a vise. Position the strut assembly in the bottom adapter of the compresser and install the special tool J26584-86 (see illustration). Be sure that the adapter captures the strut and that the locating pins are engaged.

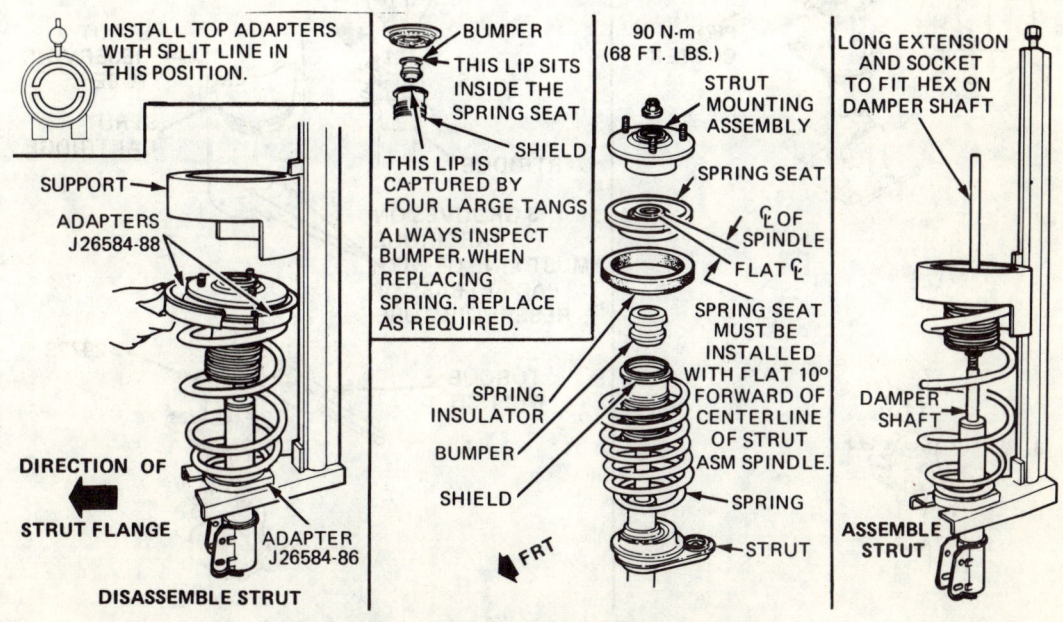

Coil spring removal and installation details

144 SUSPENSION AND STEERING

3. Rotate the strut assembly so that the top mounting assembly lip aligns with the compressor support notch. Insert two top adapters (J26584-88) between the top mounting assembly and the top spring seat. Position the adapters so that the split lines are in the 3 o'clock and 9 o'clock positions.

4. Using a 1 in. socket, turn the screw on top of the compressor clockwise until the top support flange contacts the adapters. Continue turning the screw until the coil spring is compressed approximately ½ in. (4 complete turns). *Never bottom the spring or the strut damper rod.*

5. Unscrew the nut from the strut damper shaft and then lift off the top mounting assembly.

6. Turn the compressor adjusting screw counterclockwise until the spring tension has been relieved. Remove the adapters and then remove the coil spring.

7. When installing a new spring, NEVER place a hard tool such as pliers or screwdriver against the polished surface of the damper shaft. The shaft can be held up with your fingers or an extension in order to prevent it from receding into the strut assembly while the spring is being compressed.

8. Installation is in the reverse order of removal.

Shock Absorbers
REMOVAL AND INSTALLATION

The internal piston rod, cylinder assembly and fluid can be replaced utilizing a service cartridge and nut. Internal threads are located inside the tube immediately below a cut line groove.

1. Remove the strut and the coil springs. Clamp the strut in a vise. Do not overtighten it as this will cause damage to the strut tube.

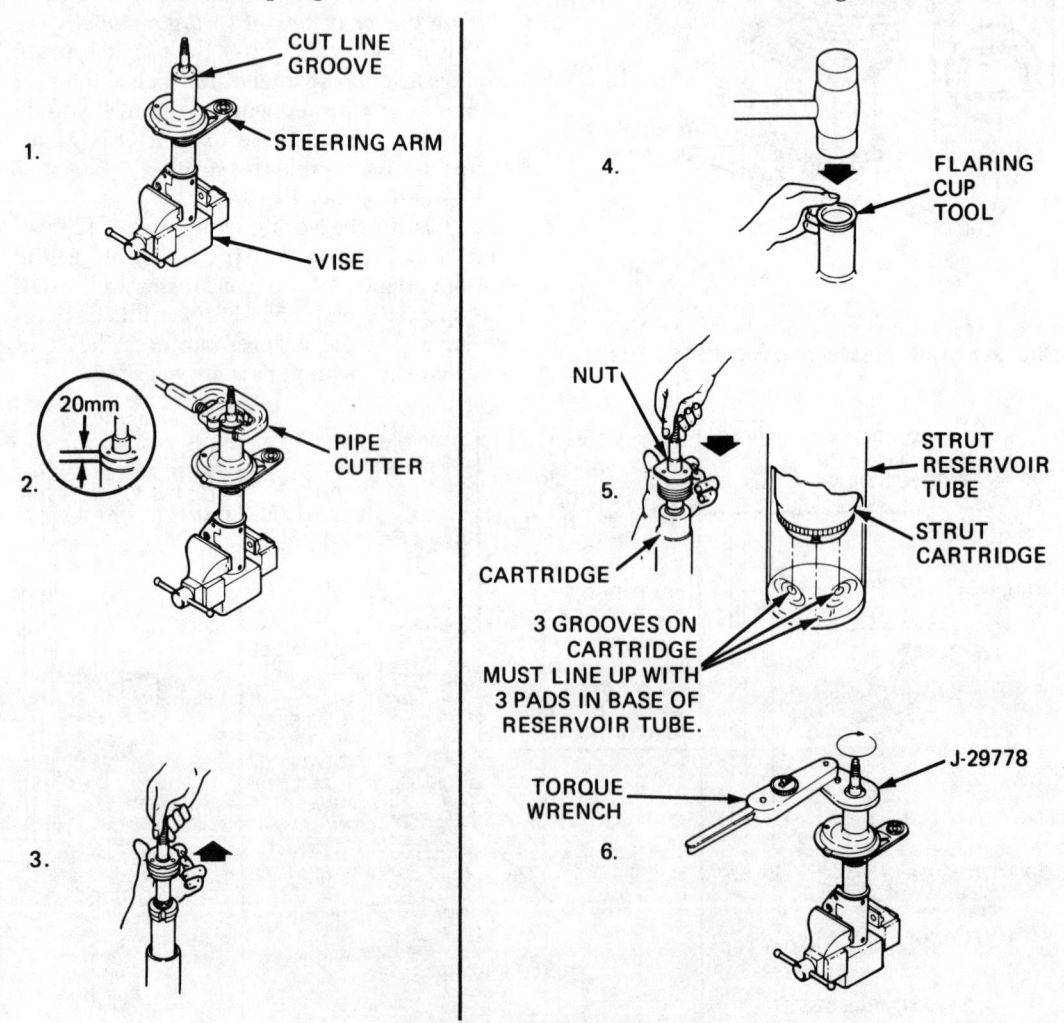

Replacing the strut cartridge

SUSPENSION AND STEERING 145

2. Locate the cut line groove just below the top edge of the strut tube. It is imperative that the groove be accurately located as any mislocation will cause inner thread damage. Using pipe cutters, cut around the groove until the tube is completely cut through.

3. Remove and discard the end cap, the cylinder and the piston rod assembly. Remove the strut assembly from the vise and pour out the old fluid.

4. Reclamp the strut in the vise. A flaring cup tool is included in the replacement cartridge kit to flare and deburr the edge that was cut on the strut tube. Place the flaring cup on the open edge of the tube and strike it with a mallet until its flat outer surface rests on the top edge of the tube. Remove the cup and discard it.

5. Try the new nut to make sure that it threads properly. If not, use the flaring cup again until it does.

6. Place the new strut cartridge into the tube. Turn the cartridge until it settles into the indentations at the base of the tube. Place the nut over the cartridge.

7. Tighten the nut to 140–170 ft. lbs. (190–230 Nm). Pull the piston rod up and down to check for proper operation.

8. Installation of the remaining components is in the reverse order of removal.

Ball Joints
INSPECTION

1. Raise and support the front of the car and let the suspension hang free.

2. Grasp the wheel at the top and the bottom and shake it in an "in-and-out" motion. Check for any horizontal movement of the

USING 1/8" DRILL, DRILL A PILOT HOLE COMPLETELY THROUGH THE RIVET.

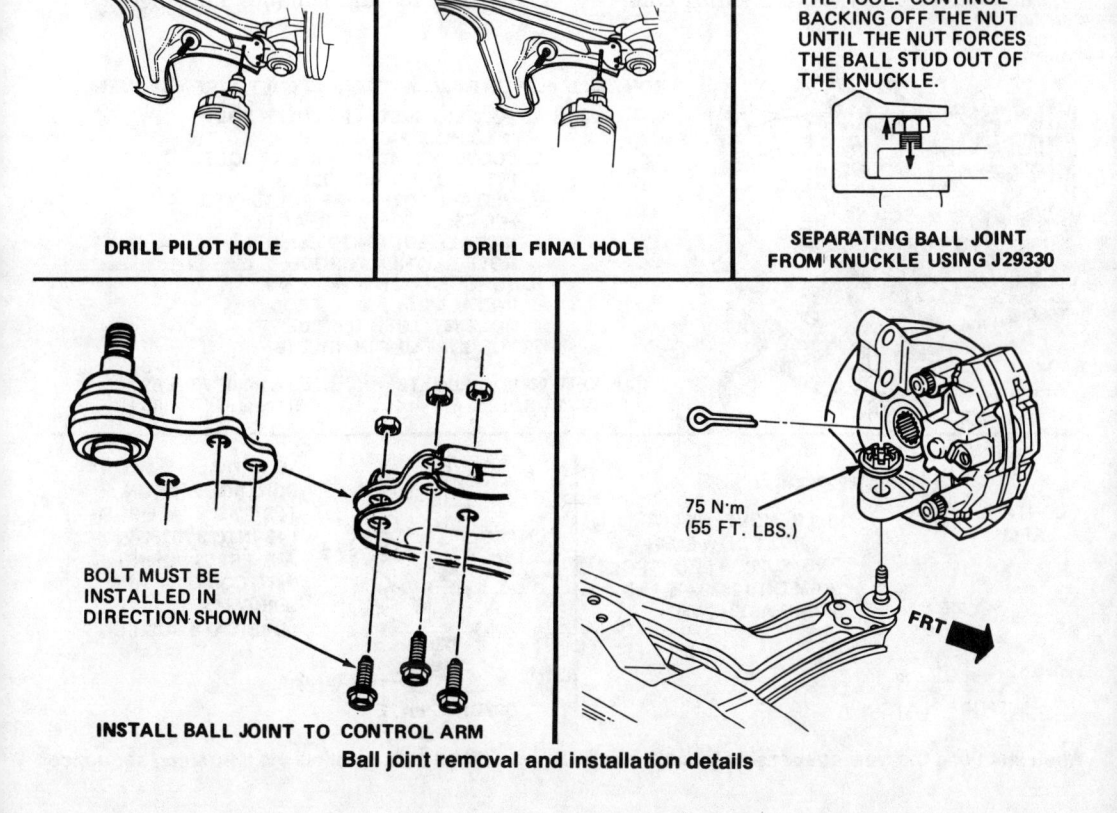

DRILL PILOT HOLE

USING A 1/2" OR 13mm DRILL, DRILL COMPLETELY THROUGH THE RIVET. REMOVE BALL JOINT. DO NOT USE EXCESSIVE FORCE TO REMOVE BALL JOINT.

DRILL FINAL HOLE

PLACE J 29330 INTO POSITION AS SHOWN. LOOSEN NUT AND BACK OFF UNTIL...

J29330

KNUCKLE

... THE NUT CONTACTS THE TOOL. CONTINUE BACKING OFF THE NUT UNTIL THE NUT FORCES THE BALL STUD OUT OF THE KNUCKLE.

SEPARATING BALL JOINT FROM KNUCKLE USING J29330

BOLT MUST BE INSTALLED IN DIRECTION SHOWN

INSTALL BALL JOINT TO CONTROL ARM

75 N·m (55 FT. LBS.)

FRT

Ball joint removal and installation details

146 SUSPENSION AND STEERING

steering knuckle relative to the lower control arm. Replace the ball joint if such movement is noted.

3. If the ball stud is disconnected from the steering knuckle and any looseness is detected, or if the ball stud can be twisted in its socket using finger pressure, replace the ball joint.

REMOVAL AND INSTALLATION

Only one ball joint is used in each lower arm. The MacPherson strut design does not use an upper ball joint.

1. Loosen the wheel nuts, raise the car, and remove the wheel.
2. Use a 1/8 in. drill bit to drill a hole through the center of each of the three ball joint rivets.
3. Use a 1/2 in. drill bit to drill completely through the rivet.
4. Use a hammer and punch to remove the rivets. Drive them out from the bottom.
5. Use the special tool J29330 or a ball joint removal tool to separate the ball joint from the steering knuckle (see illustration). Don't forget to remove the cotter pin.
6. Disconnect the stabilizer bar from the lower control arm. Remove the ball joint.
7. Install the new ball joint into the control arm with the three bolts supplied as shown. Installation of the remaining components is in the reverse order of removal. Use a new cotter pin when installing the castellated nut on the ball joint. Check the toe setting and adjust as necessary.

Control Arm

REMOVAL AND INSTALLATION

1. Raise and support the front of the car. Remove the wheel.
2. Disconnect the stabilizer bar from the control arm and/or support.
3. Separate the ball joint from the steering knuckle as previously detailed.
4. Remove the two control arm-to-support bolts and remove the control arm.
5. If control arm support bar removal is necessary, unscrew the six mounting bolts and remove the support.
6. Installation is in the reverse order of removal. Tighten the control arm support rail bolts in the sequence shown. Check the toe and adjust as necessary.

Wheel Bearings

The front wheel bearings are sealed, non-adjustable units which require no periodic attention. They are bolted to the steering knuckle by means of an integral flange.

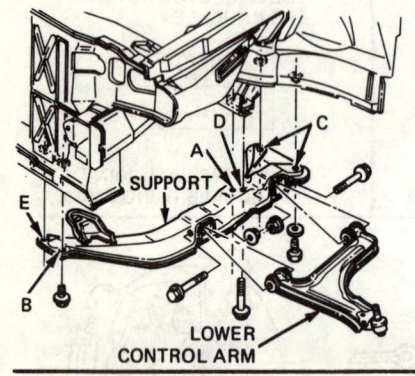

FRONT SUSP SUPPORT ASM ATTACHING BOLT/SCREW SEQUENCE
1. LOOSELY INSTALL CENTER BOLT INTO HOLE (A).
2. LOOSELY INSTALL TIE BAR BOLT INTO OUTBOARD HOLE (B).
3. INSTALL BOTH REAR BOLTS INTO HOLES (C) TORQUE REAR BOLTS.
4. INSTALL BOLT INTO CENTER HOLE(D), THEN TORQUE.
5. TORQUE BOLT IN HOLE (A).
6. INSTALL BOLT INTO FRONT HOLE (E), THEN TORQUE.
7. TORQUE BOLT IN HOLE (B).

SUPPORT-TO-BODY BOLTS . . . . 90 N·m (63 FT. LBS.)
LCA PIVOT BOLTS . . . . 95 N·m (67 FT. LBS.)

SUPPORT
LOWER CONTROL ARM

CONTROL ARM — J 29792-1
J 29797-2
SUPPORT PLATE

TO REMOVE, INSERT J 29792-1 INTO BUSHING, SUPPORT CONTROL ARM ON J 29792-2, AND PRESS AS SHOWN.

CONTROL ARM — J 29792-2
J 29792-3
SUPPORT PLATE

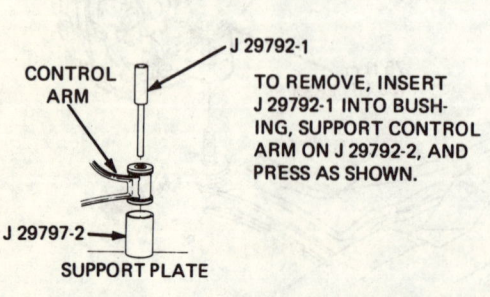

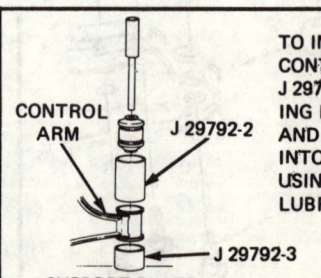

TO INSTALL, SUPPORT CONTROL ARM ON J 29792-3, PLACE BUSHING INTO J 29792-2, AND PRESS BUSING INTO CONTROL ARM USING J 29792-1. LUBRICATE BUSHING.

When installing the front suspension (control arm) support rail, be sure to follow the tightening sequence

SUSPENSION AND STEERING 147

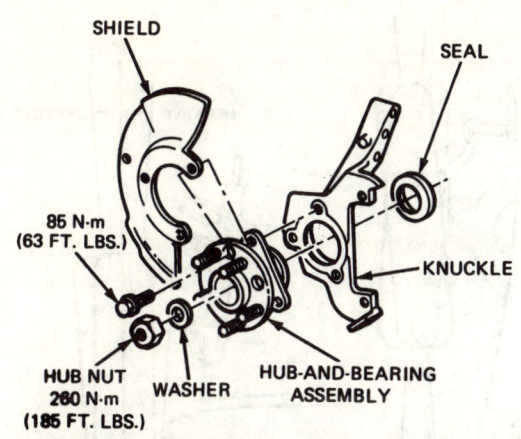

Exploded view of the hub and bearing attachment to the steering knuckle

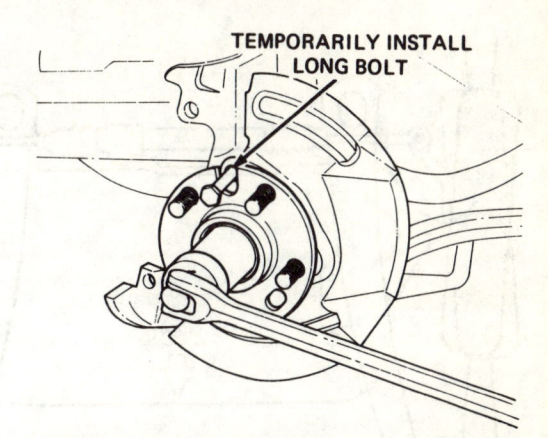

Insert a bolt into the rotor when installing the hub nut

REPLACEMENT

You will need a special tool to pull the bearing free of the halfshaft, G.M. tool no. J-28733 or the equivalent. You should also use a halfshaft boot protector, G.M. tool no. J-28712 or the equivalent to protect the parts from damage.

1. Remove the wheel cover, loosen the hub nut, and raise and support the car. Remove the front wheel.
2. Install the boot cover, G.M. part no. J-28712 or the equivalent.
3. Remove and discard the hub nut. Be sure to use a new one on assembly, not the old one.
4. Remove the brake caliper and rotor:
  a. Remove the allen head caliper mounting bolts;
  b. Remove the caliper from the knuckle and suspend from a length of wire. Do not allow the caliper to hang from the brake hose. Pull the rotor from the knuckle.
5. Remove the three hub and bearing at-

Use a seal driver when installing the new seal into the knuckle

taching bolts. If the old bearing is to be reused, match mark the bolts and holes for installation. The brake rotor splash shield will have to come off, too.

6. Attach a puller, G.M. part no. J-28733 or the equivalent, and remove the bearing. If corrosion is present, make sure the bearing is loose in the knuckle before using the puller.
7. Clean the mating surfaces of all dirt and corrosion. Check the knuckle bore and knuckle seal for damage. If a new bearing is to be installed, remove the old knuckle seal and install a new one. Grease the lips of the new seal before installation; install with a seal driver made for the purpose, G.M. tool no. J-28671 or the equivalent.
8. Push the bearing onto the halfshaft. Install a new washer and hub nut.
9. Tighten the new hub nut on the halfshaft until the bearing is seated. If the rotor and hub start to rotate as the hub nut is tightened, insert a long bolt through the cut-out in the hub assembly to prevent rotation. Do not apply full torque to the hub nut at this time—just seat the bearing.
10. Install the brake shield and the bearing retaining bolts. Tighten the bolts evenly to 63 ft. lbs. (85 Nm).
11. Install the caliper and rotor. Be sure that the caliper hose isn't twisted. Install the caliper bolts and tighten to 21–35 ft. lbs. (28–47 Nm.).
12. Install the wheel. Lower the car. Tighten the hub nut to 185 ft. lbs. (260 Nm.).

Front End Alignment

The toe setting is the only adjustment normally required on a J-car. However, in spe-

148 SUSPENSION AND STEERING

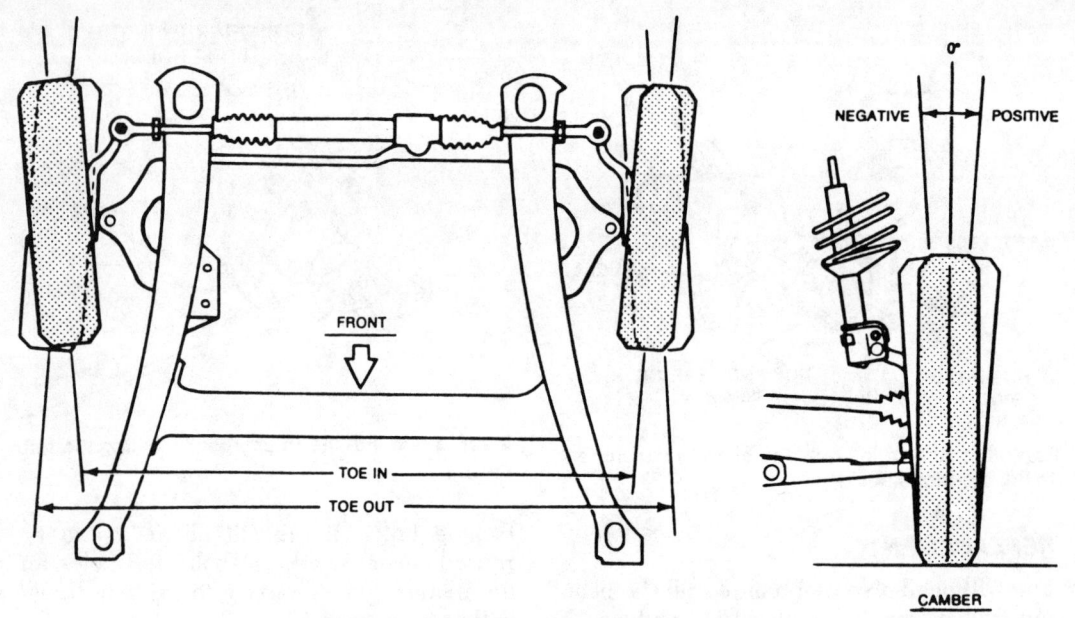

Wheel alignment: toe (left) and camber (right)

cial circumstances, such as damage due to road hazard, collision, etc., camber may be adjusted after modifying the strut as detailed earlier in this chapter. Caster is not adjustable.

CAMBER

Camber is the inward or outward tilt from the vertical, measured in degrees, of the front wheels at the top. An onward tilt gives the wheel positive camber; an inward tilt is called negative camber. Proper camber is critical to assure even tire wear.

1. Modify the suspension strut as detailed earlier.
2. Loosen the strut-to-knuckle bolts just enough to allow movement between the strut and the knuckle.
3. Grasp the top of the tire and move it in or out until the proper specification is obtained.
4. Tighten both bolts just enough to hold the adjustment. Remove the wheels and tighten the bolts to the proper specifications.
5. Replace the wheels.

TOE

Toe is the amount, measured in a fraction of a millimeter, that the wheels are closer together at one end than the other. Toe-in means that the front wheels are closer together at the front than the rear; toe-out means the rear of the front wheels are closer together than the front. J-cars are designed to have a slight amount of toe-out.

Toe is adjusted by turning the tie rods. It must be checked after camber has been adjusted, but it can be adjusted without disturbing the camber setting. You can make this adjustment without special equipment if you make very careful measurements. The wheels must be straight ahead.

1. Toe can be determined by measuring the distance between the centers of the tire treads, at the front of the tire and at the rear. If the tread pattern makes this impossible, you can measure between the edges of the wheel rims, but make sure to move the car forward and measure in a couple of places to

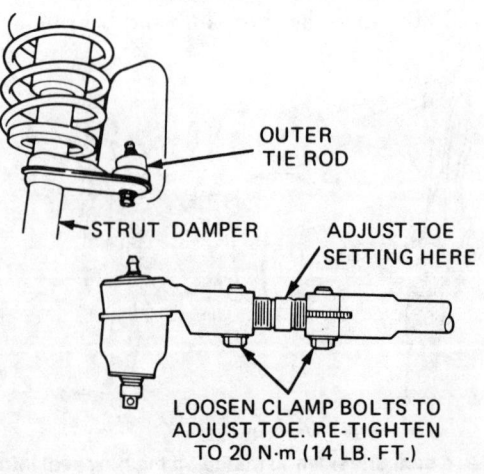

Toe adjustment is made at the tie rods

SUSPENSION AND STEERING 149

Wheel Alignment Specifications

Camber (positive)		Toe	
Range (degrees)	Preferred (degrees)	Range (degrees)	Preferred (degrees)
.10–1.10	.60	0–.250 ①	.125 ①

① Toe-out

avoid errors caused by bent rims or wheel runout.

2. If the measurement is not within specifications, loosen the nuts at the steering knuckle end of the tie rod, and remove the tie rod boot clamps. Rotate the tie rods to align the toe to specifications. Rotate the tie rods evenly, or the steering wheel will be crooked when you're done.

3. When the adjustment is correct, tighten the nuts to 14 ft. lbs. (20 Nm.). Adjust the boots and tighten the clamps.

REAR SUSPENSION

J-cars have a semi-independent rear suspension system which consists of an axle with trailing arms and a twisting cross beam, two coil springs and two shock absorbers. The axle assembly attaches to the body through a rubber bushing located at the front of each control arm. A stabilizer bar is available as an option.

Two coil springs are used, each being retained between a seat in the underbody and one on the control arm. A rubber cushion is used to isolate the coil spring upper end from the underbody seat, while the lower end sits on a combination bumper and spring insulator.

The double acting shock absorbers are filled with a calibrated amount of fluid and sealed during production. They are non-adjustable, non-refillable and cannot be disassembled.

A single unit hub and bearing assembly is bolted to both ends of the rear axle assembly; it is a sealed unit and must be replaced as one if found to be defective.

Shock Absorbers

TESTING

Visually inspect the shock absorber. If there is evidence of leakage and the shock absorber is covered with oil, the shock is defective and should be replaced.

If there is no sign of excessive leakage (a small amount of weeping is normal) bounce

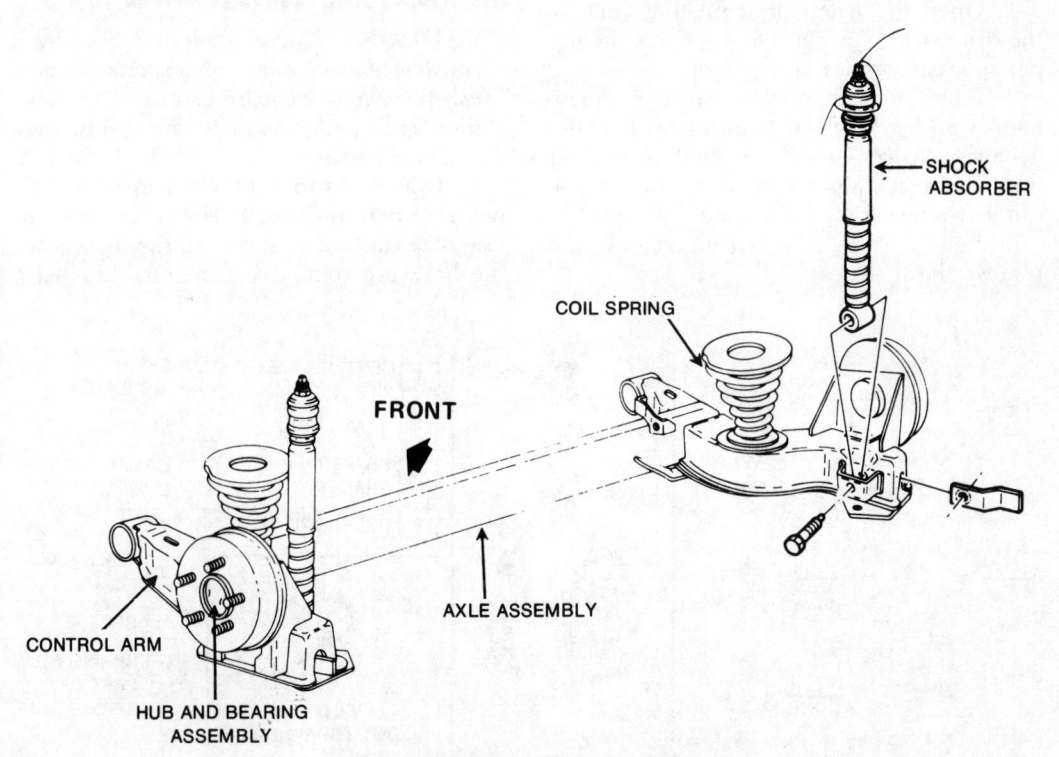

Rear axle and suspension components

SUSPENSION AND STEERING

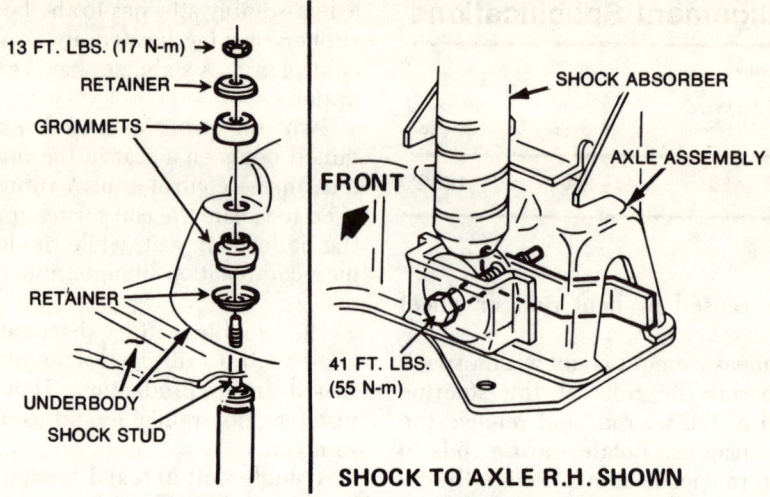

Shock absorber mounting details; top (left) and bottom (right)

the car at one corner by pressing down on the fender or bumper and releasing. When you have the car bouncing as much as you can, release the fender or bumper. The car should stop bouncing after the first rebound. If the bouncing continues past the center point of the bounce more than once, the shock absorbers are worn and should be replaced.

REMOVAL AND INSTALLATION

1. Open the hatch or trunk lid, remove the trim cover if present, and remove the upper shock absorber nut.
2. Raise and support the car at a convenient working height if you desire. It is not necessary to remove the weight of the car from the shock absorbers, however, so you can leave the car on the ground if you prefer.
3. Remove the lower attaching bolt and remove the shock.

4. If new shock absorbers are being installed, repeatedly compress them while inverted and extend them in their normal upright position. This will purge them of air.
5. Install the shocks in the reverse order of removal. Tighten the lower mount nut and bolt to 55 ft. lbs. (41 Nm.), the upper to 13 ft. lbs. (17 Nm.).

Springs
REMOVAL AND INSTALLATION

CAUTION: *The coil springs are under a considerable amount of tension. Be very careful when removing or installing them; they can exert enough force to cause very serious injuries.*

1. Raise and support the car on a hoist. Do not use a twin-post hoist. The swing arc of the axle may cause it to slip from the hoist when the bolts are removed. If a suitable hoist is

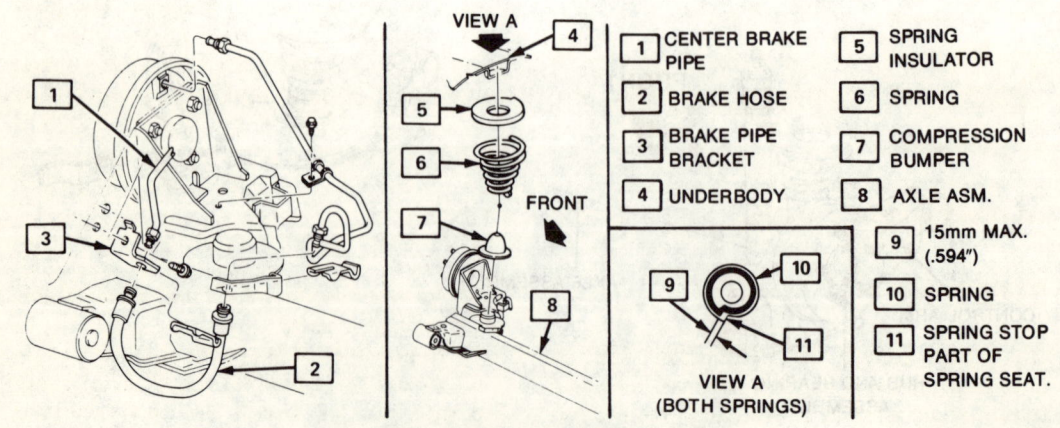

Coil spring removal and installation details

SUSPENSION AND STEERING

not available, raise and support the car on jackstands, and use a jack under the axle.

2. Support the axle with a jack that can be raised and lowered.

3. Remove the brake hose attaching brackets (right and left), allowing the hoses to hang freely. Do not disconnect the hoses.

4. Remove both shock absorber lower attaching bolts from the axle.

5. Lower the axle. Remove the coil spring and insulator.

6. To install, position the spring and insulator on the axle. The leg on the upper coil of the spring must be parallel to the axle, facing the lefthand side of the car.

7. Install the shock absorber bolts. Tighten to 41 ft. lbs. (55 Nm.). Install the brake line brackets. Tighten to 8 ft. lbs. (11 Nm.).

Rear Hub and Bearing

REMOVAL AND INSTALLATION

1. Loosen the wheel lug nuts. Raise and support the car and remove the wheel.

2. Remove the brake drum. Removal procedures are covered in the next chapter, if needed.

NOTE: *Do not hammer on the brake drum to remove; damage to the bearing will result.*

3. Remove the four hub and bearing retaining bolts and remove the assembly from the axle. The top rear attaching bolt will not clear the brake shoe when removing the hub and bearing assembly. Partially remove the hub and bearing assembly prior to removing this bolt.

4. Installation is the reverse. Hub and bearing bolt torque is 39 ft. lbs. (52 Nm.).

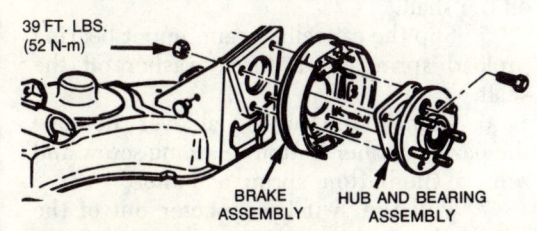

Rear hub and bearing assembly

STEERING

All J-cars except the Cimarron use an aluminum-housed Saginaw manual rack and pinion steering gear as standard equipment. The pinion is supported by and turns in a sealed ball bearing at the top and a pressed-in roller bearing at the bottom. The rack moves in bushings pressed into each end of the rack housing.

Wear compensation occurs through the action of an adjuster spring which forces the rack against the pinion teeth. This adjuster eliminates the need for periodic pinion preload adjustments. Preload is adjustable only at overhaul.

The inner tie rod assemblies are bolted to the front of the rack. A special bushing is used, allowing both rocking and rotating motion of the tie rods.

Any service other than replacement of the outer tie rods or the boots requires removal of the unit from the car.

The power rack and pinion steering gear is optional on the Cavalier, J-2000, Skyhawk and Starfire while it is standard equipment on the Cavalier CL and the Cimarron; it is an integral unit and shares most features with the manual gear. A rotary control valve directs the hydraulic fluid to either side of the rack piston. The integral rack piston is attached to the rack and converts the hydraulic pressure into left or right linear motion. A vane-type constant displacement pump with integral reservoir provides hydraulic pressure. No in-car adjustments are necessary or possible on the system, except for periodic belt tension checks and adjustments for the pump. See Chapter One for belt tension adjustments.

Steering Wheel

REMOVAL AND INSTALLATION

Standard Wheel

1. Disconnect the negative cable at the battery.

2. Pull the pad from the wheel. The horn lead is attached to the pad at one end; the other end of the pad has a wire with a spade connector. The horn lead is disconnected by pushing and turning; the spade connector is simply unplugged.

3. Remove the retainer under the pad (if so equipped).

4. Remove the steering shaft nut.

5. There should be alignment marks already present on the wheel and shaft. If not, matchmark the parts.

6. Remove the wheel with a puller.

7. Install the wheel on the shaft, aligning the matchmarks. Install the shaft nut and tighten to 30 ft. lbs. (40 Nm.).

SUSPENSION AND STEERING

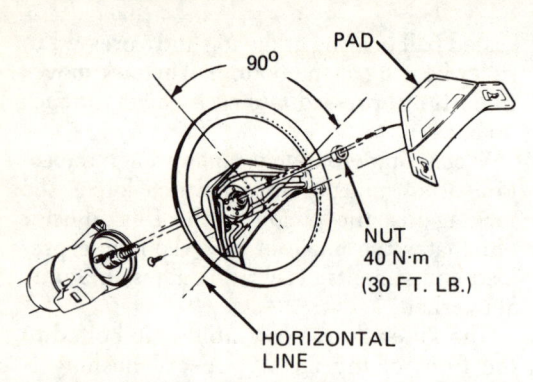

Standard steering wheel removal

8. Install the retainer.
9. Plug in the spade connector, and push and turn the horn lead to connect. Install the pad. Connect the negative battery cable.

Sport Wheel

1. Disconnect the negative cable at the battery.
2. Pry the center cap from the wheel.
3. Remove the retainer (if so equipped).
4. Remove the shaft nut.
5. If the wheel and shaft do not have factory-installed alignment marks, matchmark the parts before removal of the wheel.
6. Install a puller and remove the wheel. A horn spring, eyelet and insulator are underneath; don't lose the parts.
7. Install the spring, eyelet and insulator into the tower on the column.
8. Align the matchmarks and install the wheel onto the shaft. Install the retaining nut and tighten to 30 ft. lbs. (40 Nm).
9. Install the retainer. Install the center cap. Connect the negative battery cable.

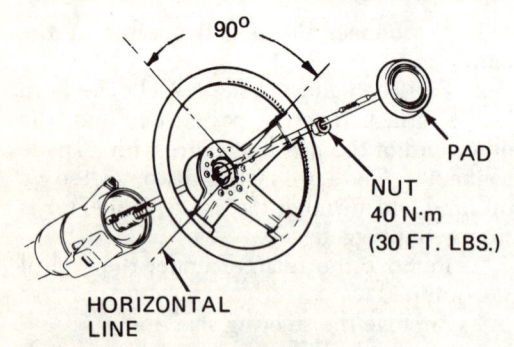

Sport steering wheel removal

Turn Signal Switch

REMOVAL AND INSTALLATION

1. Remove the steering wheel. Remove the trim cover.

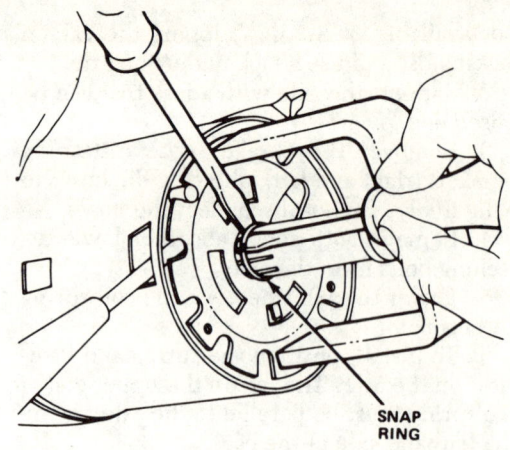

Depress the lock plate and remove the snap ring

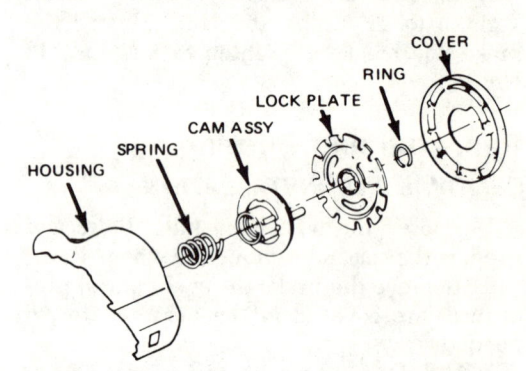

Remove these parts to get at the turn signal switch

2. Pry the cover from the steering column.
3. Position a U-shaped lockplate compressing tool on the end of the steering shaft and compress the lock plate by turning the shaft nut clockwise. Pry the wire snap-ring out of the shaft groove.
4. Remove the tool and lift the lockplate off the shaft.
5. Slip the cancelling cam, upper bearing preload spring, and thrust washer off the shaft.
6. Remove the turn signal lever. Remove the hazard flasher button retaining screw and remove the button, spring and knob.
7. Pull the switch connector out of the mast jacket and tape the upper part to facilitate switch removal. Attach a long piece of wire to the turn signal switch connector. When installing the turn signal switch, feed this wire through the column first, and then use this wire to pull the switch connector into position. On tilt wheels, place the turn signal and shifter housing in low position and remove the harness cover.

SUSPENSION AND STEERING 153

8. Remove the three switch mounting screws. Remove the switch by pulling it straight up while guiding the wiring harness cover through the column.

9. Install the replacement switch by working the connector and cover down through the housing and under the bracket. On tilt models, the connector is worked down through the housing, under the bracket, and then the cover is installed on the harness.

10. Install the switch mounting screws and the connector on the mast jacket bracket. Install the column-to-dash trim plate.

11. Install the flasher knob and the turn signal lever.

12. With the turn signal lever in neutral and the flasher knob out, slide the thrust washer, upper bearing preload spring, and cancelling cam onto the shaft.

13. Position the lock plate on the shaft and press it down until a new snap-ring can be inserted in the shaft groove. Always use a new snap-ring when assembling.

14. Install the cover and the steering wheel.

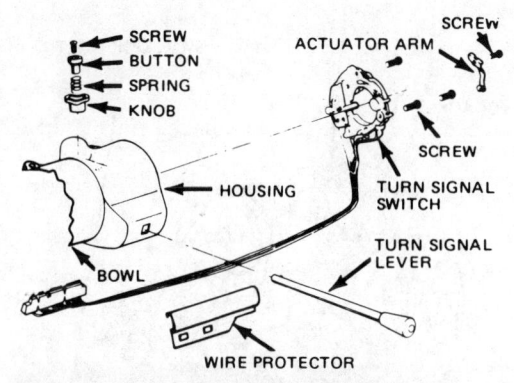

Turn signal switch installation details

Ignition Switch

REMOVAL AND INSTALLATION

The switch is located inside the channel section of the brake pedal support and is completely inaccessible without first lowering the steering column. The switch is actuated by a rod and rack assembly. A gear on the end of the lock cylinder engages the toothed upper end of the rod.

1. Lower the steering column; be sure to properly support it.

2. Put the switch in the "Off-Unlocked" position. With the cylinder removed, the rod is in "Off-Unlocked" position when it is in the next to the uppermost detent.

3. Remove the two switch screws and remove the switch assembly.

4. Before installing, place the new switch in "Off-Unlocked" position and make sure the lock cylinder and actuating rod are in "Off-Unlocked" position (second detent from the top).

5. Install the activating rod into the switch and assemble the switch on the column. Tighten the mounting screws. Use only the specified screws, since overlength screws could impair the collapsibility of the column.

6. Reinstall the steering column.

Ignition Lock Cylinder

REMOVAL AND INSTALLATION

1. Remove the steering wheel.
2. Turn the lock to the Run position.
3. Remove the lock plate, turn signal switch or combination switch, and the key warning buzzer switch. The warning buzzer switch can be fished out with a bent paper clip.

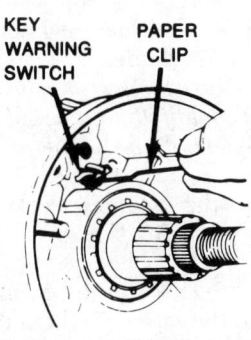

Remove the key warning buzzer switch with a paper clip

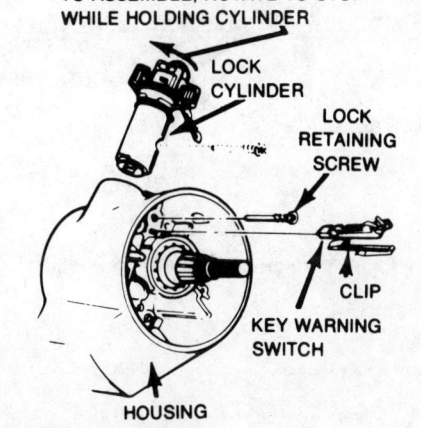

Lock cylinder installation

154 SUSPENSION AND STEERING

4. Remove the lock cylinder retaining screw and lock cylinder.
CAUTION: *If the screw is dropped on removal, it could fall into the column, requiring complete disassembly to retrieve the screw.*
5. Rotate the cylinder clockwise to align the cylinder key with the keyway in the housing.
6. Push the lock all the way in.
7. Install the screw. Tighten to 15 in. lbs.
8. The rest of installation is the reverse of removal. Turn the lock to Run to install the key warning buzzer switch, which is simply pushed down into place.

Tie Rod Ends
REMOVAL AND INSTALLATION
1. Loosen both pinch bolts at the outer tie-rod.
2. Remove the tie-rod end from the strut assembly using a suitable removal tool.
3. Unscrew the outer tie-rod end from the tie-rod adjuster, counting the number of revolutions required before they are disconnected.
4. Install the new tie-rod end, screwing it on the same number of revolutions as counted in Step 3. When the tie-rod end is installed, the tie-rod adjuster must be centered between the tie-rod and the tie-rod end, with an equal number of threads exposed on both sides of the adjuster nut. Tighten the pinch bolts to 20 ft. lbs.
5. Install the tie-rod end to the strut assembly and tighten to 50 ft. lbs. If the cotter pin cannot be installed, tighten the nut up to $1/16$ in. further. *Never back off the nut to align the holes for the cotter pin.*
6. Have the front end alignment adjusted.

Power Steering Pump
REMOVAL AND INSTALLATION
1. Disconnect the negative battery cable.
2. Disconnect the vent hole at the carburetor.
3. Loosen the adjusting bolt and pivot bolt on the pump, then remove the pump's drive belt.
4. Remove the three pump-to-bracket bolts and remove the adjusting bolt.
5. Remove the high pressure fitting from the pump.
6. Disconnect the reservoir-to-pump hose from the pump.
7. Remove the pump.
8. Installation is in the reverse order of removal. Adjust the belt tension and bleed the system.

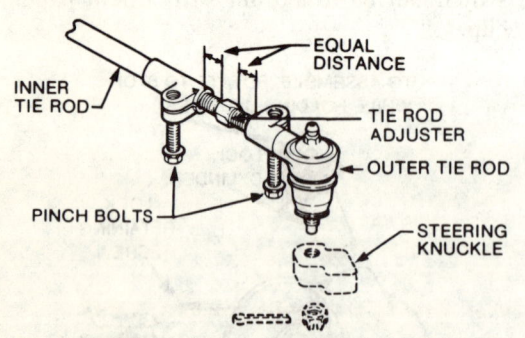

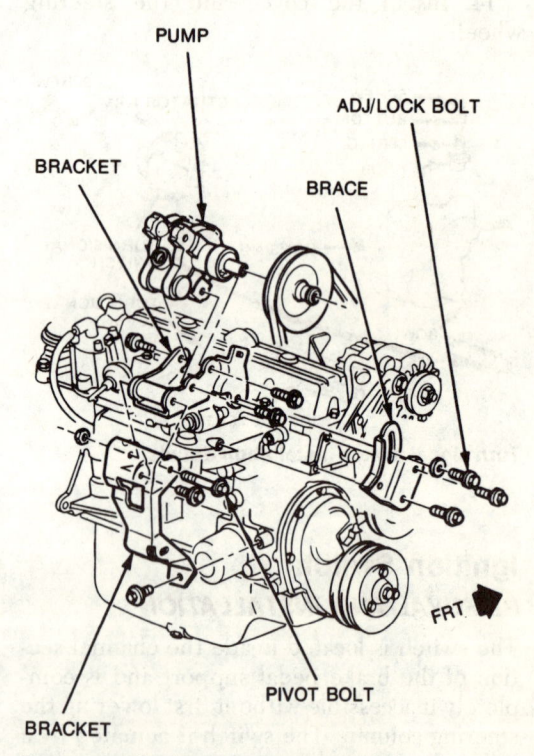

Tie rod end removal and installation details

Power steering pump removal details

SUSPENSION AND STEERING 155

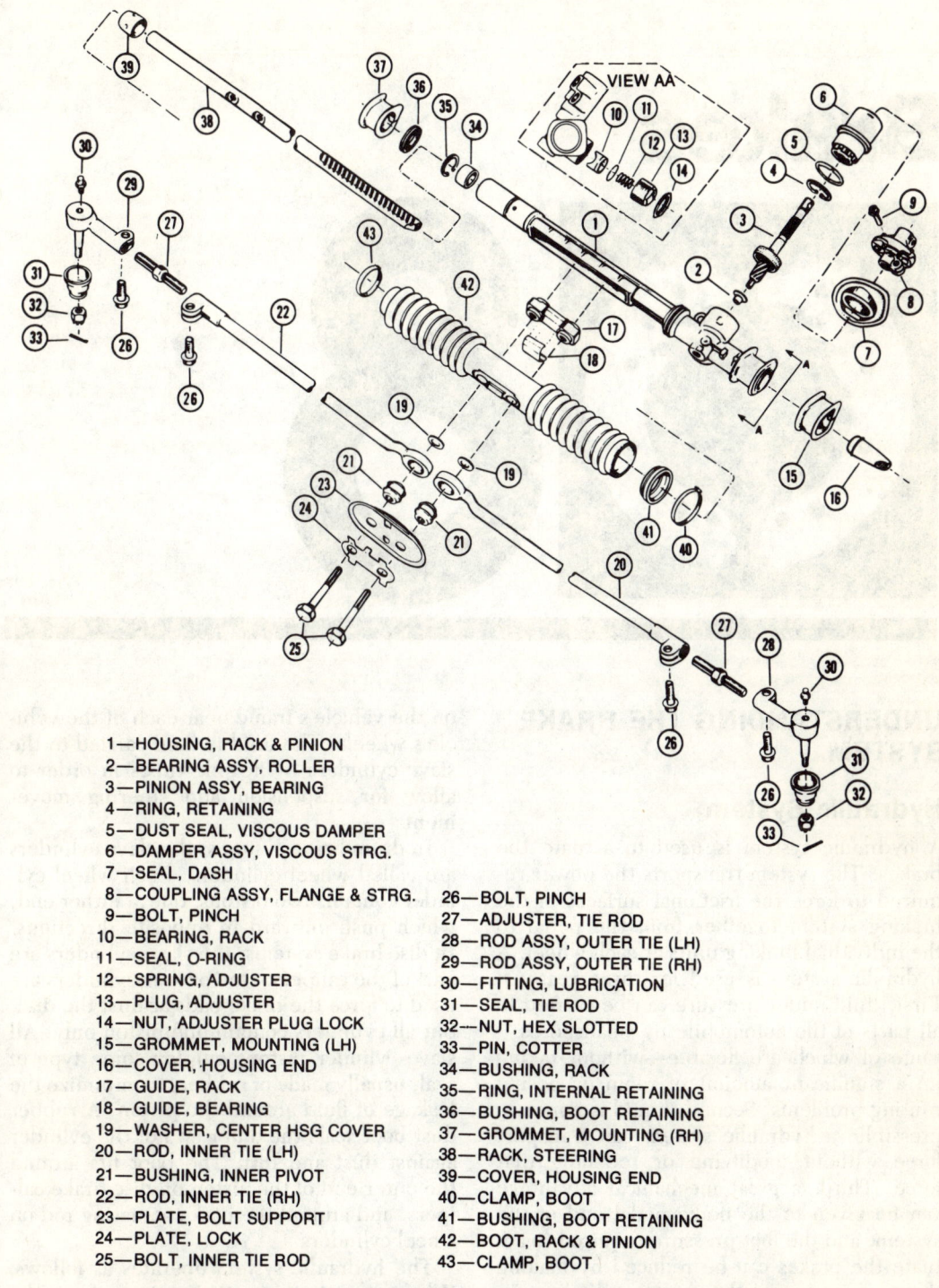

1—HOUSING, RACK & PINION
2—BEARING ASSY, ROLLER
3—PINION ASSY, BEARING
4—RING, RETAINING
5—DUST SEAL, VISCOUS DAMPER
6—DAMPER ASSY, VISCOUS STRG.
7—SEAL, DASH
8—COUPLING ASSY, FLANGE & STRG.
9—BOLT, PINCH
10—BEARING, RACK
11—SEAL, O-RING
12—SPRING, ADJUSTER
13—PLUG, ADJUSTER
14—NUT, ADJUSTER PLUG LOCK
15—GROMMET, MOUNTING (LH)
16—COVER, HOUSING END
17—GUIDE, RACK
18—GUIDE, BEARING
19—WASHER, CENTER HSG COVER
20—ROD, INNER TIE (LH)
21—BUSHING, INNER PIVOT
22—ROD, INNER TIE (RH)
23—PLATE, BOLT SUPPORT
24—PLATE, LOCK
25—BOLT, INNER TIE ROD
26—BOLT, PINCH
27—ADJUSTER, TIE ROD
28—ROD ASSY, OUTER TIE (LH)
29—ROD ASSY, OUTER TIE (RH)
30—FITTING, LUBRICATION
31—SEAL, TIE ROD
32—NUT, HEX SLOTTED
33—PIN, COTTER
34—BUSHING, RACK
35—RING, INTERNAL RETAINING
36—BUSHING, BOOT RETAINING
37—GROMMET, MOUNTING (RH)
38—RACK, STEERING
39—COVER, HOUSING END
40—CLAMP, BOOT
41—BUSHING, BOOT RETAINING
42—BOOT, RACK & PINION
43—CLAMP, BOOT

Exploded view of the manual rack and pinion steering gear (power similiar)

Brakes

UNDERSTANDING THE BRAKE SYSTEM

Hydraulic System

A hydraulic system is used to actuate the brakes. The system transports the power required to force the frictional surfaces of the braking system together from the pedal to the individual braking units at each wheel. A hydraulic system is used for three reasons. First, fluid under pressure can be carried to all parts of the automobile by small hoses—some of which are flexible—without taking up a significant amount of room or posing routing problems. Second, liquid is noncompressible; a hydraulic system can transport force without modifying or reducing that force. Third, a great mechanical advantage can be given to the brake pedal end of the system, and the foot pressure required to actuate the brakes can be reduced by making the surface area of the master cylinder pistons smaller than that of any of the pistons in the wheel cylinders or calipers.

The master cylinder consists of a fluid reservoir and a double cylinder and piston assembly. Double type master cylinders are designed to separate the front and rear braking systems hydraulically in case of a leak.

Steel lines carry the brake fluid to a point on the vehicle's frame near each of the vehicle's wheels. The fluid is then carried to the slave cylinders by flexible tubes in order to allow for suspension and steering movements.

In drum brake systems, the slave cylinders are called wheel cylinders. Each wheel cylinder contains two pistons, one at either end, which push outward in opposite directions. In disc brake systems, the slave cylinders are part of the calipers. One or four cylinders are used to force the brake pads against the disc, but all cylinders contain one piston only. All slave cylinder pistons employ some type of seal, usually made of rubber, to minimize the leakage of fluid around the piston. A rubber dust boot seals the outer end of the cylinder against dust and dirt. The boot fits around the outer end of the piston on disc brake calipers, and around the brake actuating rod on wheel cylinders.

The hydraulic system operates as follows: When at rest, the entire system, from the pistons in the master cylinder to those in the wheel cylinders or calipers, is full of brake fluid. Upon application of the brake pedal, fluid trapped in front of the master cylinder pistons is forced through the lines to the slave cylinders. Here, it forces the pistons outward, in the case of drum brakes, and inward toward the disc, in the case of disc brakes. The motion of the pistons is opposed by return springs mounted outside the cylinders in drum brakes, and by internal springs or spring seals in disc brakes.

Upon release of the brake pedal, a spring located inside the master cylinder immediately returns the master cylinder pistons to the normal position. The pistons contain check valves and the master cylinder has compensating ports drilled in it. These are uncovered as the pistons reach their normal position. The piston check valves allow fluid to flow toward the wheel cylinders or calipers as the pistons withdraw. Then, as the return springs force the brake pads or shoes into the released position, the excess fluid returns to the master cylinder fluid reservoir through the compensating ports. It is during the time the pedal is in the released position that any fluid that has leaked out of the system will be replaced through the compensating ports.

Dual circuit master cylinders employ two pistons, located one behind the other, in the same cylinder. The primary piston is actuated directly by mechanical linkage from the brake pedal. The secondary piston is actuated by fluid trapped between the two pistons. If a leak develops in front of the secondary piston, it moves forward until it bottoms against the front of the master cylinder, and the fluid trapped between the pistons will operate the rear brakes. If the rear brakes develop a leak, the primary piston will move forward until direct contact with the secondary piston takes place, and it will force the secondary piston to actuate the front brakes. In either case, the brake pedal moves farther when the brakes are applied, and less braking power is available.

All dual-circuit systems use a distributor switch to warn the driver when only half of the brake system is operational. This switch is located in a valve body which is mounted on the master cylinder. A hydraulic piston receives pressure from both circuits, each circuit's pressure being applied to one end of the piston. When the pressures are in balance, the piston remains stationary. When one circuit has a leak, however, the greater pressure in that circuit during application of the brakes will push the piston to one side, closing the distributor switch and activating the brake warning light.

In disc brake systems, this valve body also contains a metering valve and, in some cases, a proportioning valve. The metering valve keeps pressure from traveling to the disc brakes on the front wheels until the brake shoes on the rear wheels have contacted the drums, ensuring that the front brakes will never be used alone. The proportioning valve throttles the pressure to the rear brakes so as to avoid rear wheel lock-up during very hard braking.

These valves may be tested by removing the lines to the front and rear brake systems and installing special brake pressure testing gauges. Front and rear system pressures are then compared as the pedal is gradually depressed. Specifications vary with the manufacturer and design of the brake system.

Brake system warning lights may be tested by depressing the brake pedal and holding it while opening one of the wheel cylinder bleeder screws. If this does not cause the light to go on, substitute a new lamp, make continuity checks, and, finally, replace the switch as necessary.

The hydraulic system may be checked for leaks by applying pressure to the pedal gradually and steadily. If the pedal sinks very slowly to the floor, the system has a leak. This is not to be confused with a springy or spongy feel due to the compreession of air within the lines. If the system leaks, there will be a gradual change in the position of the pedal with a constant pressure.

Check for leaks along all lines and at wheel cylinders. If no external leaks are apparent, the problem is inside the master cylinder.

Disc Brakes

Instead of the traditional expanding brakes that press outward against a circular drum, disc brake systems utilize a cast iron disc with brake pads positioned on either side of it. Braking effect is achieved in a manner similar to the way you would squeeze a spinning phonograph record between your fingers. The disc (rotor) is a one-piece casting with cooling fins between the two braking surfaces. This enables air to circulate between the braking surfaces making them less sensitive to heat buildup and more resistant to fade. Dirt and water do not affect braking action since contaminants are thrown off by the centrifugal action of the rotor or scraped off by the pads. Also, the equal clamping action of the two brake pads tends to ensure uniform, straightline stops. All disc brakes are inherently self-adjusting.

Drum Brakes

Drum brakes employ two brake shoes mounted on a stationary backing plate. These shoes are positioned inside a circular cast iron drum which rotates with the wheel assembly. The shoes are held in place by springs; this allows them to slide toward the drums (when they are applied) while keeping the linings and drums in alignment. The shoes are actuated by a wheel cylinder which is mounted at the top of the backing plate. When the brakes are applied, hydraulic pressure forces the wheel cylinder's two actuating links outward. Since these links bear directly against the top of the brake shoes, the tops of the shoes are then forced outward against the inner side of the drum. This action forces the bottoms of the two shoes to contact the brake drum by rotating the entire assembly slightly (known as servo action). When pressure within the wheel cylinder is relaxed, return springs pull the shoes back away from the drum.

The drum brakes are designed to self-adjust during application when the car is moving in reverse. This motion causes both shoes to rotate very slightly with the drum, rocking an adjusting lever, thereby causing rotation of the adjusting screw by means of an actuating lever.

Power Brake Boosters

Power brakes operate just as standard brake systems except in the actuation of the master cylinder pistons. A vacuum diaphragm is located on the front of the master cylinder and assists the driver in applying the brakes, reducing both the effort and travel he must put into moving the brake pedal.

The vacuum diaphragm housing is connected to the intake manifold by a vacuum hose. A check valve is placed at the point where the hose enters the diaphragm housing, so that during periods of low manifold vacuum brake assist vacuum will not be lost.

Depressing the brake pedal closes off the vacuum source and allows atmospheric pressure to enter on one side of the diaphragm. This causes the master cylinder pistons to move and apply the brakes. When the brake pedal is released, vacuum is applied to both sides of the diaphragm, and return springs return the diaphragm and master cylinder pistons to the released position. If the vacuum fails, the brake pedal rod will butt against the end of the master cylinder actuating rod, and direct mechanical application will occur as the pedal is depressed.

The hydraulic and mechanical problems that apply to conventional brake systems also apply to power brakes, and should be checked for if the following tests do not reveal the problem.

Test for a system vacuum leak as described below:

1. Operate the engine at idle with the transaxle in Neutral without touching the brake pedal for at least one minute.
2. Turn off the engine, and wait one minute.
3. Test for the presence of assist vacuum by depressing the brake pedal and releasing it several times. Light application will produce less and less pedal travel, if vacuum was present. If there is no vacuum, air is leaking into the system somewhere.

Test for system operation as follows:

1. Pump the brake pedal (with engine off) until the supply vacuum is entirely gone.
2. Put a light, steady pressure on the pedal.
3. Start the engine, and operate it at idle with the transaxle in Neutral. If the system is operating, the brake pedal should fall toward the floor if constant pressure is maintained on the pedal.

Power brake systems may be tested for hydraulic leaks just as ordinary systems are tested, except that the engine should be idling with the transaxle in Neutral throughout the test.

BRAKE SYSTEM

The J-cars have a diagonally-split hydraulic system. This differs from conventional practice in that the left front and right rear brakes are on one hydraulic circuit, and the right front and left rear are on the other.

A diagonally-split system necessitates the use of a special master cylinder design. The J-car master cylinder incorporates the functions of a standard tandem master cylinder, plus a warning light switch and proportioning valves. Additionally, the master cylinder is designed with a quick take-up feature which provides a large volume of fluid to the brakes at low pressure when the brakes are initially applied. The low pressure fluid acts to quickly fill the large displacement requirements of the system.

BRAKES 159

The front disc brakes are single piston sliding caliper units. Fluid pressure acts equally against the piston and the bottom of the piston bore in the caliper. This forces the piston outward until the pad contacts the rotor. The force on the caliper bore forces the caliper to slide over, carrying the other pad into contact with the other side of the rotor. The disc brakes are self-adjusting.

Rear drum brakes are conventional duo-servo units. A dual piston wheel cylinder, mounted to the top of the backing plate, actuates both brake shoes. Wheel cylinder force to the shoes is supplemented by the tendency of the shoes to wrap into the drum (servo action). An actuating link, pivot and lever serve to automatically engage the adjuster as the brakes are applied when the car is moving in reverse. Provisions for manual adjustment are also provided. The rear brakes also serve as the parking brakes; linkage is mechanical.

Vacuum boost is a standard. The booster is a conventional tandem vacuum unit.

ADJUSTMENT
Disc Brakes

The front disc brakes are inherently self-adjusting. No adjustments are either necessary or possible.

Drum Brakes

The drum brakes are designed to self-adjust when applied with the car moving in reverse. However, they can also be adjusted manually. This manual adjustment should also be performed whenever the linings are replaced.

1. Use a punch to knock out the stamped area on the brake drum. If this is done with the drum installed on the car, the drum must then be removed to clean out all metal pieces. After adjustments are complete, obtain a hole cover from your dealer (Part no. 4874119 or the equivalent) to prevent entry of dirt and water into the brakes.
2. Use an awl, a screwdriver, or an adjusting tool especially made for the purpose to turn the brake adjusting screw star wheel. Expand the shoes until the drum can just barely be turned by hand.
3. Back off the adjusting screw 30 notches. If the shoes still are dragging lightly, back off the adjusting screw one or two additional notches. If the brakes still drag, the parking brake adjustment is incorrect or the parking brake is applied. Fix and start over.
4. Install the hole cover into the drum.
5. Check the parking brake adjustment.

On some models, no marked area or stamped area is present on the drum. In this case, a hole must be drilled in the backing plate:

1. All backing plates have two round flat areas in the lower half through which the parking brake cable is installed. Drill a ½ in. hole into the round flat area on the backing plate opposite the parking brake cable. This will allow access to the star wheel.
2. After drilling the hole, remove the drum and remove all metal particles. Install a hole plug (Part no. 4874119 or the equivalent) to prevent the entry of water or dirt.

HYDRAULIC SYSTEM

Master Cylinder
REMOVAL AND INSTALLATION

1. Unplug the electrical connector from the master cylinder.
2. Place a number of cloths or a container under the master cylinder to catch the brake fluid. Disconnect the brake tubes from the master cylinder; use a flare nut wrench if one is available. Tape over open ends of the tubes.

NOTE: *Brake fluid eats paint. Wipe up any spilled fluid immediately, then flush the area with clear water.*

3. Remove the two nuts attaching the master cylinder to the booster or firewall.
4. Remove the master cylinder.
5. To install, attach the master cylinder to

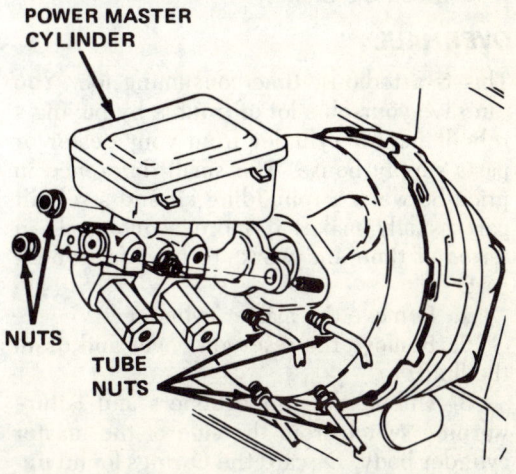

Master cylinder removal and installation details

160 BRAKES

Exploded view of the master cylinder

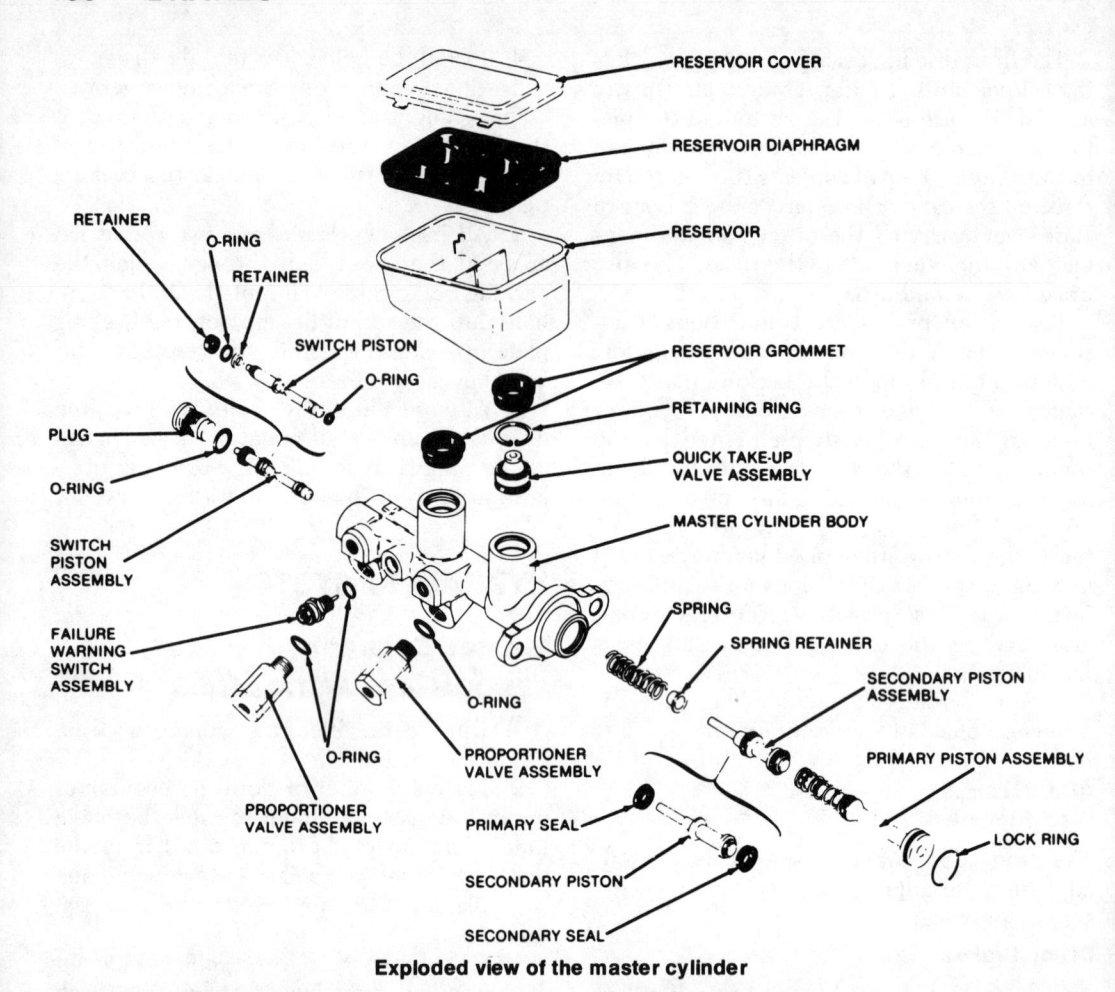

the booster with the nuts. Torque to 22–30 ft. lbs. (30–45 Nm.).

6. Remove the tape from the lines and connect to the master cylinder. Torque to 10–15 ft. lbs. (13–20 Nm.). Connect the electrical lead.

7. Bleed the brakes.

OVERHAUL

This is a tedious, time-consuming job. You can save yourself a lot of trouble by buying a rebuilt master cylinder from your dealer or parts supply house. The small difference in price between a rebuilding kit and a rebuilt part usually makes it more economical, in terms of time and work, to buy the rebuilt part.

1. Remove the master cylinder.
2. Remove the reservoir cover and drain the fluid.
3. Unbolt the proportioners and failure warning switch from the side of the master cylinder body. Discard the O-rings found under the proportioners. Use new ones on installation. There may or may not be an O-ring under the original equipment failure warning switch. If there is, discard it. In either case, use an O-ring upon assembly.

4. Clamp the master cylinder body in a vise, taking care not to crush it. Depress the primary piston with a wooden dowel and remove the lock ring with a pair of snap-ring pliers.

5. The primary and secondary pistons can be removed by applying compressed air into one of the outlets at the end of the cylinder and plugging the other three outlets. The primary piston must be replaced as an assembly if the seals are bad. The secondary piston seals are replaceable. Install these new seals with the lips facing outwards.

6. Inspect the bore for corrosion. If any corrosion is evident, the master cylinder body must be replaced. Do not attempt to polish the bore with crocus cloth, sandpaper, or anything else. The body is aluminum; polishing the bore won't work.

7. To remove the failure warning switch

BRAKES 161

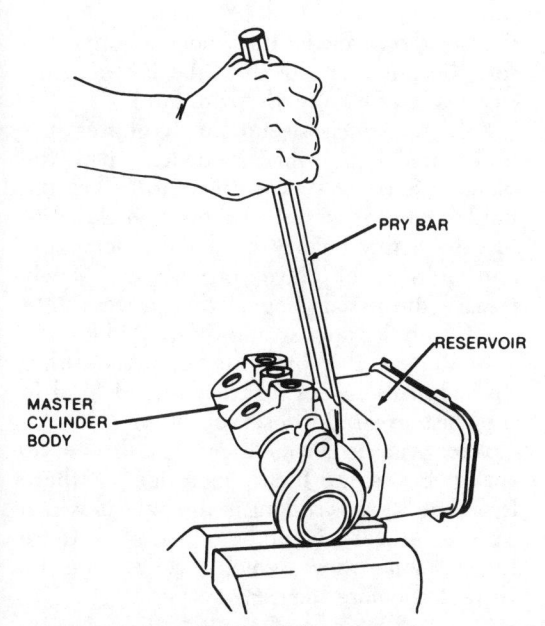

Removing the master cylinder reservoir

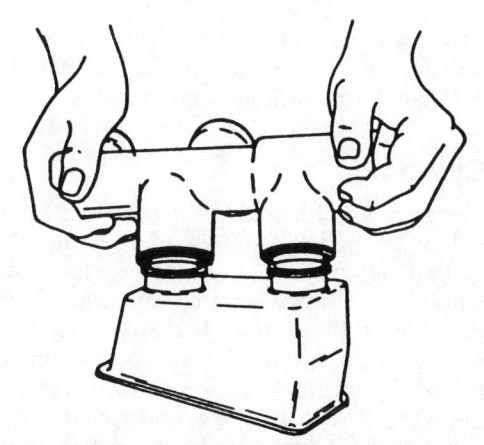

Install the master cylinder body to the reservoir with a rocking motion

piston assembly, remove the allen head plug from the end of the bore and withdraw the assembly with a pair of needlenose pliers. The switch piston assembly seals are replaceable.

8. The reservoir can be removed from the master cylinder body if necessary. Clamp the body in a vise by its mounting flange. Use a prey bar to remove the reservoir. If the reservoir is removed, remove the reservoir grommets and discard them. The quick take-up valves under the grommets are accessible after the retaining snap-rings are removed. Use snap-ring pliers; no other tool will work.

9. Clean all parts in denatured alcohol and allow to air dry. Do not use anything else to clean, and do not wipe dry with a rag, which will leave bits of lint behind. Inspect all parts for corrosion or wear. Generally, it is best to replace *all* rubber parts whenever the master cylinder is disassembled, and replace any metal part which shows any sign whatsoever of wear or corrosion.

10. Lubricate all parts with clean brake fluid before assembly.

11. Install the quick take-up valves into the master cylinder body and secure with the snap-rings. Make sure the snap-rings are properly seated in their grooves. Lubricate the new reservoir grommets with clean brake fluid and press them into the master cylinder.

12. Install the reservoir into the grommets by placing the reservoir on its lid and pressing the master cylinder body down onto it with a rocking motion.

13. Lubricate the switch piston assembly with clean brake fluid. Install new O-rings and retainers on the piston. Install the piston assembly into the master cylinder and secure with the plug, using a new O-ring on the plug. Torque is 40–140 in. lbs (5–16 Nm.).

14. Assemble the new secondary piston seals onto the piston. Lubricate the parts with clean brake fluid, then install the spring, spring retainer and secondary piston into the cylinder. Install the primary piston, depress, and install the lock ring.

15. Install new O-rings on the proportioners and the failure warning switch. Install the proportioners and torque to 18–30 ft. lbs. (25–40 Nm.). Install the failure warning switch and torque to 15–50 in. lbs. (2–6 Nm.).

16. Clamp the master cylinder body upright into a vise by one of the mounting flanges. Fill the reservoir with fresh brake fluid. Pump the piston with a dowel until fluid squirts from the outlet ports. Continue pumping until the expelled fluid is free of air bubbles.

17. Install the master cylinder, and bleed the brakes. Check the brake system for proper operation. Do not move the car until a "hard" brake pedal is obtained and the brake system has been thoroughly checked for soundness.

Proportioning Valves and Failure Warning Switch

These parts are installed in the master cylinder body. No separate proportioning or metering valve is used. Replacement of these parts requires disassembly of the master cylinder. See the preceding master cylinder overhaul for replacement instructions.

Bleeding

The purpose of bleeding the brakes is to expel air trapped in the hydraulic system. The system must be bled whenever the pedal feels spongy, indicating that compressible air has entered the system. It must also be bled whenever the system has been opened or repaired. You will need a helper for this job.

CAUTION: *Never reuse brake fluid which has been bled from the brake system.*

1. The sequence for bleeding is right rear, left front, left rear and right front. If the car has power brakes, remove the vacuum by applying the brakes several times. Do not run the engine while bleeding the brakes.

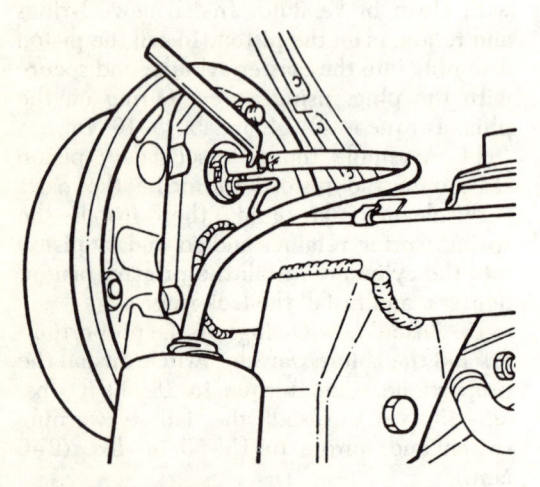

Bleeding the brakes

2. Clean all the bleeder screws. You may want to give each one a shot of penetrating solvent to loosen it up; seizure is a common problem with bleeder screws, which then break off, sometimes requiring replacement of the part to which they are attached.

3. Fill the master cylinder with DOT 3 brake fluid.

NOTE: *Brake fluid absorbs moisture from the air. Don't leave the master cylinder or the fluid container uncovered any longer than necessary. Be careful handling the fluid—it eats paint.*

Check the level of the fluid often when bleeding, and refill the reservoirs as necessary. Don't let them run dry, or you will have to repeat the process.

4. Attach a length of clear vinyl tubing to the bleeder screw on the wheel cylinder. Insert the other end of the tube into a clear, clean jar half filled with brake fluid.

5. Have your assistant slowly depress the brake pedal. As this is done, open the bleeder screw ⅓–½ of a turn, and allow the fluid to run through the tube. Then close the bleeder screw before the pedal reaches the end of its travel. Have your assistant slowly release the pedal. Repeat this process until no air bubbles appear in the expelled fluid.

6. Repeat the procedure on the other three brakes, checking the level of fluid in the master cylinder reservoir often.

After you're done, there should be no sponginess in the brake pedal feel. If there is, either there is still air in the line, in which case the process should be repeated, or there is a leak somewhere, which of course must be corrected before the car is moved.

FRONT DISC BRAKES

Pads

INSPECTION

The pad thickness should be inspected every time that the tires are removed for rotation. The outer pad can be checked by looking in at each end, which is the point at which the highest rate of wear occurs. The inner pad can be checked by looking down through the inspection hole in the top of the caliper. If the thickness of the pad is worn to within 0.030 in. (0.76 mm) of the rivet at either end of the pad, all the pads should be replaced. This is the factory-recommended measurement; your state's automobile inspection laws may not agree with this.

NOTE: *Always replace all pads on both front wheels at the same time. Failure to do so will result in uneven braking action and premature wear.*

REMOVAL AND INSTALLATION

1. Siphon ⅔ of the brake fluid from the master cylinder reservoir. Loosen the wheel lug nuts and raise the car. Remove the wheel.

2. Position a C-clamp across the caliper so that it presses on the pads and tighten it until the caliper piston bottoms in its bore.

NOTE: *If you haven't removed some brake fluid from the master cylinder, it will overflow when the piston is retracted.*

3. Remove the C-clamp.

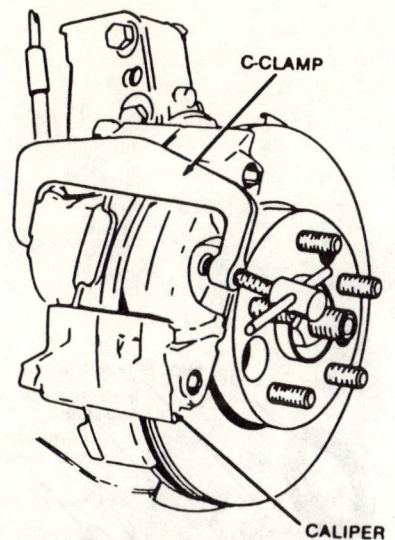

BRAKES 163

Install a C-clamp to retract the disc brake pads

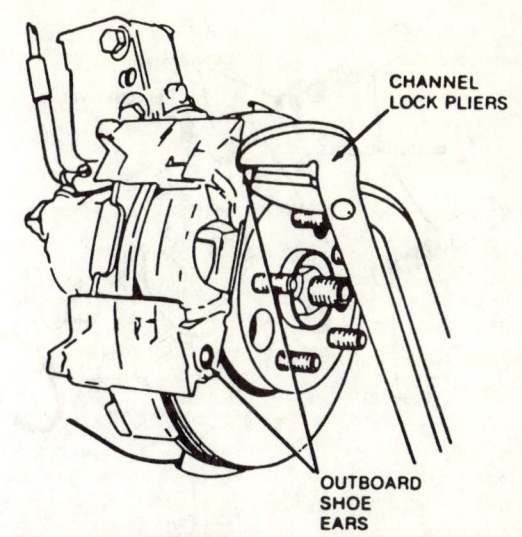

Bend the outboard pad ears into place with a large pair of slip-joint pliers

4. Remove the allen head caliper mounting bolts. Inspect the bolts for corrosion, and replace as necessary.

5. Remove the caliper from the steering knuckle and suspend it from the body of the car with a length of wire. Do not allow the caliper to hang by its hose.

6. Remove the pad retaining springs and remove the pads from the caliper.

7. Remove the plastic sleeves and the rubber bushings from the mounting bolt holes.

8. Install new sleeves and bushings. Lubricate the sleeves with a light coating of silicone grease before installation. These parts must always be replaced when the pads are replaced. The parts are usually included in the pad replacement kits.

9. Install the outboard pad into the caliper.

10. Install the retainer spring on the inboard pad. A new spring should be included in the pad replacement kit.

11. Install the new inboard pad into the caliper. The retention lugs fit into the piston.

12. Use a large pair of slip joint pliers to bend the outer pad ears down over the caliper.

13. Install the caliper onto the steering knuckle. Tighten the mounting bolts to 21–35 ft. lbs. (28–47 Nm.). Install the wheel and lower the car. Fill the master cylinder to its proper level with fresh brake fluid meeting DOT 3 specifications. Since the brake hose wasn't disconnected, it isn't really necessary to bleed the brakes, although most mechanics do this as a matter of course.

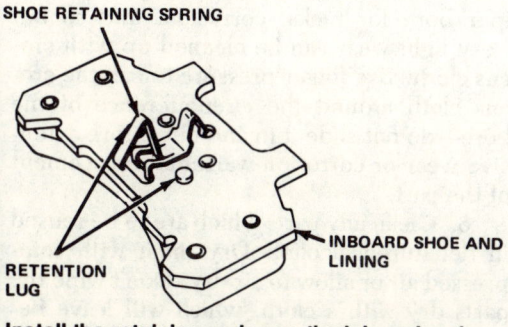

Caliper

REMOVAL AND INSTALLATION

1. Follow Steps 1, 2 and 3 of the pad replacement procedure.

2. Before removing the caliper mounting bolts, remove the bolt holding the brake hose to the caliper.

3. Remove the allen head caliper mounting bolts. Inspect them for corrosion and replace them if necessary.

4. Installation is the reverse. Mounting bolt torque is 21–35 ft. lbs. (28–47 Nm.) for the caliper. The brake hose fitting should be tightened to 18–30 ft. lbs. (24–40 Nm.).

OVERHAUL

1. Remove the caliper.
2. Remove the pads.
3. Place some cloths or a slat of wood in front of the piston. Remove the piston by applying compressed air to the fluid inlet fit-

Install the retaining spring on the inboard pad

164 BRAKES

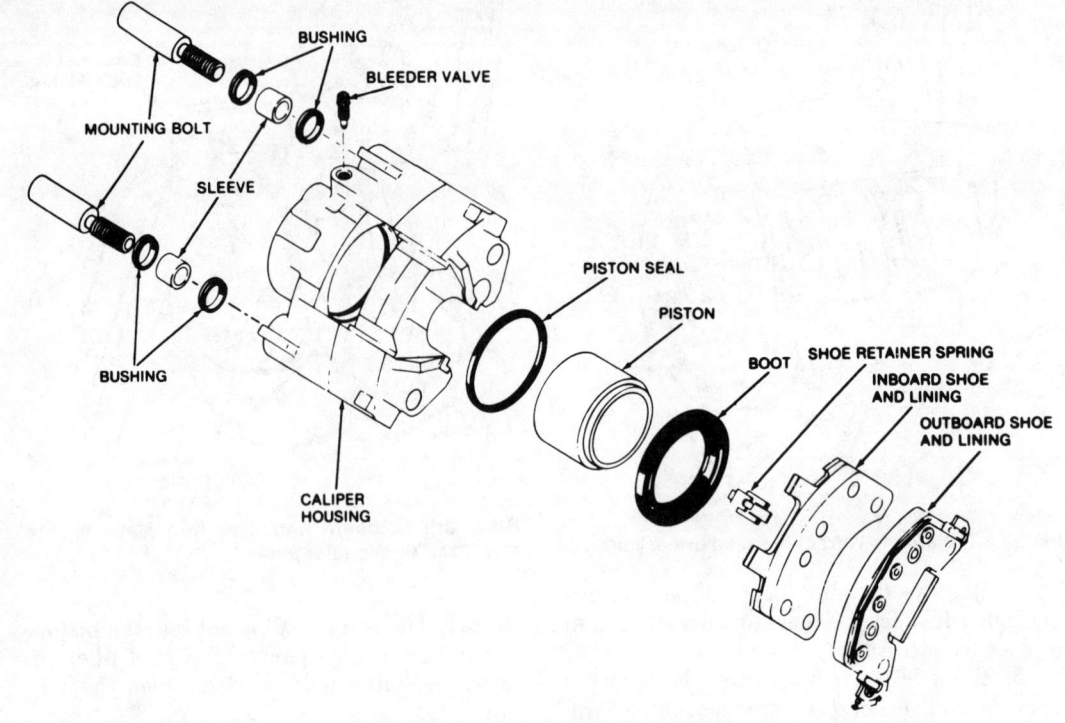

Exploded view of the disc brake caliper

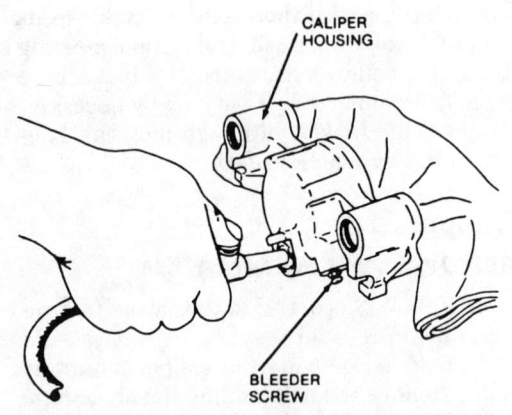

Use air pressure to remove the piston from the bore

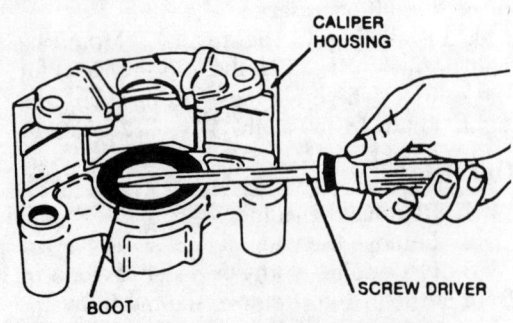

Remove the piston boot with a screwdriver

ting. Use just enough air pressure to ease the piston from the bore.

CAUTION: *Do not try to catch the piston with your fingers, which can result in serious injury.*

4. Remove the piston boot with a screwdriver, working carefully so that the piston bore is not scratched.

5. Remove the bleeder screw.

6. Inspect the piston for scoring, nicks, corrosion, wear, etc., and damaged or worn chrome plating. Replace the piston if any defects are found.

7. Remove the piston seal from the caliper bore groove using a piece of pointed wood or plastic. Do not use a screwdriver, which will damage the bore. Inspect the caliper bore for nicks, corrosion, and so on. Very light wear can be cleaned up with crocus cloth. Use finger pressure to rub the crocus cloth around the circumference of the bore—do not slide it in and out. More extensive wear or corrosion warrants replacement of the part.

8. Clean any parts which are to be reused in denatured alcohol. Dry them with compressed air or allow to air dry. Don't wipe the parts dry with a cloth, which will leave behind bits of lint.

9. Lubricate the new seal, provided in the repair kit, with clean brake fluid. Install the seal in its groove, making sure it is fully seated and not twisted.

10. Install the new dust boot on the piston. Lubricate the bore of the caliper with clean brake fluid and insert the piston into its bore. Position the boot in the caliper housing and seat with a seal driver of the appropriate size, or G.M. tool no. J-29077.

11. Install the bleeder screw, tightening to 80–140 in. lbs (9–16 Nm.). Do not overtighten.

12. Install the pads, install the caliper, and bleed the brakes.

Disc (Rotor)

REMOVAL AND INSTALLATION

1. Remove the caliper.
2. Remove the rotor.
3. Installation is the reverse.

INSPECTION

1. Check the rotor surface for wear or scoring. Deep scoring, grooves or rust pitting can be removed by refacing, a job to be referred to your local machine shop or garage. Minimum thickness is stamped on the rotor (0.830 in., or 21.08 mm). If the rotor will be thinner than this after refinishing, it must be replaced.

2. Check the rotor parallelism; it must vary less than 0.0005 in. (0.013 mm) measured at four or more points around the circumference. Make all measurements at the same distance in from the edge of the rotor.

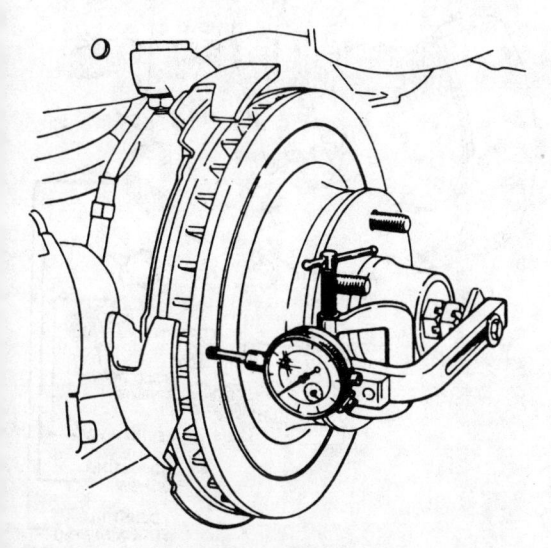

Check the runout with a dial indicator

Refinish the rotor if it fails to meet this specification.

3. Measure the disc runout with a dial indicator. If runout exceeds 0.005 in. (0.127 mm), and the wheel bearings are OK (if runout is being measured with the disc on the car), the rotor must be refaced or replaced as necessary.

Wheel Bearings

Adjustment, removal and installation procedures can all be found in Chapter 7.

REAR DRUM BRAKES

Brake Drums

REMOVAL AND INSTALLATION

1. Loosen the wheel lug nuts. Raise and support the car. Mark the relationship of the wheel to the axle and remove the wheel.

2. Mark the relationship of the drum to the axle and remove the drum. If it cannot be slipped off easily, check to see that the parking brake is fully released. If so, the brake shoes are probably locked against the drum. See the "Adjustment" section earlier in this chapter for details on how to back off the adjuster.

3. Installation is the reverse. Be sure to align the matchmarks made during removal. Lug nut torque is 102 ft. lbs. (140 Nm.).

INSPECTION

1. After removing the brake drum, wipe out the accumulated dust with a damp cloth.
   WARNING: *Do not blow the brake dust out of the drums with compressed air or lungpower. Brake linings contain asbestos, a known cancer causing substance. Dispose of the cloth used to clean the parts after use.*

2. Inspect the drums for cracks, deep grooves, roughness, scoring, or out-of-roundness. Replace any drum which is cracked; do not try to weld it up.

3. Smooth any slight scores by polishing the friction surface with fine emery cloth. Heavy or extensive scoring will cause excessive lining wear and should be removed from the drum through resurfacing, a job to be referred to your local machine shop or garage. The maximum finished diameter of the drums is 7.90 in. (200.64 mm). The drum

166 BRAKES

must be replaced if the diameter is 7.93 in. (201.40 mm) or greater.

Brake Shoes

INSPECTION

After removing the brake drum, inspect the brake shoes. If the lining is worn down to within 1/32 in. (0.76 mm) of a rivet, the shoes must be replaced.

NOTE: *This figure may disagree with your state's automobile inspection laws.*

If the brake lining is soaked with brake fluid or grease, it must be replaced. If this is the case, the brake drum should be sanded with crocus cloth to remove all traces of brake fluid, and the wheel cylinders should be rebuilt. Clean all grit from the friction surface of the drum before replacing it.

If the lining is chipped, cracked, or otherwise damaged, it must be replaced with a new lining.

NOTE: *Always replace the brake linings in sets of two on both ends of the axle. Never replace just one shoe, or both shoes on one side.*

Check the condition of the shoes, retracting springs, and hold-down springs for signs of overheating. If the shoes or springs have a slight blue color, this indicates overheating and replacement of the shoes and springs is recommended. The wheel cylinders should be rebuilt as a precaution against future problems.

REMOVAL AND INSTALLATION

1. Loosen the lug nuts on the wheel to be serviced, raise and support the car, and remove the wheel and brake drum.

NOTE: *It is not really necessary to remove the hub and wheel bearing assembly from the axle, but it does make the job easier. If you can work with the hub and bearing assembly in place, skip down to Step 3.*

2. Remove the four hub and bearing assembly retaining bolts and remove the assembly from the axle.

3. Remove the return springs from the

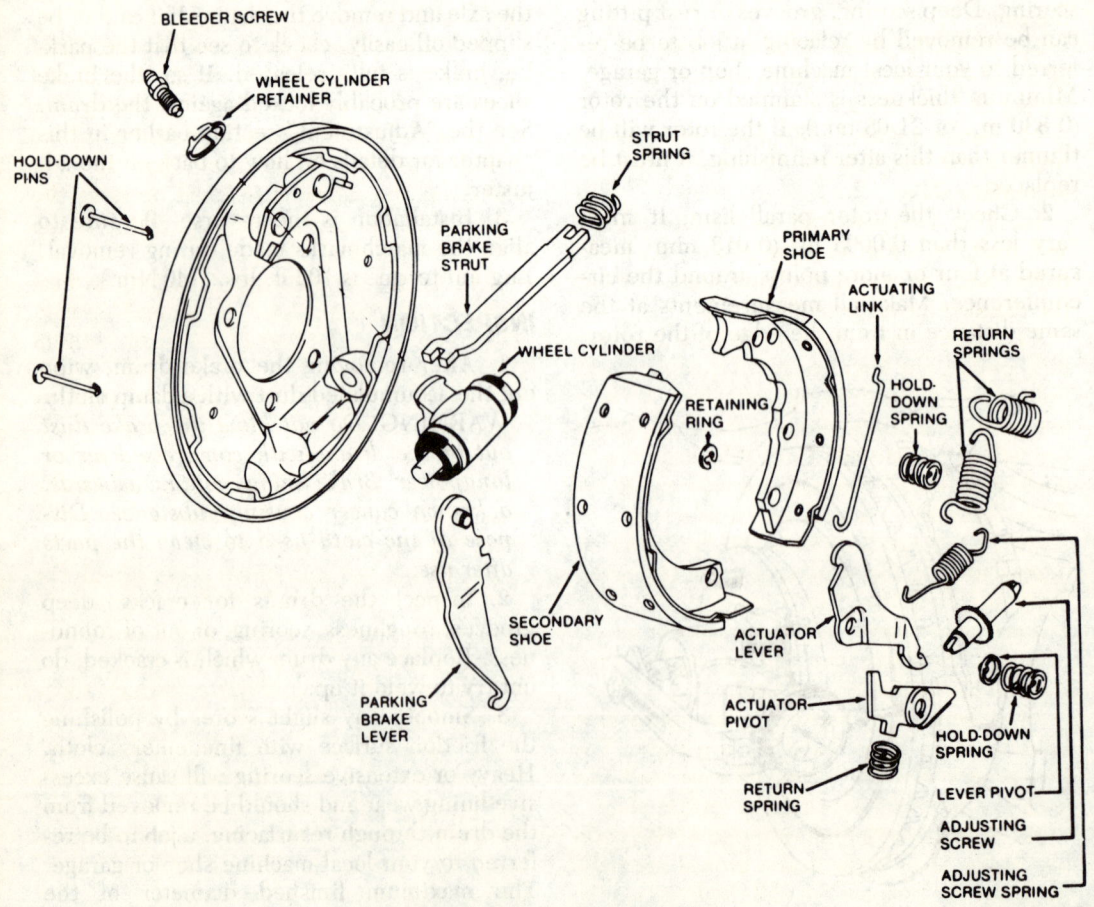

Exploded view of the drum brakes

shoes with a pair of needle nose pliers. There are also special brake spring pliers for this job.

4. Remove the hold down springs by gripping them with a pair of pliers, then pressing down and turning 90°. There are special tools to grab and turn these parts, but pliers work fairly well.

5. Remove the shoe hold-down pins from behind the brake backing plate. They will simply slide out once the hold-down spring tension is relieved.

6. Lift up the actuator lever for the self-adjusting mechanism and remove the actuating link. Remove the actuator lever, pivot, and the pivot return spring.

7. Spread the shoes apart to clear the wheel cylinder pistons and remove the parking brake strut and spring.

8. If the hub and bearing assembly is still in place, spread the shoes far enough apart to clear it.

9. Disconnect the parking brake cable from the lever. Remove the shoes, still connected by their adjusting screw spring, from the car.

10. With the shoes removed, note the position of the adjusting spring and remove the spring and adjusting screw.

11. Remove the C-clip from the parking brake lever and remove the lever from the secondary shoe.

12. Use a damp cloth to remove all dirt and dust from the backing plate and brake parts. See the warning about brake dust in the drum removal procedure.

13. Check the wheel cylinders by carefully pulling the lower edges of the wheel cylinder boots away from the cylinders. If there is excessive leakage, the inside of the cylinder will be moist with fluid. If leakage exists, a wheel cylinder overhaul is in order. Do not delay, because brake failure could result.

NOTE: *A small amount of fluid will be present to act as a lubricant for the wheel cylinder pistons. Fluid spilling from the boot center hole, after the piston is removed, indicates cup leakage and the necessity for cylinder overhaul.*

14. Check the backing plate attaching bolts to make sure that they are tight. Use fine emery cloth to clean all rust and dirt from the shoe contact surfaces on the plate.

15. Lubricate the fulcrum end of the parking brake lever with brake grease specially made for the purpose. Install the lever on the secondary shoe and secure with the C-clip.

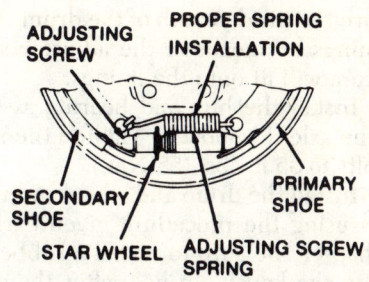

Proper spring installation is with the coils over the adjuster, not the star wheel

16. Install the adjusting screw and spring on the shoes, connecting them together. The coils of the spring must *not* be over the star wheel on the adjuster. The left and right hand springs are *not* interchangeable. Do not mix them up.

17. Lubricate the shoe contact surfaces on the backing plate with the brake grease. Be certain when you are using this stuff that none of it actually gets on the linings or drums. Apply the same grease to the point where the parking brake cable contacts the plate. Use the grease sparingly.

18. Spread the shoe assemblies apart and connect the parking brake cable. Install the shoes on the backing plate, engaging the shoes at the top temporarily with the wheel cylinder pistons. Make sure that the star wheel on the adjuster is lined up with the adjusting hole in the backing plate, if the hole is back there.

19. Spread the shoes apart slightly and install the parking brake strut and spring. Make sure that the end of the strut without the spring engages the parking brake lever. The end with the spring engages the primary shoe (the one with the shorter lining).

20. Install the actuator pivot, lever and return spring. Install the actuating link in the shoe retainer. Lift up the actuator lever and hook the link into the lever.

21. Install the hold-down pins through the back of the plate, install the lever pivots and hold-down springs. Install the shoe return springs with a pair of pliers. Be very careful not to stretch or otherwise distort these springs.

22. Take a look at everything. Make sure the linings are in the right place, the self-adjusting mechanism is correctly installed, and the parking brake parts are all hooked up. If in doubt, remove the other wheel and take a look at that one for comparison.

23. Measure the width of the linings, then

168 BRAKES

measure the inside width of the drum. Adjust the linings by means of the adjuster so that the drum will fit onto the linings.

24. Install the hub and bearing assembly onto the axle if removed. Tighten the retaining bolts to 35 ft. lbs. (55 Nm.).

25. Install the drum and wheel. Adjust the brakes using the procedure given earlier in this chapter. Be sure to install a rubber hole cover in the knock-out hole after the adjustment is complete. Adjust the parking brake.

26. Lower the car and check the pedal for any sponginess or lack of a "hard" feel. Check the braking action and the parking brake. The brakes must not be applied severely immediately after installation. They should be used moderately for the first 200 miles of city driving or 1000 miles of highway driving, to allow the linings to conform to the shape of the drum.

Wheel Cylinders

REMOVAL AND INSTALLATION

1. Loosen the wheel lug nuts, raise and support the car, and remove the wheel. Remove the drum and brake shoes. Leave the hub and wheel bearing assembly in place.

2. Remove any dirt from around the brake line fitting. Disconnect the brake line.

3. Remove the wheel cylinder retainer by using two awls or punches with a tip diameter of 1/8 in. or less. Insert the awls or punches into the access slots between the wheel cylinder pilot and retainer locking tabs. Bend both tabs away simultaneously. Remove the wheel cylinder from the backing plate.

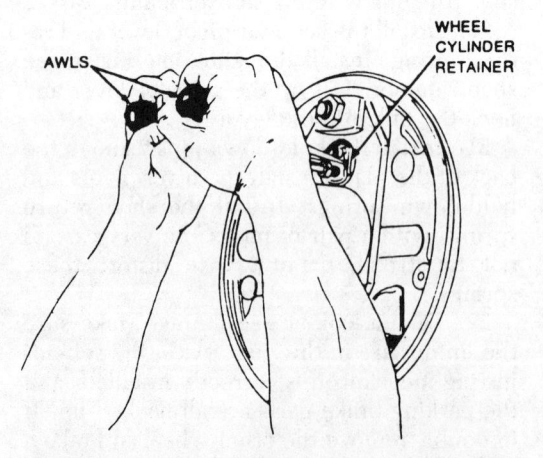

Remove the wheel cylinder retainer from the backing plate with a pair of awls or punches

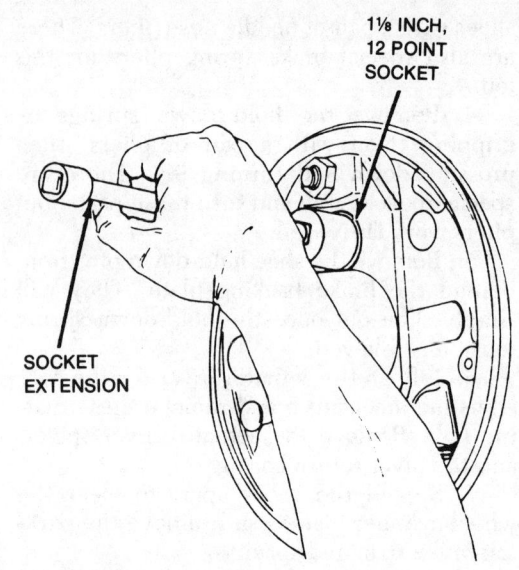

Installing a new retainer

4. To install, position the wheel cylinder against the backing plate and hold it in place with a wooden block between the wheel cylinder and the hub and bearing assembly.

5. Install a new retainer over the wheel cylinder abutment on the rear of the backing plate by pressing it into place with a 1 1/8 in. 12-point socket and an extension.

6. Install a new bleeder screw into the wheel cylinder. Install the brake line and tighten to 10–15 ft. lbs. (13–20 Nm.).

7. The rest of installation is the reverse of removal. After the drum is installed, bleed the brakes using the procedure outlined earlier in this chapter.

OVERHAUL

As is the case with master cylinders, overhaul kits are available for the wheel cylinders. And, as is the case with master cylinders, it is usually more profitable to simply buy new

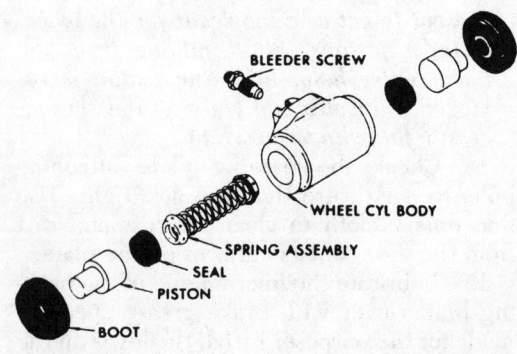

Exploded view of a wheel cylinder

BRAKES

or rebuilt wheel cylinders rather than rebuilding them. When rebuilding wheel cylinders, avoid getting any contaminants in the system. Always install new high-quality brake fluid; the use of improper fluid will swell and deteriorate the rubber parts.

1. Remove the wheel cylinders.
2. Remove the rubber boots from the cylinder ends. Discard the boots.
3. Remove and discard the pistons and cups.
4. Wash the cylinder and metal parts in denatured alcohol.

CAUTION: *Never use mineral-based solvents to clean the brake parts.*

5. Allow the parts to air dry and inspect the cylinder bore for corrosion or wear. Light corrosion can be cleaned up with crocus cloth; use finger pressure and rotate the cloth around the circumference of the bore. Do not move the cloth in and out. Any deep corrosion or pitting or wear warrants replacement of the parts.
6. Rinse the parts and allow to dry. Do not dry with a rag, which will leave bits of lint behind.
7. Lubricate the cylinder bore with clean brake fluid. Insert the spring assembly.
8. Install new cups. Do not lubricate prior to assembly.
9. Install the new pistons.
10. Press the new boots onto the cylinders by hand. Do not lubricate prior to assembly.
11. Install the wheel cylinders. Bleed the brakes after installation of the drum.

Vacuum Booster

REMOVAL AND INSTALLATION

1. Remove the master cylinder from the booster. It is not necessary to disconnect the lines from the master cylinder. Just move the cylinder aside.

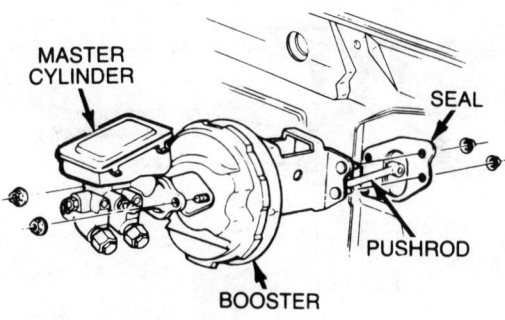

Vacuum booster mounting

2. Disconnect the vacuum booster pushrod from the brake pedal inside the car. It is retained by a bolt. A spring washer lives under the bolt head, and a flat washer goes on the other side of the pushrod eye, next to the pedal arm.
3. Remove the four attaching nuts from inside the car. Remove the booster.
4. Install the booster on the firewall. Tighten the mounting nuts to 22–33 ft. lbs. (30–45 Nm.).
5. Connect the pushrod to the brake pedal.
6. Install the master cylinder. Mounting torque is 22–33 ft. lbs. (30–45 Nm).

OVERHAUL

This job is not difficult, but requires a number of special tools which are expensive, especially if they're to be used only once. Generally, it's better to leave this job to your dealer, or buy a rebuilt vacuum booster and install it yourself.

PARKING BRAKE

ADJUSTMENT

1. Raise and support the car with both rear wheels off the ground.

Brake Specifications

Model	Lug Nut Torque (ft. lb.)	Master Cylinder Bore	Brake Disc Minimum Thickness	Brake Disc Maximum Run-Out	Brake Drum Diameter	Brake Drum Max Machine O/S	Brake Drum Max Wear Limit	Minimum Lining Thickness Front	Minimum Lining Thickness Rear
All	102	.866	.830	.004	7.88	7.90	7.93	①	①

① Minimum lining thickness is to $1/32$ of rivet
NOTE: *Minimum lining thickness is as recommended by the manufacturer. Because of variations in state inspection regulations, the minimum allowable thickness may be different than recommended by the manufacturer.*

170 BRAKES

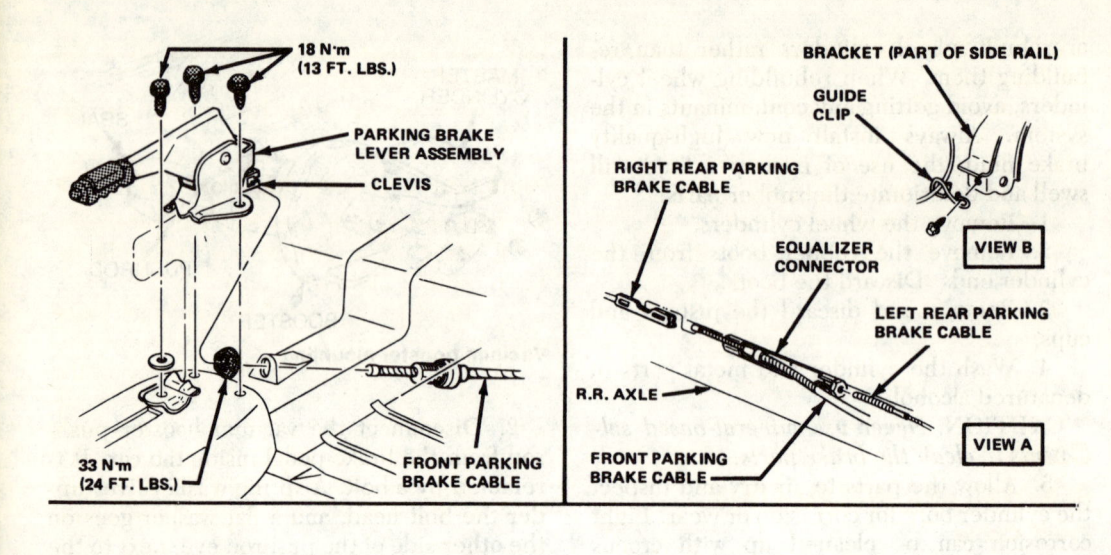

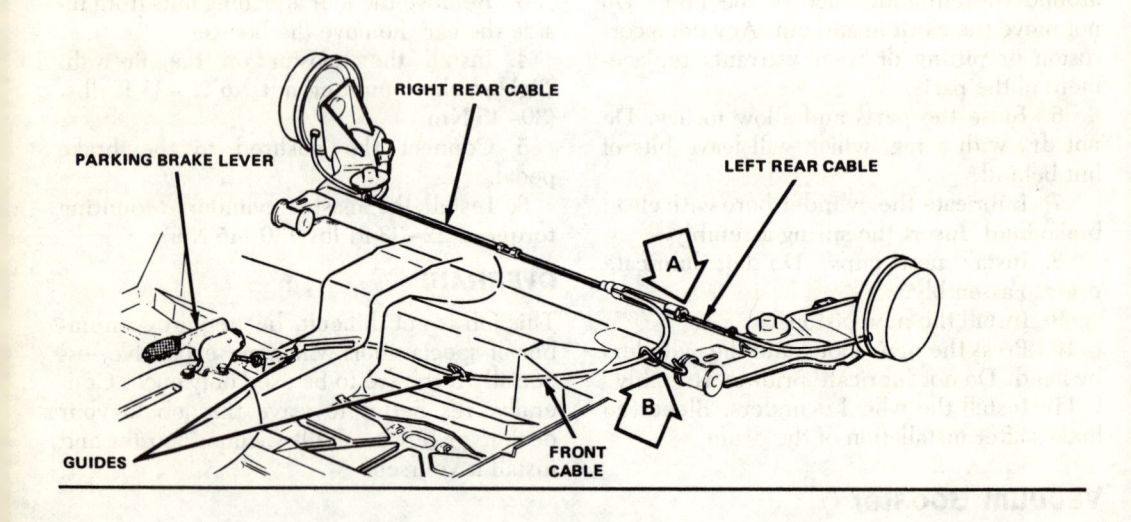

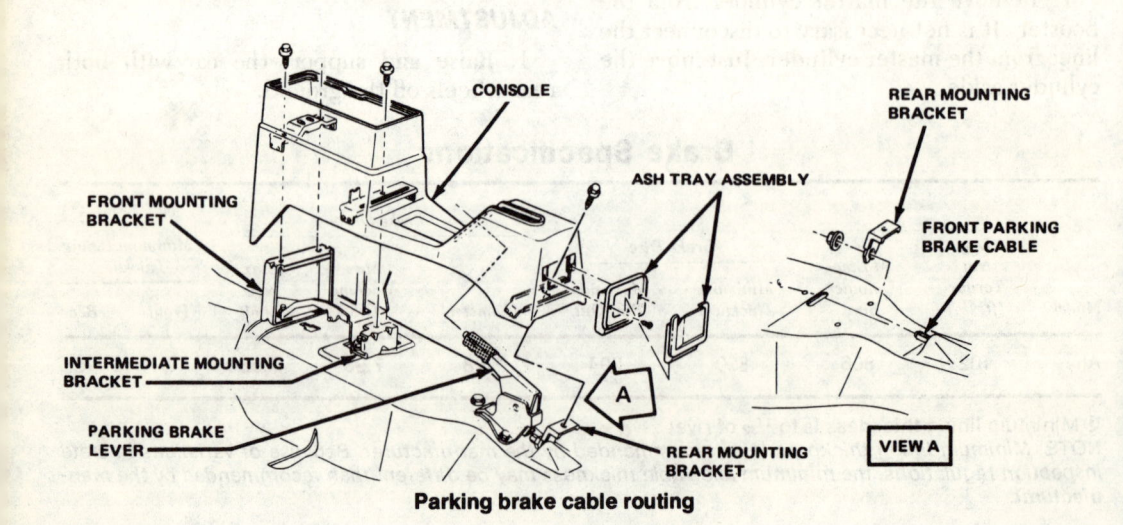

Parking brake cable routing

2. Pull the parking brake lever exactly two ratchet clicks.
3. Loosen the equalizer locknut, then tighten the adjusting nut until the left rear wheel can just be turned backward using two hands, but is locked in forward rotation.
4. Tighten the locknut.
5. Release the parking brake. Rotate the rear wheels—there should be no drag.
6. Lower the car.

Cable

REMOVAL AND INSTALLATION
Front Cable

1. Place the gear selector in Neutral and apply the parking brake.
2. Remove the center console as detailed in Chapter 5.
3. Disconnect the parking brake cable from the lever.
4. Remove the cable retaining nut and the bracket securing the front cable to the floor panel.
5. Raise the car and loosen the equalizer nut.
6. Loosen the catalytic converter shield and then remove the parking brake cable from the body.
7. Disconnect the cable from the equalizer and then remove the cable from the guide and the underbody clips.
8. Reverse the procedure and adjust the cable.

Right and Left Rear Cables

1. Raise and support the rear of the car.
2. Back off the equalizer nut until the cable tension is eliminated.
3. Remove the tires, wheels and brake drums.
4. Insert a screwdriver between the brake shoe and the top part of the brake adjuster bracket. Push the bracket to the front and then release the top brake adjuster rod.
5. Remove the rear hold down spring. Remove the actuator lever and the lever return spring.
6. Remove the adjuster screw spring.
7. Remove the top rear brake shoe return spring.
8. Unhook the parking brake cable from the parking brake lever.
9. Depress the conduit fitting retaining tangs and then remove the conduit fitting from the backing plate.
10. Remove the cable end button from the connector.
11. Depress the conduit fitting retaining tangs and remove the conduit fitting from the axle bracket.
12. Reverse the procedure to install and adjust the cable.

Body 9

You can repair most minor auto body damage yourself. Minor damage usually falls into one of several categories: (1) small scratches and dings in the paint that can be repaired without the use of body filler, (2) deep scratches and dents that require body filler, but do not require pulling, or hammering metal back into shape and (3) rust-out repairs. The repair sequences illustrated in this chapter are typical of these types of repairs. If you want to get involved in more complicated repairs including pulling or hammering sheet metal back into shape, you will probably need more detailed instructions. Chilton's *Minor Auto Body Repair, 2nd Edition* is a comprehensive guide to repairing auto body damage yourself.

TOOLS AND SUPPLIES

The list of tools and equipment you may need to fix minor body damage ranges from very basic hand tools to a wide assortment of specialized body tools. Most minor scratches, dings and rust holes can be fixed using an electric drill, wire wheel or grinder attachment, half-round plastic file, sanding block, various grades of sandpaper (#36, which is coarse through #600, which is fine) in both wet and dry types, auto body plastic, primer, touch-up paint, spreaders, newspaper and masking tape.

Most manufacturers of auto body repair products began supplying materials to professionals. Their knowledge of the best, most-used products has been translated into body repair kits for the do-it-yourselfer. Kits are available from a number of manufacturers and contain the necessary materials in the required amounts for the repair identified on the package.

Kits are available for a wide variety of uses, including:
- Rusted out metal
- All purpose kit for dents and holes
- Dents and deep scratches
- Fiberglass repair kit
- Epoxy kit for restyling.

Kits offer the advantage of buying what you need for the job. There is little waste and little chance of materials going bad from not being used. The same manufacturers also merchandise all of the individual products used—spreaders, dent pullers, fiberglass cloth, polyester resin, cream hardener, body filler, body files, sandpaper, sanding discs and holders, primer, spray paint, etc.

CAUTION: *Most of the products you will be using contain harmful chemicals, so be extremely careful. Always read the complete label before opening the containers. When*

BODY 173

you put them away for future use, be sure they are out of children's reach!

Most auto body repair kits contain all the materials you need to do the job right in the kit. So, if you have a small rust spot or dent you want to fix, check the contents of the kit before you run out and buy any additional tools.

ALIGNING BODY PANELS

Doors

There are several methods of adjusting doors. Your vehicle will probably use one of those illustrated.

Whenever a door is removed and is to be reinstalled, you should matchmark the position of the hinges on the door pillars. The holes of the hinges and/or the hinge attaching points are usually oversize to permit alignment of doors. The striker plate is also moveable, through oversize holes, permitting up-and-down, in-and-out and fore-and-aft movement. Fore-and-aft movement is made by adding or subtracting shims from behind the striker and pillar post. The striker should be adjusted so that the door closes fully and remains closed, yet enters the lock freely.

DOOR HINGES

Don't try to cover up poor door adjustment with a striker plate adjustment. The gap on each side of the door should be equal and uniform and there should be no metal-to-metal contact as the door is opened or closed.

1. Determine which hinge bolts must be loosened to move the door in the desired direction.
2. Loosen the hinge bolt(s) just enough to allow the door to be moved with a padded pry bar.
3. Move the door a small amount and check the fit, after tightening the bolts. Be sure that there is no bind or interference with adjacent panels.
4. Repeat this until the door is properly positioned, and tighten all the bolts securely.

Hood, Trunk or Tailgate

As with doors, the outline of hinges should be scribed before removal. The hood and trunk can be aligned by loosening the hinge bolts in their slotted mounting holes and moving the hood or trunk lid as necessary.

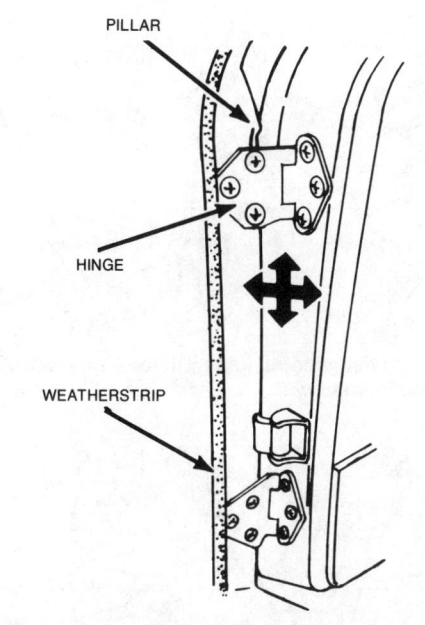

Door hinge adjustment

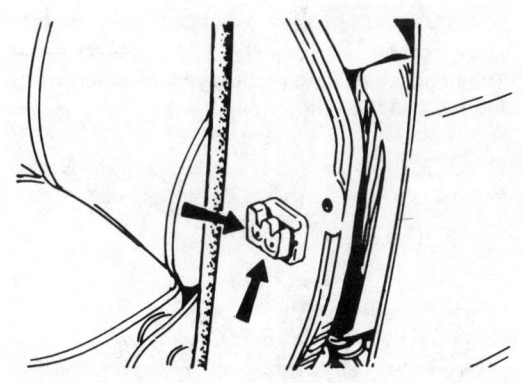

Move the door striker as indicated by arrows

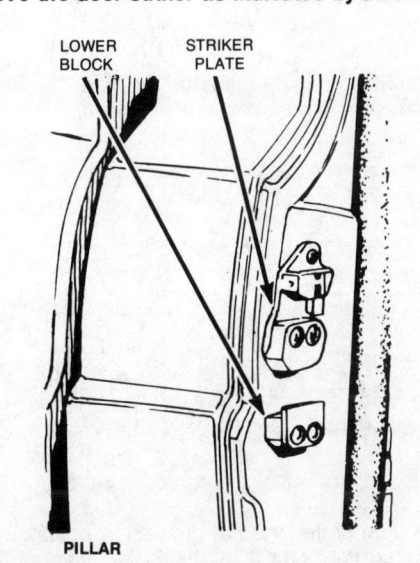

Striker plate and lower block

174 BODY

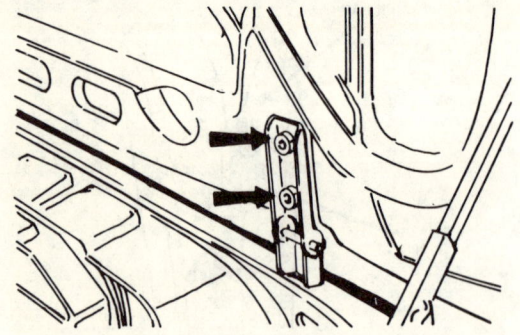

Loosen the hinge boots to permit fore-and-aft and horizontal adjustment

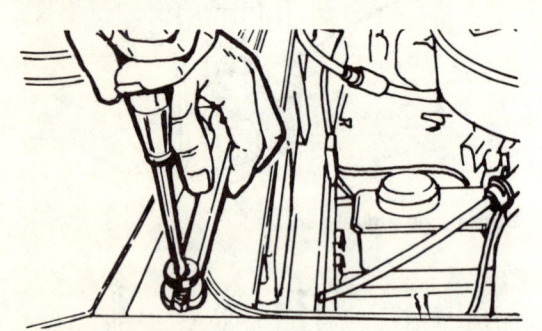

The hood is adjusted vertically by stop-screws at the front and/or rear

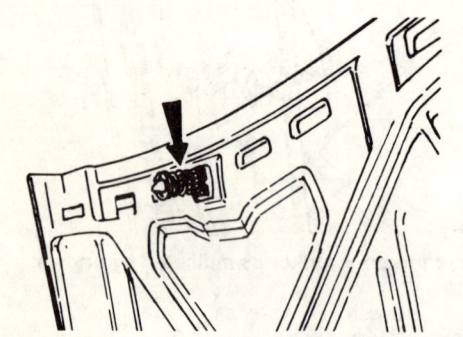

The hood pin can be adjusted for proper lock engagement

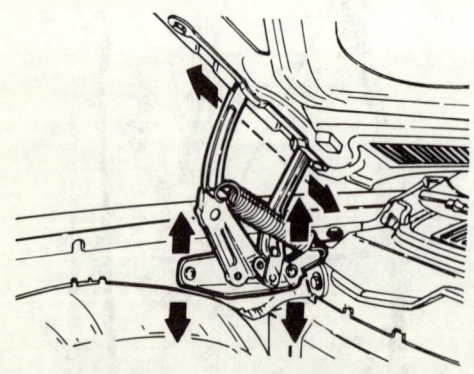

The height of the hood at the rear is adjusted by loosening the bolts that attach the hinge to the body and moving the hood up or down

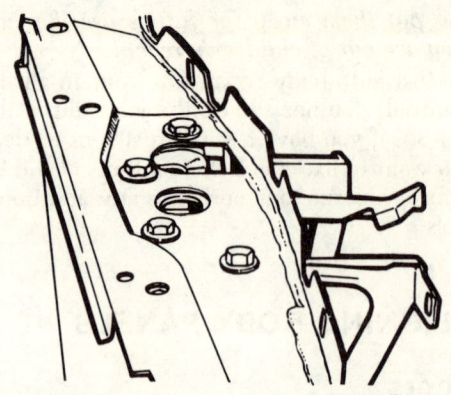

The base of the hood lock can also be repositioned slightly to give more positive lock engagement

The hood and trunk have adjustable catch locations to regulate lock engagement. Bumpers at the front and/or rear of the hood provide a vertical adjustment and the hood lockpin can be adjusted for proper engagement.

The tailgate on the station wagon can be adjusted by loosening the hinge bolts in their slotted mounting holes and moving the tailgate on its hinges. The latchplate and latch striker at the bottom of the tailgate opening can be adjusted to stop rattle. An adjustable bumper is located on each side.

RUST, UNDERCOATING, AND RUSTPROOFING

Rust

Rust is an electrochemical process. It works on ferrous metals (iron and steel) from the inside out due to exposure of unprotected surfaces to air and moisture. The possibility of rust exists practically nationwide—anywhere humidity, industrial pollution or chemical salts are present, rust can form. In coastal areas, the problem is high humidity and salt air; in snowy areas, the problem is chemical salt (de-icer) used to keep the roads clear, and in industrial areas, sulphur dioxide is present in the air from industrial pollution and is changed to sulphuric acid when it rains. The rusting process is accelerated by high temperatures, especially in snowy areas, when vehicles are driven over slushy roads and then left overnight in a heated garage.

Automotive styling also can be a contributor to rust formation. Spot welding of panels creates small pockets that trap moisture and form an environment for rust formation. Fortunately, auto manufacturers have been working hard to increase the corrosion protection of their products. Galvanized sheet metal enjoys much wider use, along with the increased use of plastic and various rust retardant coatings. Manufacturers are also designing out areas in the body where rust-forming moisture can collect.

To prevent rust, you must stop it before it gets started. On new vehicles, there are two ways to accomplish this.

First, the car or truck should be treated with a commercial rustproofing compound. There are many different brands of franchised rustproofers, but most processes involve spraying a waxy "self-healing" compound under the chassis, inside rocker panels, inside doors and fender liners and similar places where rust is likely to form. Prices for a quality rustproofing job range from $100–$250, depending on the area, the brand name and the size of the vehicle.

Ideally, the vehicle should be rustproofed as soon as possible following the purchase. The surfaces of the car or truck have begun to oxidize and deteriorate during shipping. In addition, the car may have sat on a dealer's lot or on a lot at the factory, and once the rust has progressed past the stage of light, powdery surface oxidation rustproofing is not likely to be worthwhile. Professional rustproofers feel that once rust has formed, rustproofing will simply seal in moisture already present. Most franchised rustproofing operations offer a 3–5 year warranty against rust-through, but will not support that warranty if the rustproofing is not applied within three months of the date of manufacture.

Undercoating should not be mistaken for rustproofing. Undercoating is a black, tarlike substance that is applied to the underside of a vehicle. Its basic function is to deaden noises that are transmitted from under the car. It simply cannot get into the crevices and seams where moisture tends to collect. In fact, it may clog up drainage holes and ventilation passages. Some undercoatings also tend to crack or peel with age and only create more moisture and corrosion attracting pockets.

The second thing you should do immediately after purchasing the car is apply a paint sealant. A sealant is a petroleum based product marketed under a wide variety of brand names. It has the same protective properties as a good wax, but bonds to the paint with a chemically inert layer that seals it from the air. If air can't get at the surface, oxidation cannot start.

The paint sealant kit consists of a base coat and a conditioning coat that should be applied every 6–8 months, depending on the manufacturer. The base coat must be applied before waxing, or the wax must first be removed.

Third, keep a garden hose handy for your car in winter. Use it a few times on nice days during the winter for underneath areas, and it will pay big dividends when spring arrives. Spraying under the fenders and other areas which even car washes don't reach will help remove road salt, dirt and other build-ups which help breed rust. Adjust the nozzle to a high-force spray. An old brush will help break up residue, permitting it to be washed away more easily.

It's a somewhat messy job, but worth it in the long run because rust often starts in those hidden areas.

At the same time, wash grime off the door sills and, more importantly, the under portions of the doors, plus the tailgate if you have a station wagon or truck. Applying a coat of wax to those areas at least once before and once during winter will help fend off rust.

When applying the wax to the under parts of the doors, you will note small drain holes. These holes often are plugged with undercoating or dirt. Make sure they are cleaned out to prevent water build-up inside the doors. A small punch or penknife will do the job.

Water from the high-pressure sprays in car washes sometimes can get into the housings for parking and taillights, so take a close look. If they contain water merely loosen the retaining screws and the water should run out.

176 BODY

Repairing Scratches and Small Dents

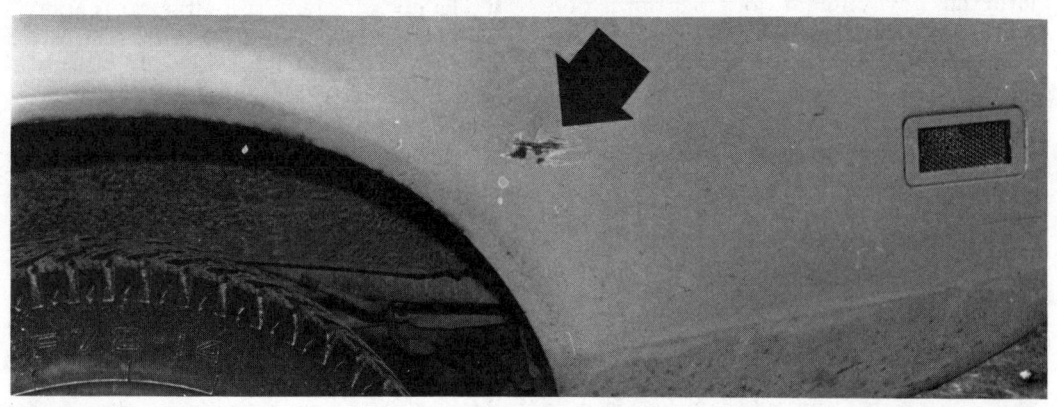

Step 1. This dent (arrow) is typical of a deep scratch or minor dent. If deep enough, the dent or scratch can be pulled out or hammered out from behind. In this case no straightening is necessary

Step 2. Using an 80-grit grinding disc on an electric drill grind the paint from the surrounding area down to bare metal. This will provide a rough surface for the body filler to grab

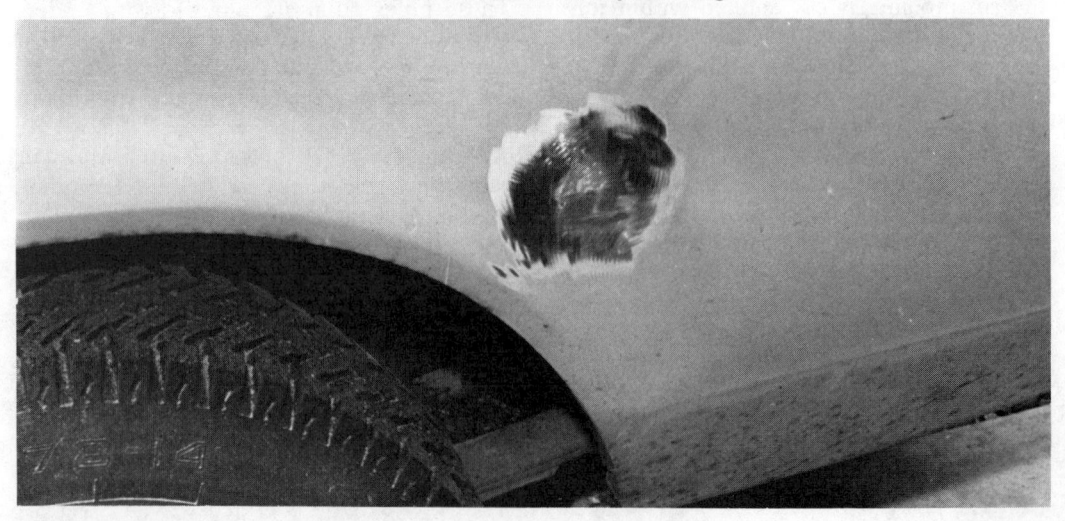

Step 3. The area should look like this when you're finished grinding

BODY 177

Step 4. Mix the body filler and cream hardener according to the directions

Step 5. Spread the body filler evenly over the entire area. Be sure to cover the area completely

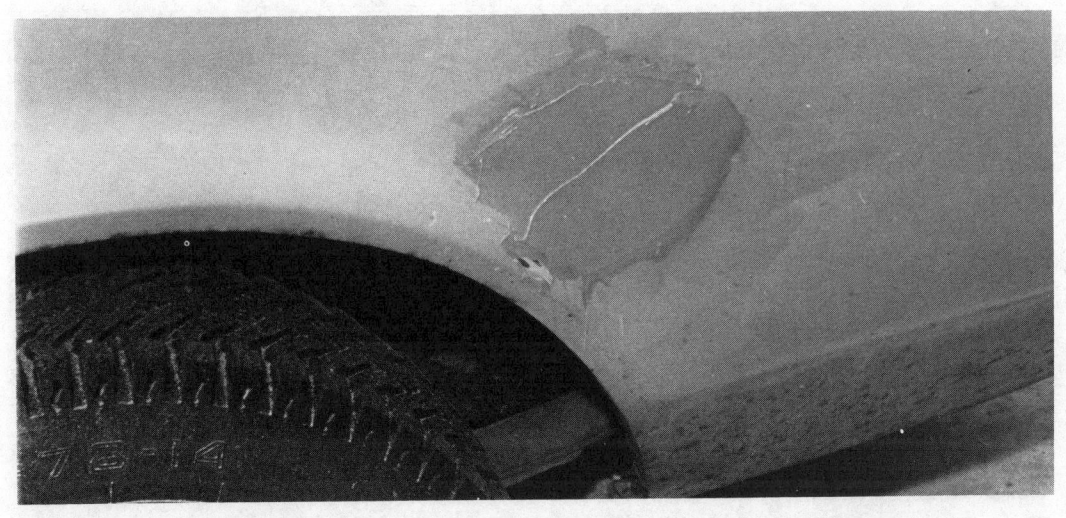

Step 6. Let the body filler dry until the surface can just be scratched with your fingernail

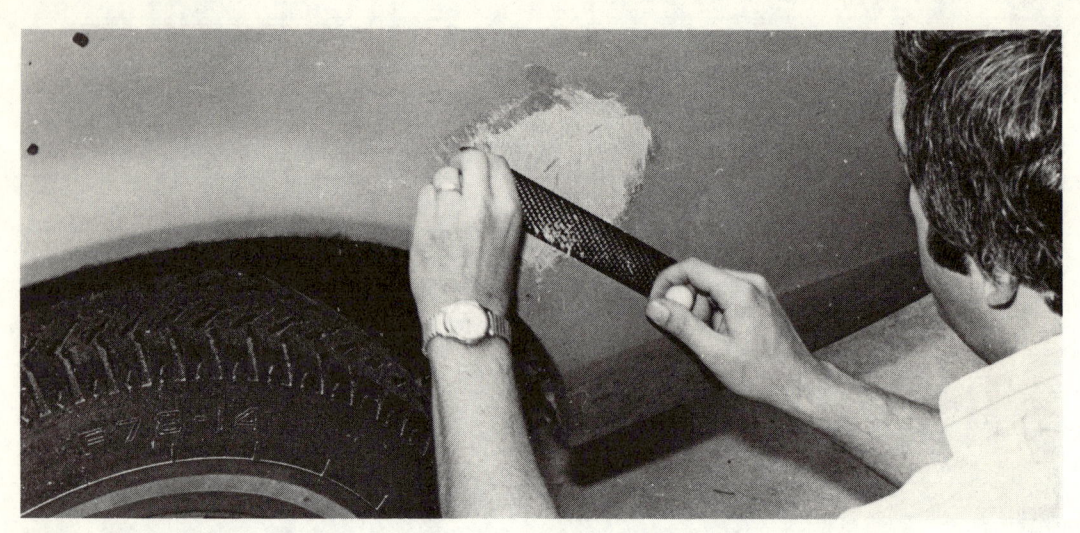

Step 7. Knock the high spots from the body filler with a body file

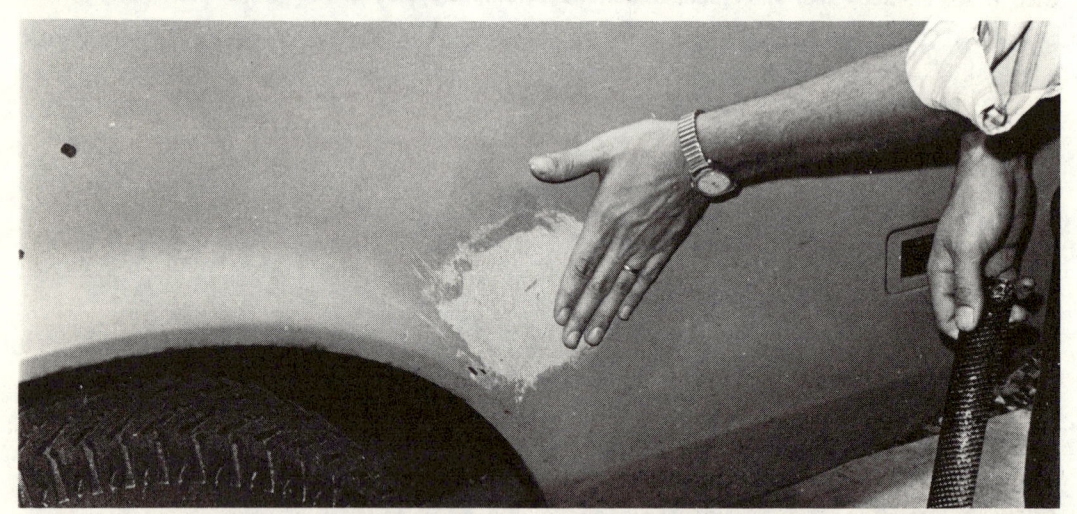

Step 8. Check frequently with the palm of your hand for high and low spots. If you wind up with low spots, you may have to apply another layer of filler

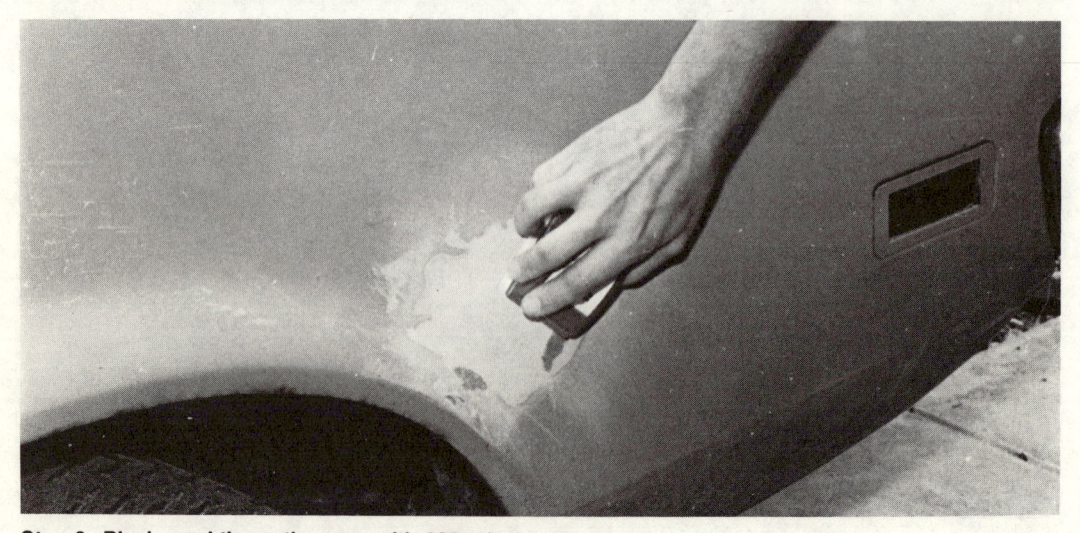

Step 9. Block sand the entire area with 320 grit paper

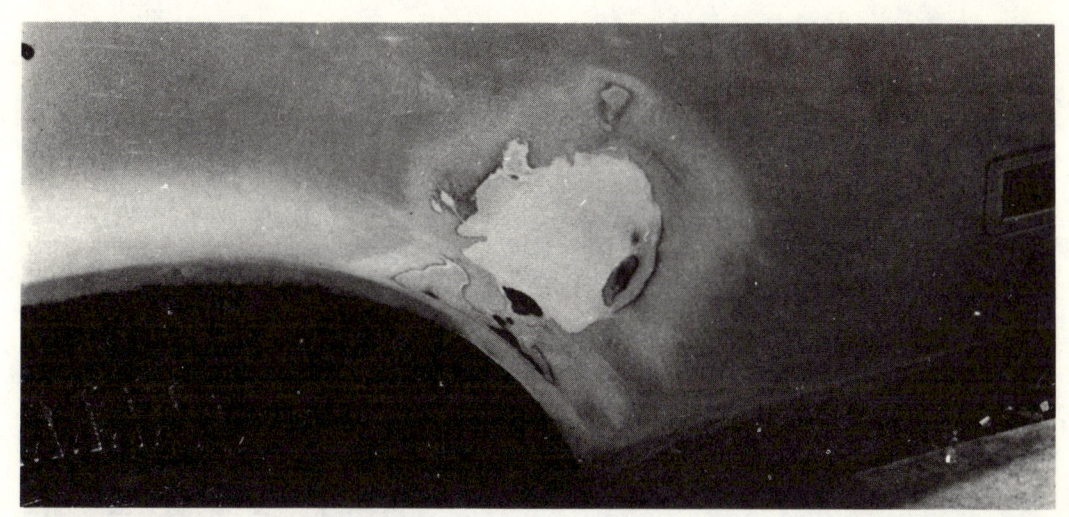

BODY 179

Step 10. When you're finished, the repair should look like this. Note the sand marks extending 2—3 inches out from the repaired area

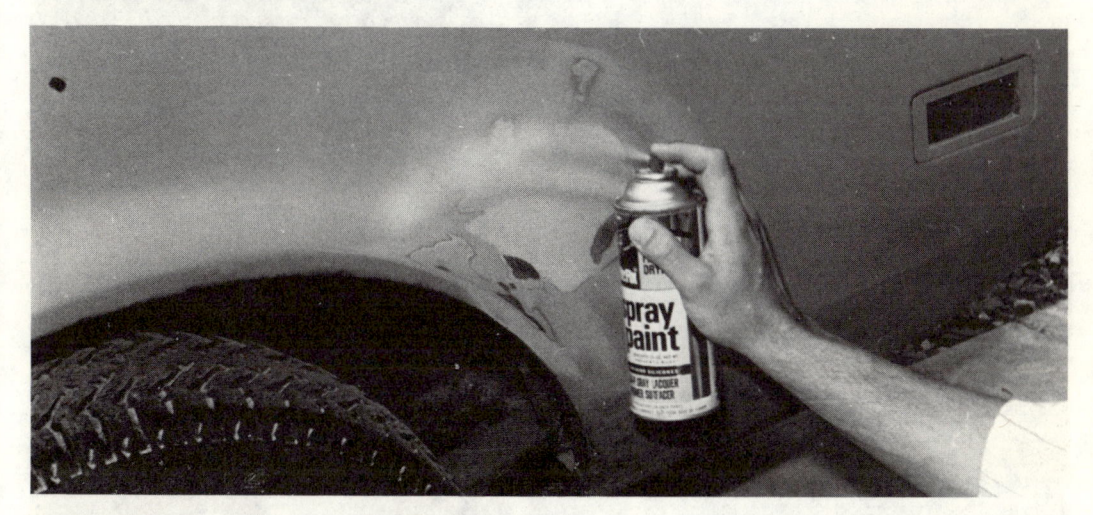

Step 11. Prime the entire area with automotive primer

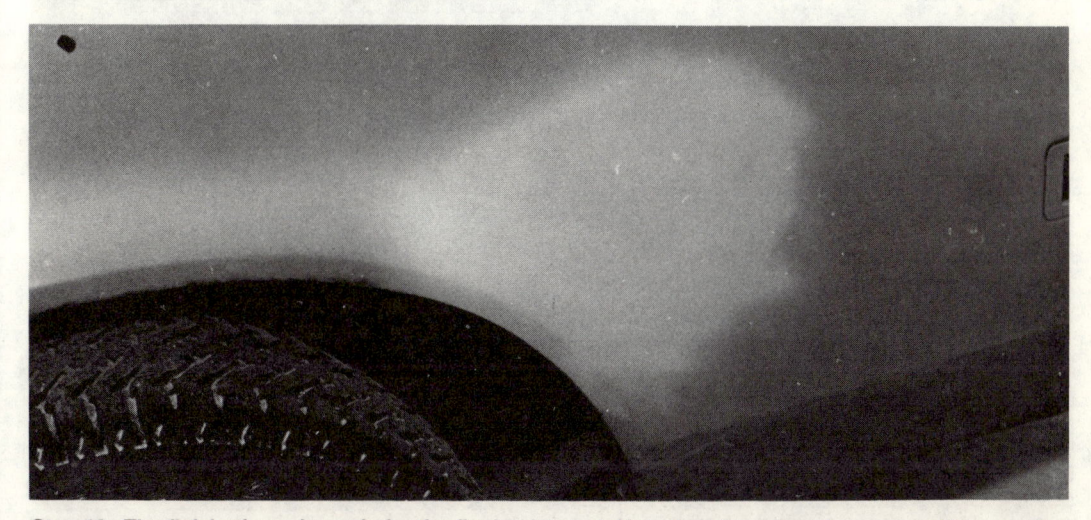

Step 12. The finished repair ready for the final paint coat. Note that the primer has covered the sanding marks (see Step 10). A repair of this size should be able to be spotpainted with good results

REPAIRING RUST HOLES

One thing you have to remember about rust: even if you grind away all the rusted metal in a panel, and repair the area with any of the kits available, *eventually* the rust will return. There are two reasons for this. One, rust is a chemical reaction that causes pressure under the repair from the inside out. That's how the blisters form. Two, the back side of the panel (and the repair) is wide open to moisture, and unpainted body filler acts like a sponge. That's why the best solution to rust problems is to remove the rusted panel and install a new one or have the rusted area cut out and a new piece of sheet metal welded in its place. The trouble with welding is the expense; sometimes it will cost more than the car or truck is worth.

One of the better solutions to do-it-yourself rust repair is the process using a fiberglass cloth repair kit (shown here). This will give a strong repair that resists cracking and moisture and is relatively easy to use. It can be used on large or small holes and also can be applied over contoured surfaces.

Step 1. Rust areas such as this are common and are easily fixed

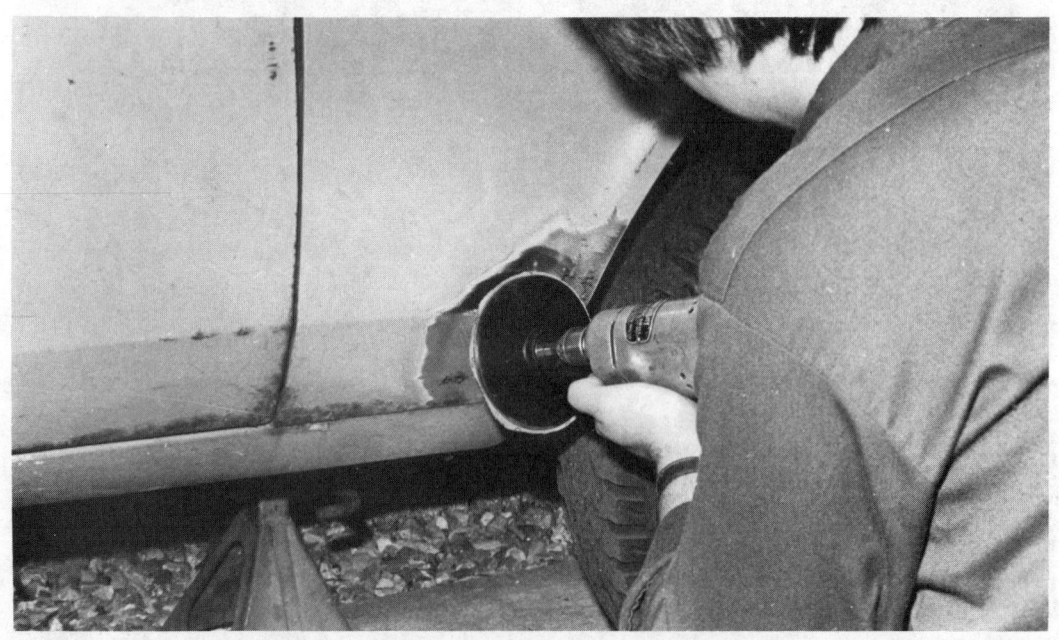

Step 2. Grind away all traces of rust with a 24-grit grinding disc. Be sure to grind back 3—4 inches from the edge of the hole down to bare metal and be sure all traces of rust are removed

BODY 181

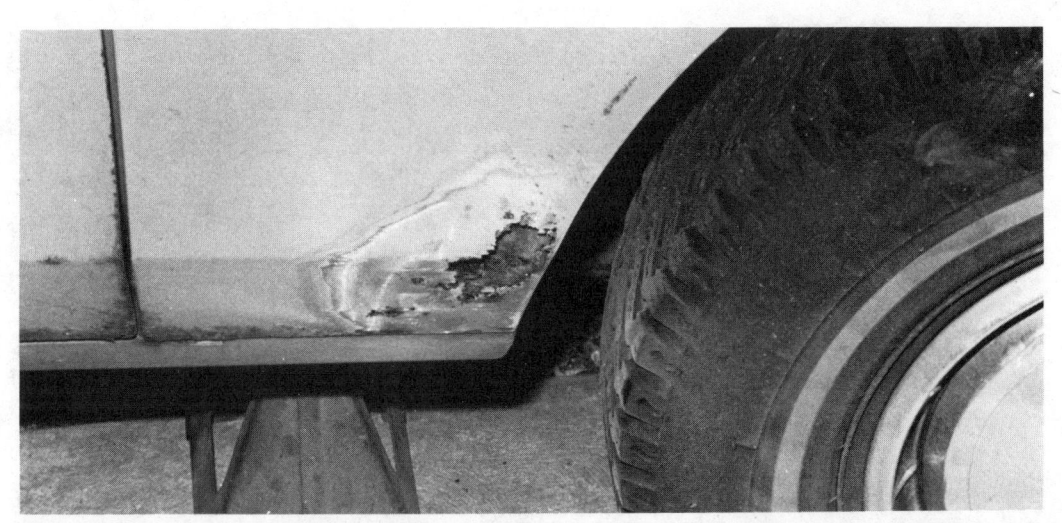

Step 3. Be sure all rust is removed from the edges of the metal. The edges must be ground back to un-rusted metal

Step 4. If you are going to use release film, cut a piece about 2" larger than the area you have sanded. Place the film over the repair and mark the sanded area on the film. Avoid any unnecessary wrinkling of the film

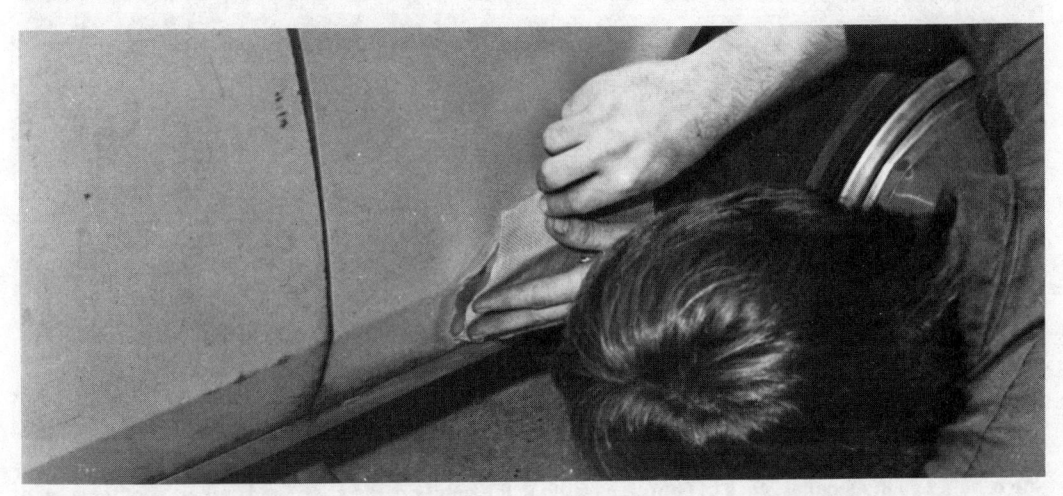

Step 5. Cut 2 pieces of fiberglass matte. One piece should be about 1" smaller than the sanded area and the second piece should be 1" smaller than the first. Use sharp scissors to avoid loose ends

182 BODY

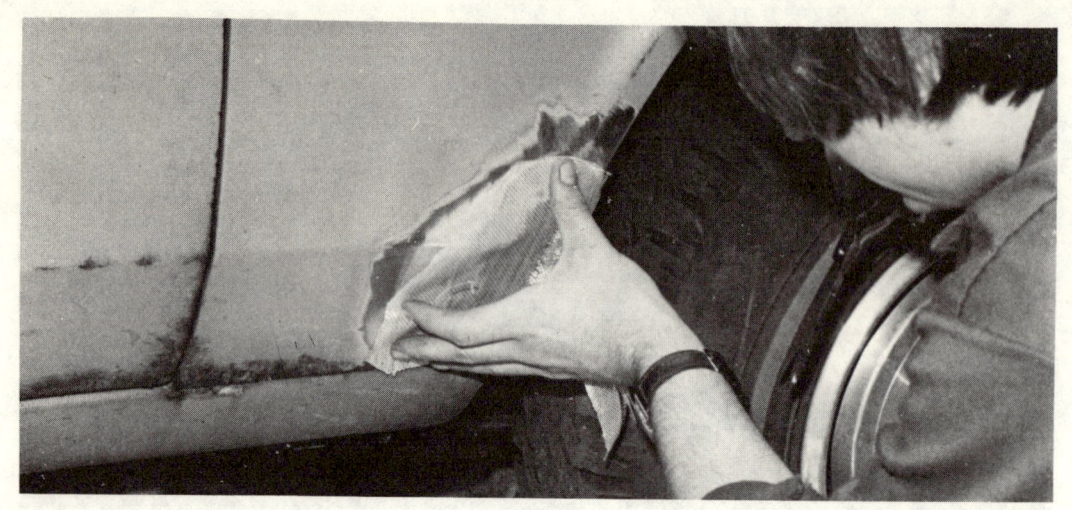

Step 6. Check the dimensions of the release film and cloth by holding them up to the repair area

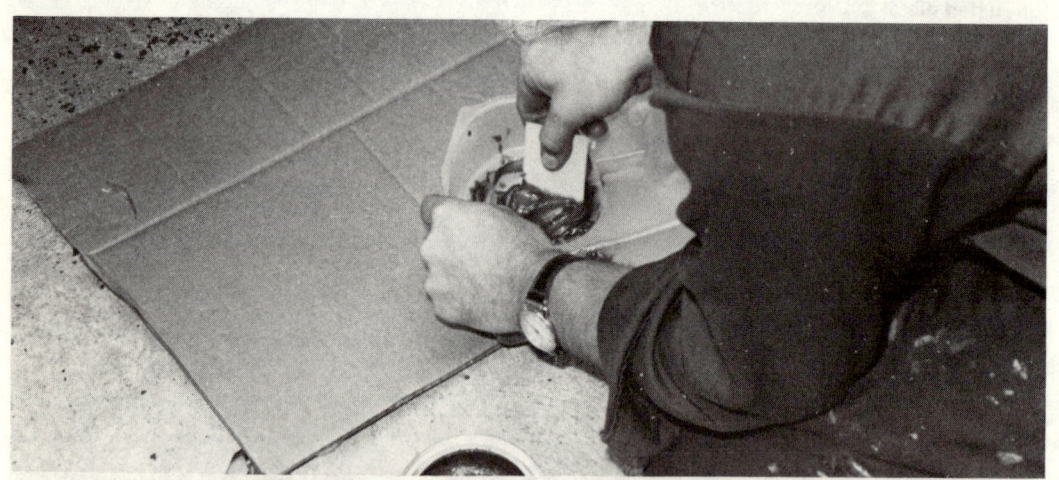

Step 7. Mix enough repair jelly and cream hardener in the mixing tray to saturate the fiberglass material or fill the repair area. Follow the directions on the container

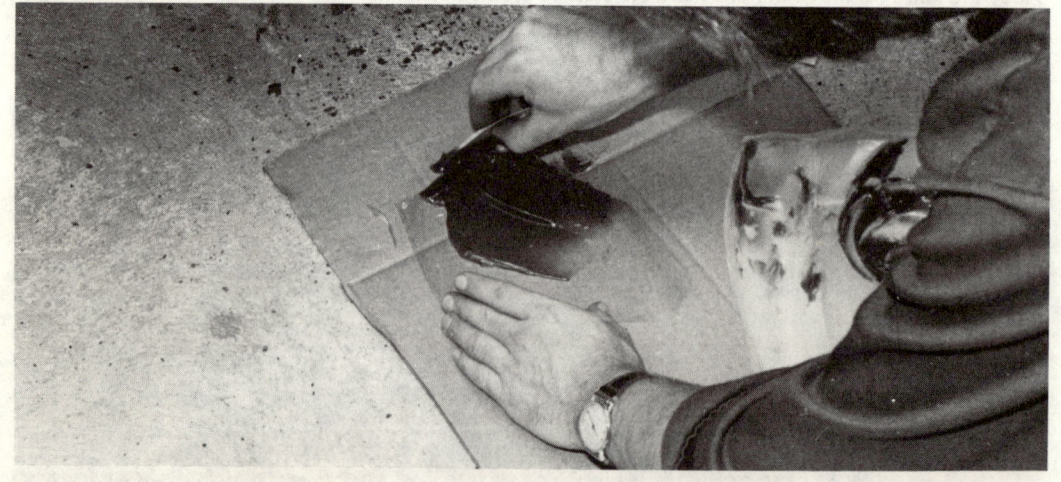

Step 8. Lay the release sheet on a flat surface and spread an even layer of filler, large enough to cover the repair. Lay the smaller piece of fiberglass cloth in the center of the sheet and spread another layer of repair jelly over the fiberglass cloth. Repeat the operation for the larger piece of cloth. If the fiberglass cloth is not used, spread the repair jelly on the release film, concentrated in the middle of the repair

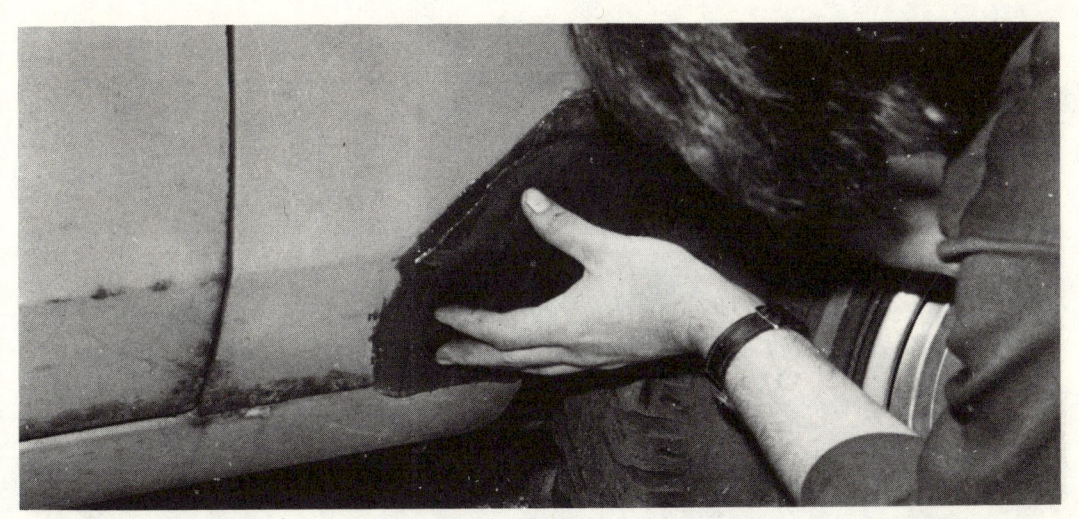

Step 9. Place the repair material over the repair area, with the release film facing outward

Step 10. Use a spreader and work from the center outward to smooth the material, following the body contours. Be sure to remove all air bubbles

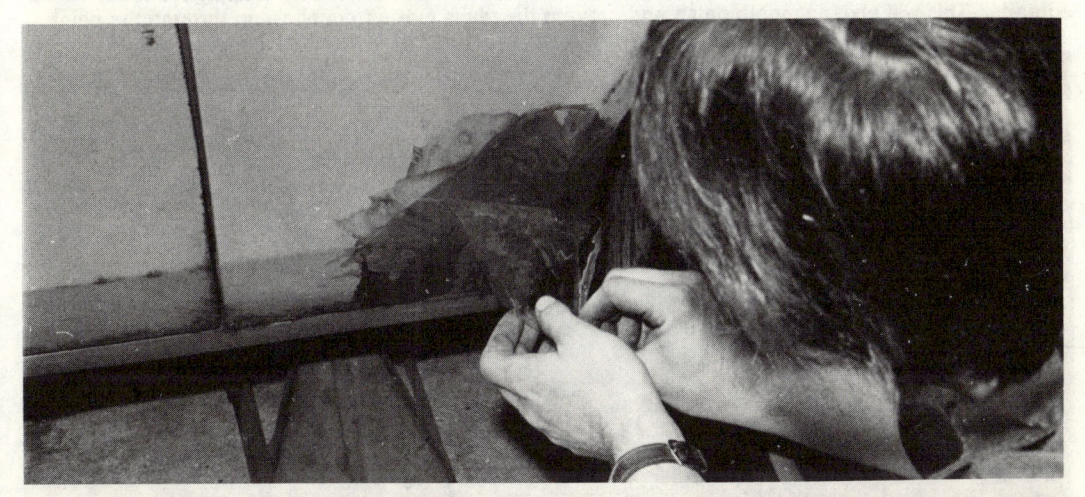

Step 11. Wait until the repair has dried tack-free and peel off the release sheet. The ideal working temperature is 65—90° F. Cooler or warmer temperatures or high humidity may require additional curing time

184 BODY

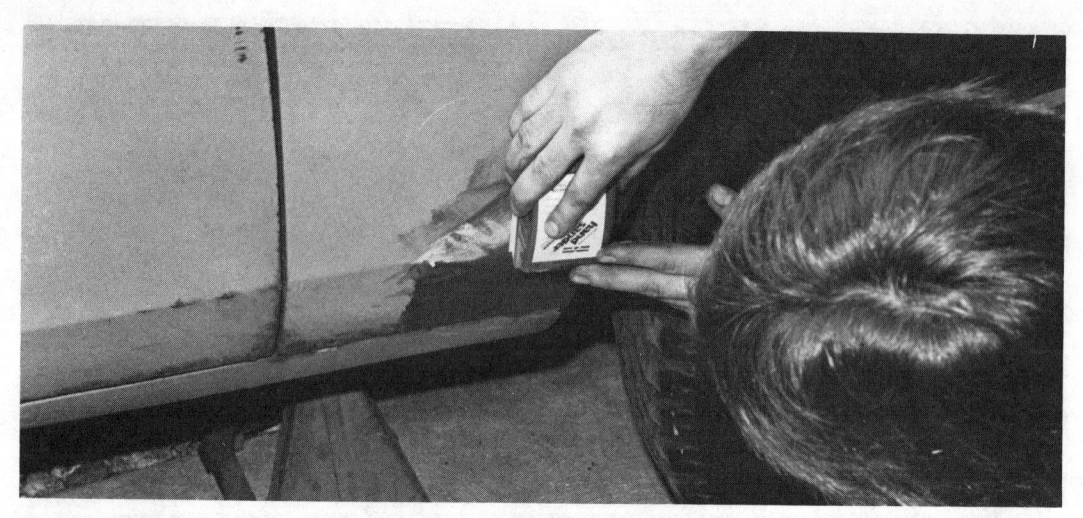

Step 12. Sand and feather-edge the entire area. The initial sanding can be done with a sanding disc on an electric drill if care is used. Finish the sanding with a block sander

Step 13. When the area is sanded smooth, mix some topcoat and hardener and apply it directly with a spreader. This will give a smooth finish and prevent the glass matte from showing through the paint

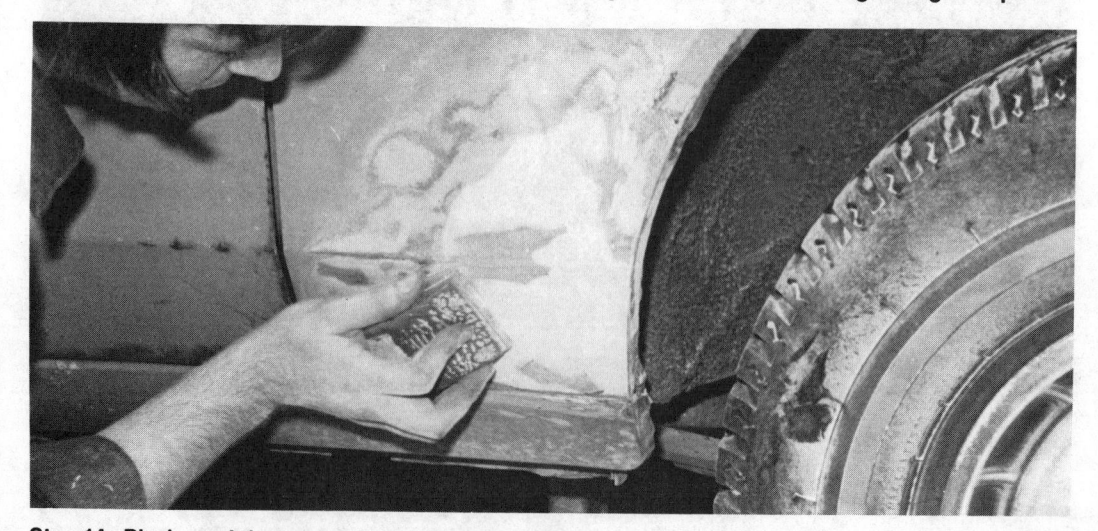

Step 14. Block sand the topcoat with finishing sandpaper

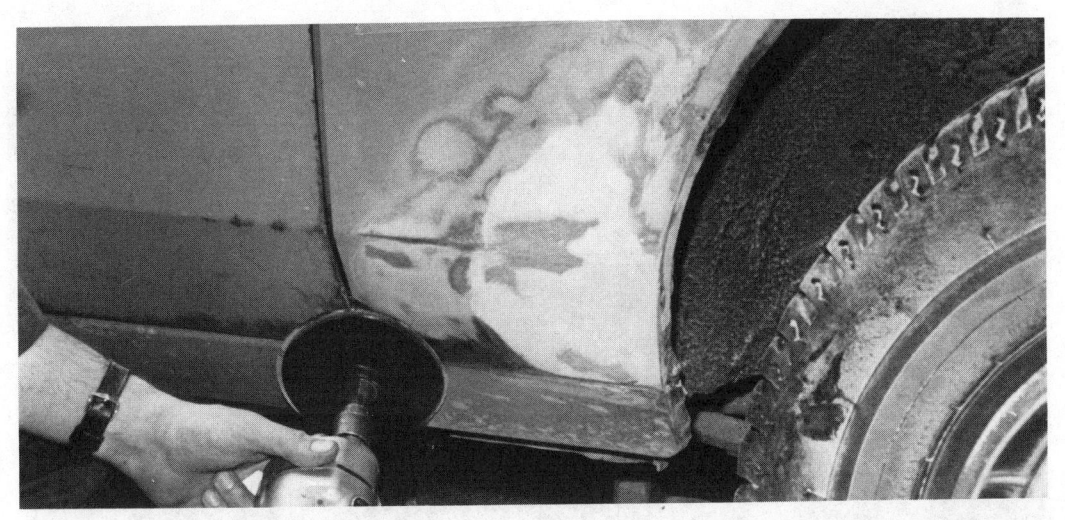

Step 15. To finish this repair, grind out the surface rust along the top edge of the rocker panel

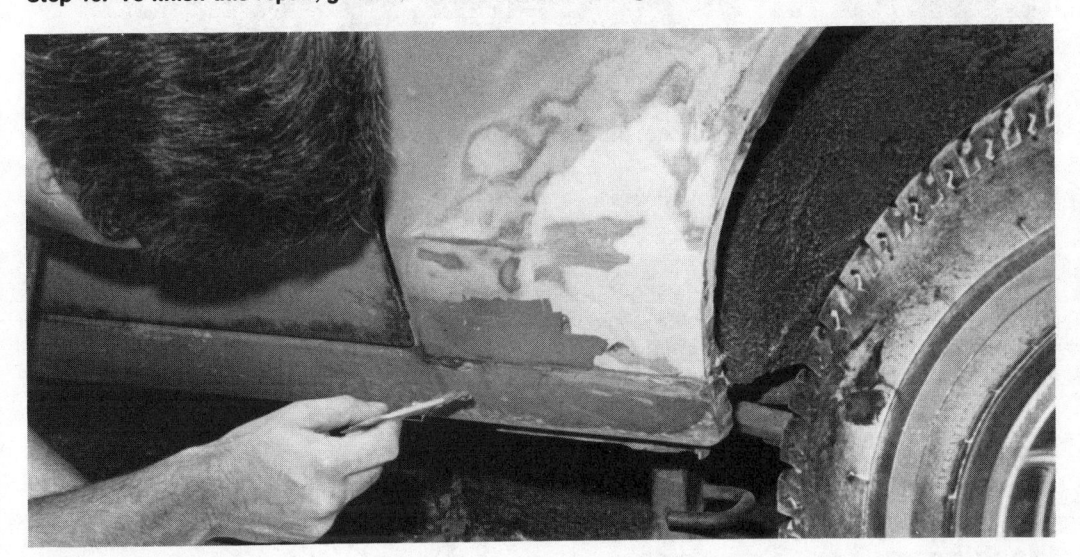

Step 16. Mix some more repair jelly and cream hardener and apply it directly over the surface

Step 17. When it dries tack-free, block sand the surface smooth

186 BODY

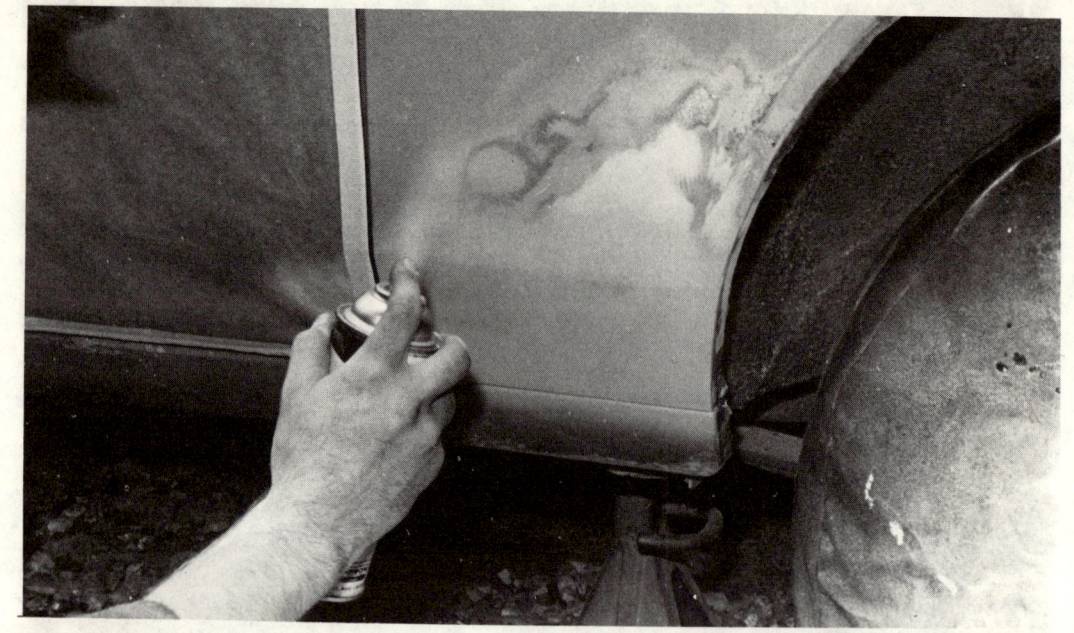

Step 18. If necessary, mask off adjacent panels and spray the entire repair with primer. You are now ready for a color coat

AUTO BODY CARE

There are hundreds—maybe thousands—of products on the market, all designed to protect or aid your car's finish in some manner. There are as many different products as there are ways to use them, but they all have one thing in common—the surface must be clean.

Washing

The primary ingredient for washing your car is water, preferably "soft" water. In many areas of the country, the local water supply is "hard" containing many minerals. The little rings or film that is left on your car's surface after it has dried is the result of "hard" water.

Since you usually can't change the local water supply, the next best thing is to dry the surface before it has a chance to dry itself.

Into the water you usually add soap. Don't use detergents or common, coarse soaps. Your car's paint never truly dries out, but is always evaporating residual oils into the air. Harsh detergents will remove these oils, causing the paint to dry faster than normal. Instead use warm water and a non-detergent soap made especially for waxed surfaces or a liquid soap made for waxed surfaces or a liquid soap made for washing dishes by hand.

Other products that can be used on painted surfaces include baking soda or plain soda water for stubborn dirt.

Wash the car completely, starting at the top, and rinse it completely clean. Abrasive grit should be loaded off under water pressure; scrubbing grit off will scratch the finish. The best washing tool is a sponge, cleaning mitt or soft towel. Whichever you choose, replace it often as each tends to absorb grease and dirt.

Other ways to get a better wash include:
• Don't wash your car in the sun or when the finish is hot.
• Use water pressure to remove caked-on dirt.
• Remove tree-sap and bird effluence immediately. Such substances will eat through wax, polish and paint.

One of the best implements to dry your car is a turkish towel or an old, soft bath towel. Anything with a deep nap will hold any dirt in suspension and not grind it into the paint.

Harder cloths will only grind the grit into the paint making more scratches. Always start drying at the top, followed by the hood and trunk and sides. You'll find there's always more dirt near the rocker panels and wheelwells which will wind up on the rest of the car if you dry these areas first.

Cleaners, Waxes and Polishes

Before going any farther you should know the function of various products.

Cleaners—remove the top layer of dead pigment or paint.

Rubbing or polishing compounds—used to remove stubborn dirt, get rid of minor scratches, smooth away imperfections and partially restore badly weathered paint.

Polishes—contain no abrasives or waxes; they shine the paint by adding oils to the paint.

Waxes—are a protective coating for the polish.

CLEANERS AND COMPOUNDS

Before you apply any wax, you'll have to remove oxidation, road film and other types of pollutants that washing alone will not remove.

The paint on your car never dries completely. There are always residual oils evaporating from the paint into the air. When enough oils are present in the paint, it has a healthy shine (gloss). When too many oils evaporate the paint takes on a whitish cast known as oxidation. The idea of polishing and waxing is to keep enough oil present in the painted surface to prevent oxidation; but when it occurs, the only recourse is to remove the top layer of "dead" paint, exposing the healthy paint underneath.

Products to remove oxidation and road film are sold under a variety of generic names—polishes, cleaner, rubbing compound, cleaner/polish, polish/cleaner, self-polishing wax, pre-wax cleaner, finish restorer and many more. Regardless of name there are two types of cleaners—abrasive cleaners (sometimes called polishing or rubbing compounds) that remove oxidation by grinding away the top layer of "dead" paint, or chemical cleaners that dissolve the "dead" pigment, allowing it to be wiped away.

Abrasive cleaners, by their nature, leave thousands of minute scratches in the finish, which must be polished out later. These should only be used in extreme cases, but are usually the only thing to use on badly oxidized paint finishes. Chemical cleaners are much milder but are not strong enough for severe cases of oxidation or weathered paint.

The most popular cleaners are liquid or paste abrasive polishing and rubbing compounds. Polishing compounds have a finer abrasive grit for medium duty work. Rubbing compounds are a coarser abrasive and for heavy duty work. Unless you are familiar with how to use compounds, be very careful. Excessive rubbing with any type of compound or cleaner can grind right through the paint to primer or bare metal. Follow the directions on the container—depending on type, the cleaner may or may not be OK for your paint. For example, some cleaners are not formulated for acrylic lacquer finishes.

When a small area needs compounding or heavy polishing, it's best to do the job by hand. Some people prefer a powered buffer for large areas. Avoid cutting through the paint along styling edges on the body. Small, hand operations where the compound is applied and rubbed using cloth folded into a thick ball allow you to work in straight lines along such edges.

To avoid cutting through on the edges when using a power buffer, try masking tape. Just cover the edge with tape while using power. Then finish the job by hand with the tape removed. Even then work carefully. The paint tends to be a lot thinner along the sharp ridges stamped into the panels.

Whether compounding by machine or by hand, only work on a small area and apply the compound sparingly. If the materials are spread too thin, or allowed to sit too long, they dry out. Once dry they lose the ability to deliver a smooth, clean finish. Also, dried out polish tends to cause the buffer to stick in one spot. This in turn can burn or cut through the finish.

WAXES AND POLISHES

Your car's finish can be protected in a number of ways. A cleaner/wax or polish/cleaner followed by wax or variations of each all provide good results. The two-step approach (polish followed by wax) is probably slightly better but consumes more time and effort. Properly fed with oils, your paint should never need cleaning, but despite the best polishing job, it won't last unless it's protected with wax. Without wax, polish must be renewed at least once a month to prevent oxidation. Years ago (some still swear by it today), the best wax was made from the Brazilian palm, the Carnuba, favored for its vegetable base and high melting point. However, modern synthetic waxes are harder, which means they protect against moisture better, and chemically inert silicone is used for a long lasting protection. The only problem with silicone wax is that it penetrates all layers of paint. To repaint or touch up a panel or car protected by silicone wax, you have to completely strip the finish to avoid "fisheyes."

Under normal conditions, silicone waxes will last 4–6 months, but you have to be careful of wax build-up from too much waxing. Too thick a coat of wax is just as bad as no wax at all; it stops the paint from breathing.

Combination cleaners/waxes have become popular lately because they remove the old layer of wax plus light oxidation, while putting on a fresh coat of wax at the same time. Some cleaners/waxes contain abrasive cleaners which require caution, although many cleaner/waxes use a chemical cleaner.

Applying Wax or Polish

You may view polishing and waxing your car as a pleasant way to spend an afternoon, or as a boring chore, but it has to be done to keep the paint on your car. Caring for the paint doesn't require special tools, but you should follow a few rules.

1. Use a good quality wax.
2. Before applying any wax or polish, be sure the surface is completely clean. Just because the car looks clean, doesn't mean it's ready for polish or wax.
3. If the finish on your car is weathered, dull, or oxidized, it will probably have to be compounded to remove the old or oxidized paint. If the paint is simply dulled from lack of care, one of the non-abrasive cleaners known as polishing compounds will do the trick. If the paint is severely scratched or really dull, you'll probably have to use a rubbing compound to prepare the finish for waxing. If you're not sure which one to use, use the polishing compound, since you can easily ruin the finish by using too strong a compound.
4. Don't apply wax, polish or compound in direct sunlight, even if the directions on the can say you can. Most waxes will not cure properly in bright sunlight and you'll probably end up with a blotchy looking finish.
5. Don't rub the wax off too soon. The result will be a wet, dull looking finish. Let the wax dry thoroughly before buffing it off.
6. A constant debate among car enthusiasts is how wax should be applied. Some maintain pastes or liquids should be applied in a circular motion, but body shop experts have long thought that this approach results in barely detectable circular abrasions, especially on cars that are waxed frequently. They advise rubbing in straight lines, especially if any kind of cleaner is involved.
7. If an applicator is not supplied with the wax, use a piece of soft cheesecloth or very soft lint-free material. The same applies to buffing the surface.

SPECIAL SURFACES

One-step combination cleaner and wax formulas shouldn't be used on many of the special surfaces which abound on cars. The one-step materials contain abrasives to achieve a clean surface under the wax top coat. The abrasives are so mild that you could clean a car every week for a couple of years without fear of rubbing through the paint. But this same level of abrasiveness might, through repeated use, damage decals used for special trim effects. This includes wide stripes, wood-grain trim and other appliques.

Painted plastics must be cleaned with care. If a cleaner is too aggressive it will cut through the paint and expose the primer. If bright trim such as polished aluminum or chrome is painted, cleaning must be performed with even greater care. If rubbing compound is being used, it will cut faster than polish.

Abrasive cleaners will dull an acrylic finish. The best way to clean these newer finishes is with a non-abrasive liquid polish. Only dirt and oxidation, not paint, will be removed.

Taking a few minutes to read the instructions on the can of polish or wax will help prevent making serious mistakes. Not all preparations will work on all surfaces. And some are intended for power application while others will only work when applied by hand.

Don't get the idea that just pouring on some polish and then hitting it with a buffer will suffice. Power equipment speeds the operation. But it also adds a measure of risk. It's very easy to damage the finish if you use the wrong methods or materials.

Caring for Chrome

Read the label on the container. Many products are formulated specifically for chrome, but others contain abrasives that will scratch the chrome finish. If it isn't recommended for chrome, don't use it.

Never use steel wool or kitchen soap pads to clean chrome. Be careful not to get chrome cleaner on paint or interior vinyl surfaces. If you do, get it off immediately.

Troubleshooting 10

This section is designed to aid in the quick, accurate diagnosis of automotive problems. While automotive repairs can be made by many people, accurate troubleshooting is a rare skill for the amateur and professional alike.

In its simplest state, troubleshooting is an exercise in logic. It is essential to realize that an automobile is really composed of a series of systems. Some of these systems are interrelated; others are not. Automobiles operate within a framework of logical rules and physical laws, and the key to troubleshooting is a good understanding of all the automotive systems.

This section breaks the car or truck down into its component systems, allowing the problem to be isolated. The charts and diagnostic road maps list the most common problems and the most probable causes of trouble. Obviously it would be impossible to list every possible problem that could happen along with every possible cause, but it will locate MOST problems and eliminate a lot of unnecessary guesswork. The systematic format will locate problems within a given system, but, because many automotive systems are interrelated, the solution to your particular problem may be found in a number of systems on the car or truck.

USING THE TROUBLESHOOTING CHARTS

This book contains all of the specific information that the average do-it-yourself mechanic needs to repair and maintain his or her car or truck. The troubleshooting charts are designed to be used in conjunction with the specific procedures and information in the text. For instance, troubleshooting a point-type ignition system is fairly standard for all models, but you may be directed to the text to find procedures for troubleshooting an individual type of electronic ignition. You will also have to refer to the specification charts throughout the book for specifications applicable to your car or truck.

TOOLS AND EQUIPMENT

The tools illustrated in Chapter 1 (plus two more diagnostic pieces) will be adequate to troubleshoot most problems. The two other tools needed are a voltmeter and an ohmmeter. These can be purchased separately or in combination, known as a VOM meter.

In the event that other tools are required, they will be noted in the procedures.

190 TROUBLESHOOTING

Troubleshooting Engine Problems

See Chapters 2, 3, 4 for more information and service procedures.

Index to Systems

System	To Test	Group
Battery	Engine need not be running	1
Starting system	Engine need not be running	2
Primary electrical system	Engine need not be running	3
Secondary electrical system	Engine need not be running	4
Fuel system	Engine need not be running	5
Engine compression	Engine need not be running	6
Engine vacuum	Engine must be running	7
Secondary electrical system	Engine must be running	8
Valve train	Engine must be running	9
Exhaust system	Engine must be running	10
Cooling system	Engine must be running	11
Engine lubrication	Engine must be running	12

Index to Problems

Problem: Symptom	Begin at Specific Diagnosis, Number
Engine Won't Start:	
Starter doesn't turn	1.1, 2.1
Starter turns, engine doesn't	2.1
Starter turns engine very slowly	1.1, 2.4
Starter turns engine normally	3.1, 4.1
Starter turns engine very quickly	6.1
Engine fires intermittently	4.1
Engine fires consistently	5.1, 6.1
Engine Runs Poorly:	
Hard starting	3.1, 4.1, 5.1, 8.1
Rough idle	4.1, 5.1, 8.1
Stalling	3.1, 4.1, 5.1, 8.1
Engine dies at high speeds	4.1, 5.1
Hesitation (on acceleration from standing stop)	5.1, 8.1
Poor pickup	4.1, 5.1, 8.1
Lack of power	3.1, 4.1, 5.1, 8.1
Backfire through the carburetor	4.1, 8.1, 9.1
Backfire through the exhaust	4.1, 8.1, 9.1
Blue exhaust gases	6.1, 7.1
Black exhaust gases	5.1
Running on (after the ignition is shut off)	3.1, 8.1
Susceptible to moisture	4.1
Engine misfires under load	4.1, 7.1, 8.4, 9.1
Engine misfires at speed	4.1, 8.4
Engine misfires at idle	3.1, 4.1, 5.1, 7.1, 8.4

Sample Section

Test and Procedure	Results and Indications	Proceed to
4.1—Check for spark: Hold each spark plug wire approximately ¼" from ground with gloves or a heavy, dry rag. Crank the engine and observe the spark.	→ If no spark is evident:	→ 4.2
	→ If spark is good in some cases:	→ 4.3
	→ If spark is good in all cases:	→ 4.6

TROUBLESHOOTING

Specific Diagnosis

This section is arranged so that following each test, instructions are given to proceed to another, until a problem is diagnosed.

Section 1—Battery

Test and Procedure	Results and Indications	Proceed to
1.1—Inspect the battery visually for case condition (corrosion, cracks) and water level.	If case is cracked, replace battery:	1.4
	If the case is intact, remove corrosion with a solution of baking soda and water (**CAUTION:** *do not get the solution into the battery*), and fill with water:	1.2
1.2—Check the battery cable connections: Insert a screwdriver between the battery post and the cable clamp. Turn the headlights on high beam, and observe them as the screwdriver is gently twisted to ensure good metal to metal contact.	If the lights brighten, remove and clean the clamp and post; coat the post with petroleum jelly, install and tighten the clamp:	1.4
	If no improvement is noted:	1.3
1.3—Test the state of charge of the battery using an individual cell tester or hydrometer.	If indicated, charge the battery. **NOTE:** *If no obvious reason exists for the low state of charge (i.e., battery age, prolonged storage), proceed to:*	1.4

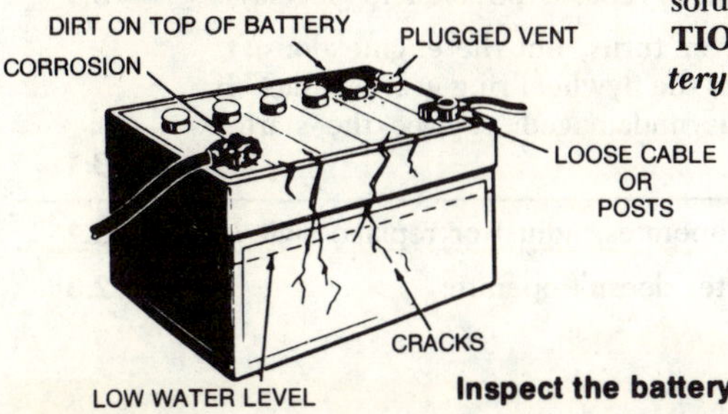

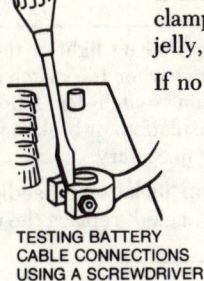

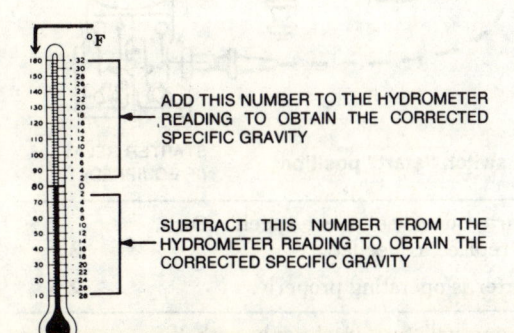

Specific Gravity (@ 80° F.)

Minimum	Battery Charge
1.260	100% Charged
1.230	75% Charged
1.200	50% Charged
1.170	25% Charged
1.140	Very Little Power Left
1.110	Completely Discharged

The effects of temperature on battery specific gravity (left) and amount of battery charge in relation to specific gravity (right)

1.4—Visually inspect battery cables for cracking, bad connection to ground, or bad connection to starter.	If necessary, tighten connections or replace the cables:	2.1

TROUBLESHOOTING

Section 2—Starting System
See Chapter 3 for service procedures

Test and Procedure	Results and Indications	Proceed to
Note: Tests in Group 2 are performed with coil high tension lead disconnected to prevent accidental starting.		
2.1—Test the starter motor and solenoid: Connect a jumper from the battery post of the solenoid (or relay) to the starter post of the solenoid (or relay).	If starter turns the engine normally:	2.2
	If the starter buzzes, or turns the engine very slowly:	2.4
	If no response, replace the solenoid (or relay).	3.1
	If the starter turns, but the engine doesn't, ensure that the flywheel ring gear is intact. If the gear is undamaged, replace the starter drive.	3.1
2.2—Determine whether ignition override switches are functioning properly (clutch start switch, neutral safety switch), by connecting a jumper across the switch(es), and turning the ignition switch to "start".	If starter operates, adjust or replace switch:	3.1
	If the starter doesn't operate:	2.3
2.3—Check the ignition switch "start" position: Connect a 12V test lamp or voltmeter between the starter post of the solenoid (or relay) and ground. Turn the ignition switch to the "start" position, and jiggle the key.	If the lamp doesn't light or the meter needle doesn't move when the switch is turned, check the ignition switch for loose connections, cracked insulation, or broken wires. Repair or replace as necessary:	3.1
	If the lamp flickers or needle moves when the key is jiggled, replace the ignition switch.	3.3

Checking the ignition switch "start" position

STARTER RELAY (IF EQUIPPED)

2.4—Remove and bench test the starter, according to specifications in the engine electrical section.	If the starter does not meet specifications, repair or replace as needed:	3.1
	If the starter is operating properly:	2.5
2.5—Determine whether the engine can turn freely: Remove the spark plugs, and check for water in the cylinders. Check for water on the dipstick, or oil in the radiator. Attempt to turn the engine using an 18" flex drive and socket on the crankshaft pulley nut or bolt.	If the engine will turn freely only with the spark plugs out, and hydrostatic lock (water in the cylinders) is ruled out, check valve timing:	9.2
	If engine will not turn freely, and it is known that the clutch and transmission are free, the engine must be disassembled for further evaluation:	Chapter 3

Section 3—Primary Electrical System

Test and Procedure	Results and Indications	Proceed to
3.1—Check the ignition switch "on" position: Connect a jumper wire between the distributor side of the coil and ground, and a 12V test lamp between the switch side of the coil and ground. Remove the high tension lead from the coil. Turn the ignition switch on and jiggle the key.	If the lamp lights:	3.2
	If the lamp flickers when the key is jiggled, replace the ignition switch:	3.3
	If the lamp doesn't light, check for loose or open connections. If none are found, remove the ignition switch and check for continuity. If the switch is faulty, replace it:	3.3

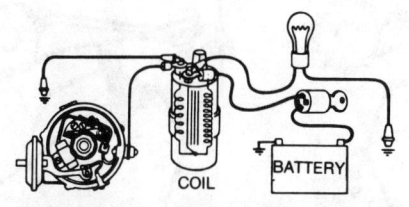

Checking the ignition switch "on" position

3.2—Check the ballast resistor or resistance wire for an open circuit, using an ohmmeter. See Chapter 3 for specific tests.	Replace the resistor or resistance wire if the resistance is zero. **NOTE:** *Some ignition systems have no ballast resistor.*	3.3

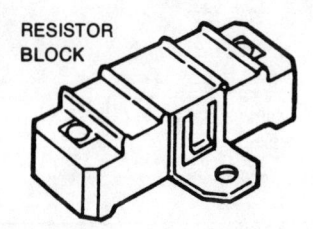

Two types of resistors

3.3—On point-type ignition systems, visually inspect the breaker points for burning, pitting or excessive wear. Gray coloring of the point contact surfaces is normal. Rotate the crankshaft until the contact heel rests on a high point of the distributor cam and adjust the point gap to specifications. On electronic ignition models, remove the distributor cap and visually inspect the armature. Ensure that the armature pin is in place, and that the armature is on tight and rotates when the engine is cranked. Make sure there are no cracks, chips or rounded edges on the armature.	If the breaker points are intact, clean the contact surfaces with fine emery cloth, and adjust the point gap to specifications. If the points are worn, replace them. On electronic systems, replace any parts which appear defective. If condition persists:	3.4

194 TROUBLESHOOTING

Test and Procedure	Results and Indications	Proceed to
3.4—On point-type ignition systems, connect a dwell-meter between the distributor primary lead and ground. Crank the engine and observe the point dwell angle. On electronic ignition systems, conduct a stator (magnetic pickup assembly) test. See Chapter 3.	On point-type systems, adjust the dwell angle if necessary. **NOTE:** *Increasing the point gap decreases the dwell angle and vice-versa.*	3.6
	If the dwell meter shows little or no reading;	3.5
	On electronic ignition systems, if the stator is bad, replace the stator. If the stator is good, proceed to the other tests in Chapter 3.	

Dwell is a function of point gap

| 3.5—On the point-type ignition systems, check the condenser for short: connect an ohmeter across the condenser body and the pigtail lead. | If any reading other than infinite is noted, replace the condenser | 3.6 |

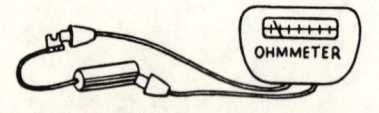

Checking the condenser for short

| 3.6—Test the coil primary resistance: On point-type ignition systems, connect an ohmmeter across the coil primary terminals, and read the resistance on the low scale. Note whether an external ballast resistor or resistance wire is used. On electronic ignition systems, test the coil primary resistance as in Chapter 3. | Point-type ignition coils utilizing ballast resistors or resistance wires should have approximately 1.0 ohms resistance. Coils with internal resistors should have approximately 4.0 ohms resistance. If values far from the above are noted, replace the coil. | 4.1 |

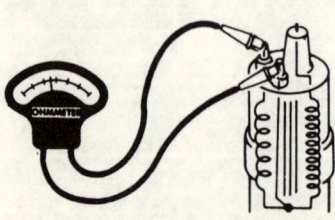

Check the coil primary resistance

TROUBLESHOOTING 195

Section 4—Secondary Electrical System
See Chapters 2–3 for service procedures

Test and Procedure	Results and Indications	Proceed to
4.1—Check for spark: Hold each spark plug wire approximately ¼" from ground with gloves or a heavy, dry rag. Crank the engine, and observe the spark.	If no spark is evident:	4.2
	If spark is good in some cylinders:	4.3
	If spark is good in all cylinders:	4.6

Check for spark at the plugs

4.2—Check for spark at the coil high tension lead: Remove the coil high tension lead from the distributor and position it approximately ¼" from ground. Crank the engine and observe spark. **CAUTION:** *This test should not be performed on engines equipped with electronic ignition.*	If the spark is good and consistent:	4.3
	If the spark is good but intermittent, test the primary electrical system starting at 3.3:	3.3
	If the spark is weak or non-existent, replace the coil high tension lead, clean and tighten all connections and retest. If no improvement is noted:	4.4
4.3—Visually inspect the distributor cap and rotor for burned or corroded contacts, cracks, carbon tracks, or moisture. Also check the fit of the rotor on the distributor shaft (where applicable).	If moisture is present, dry thoroughly, and retest per 4.1:	4.1
	If burned or excessively corroded contacts, cracks, or carbon tracks are noted, replace the defective part(s) and retest per 4.1:	4.1
	If the rotor and cap appear intact, or are only slightly corroded, clean the contacts thoroughly (including the cap towers and spark plug wire ends) and retest per 4.1:	
	If the spark is good in all cases:	4.6
	If the spark is poor in all cases:	4.5

Inspect the distributor cap and rotor

196 TROUBLESHOOTING

Test and Procedure	Results and Indications	Proceed to
4.4—Check the coil secondary resistance: On point-type systems connect an ohmmeter across the distributor side of the coil and the coil tower. Read the resistance on the high scale of the ohmmeter. On electronic ignition systems, see Chapter 3 for specific tests.	The resistance of a satisfactory coil should be between 4,000 and 10,000 ohms. If resistance is considerably higher (i.e., 40,000 ohms) replace the coil and retest per 4.1. **NOTE:** *This does not apply to high performance coils.*	

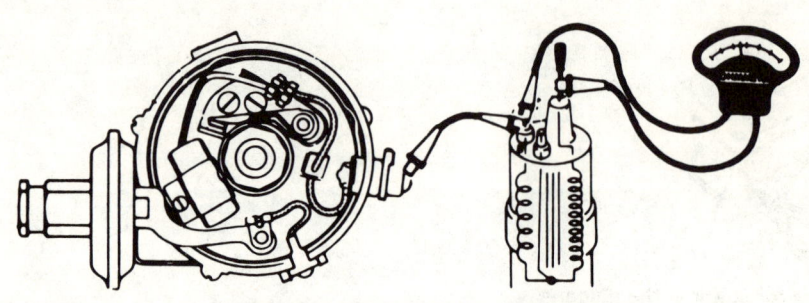

Testing the coil secondary resistance

4.5—Visually inspect the spark plug wires for cracking or brittleness. Ensure that no two wires are positioned so as to cause induction firing (adjacent and parallel). Remove each wire, one by one, and check resistance with an ohmmeter.	Replace any cracked or brittle wires. If any of the wires are defective, replace the entire set. Replace any wires with excessive resistance (over 8000 Ω per foot for suppression wire), and separate any wires that might cause induction firing.	4.6

Misfiring can be the result of spark plug leads to adjacent, consecutively firing cylinders running parallel and too close together

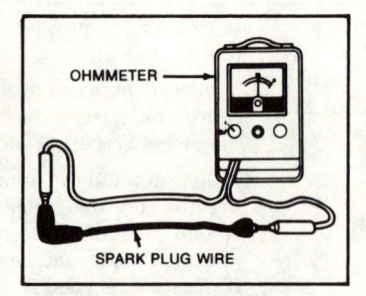

On point-type ignition systems, check the spark plug wires as shown. On electronic ignitions, do not remove the wire from the distributor cap terminal; instead, test through the cap

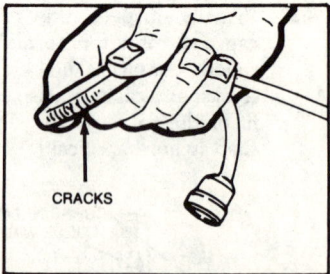

Spark plug wires can be checked visually by bending them in a loop over your finger. This will reveal any cracks, burned or broken insulation. Any wire with cracked insulation should be replaced

4.6—Remove the spark plugs, noting the cylinders from which they were removed, and evaluate according to the color photos in the middle of this book.	See following.	**See following.**

TROUBLESHOOTING 197

Test and Procedure	Results and Indications	Proceed to
4.7—Examine the location of all the plugs.	The following diagrams illustrate some of the conditions that the location of plugs will reveal.	**4.8**

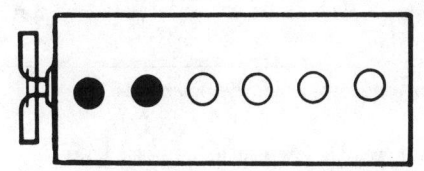

Two adjacent plugs are fouled in a 6-cylinder engine, 4-cylinder engine or either bank of a V-8. This is probably due to a blown head gasket between the two cylinders

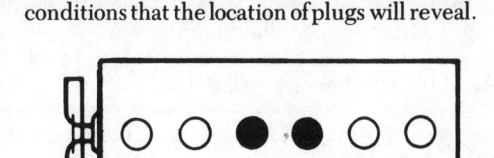

The two center plugs in a 6-cylinder engine are fouled. Raw fuel may be "boiled" out of the carburetor into the intake manifold after the engine is shut-off. Stop-start driving can also foul the center plugs, due to overly rich mixture. Proper float level, a new float needle and seat or use of an insulating spacer may help this problem

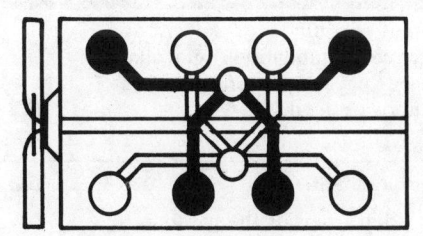

An unbalanced carburetor is indicated. Following the fuel flow on this particular design shows that the cylinders fed by the right-hand barrel are fouled from overly rich mixture, while the cylinders fed by the left-hand barrel are normal

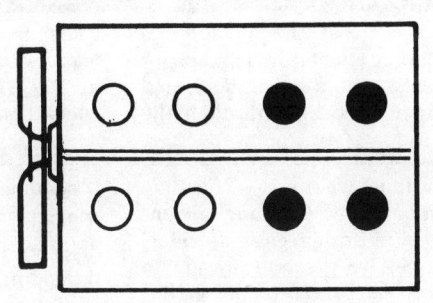

If the four rear plugs are overheated, a cooling system problem is suggested. A thorough cleaning of the cooling system may restore coolant circulation and cure the problem

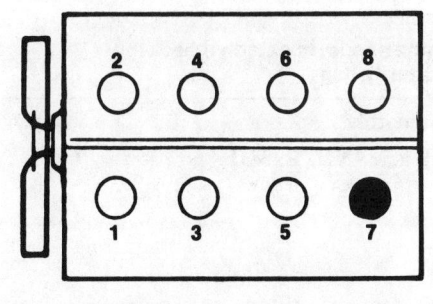

Finding one plug overheated may indicate an intake manifold leak near the affected cylinder. If the overheated plug is the second of two adjacent, consecutively firing plugs, it could be the result of ignition cross-firing. Separating the leads to these two plugs will eliminate cross-fire

Occasionally, the two rear plugs in large, lightly used V-8's will become oil fouled. High oil consumption and smoky exhaust may also be noticed. It is probably due to plugged oil drain holes in the rear of the cylinder head, causing oil to be sucked in around the valve stems. This usually occurs in the rear cylinders first, because the engine slants that way

TROUBLESHOOTING

Test and Procedure	Results and Indications	Proceed to
4.8—Determine the static ignition timing. Using the crankshaft pulley timing marks as a guide, locate top dead center on the compression stroke of the number one cylinder.	The rotor should be pointing toward the No. 1 tower in the distributor cap, and, on electronic ignitions, the armature spoke for that cylinder should be lined up with the stator.	4.8
4.9—Check coil polarity: Connect a voltmeter negative lead to the coil high tension lead, and the positive lead to ground (**NOTE:** *Reverse the hook-up for positive ground systems*). Crank the engine momentarily. **Checking coil polarity**	If the voltmeter reads up-scale, the polarity is correct: If the voltmeter reads down-scale, reverse the coil polarity (switch the primary leads):	5.1 5.1

Section 5—Fuel System
See Chapter 4 for service procedures

Test and Procedure	Results and Indications	Proceed to
5.1—Determine that the air filter is functioning efficiently: Hold paper elements up to a strong light, and attempt to see light through the filter.	Clean permanent air filters in solvent (or manufacturer's recommendation), and allow to dry. Replace paper elements through which light cannot be seen:	5.2
5.2—Determine whether a flooding condition exists: Flooding is identified by a strong gasoline odor, and excessive gasoline present in the throttle bore(s) of the carburetor. **If the engine floods repeatedly, check the choke butterfly flap**	If flooding is not evident: If flooding is evident, permit the gasoline to dry for a few moments and restart. If flooding doesn't recur: If flooding is persistent:	5.3 5.7 5.5
5.3—Check that fuel is reaching the carburetor: Detach the fuel line at the carburetor inlet. Hold the end of the line in a cup (not styrofoam), and crank the engine. **Check the fuel pump by disconnecting the output line (fuel pump-to-carburetor) at the carburetor and operating the starter briefly**	If fuel flows smoothly: If fuel doesn't flow (**NOTE:** *Make sure that there is fuel in the tank*), or flows erratically:	5.7 5.4

TROUBLESHOOTING

Test and Procedure	Results and Indications	Proceed to
5.4—Test the fuel pump: Disconnect all fuel lines from the fuel pump. Hold a finger over the input fitting, crank the engine (with electric pump, turn the ignition or pump on); and feel for suction.	If suction is evident, blow out the fuel line to the tank with low pressure compressed air until bubbling is heard from the fuel filler neck. Also blow out the carburetor fuel line (both ends disconnected):	5.7
	If no suction is evident, replace or repair the fuel pump:	5.7
	NOTE: *Repeated oil fouling of the spark plugs, or a no-start condition, could be the result of a ruptured vacuum booster pump diaphragm, through which oil or gasoline is being drawn into the intake manifold (where applicable).*	
5.5—Occasionally, small specks of dirt will clog the small jets and orifices in the carburetor. With the engine cold, hold a flat piece of wood or similar material over the carburetor, where possible, and crank the engine.	If the engine starts, but runs roughly the engine is probably not run enough.	
	If the engine won't start:	5.9
5.6—Check the needle and seat: Tap the carburetor in the area of the needle and seat.	If flooding stops, a gasoline additive (e.g., Gumout) will often cure the problem:	5.7
	If flooding continues, check the fuel pump for excessive pressure at the carburetor (according to specifications). If the pressure is normal, the needle and seat must be removed and checked, and/or the float level adjusted:	5.7
5.7—Test the accelerator pump by looking into the throttle bores while operating the throttle.	If the accelerator pump appears to be operating normally:	5.8
	If the accelerator pump is not operating, the pump must be reconditioned. Where possible, service the pump with the carburetor(s) installed on the engine. If necessary, remove the carburetor. Prior to removal:	5.8

Check for gas at the carburetor by looking down the carburetor throat while someone moves the accelerator

5.8—Determine whether the carburetor main fuel system is functioning: Spray a commercial starting fluid into the carburetor while attempting to start the engine.	If the engine starts, runs for a few seconds, and dies:	5.9
	If the engine doesn't start:	6.1

TROUBLESHOOTING

Test and Procedure	Results and Indications	Proceed to
5.9—Uncommon fuel system malfunctions: See below:	If the problem is solved: If the problem remains, remove and recondition the carburetor.	6.1

Condition	Indication	Test	Prevailing Weather Conditions	Remedy
Vapor lock	Engine will not restart shortly after running.	Cool the components of the fuel system until the engine starts. Vapor lock can be cured faster by draping a wet cloth over a mechanical fuel pump.	Hot to very hot	Ensure that the exhaust manifold heat control valve is operating. Check with the vehicle manufacturer for the recommended solution to vapor lock on the model in question.
Carburetor icing	Engine will not idle, stalls at low speeds.	Visually inspect the throttle plate area of the throttle bores for frost.	High humidity, 32–40° F.	Ensure that the exhaust manifold heat control valve is operating, and that the intake manifold heat riser is not blocked.
Water in the fuel	Engine sputters and stalls; may not start.	Pump a small amount of fuel into a glass jar. Allow to stand, and inspect for droplets or a layer of water.	High humidity, extreme temperature changes.	For droplets, use one or two cans of commercial gas line anti-freeze. For a layer of water, the tank must be drained, and the fuel lines blown out with compressed air.

Section 6—Engine Compression
See Chapter 3 for service procedures

6.1—Test engine compression: Remove all spark plugs. Block the throttle wide open. Insert a compression gauge into a spark plug port, crank the engine to obtain the maximum reading, and record.	If compression is within limits on all cylinders:	7.1
	If gauge reading is extremely low on all cylinders:	6.2
	If gauge reading is low on one or two cylinders: (If gauge readings are identical and low on two or more adjacent cylinders, the head gasket must be replaced.)	6.2

Checking compression

6.2—Test engine compression (wet): Squirt approximately 30 cc. of engine oil into each cylinder, and retest per 6.1.	If the readings improve, worn or cracked rings or broken pistons are indicated:	See Chapter 3
	If the readings do not improve, burned or excessively carboned valves or a jumped timing chain are indicated: **NOTE:** *A jumped timing chain is often indicated by difficult cranking.*	7.1

TROUBLESHOOTING 201

Section 7—Engine Vacuum
See Chapter 3 for service procedures

Test and Procedure	Results and Indications	Proceed to
7.1—Attach a vacuum gauge to the intake manifold beyond the throttle plate. Start the engine, and observe the action of the needle over the range of engine speeds.	See below.	**See below**

INDICATION: normal engine in good condition

Proceed to: 8.1

Normal engine
Gauge reading: steady, from 17–22 in./Hg.

INDICATION: sticking valves or ignition miss

Proceed to: 9.1, 8.3

Sticking valves
Gauge reading: intermittent fluctuation at idle

INDICATION: late ignition or valve timing, low compression, stuck throttle valve, leaking carburetor or manifold gasket

Proceed to: 6.1

Incorrect valve timing
Gauge reading: low (10–15 in./Hg) but steady

INDICATION: improper carburetor adjustment or minor intake leak.

Proceed to: 7.2

Carburetor requires adjustment
Gauge reading: drifting needle

INDICATION: ignition miss, blown cylinder head gasket, leaking valve or weak valve spring

Proceed to: 8.3, 6.1

Blown head gasket
Gauge reading: needle fluctuates as engine speed increases

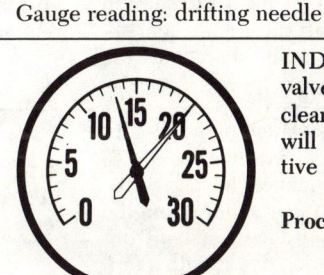

INDICATION: burnt valve or faulty valve clearance. Needle will fall when defective valve operates

Proceed to: 9.1

Burnt or leaking valves
Gauge reading: steady needle, but drops regularly

INDICATION: choked muffler, excessive back pressure in system

Proceed to: 10.1

Clogged exhaust system
Gauge reading: gradual drop in reading at idle

INDICATION: worn valve guides

Proceed to: 9.1

Worn valve guides
Gauge reading: needle vibrates excessively at idle, but steadies as engine speed increases

White pointer = steady gauge hand   Black pointer = fluctuating gauge hand

202 TROUBLESHOOTING

Test and Procedure	Results and Indications	Proceed to
7.2—Attach a vacuum gauge per 7.1, and test for an intake manifold leak. Squirt a small amount of oil around the intake manifold gaskets, carburetor gaskets, plugs and fittings. Observe the action of the vacuum gauge.	If the reading improves, replace the indicated gasket, or seal the indicated fitting or plug: If the reading remains low:	8.1 7.3
7.3—Test all vacuum hoses and accessories for leaks as described in 7.2. Also check the carburetor body (dashpots, automatic choke mechanism, throttle shafts) for leaks in the same manner.	If the reading improves, service or replace the offending part(s): If the reading remains low:	8.1 6.1

Section 8—Secondary Electrical System
See Chapter 2 for service procedures

Test and Procedure	Results and Indications	Proceed to
8.1—Remove the distributor cap and check to make sure that the rotor turns when the engine is cranked. Visually inspect the distributor components.	Clean, tighten or replace any components which appear defective.	8.2
8.2—Connect a timing light (per manufacturer's recommendation) and check the dynamic ignition timing. Disconnect and plug the vacuum hose(s) to the distributor if specified, start the engine, and observe the timing marks at the specified engine speed.	If the timing is not correct, adjust to specifications by rotating the distributor in the engine: (Advance timing by rotating distributor opposite normal direction of rotor rotation, retard timing by rotating distributor in same direction as rotor rotation.)	8.3
8.3—Check the operation of the distributor advance mechanism(s): To test the mechanical advance, disconnect the vacuum lines from the distributor advance unit and observe the timing marks with a timing light as the engine speed is increased from idle. If the mark moves smoothly, without hesitation, it may be assumed that the mechanical advance is functioning properly. To test vacuum advance and/or retard systems, alternately crimp and release the vacuum line, and observe the timing mark for movement. If movement is noted, the system is operating.	If the systems are functioning: If the systems are not functioning, remove the distributor, and test on a distributor tester:	8.4 8.4
8.4—Locate an ignition miss: With the engine running, remove each spark plug wire, one at a time, until one is found that doesn't cause the engine to roughen and slow down.	When the missing cylinder is identified:	4.1

Section 9—Valve Train
See Chapter 3 for service procedures

Test and Procedure	Results and Indications	Proceed to
9.1—Evaluate the valve train: Remove the valve cover, and ensure that the valves are adjusted to specifications. A mechanic's stethoscope may be used to aid in the diagnosis of the valve train. By pushing the probe on or near push rods or rockers, valve noise often can be isolated. A timing light also may be used to diagnose valve problems. Connect the light according to manufacturer's recommendations, and start the engine. Vary the firing moment of the light by increasing the engine speed (and therefore the ignition advance), and moving the trigger from cylinder to cylinder. Observe the movement of each valve.	Sticking valves or erratic valve train motion can be observed with the timing light. The cylinder head must be disassembled for repairs.	See Chapter 3
9.2—Check the valve timing: Locate top dead center of the No. 1 piston, and install a degree wheel or tape on the crankshaft pulley or damper with zero corresponding to an index mark on the engine. Rotate the crankshaft in its direction of rotation, and observe the opening of the No. 1 cylinder intake valve. The opening should correspond with the correct mark on the degree wheel according to specifications.	If the timing is not correct, the timing cover must be removed for further investigation.	See Chapter 3

Section 10—Exhaust System

Test and Procedure	Results and Indications	Proceed to
10.1—Determine whether the exhaust manifold heat control valve is operating: Operate the valve by hand to determine whether it is free to move. If the valve is free, run the engine to operating temperature and observe the action of the valve, to ensure that it is opening.	If the valve sticks, spray it with a suitable solvent, open and close the valve to free it, and retest.	
	If the valve functions properly:	10.2
	If the valve does not free, or does not operate, replace the valve:	10.2
10.2—Ensure that there are no exhaust restrictions: Visually inspect the exhaust system for kinks, dents, or crushing. Also note that gases are flowing freely from the tailpipe at all engine speeds, indicating no restriction in the muffler or resonator.	Replace any damaged portion of the system:	11.1

TROUBLESHOOTING

Section 11—Cooling System
See Chapter 3 for service procedures

Test and Procedure	Results and Indications	Proceed to
11.1—Visually inspect the fan belt for glazing, cracks, and fraying, and replace if necessary. Tighten the belt so that the longest span has approximately ½" play at its midpoint under thumb pressure (see Chapter 1).	Replace or tighten the fan belt as necessary:	11.2
11.2—Check the fluid level of the cooling system.	If full or slightly low, fill as necessary:	11.5
	If extremely low:	11.3
11.3—Visually inspect the external portions of the cooling system (radiator, radiator hoses, thermostat elbow, water pump seals, heater hoses, etc.) for leaks. If none are found, pressurize the cooling system to 14–15 psi.	If cooling system holds the pressure:	11.5
	If cooling system loses pressure rapidly, reinspect external parts of the system for leaks under pressure. If none are found, check dipstick for coolant in crankcase. If no coolant is present, but pressure loss continues:	11.4
	If coolant is evident in crankcase, remove cylinder head(s), and check gasket(s). If gaskets are intact, block and cylinder head(s) should be checked for cracks or holes.	
	If the gasket(s) is blown, replace, and purge the crankcase of coolant:	12.6
	NOTE: *Occasionally, due to atmospheric and driving conditions, condensation of water can occur in the crankcase. This causes the oil to appear milky white. To remedy, run the engine until hot, and change the oil and oil filter.*	
11.4—Check for combustion leaks into the cooling system: Pressurize the cooling system as above. Start the engine, and observe the pressure gauge. If the needle fluctuates, remove each spark plug wire, one at a time, noting which cylinder(s) reduce or eliminate the fluctuation.	Cylinders which reduce or eliminate the fluctuation, when the spark plug wire is removed, are leaking into the cooling system. Replace the head gasket on the affected cylinder bank(s).	

Checking belt tension

Pressurizing the cooling system

TROUBLESHOOTING

Test and Procedure	Results and Indications	Proceed to
11.5—Check the radiator pressure cap: Attach a radiator pressure tester to the radiator cap (wet the seal prior to installation). Quickly pump up the pressure, noting the point at which the cap releases.	If the cap releases within ± 1 psi of the specified rating, it is operating properly:	11.6
	If the cap releases at more than ± 1 psi of the specified rating, it should be replaced:	11.6

Checking radiator pressure cap

Test and Procedure	Results and Indications	Proceed to
11.6—Test the thermostat: Start the engine cold, remove the radiator cap, and insert a thermometer into the radiator. Allow the engine to idle. After a short while, there will be a sudden, rapid increase in coolant temperature. The temperature at which this sharp rise stops is the thermostat opening temperature.	If the thermostat opens at or about the specified temperature:	11.7
	If the temperature doesn't increase: (If the temperature increases slowly and gradually, replace the thermostat.)	11.7
11.7—Check the water pump: Remove the thermostat elbow and the thermostat, disconnect the coil high tension lead (to prevent starting), and crank the engine momentarily.	If coolant flows, replace the thermostat and retest per 11.6:	11.6
	If coolant doesn't flow, reverse flush the cooling system to alleviate any blockage that might exist. If system is not blocked, and coolant will not flow, replace the water pump.	

Section 12—Lubrication
See Chapter 3 for service procedures

Test and Procedure	Results and Indications	Proceed to
12.1—Check the oil pressure gauge or warning light: If the gauge shows low pressure, or the light is on for no obvious reason, remove the oil pressure sender. Install an accurate oil pressure gauge and run the engine momentarily.	If oil pressure builds normally, run engine for a few moments to determine that it is functioning normally, and replace the sender.	—
	If the pressure remains low:	12.2
	If the pressure surges:	12.3
	If the oil pressure is zero:	12.3
12.2—Visually inspect the oil: If the oil is watery or very thin, milky, or foamy, replace the oil and oil filter.	If the oil is normal:	12.3
	If after replacing oil the pressure remains low:	12.3
	If after replacing oil the pressure becomes normal:	—

206 TROUBLESHOOTING

Test and Procedure	Results and Indications	Proceed to
12.3—Inspect the oil pressure relief valve and spring, to ensure that it is not sticking or stuck. Remove and thoroughly clean the valve, spring, and the valve body.	If the oil pressure improves: If no improvement is noted:	— 12.4
12.4—Check to ensure that the oil pump is not cavitating (sucking air instead of oil): See that the crankcase is neither over nor underfull, and that the pickup in the sump is in the proper position and free from sludge.	Fill or drain the crankcase to the proper capacity, and clean the pickup screen in solvent if necessary. If no improvement is noted:	12.5
12.5—Inspect the oil pump drive and the oil pump:	If the pump drive or the oil pump appear to be defective, service as necessary and retest per 12.1: If the pump drive and pump appear to be operating normally, the engine should be disassembled to determine where blockage exists:	12.1 See Chapter 3
12.6—Purge the engine of ethylene glycol coolant: Completely drain the crankcase and the oil filter. Obtain a commercial butyl cellosolve base solvent, designated for this purpose, and follow the instructions precisely. Following this, install a new oil filter and refill the crankcase with the proper weight oil. The next oil and filter change should follow shortly thereafter (1000 miles).		

TROUBLESHOOTING EMISSION CONTROL SYSTEMS

See Chapter 4 for procedures applicable to individual emission control systems used on specific combinations of engine/transmission/model.

TROUBLESHOOTING THE CARBURETOR
See Chapter 4 for service procedures

Carburetor problems cannot be effectively isolated unless all other engine systems (particularly ignition and emission) are functioning properly and the engine is properly tuned.

TROUBLESHOOTING

Condition	Possible Cause
Engine cranks, but does not start	1. Improper starting procedure 2. No fuel in tank 3. Clogged fuel line or filter 4. Defective fuel pump 5. Choke valve not closing properly 6. Engine flooded 7. Choke valve not unloading 8. Throttle linkage not making full travel 9. Stuck needle or float 10. Leaking float needle or seat 11. Improper float adjustment
Engine stalls	1. Improperly adjusted idle speed or mixture **Engine hot** 2. Improperly adjusted dashpot 3. Defective or improperly adjusted solenoid 4. Incorrect fuel level in fuel bowl 5. Fuel pump pressure too high 6. Leaking float needle seat 7. Secondary throttle valve stuck open 8. Air or fuel leaks 9. Idle air bleeds plugged or missing 10. Idle passages plugged **Engine Cold** 11. Incorrectly adjusted choke 12. Improperly adjusted fast idle speed 13. Air leaks 14. Plugged idle or idle air passages 15. Stuck choke valve or binding linkage 16. Stuck secondary throttle valves 17. Engine flooding—high fuel level 18. Leaking or misaligned float
Engine hesitates on acceleration	1. Clogged fuel filter 2. Leaking fuel pump diaphragm 3. Low fuel pump pressure 4. Secondary throttle valves stuck, bent or misadjusted 5. Sticking or binding air valve 6. Defective accelerator pump 7. Vacuum leaks 8. Clogged air filter 9. Incorrect choke adjustment (engine cold)
Engine feels sluggish or flat on acceleration	1. Improperly adjusted idle speed or mixture 2. Clogged fuel filter 3. Defective accelerator pump 4. Dirty, plugged or incorrect main metering jets 5. Bent or sticking main metering rods 6. Sticking throttle valves 7. Stuck heat riser 8. Binding or stuck air valve 9. Dirty, plugged or incorrect secondary jets 10. Bent or sticking secondary metering rods. 11. Throttle body or manifold heat passages plugged 12. Improperly adjusted choke or choke vacuum break.
Carburetor floods	1. Defective fuel pump. Pressure too high. 2. Stuck choke valve 3. Dirty, worn or damaged float or needle valve/seat 4. Incorrect float/fuel level 5. Leaking float bowl

TROUBLESHOOTING

Condition	Possible Cause
Engine idles roughly and stalls	1. Incorrect idle speed 2. Clogged fuel filter 3. Dirt in fuel system or carburetor 4. Loose carburetor screws or attaching bolts 5. Broken carburetor gaskets 6. Air leaks 7. Dirty carburetor 8. Worn idle mixture needles 9. Throttle valves stuck open 10. Incorrectly adjusted float or fuel level 11. Clogged air filter
Engine runs unevenly or surges	1. Defective fuel pump 2. Dirty or clogged fuel filter 3. Plugged, loose or incorrect main metering jets or rods 4. Air leaks 5. Bent or sticking main metering rods 6. Stuck power piston 7. Incorrect float adjustment 8. Incorrect idle speed or mixture 9. Dirty or plugged idle system passages 10. Hard, brittle or broken gaskets 11. Loose attaching or mounting screws 12. Stuck or misaligned secondary throttle valves
Poor fuel economy	1. Poor driving habits 2. Stuck choke valve 3. Binding choke linkage 4. Stuck heat riser 5. Incorrect idle mixture 6. Defective accelerator pump 7. Air leaks 8. Plugged, loose or incorrect main metering jets 9. Improperly adjusted float or fuel level 10. Bent, misaligned or fuel-clogged float 11. Leaking float needle seat 12. Fuel leak 13. Accelerator pump discharge ball not seating properly 14. Incorrect main jets
Engine lacks high speed performance or power	1. Incorrect throttle linkage adjustment 2. Stuck or binding power piston 3. Defective accelerator pump 4. Air leaks 5. Incorrect float setting or fuel level 6. Dirty, plugged, worn or incorrect main metering jets or rods 7. Binding or sticking air valve 8. Brittle or cracked gaskets 9. Bent, incorrect or improperly adjusted secondary metering rods 10. Clogged fuel filter 11. Clogged air filter 12. Defective fuel pump

TROUBLESHOOTING FUEL INJECTION PROBLEMS

Each fuel injection system has its own unique components and test procedures, for which it is impossible to generalize. Refer to Chapter 4 of this Repair & Tune-Up Guide for specific test and repair procedures, if the vehicle is equipped with fuel injection.

TROUBLESHOOTING ELECTRICAL PROBLEMS

See Chapter 5 for service procedures

For any electrical system to operate, it must make a complete circuit. This simply means that the power flow from the battery must make a complete circle. When an electrical component is operating, power flows from the battery to the component, passes through the component causing it to perform its function (lighting a light bulb), and then returns to the battery through the ground of the circuit. This ground is usually (but not always) the metal part of the car or truck on which the electrical component is mounted.

Perhaps the easiest way to visualize this is to think of connecting a light bulb with two wires attached to it to the battery. If one of the two wires attached to the light bulb were attached to the negative post of the battery and the other were attached to the positive post of the battery, you would have a complete circuit. Current from the battery would flow to the light bulb, causing it to light, and return to the negative post of the battery.

The normal automotive circuit differs from this simple example in two ways. First, instead of having a return wire from the bulb to the battery, the light bulb returns the current to the battery through the chassis of the vehicle. Since the negative battery cable is attached to the chassis and the chassis is made of electrically conductive metal, the chassis of the vehicle can serve as a ground wire to complete the circuit. Secondly, most automotive circuits contain switches to turn components on and off as required.

Every complete circuit from a power source must include a component which is using the power from the power source. If you were to disconnect the light bulb from the wires and touch the two wires together (don't do this) the power supply wire to the component would be grounded before the normal ground connection for the circuit.

Because grounding a wire from a power source makes a complete circuit—less the required component to use the power—this phenomenon is called a short circuit. Common causes are: broken insulation (exposing the metal wire to a metal part of the car or truck), or a shorted switch.

Some electrical components which require a large amount of current to operate also have a relay in their circuit. Since these circuits carry a large amount of current, the thickness of the wire in the circuit (gauge size) is also greater. If this large wire were connected from the component to the control switch on the instrument panel, and then back to the component, a voltage drop would occur in the circuit. To prevent this potential drop in voltage, an electromagnetic switch (relay) is used. The large wires in the circuit are connected from the battery to one side of the relay, and from the opposite side of the relay to the component. The relay is normally open, preventing current from passing through the circuit. An additional, smaller, wire is connected from the relay to the control switch for the circuit. When the control switch is turned on, it grounds the smaller wire from the relay and completes the circuit. This closes the relay and allows current to flow from the battery to the component. The horn, headlight, and starter circuits are three which use relays.

It is possible for larger surges of current to pass through the electrical system of your car or truck. If this surge of current were to reach an electrical component, it could burn it out. To prevent this, fuses, circuit breakers or fusible links are connected into the current supply wires of most of the major electrical systems. When an electrical current of excessive power passes through the component's fuse, the fuse blows out and breaks the circuit, saving the component from destruction.

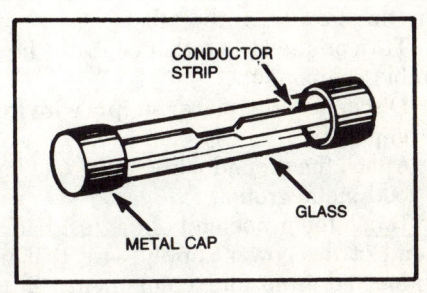

Typical automotive fuse

A circuit breaker is basically a self-repairing fuse. The circuit breaker opens the circuit the same way a fuse does. However, when either the short is removed from the circuit or the surge subsides, the circuit breaker resets itself and does not have to be replaced as a fuse does.

A fuse link is a wire that acts as a fuse. It is normally connected between the starter relay and the main wiring harness. This connection is usually under the hood. The fuse link (if installed) protects all the

210 TROUBLESHOOTING

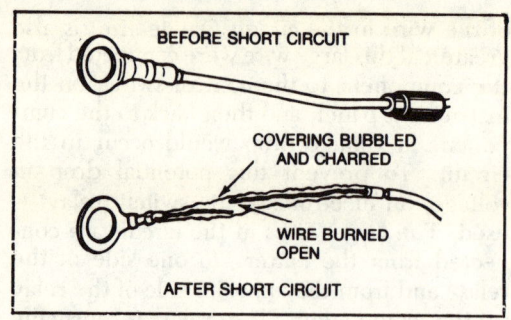

Most fusible links show a charred, melted insulation when they burn out

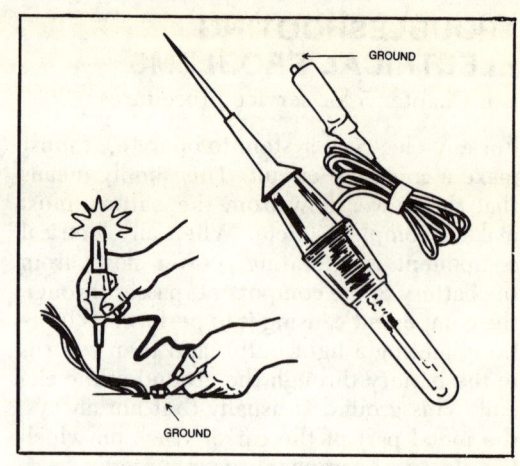

The test light will show the presence of current when touched to a hot wire and grounded at the other end

chassis electrical components, and is the probable cause of trouble when none of the electrical components function, unless the battery is disconnected or dead.

Electrical problems generally fall into one of three areas:

1. The component that is not functioning is not receiving current.
2. The component itself is not functioning.
3. The component is not properly grounded.

The electrical system can be checked with a test light and a jumper wire. A test light is a device that looks like a pointed screwdriver with a wire attached to it and has a light bulb in its handle. A jumper wire is a piece of insulated wire with an alligator clip attached to each end.

If a component is not working, you must follow a systematic plan to determine which of the three causes is the villain.

1. Turn on the switch that controls the inoperable component.
2. Disconnect the power supply wire from the component.
3. Attach the ground wire on the test light to a good metal ground.
4. Touch the probe end of the test light to the end of the power supply wire that was disconnected from the component. If the component is receiving current, the test light will go on.

NOTE: *Some components work only when the ignition switch is turned on.*

If the test light does not go on, then the problem is in the circuit between the battery and the component. This includes all the switches, fuses, and relays in the system. Follow the wire that runs back to the battery. The problem is an open circuit between the battery and the component. If the fuse is blown and, when replaced, immediately blows again, there is a short circuit in the system which must be located and repaired. If there is a switch in the system, bypass it with a jumper wire. This is done by connecting one end of the jumper wire to the power supply wire into the switch and the other end of the jumper wire to the wire coming out of the switch. If the test light lights with the jumper wire installed, the switch or whatever was bypassed is defective.

NOTE: *Never substitute the jumper wire for the component, since it is required to use the power from the power source.*

5. If the bulb in the test light goes on, then the current is getting to the component that is not working. This eliminates the first of the three possible causes. Connect the power supply wire and connect a jumper wire from the component to a good metal ground. Do this with the switch which controls the component turned on, and also the ignition switch turned on if it is required for the component to work. If the component works with the jumper wire installed, then it has a bad ground. This is usually caused by the metal area on which the component mounts to the chassis being coated with some type of foreign matter.

6. If neither test located the source of the trouble, then the component itself is defective. Remember that for any electrical system to work, all connections must be clean and tight.

TROUBLESHOOTING

Troubleshooting Basic Turn Signal and Flasher Problems
See Chapter 5 for service procedures

Most problems in the turn signals or flasher system can be reduced to defective flashers or bulbs, which are easily replaced. Occasionally, the turn signal switch will prove defective.

F = Front   R = Rear   ● = Lights off   ○ = Lights on

Condition		Possible Cause
Turn signals light, but do not flash	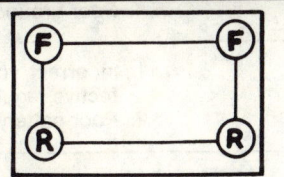	Defective flasher
No turn signals light on either side	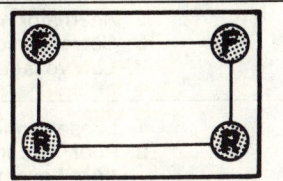	Blown fuse. Replace if defective. Defective flasher. Check by substitution. Open circuit, short circuit or poor ground.
Both turn signals on one side don't work	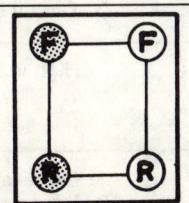	Bad bulbs. Bad ground in both (or either) housings.
One turn signal light on one side doesn't work	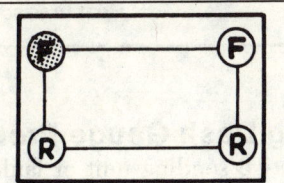	Defective bulb. Corrosion in socket. Clean contacts. Poor ground at socket.
Turn signal flashes too fast or too slowly	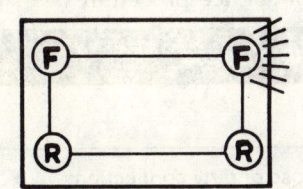	Check any bulb on the side flashing too fast. A heavy-duty bulb is probably installed in place of a regular bulb. Check the bulb flashing too slowly. A standard bulb was probably installed in place of a heavy-duty bulb. Loose connections or corrosion at the bulb socket.
Indicator lights don't work in either direction		Check if the turn signals are working. Check the dash indicator lights. Check the flasher by substitution.
One indicator light doesn't light		On systems with one dash indicator: See if the lights work on the same side. Often the filaments have been reversed in systems combining stoplights with taillights and turn signals. Check the flasher by substitution. On systems with two indicators: Check the bulbs on the same side. Check the indicator light bulb. Check the flasher by substitution.

Troubleshooting Lighting Problems
See Chapter 5 for service procedures

Condition	Possible Cause
One or more lights don't work, but others do	1. Defective bulb(s) 2. Blown fuse(s) 3. Dirty fuse clips or light sockets 4. Poor ground circuit
Lights burn out quickly	1. Incorrect voltage regulator setting or defective regulator 2. Poor battery/alternator connections
Lights go dim	1. Low/discharged battery 2. Alternator not charging 3. Corroded sockets or connections 4. Low voltage output
Lights flicker	1. Loose connection 2. Poor ground. (Run ground wire from light housing to frame) 3. Circuit breaker operating (short circuit)
Lights "flare"—Some flare is normal on acceleration—If excessive, see "Lights Burn Out Quickly"	High voltage setting
Lights glare—approaching drivers are blinded	1. Lights adjusted too high 2. Rear springs or shocks sagging 3. Rear tires soft

Troubleshooting Dash Gauge Problems

Most problems can be traced to a defective sending unit or faulty wiring. Occasionally, the gauge itself is at fault. See Chapter 5 for service procedures.

Condition	Possible Cause
COOLANT TEMPERATURE GAUGE	
Gauge reads erratically or not at all	1. Loose or dirty connections 2. Defective sending unit. 3. Defective gauge. To test a bi-metal gauge, remove the wire from the sending unit. Ground the wire for an instant. If the gauge registers, replace the sending unit. To test a magnetic gauge, disconnect the wire at the sending unit. With ignition ON gauge should register COLD. Ground the wire; gauge should register HOT.
AMMETER GAUGE—TURN HEADLIGHTS ON (DO NOT START ENGINE). NOTE REACTION	
Ammeter shows charge Ammeter shows discharge Ammeter does not move	1. Connections reversed on gauge 2. Ammeter is OK 3. Loose connections or faulty wiring 4. Defective gauge

TROUBLESHOOTING

Condition	Possible Cause

OIL PRESSURE GAUGE

Gauge does not register or is inaccurate	1. On mechanical gauge, Bourdon tube may be bent or kinked. 2. Low oil pressure. Remove sending unit. Idle the engine briefly. If no oil flows from sending unit hole, problem is in engine. 3. Defective gauge. Remove the wire from the sending unit and ground it for an instant with the ignition ON. A good gauge will go to the top of the scale. 4. Defective wiring. Check the wiring to the gauge. If it's OK and the gauge doesn't register when grounded, replace the gauge. 5. Defective sending unit.

ALL GAUGES

All gauges do not operate All gauges read low or erratically All gauges pegged	1. Blown fuse 2. Defective instrument regulator 3. Defective or dirty instrument voltage regulator 4. Loss of ground between instrument voltage regulator and frame 5. Defective instrument regulator

WARNING LIGHTS

Light(s) do not come on when ignition is ON, but engine is not started Light comes on with engine running	1. Defective bulb 2. Defective wire 3. Defective sending unit. Disconnect the wire from the sending unit and ground it. Replace the sending unit if the light comes on with the ignition ON. 4. Problem in individual system 5. Defective sending unit

Troubleshooting Clutch Problems

It is false economy to replace individual clutch components. The pressure plate, clutch plate and throwout bearing should be replaced as a set, and the flywheel face inspected, whenever the clutch is overhauled. See Chapter 6 for service procedures.

Condition	Possible Cause
Clutch chatter	1. Grease on driven plate (disc) facing 2. Binding clutch linkage or cable 3. Loose, damaged facings on driven plate (disc) 4. Engine mounts loose 5. Incorrect height adjustment of pressure plate release levers 6. Clutch housing or housing to transmission adapter misalignment 7. Loose driven plate hub
Clutch grabbing	1. Oil, grease on driven plate (disc) facing 2. Broken pressure plate 3. Warped or binding driven plate. Driven plate binding on clutch shaft
Clutch slips	1. Lack of lubrication in clutch linkage or cable (linkage or cable binds, causes incomplete engagement) 2. Incorrect pedal, or linkage adjustment 3. Broken pressure plate springs 4. Weak pressure plate springs 5. Grease on driven plate facings (disc)

Troubleshooting Clutch Problems (cont.)

Condition	Possible Cause
Incomplete clutch release	1. Incorrect pedal or linkage adjustment or linkage or cable binding 2. Incorrect height adjustment on pressure plate release levers 3. Loose, broken facings on driven plate (disc) 4. Bent, dished, warped driven plate caused by overheating
Grinding, whirring grating noise when pedal is depressed	1. Worn or defective throwout bearing 2. Starter drive teeth contacting flywheel ring gear teeth. Look for milled or polished teeth on ring gear.
Squeal, howl, trumpeting noise when pedal is being released (occurs during first inch to inch and one-half of pedal travel)	Pilot bushing worn or lack of lubricant. If bushing appears OK, polish bushing with emery cloth, soak lube wick in oil, lube bushing with oil, apply film of chassis grease to clutch shaft pilot hub, reassemble. NOTE: Bushing wear may be due to misalignment of clutch housing or housing to transmission adapter
Vibration or clutch pedal pulsation with clutch disengaged (pedal fully depressed)	1. Worn or defective engine transmission mounts 2. Flywheel run out. (Flywheel run out at face not to exceed 0.005″) 3. Damaged or defective clutch components

Troubleshooting Manual Transmission Problems
See Chapter 6 for service procedures

Condition	Possible Cause
Transmission jumps out of gear	1. Misalignment of transmission case or clutch housing. 2. Worn pilot bearing in crankshaft. 3. Bent transmission shaft. 4. Worn high speed sliding gear. 5. Worn teeth or end-play in clutch shaft. 6. Insufficient spring tension on shifter rail plunger. 7. Bent or loose shifter fork. 8. Gears not engaging completely. 9. Loose or worn bearings on clutch shaft or mainshaft. 10. Worn gear teeth. 11. Worn or damaged detent balls.
Transmission sticks in gear	1. Clutch not releasing fully. 2. Burred or battered teeth on clutch shaft, or sliding sleeve. 3. Burred or battered transmission mainshaft. 4. Frozen synchronizing clutch. 5. Stuck shifter rail plunger. 6. Gearshift lever twisting and binding shifter rail. 7. Battered teeth on high speed sliding gear or on sleeve. 8. Improper lubrication, or lack of lubrication. 9. Corroded transmission parts. 10. Defective mainshaft pilot bearing. 11. Locked gear bearings will give same effect as stuck in gear.
Transmission gears will not synchronize	1. Binding pilot bearing on mainshaft, will synchronize in high gear only. 2. Clutch not releasing fully. 3. Detent spring weak or broken. 4. Weak or broken springs under balls in sliding gear sleeve. 5. Binding bearing on clutch shaft, or binding countershaft. 6. Binding pilot bearing in crankshaft. 7. Badly worn gear teeth. 8. Improper lubrication. 9. Constant mesh gear not turning freely on transmission mainshaft. Will synchronize in that gear only.

TROUBLESHOOTING 215

Condition	Possible Cause
Gears spinning when shifting into gear from neutral	1. Clutch not releasing fully. 2. In some cases an extremely light lubricant in transmission will cause gears to continue to spin for a short time after clutch is released. 3. Binding pilot bearing in crankshaft.
Transmission noisy in all gears	1. Insufficient lubricant, or improper lubricant. 2. Worn countergear bearings. 3. Worn or damaged main drive gear or countergear. 4. Damaged main drive gear or mainshaft bearings. 5. Worn or damaged countergear anti-lash plate.
Transmission noisy in neutral only	1. Damaged main drive gear bearing. 2. Damaged or loose mainshaft pilot bearing. 3. Worn or damaged countergear anti-lash plate. 4. Worn countergear bearings.
Transmission noisy in one gear only	1. Damaged or worn constant mesh gears. 2. Worn or damaged countergear bearings. 3. Damaged or worn synchronizer.
Transmission noisy in reverse only	1. Worn or damaged reverse idler gear or idler bushing. 2. Worn or damaged mainshaft reverse gear. 3. Worn or damaged reverse countergear. 4. Damaged shift mechanism.

TROUBLESHOOTING AUTOMATIC TRANSMISSION PROBLEMS

Keeping alert to changes in the operating characteristics of the transmission (changing shift points, noises, etc.) can prevent small problems from becoming large ones. If the problem cannot be traced to loose bolts, fluid level, misadjusted linkage, clogged filters or similar problems, you should probably seek professional service.

Transmission Fluid Indications

The appearance and odor of the transmission fluid can give valuable clues to the overall condition of the transmission. Always note the appearance of the fluid when you check the fluid level or change the fluid. Rub a small amount of fluid between your fingers to feel for grit and smell the fluid on the dipstick.

If the fluid appears:	It indicates:
Clear and red colored	Normal operation
Discolored (extremely dark red or brownish) or smells burned	Band or clutch pack failure, usually caused by an overheated transmission. Hauling very heavy loads with insufficient power or failure to change the fluid often result in overheating. Do not confuse this appearance with newer fluids that have a darker red color and a strong odor (though not a burned odor).
Foamy or aerated (light in color and full of bubbles)	1. The level is too high (gear train is churning oil) 2. An internal air leak (air is mixing with the fluid). Have the transmission checked professionally.
Solid residue in the fluid	Defective bands, clutch pack or bearings. Bits of band material or metal abrasives are clinging to the dipstick. Have the transmission checked professionally.
Varnish coating on the dipstick	The transmission fluid is overheating

TROUBLESHOOTING DRIVE AXLE PROBLEMS

First, determine when the noise is most noticeable.

Drive Noise: Produced under vehicle acceleration.

Coast Noise: Produced while coasting with a closed throttle.

Float Noise: Occurs while maintaining constant speed (just enough to keep speed constant) on a level road.

External Noise Elimination

It is advisable to make a thorough road test to determine whether the noise originates in the rear axle or whether it originates from the tires, engine, transmission, wheel bearings or road surface. Noise originating from other places cannot be corrected by servicing the rear axle.

ROAD NOISE

Brick or rough surfaced concrete roads produce noises that seem to come from the rear axle. Road noise is usually identical in Drive or Coast and driving on a different type of road will tell whether the road is the problem.

TIRE NOISE

Tire noise can be mistaken as rear axle noise, even though the tires on the front are at fault. Snow tread and mud tread tires or tires worn unevenly will frequently cause vibrations which seem to originate elsewhere; *temporarily, and for test purposes only,* inflate the tires to 40–50 lbs. This will significantly alter the noise produced by the tires, but will not alter noise from the rear axle. Noises from the rear axle will normally cease at speeds below 30 mph on coast, while tire noise will continue at lower tone as speed is decreased. The rear axle noise will usually change from drive conditions to coast conditions, while tire noise will not. Do not forget to lower the tire pressure to normal after the test is complete.

ENGINE/TRANSMISSION NOISE

Determine at what speed the noise is most pronounced, then stop in a quiet place. With the transmission in Neutral, run the engine through speeds corresponding to road speeds where the noise was noticed. Noises produced with the vehicle standing still are coming from the engine or transmission.

FRONT WHEEL BEARINGS

Front wheel bearing noises, sometimes confused with rear axle noises, will not change when comparing drive and coast conditions. While holding the speed steady, lightly apply the footbrake. This will often cause wheel bearing noise to lessen, as some of the weight is taken off the bearing. Front wheel bearings are easily checked by jacking up the wheels and spinning the wheels. Shaking the wheels will also determine if the wheel bearings are excessively loose.

REAR AXLE NOISES

Eliminating other possible sources can narrow the cause to the rear axle, which normally produces noise from worn gears or bearings. Gear noises tend to peak in a narrow speed range, while bearing noises will usually vary in pitch with engine speeds.

Noise Diagnosis

The Noise Is:	Most Probably Produced By:
1. Identical under Drive or Coast	Road surface, tires or front wheel bearings
2. Different depending on road surface	Road surface or tires
3. Lower as speed is lowered	Tires
4. Similar when standing or moving	Engine or transmission
5. A vibration	Unbalanced tires, rear wheel bearing, unbalanced driveshaft or worn U-joint
6. A knock or click about every two tire revolutions	Rear wheel bearing
7. Most pronounced on turns	Damaged differential gears
8. A steady low-pitched whirring or scraping, starting at low speeds	Damaged or worn pinion bearing
9. A chattering vibration on turns	Wrong differential lubricant or worn clutch plates (limited slip rear axle)
10. Noticed only in Drive, Coast or Float conditions	Worn ring gear and/or pinion gear

TROUBLESHOOTING

Troubleshooting Steering & Suspension Problems

Condition	Possible Cause
Hard steering (wheel is hard to turn)	1. Improper tire pressure 2. Loose or glazed pump drive belt 3. Low or incorrect fluid 4. Loose, bent or poorly lubricated front end parts 5. Improper front end alignment (excessive caster) 6. Bind in steering column or linkage 7. Kinked hydraulic hose 8. Air in hydraulic system 9. Low pump output or leaks in system 10. Obstruction in lines 11. Pump valves sticking or out of adjustment 12. Incorrect wheel alignment
Loose steering (too much play in steering wheel)	1. Loose wheel bearings 2. Faulty shocks 3. Worn linkage or suspension components 4. Loose steering gear mounting or linkage points 5. Steering mechanism worn or improperly adjusted 6. Valve spool improperly adjusted 7. Worn ball joints, tie-rod ends, etc.
Veers or wanders (pulls to one side with hands off steering wheel)	1. Improper tire pressure 2. Improper front end alignment 3. Dragging or improperly adjusted brakes 4. Bent frame 5. Improper rear end alignment 6. Faulty shocks or springs 7. Loose or bent front end components 8. Play in Pitman arm 9. Steering gear mountings loose 10. Loose wheel bearings 11. Binding Pitman arm 12. Spool valve sticking or improperly adjusted 13. Worn ball joints
Wheel oscillation or vibration transmitted through steering wheel	1. Low or uneven tire pressure 2. Loose wheel bearings 3. Improper front end alignment 4. Bent spindle 5. Worn, bent or broken front end components 6. Tires out of round or out of balance 7. Excessive lateral runout in disc brake rotor 8. Loose or bent shock absorber or strut
Noises (see also "Troubleshooting Drive Axle Problems")	1. Loose belts 2. Low fluid, air in system 3. Foreign matter in system 4. Improper lubrication 5. Interference or chafing in linkage 6. Steering gear mountings loose 7. Incorrect adjustment or wear in gear box 8. Faulty valves or wear in pump 9. Kinked hydraulic lines 10. Worn wheel bearings
Poor return of steering	1. Over-inflated tires 2. Improperly aligned front end (excessive caster) 3. Binding in steering column 4. No lubrication in front end 5. Steering gear adjusted too tight
Uneven tire wear (see "How To Read Tire Wear")	1. Incorrect tire pressure 2. Improperly aligned front end 3. Tires out-of-balance 4. Bent or worn suspension parts

218   TROUBLESHOOTING

HOW TO READ TIRE WEAR

The way your tires wear is a good indicator of other parts of the suspension. Abnormal wear patterns are often caused by the need for simple tire maintenance, or for front end alignment.

Excessive wear at the center of the tread indicates that the air pressure in the tire is consistently too high. The tire is riding on the center of the tread and wearing it prematurely. Occasionally, this wear pattern can result from outrageously wide tires on narrow rims. The cure for this is to replace either the tires or the wheels.

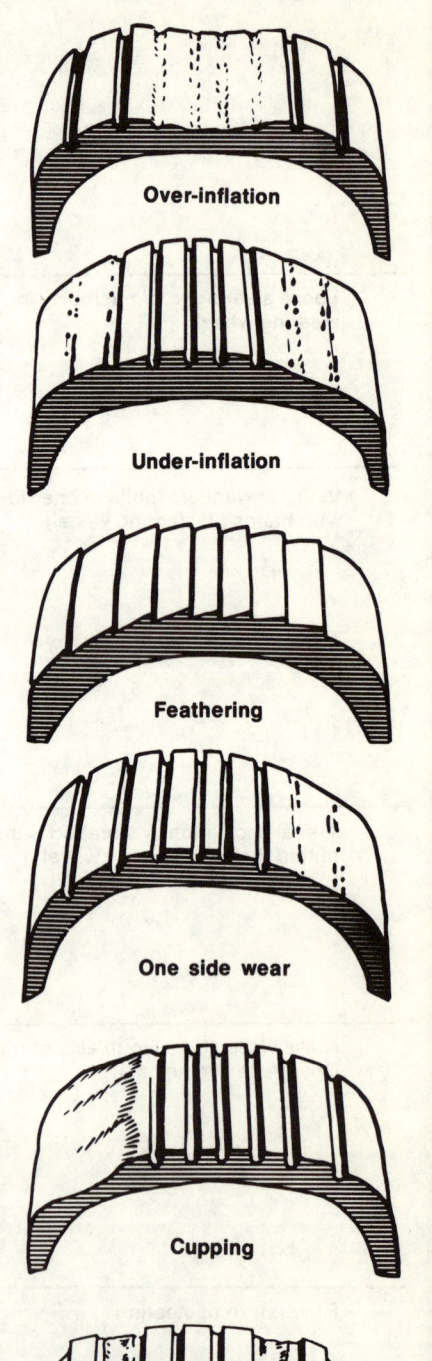

Over-inflation

This type of wear usually results from consistent under-inflation. When a tire is under-inflated, there is too much contact with the road by the outer treads, which wear prematurely. When this type of wear occurs, and the tire pressure is known to be consistently correct, a bent or worn steering component or the need for wheel alignment could be indicated.

Under-inflation

Feathering is a condition when the edge of each tread rib develops a slightly rounded edge on one side and a sharp edge on the other. By running your hand over the tire, you can usually feel the sharper edges before you'll be able to see them. The most common causes of feathering are incorrect toe-in setting or deteriorated bushings in the front suspension.

Feathering

When an inner or outer rib wears faster than the rest of the tire, the need for wheel alignment is indicated. There is excessive camber in the front suspension, causing the wheel to lean too much putting excessive load on one side of the tire. Misalignment could also be due to sagging springs, worn ball joints, or worn control arm bushings. Be sure the vehicle is loaded the way it's normally driven when you have the wheels aligned.

One side wear

Cups or scalloped dips appearing around the edge of the tread almost always indicate worn (sometimes bent) suspension parts. Adjustment of wheel alignment alone will seldom cure the problem. Any worn component that connects the wheel to the suspension can cause this type of wear. Occasionally, wheels that are out of balance will wear like this, but wheel imbalance usually shows up as bald spots between the outside edges and center of the tread.

Cupping

Second-rib wear is usually found only in radial tires, and appears where the steel belts end in relation to the tread. It can be kept to a minimum by paying careful attention to tire pressure and frequently rotating the tires. This is often considered normal wear but excessive amounts indicate that the tires are too wide for the wheels.

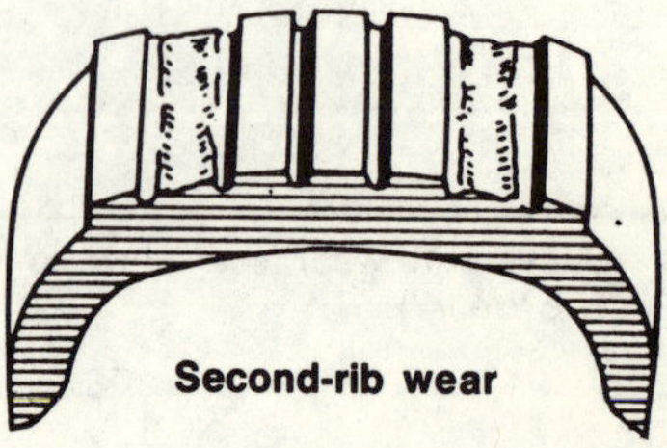

Second-rib wear

TROUBLESHOOTING

Troubleshooting Disc Brake Problems

Condition	Possible Cause
Noise—groan—brake noise emanating when slowly releasing brakes (creep-groan)	Not detrimental to function of disc brakes—no corrective action required. (This noise may be eliminated by slightly increasing or decreasing brake pedal efforts.)
Rattle—brake noise or rattle emanating at low speeds on rough roads, (front wheels only).	1. Shoe anti-rattle spring missing or not properly positioned. 2. Excessive clearance between shoe and caliper. 3. Soft or broken caliper seals. 4. Deformed or misaligned disc. 5. Loose caliper.
Scraping	1. Mounting bolts too long. 2. Loose wheel bearings. 3. Bent, loose, or misaligned splash shield.
Front brakes heat up during driving and fail to release	1. Operator riding brake pedal. 2. Stop light switch improperly adjusted. 3. Sticking pedal linkage. 4. Frozen or seized piston. 5. Residual pressure valve in master cylinder. 6. Power brake malfunction. 7. Proportioning valve malfunction.
Leaky brake caliper	1. Damaged or worn caliper piston seal. 2. Scores or corrosion on surface of cylinder bore.
Grabbing or uneven brake action—Brakes pull to one side	1. Causes listed under "Brakes Pull". 2. Power brake malfunction. 3. Low fluid level in master cylinder. 4. Air in hydraulic system. 5. Brake fluid, oil or grease on linings. 6. Unmatched linings. 7. Distorted brake pads. 8. Frozen or seized pistons. 9. Incorrect tire pressure. 10. Front end out of alignment. 11. Broken rear spring. 12. Brake caliper pistons sticking. 13. Restricted hose or line. 14. Caliper not in proper alignment to braking disc. 15. Stuck or malfunctioning metering valve. 16. Soft or broken brake seals. 17. Loose caliper.
Brake pedal can be depressed without braking effect	1. Air in hydraulic system or improper bleeding procedure. 2. Leak past primary cup in master cylinder. 3. Leak in system. 4. Rear brakes out of adjustment. 5. Bleeder screw open.
Excessive pedal travel	1. Air, leak, or insufficient fluid in system or caliper. 2. Warped or excessively tapered shoe and lining assembly. 3. Excessive disc runout. 4. Rear brake adjustment required. 5. Loose wheel bearing adjustment. 6. Damaged caliper piston seal. 7. Improper brake fluid (boil). 8. Power brake malfunction. 9. Weak or soft hoses.

Troubleshooting Disc Brake Problems (cont.)

Condition	Possible Cause
Brake roughness or chatter (pedal pumping)	1. Excessive thickness variation of braking disc. 2. Excessive lateral runout of braking disc. 3. Rear brake drums out-of-round. 4. Excessive front bearing clearance.
Excessive pedal effort	1. Brake fluid, oil or grease on linings. 2. Incorrect lining. 3. Frozen or seized pistons. 4. Power brake malfunction. 5. Kinked or collapsed hose or line. 6. Stuck metering valve. 7. Scored caliper or master cylinder bore. 8. Seized caliper pistons.
Brake pedal fades (pedal travel increases with foot on brake)	1. Rough master cylinder or caliper bore. 2. Loose or broken hydraulic lines/connections. 3. Air in hydraulic system. 4. Fluid level low. 5. Weak or soft hoses. 6. Inferior quality brake shoes or fluid. 7. Worn master cylinder piston cups or seals.

Troubleshooting Drum Brakes

Condition	Possible Cause
Pedal goes to floor	1. Fluid low in reservoir. 2. Air in hydraulic system. 3. Improperly adjusted brake. 4. Leaking wheel cylinders. 5. Loose or broken brake lines. 6. Leaking or worn master cylinder. 7. Excessively worn brake lining.
Spongy brake pedal	1. Air in hydraulic system. 2. Improper brake fluid (low boiling point). 3. Excessively worn or cracked brake drums. 4. Broken pedal pivot bushing.
Brakes pulling	1. Contaminated lining. 2. Front end out of alignment. 3. Incorrect brake adjustment. 4. Unmatched brake lining. 5. Brake drums out of round. 6. Brake shoes distorted. 7. Restricted brake hose or line. 8. Broken rear spring. 9. Worn brake linings. 10. Uneven lining wear. 11. Glazed brake lining. 12. Excessive brake lining dust. 13. Heat spotted brake drums. 14. Weak brake return springs. 15. Faulty automatic adjusters. 16. Low or incorrect tire pressure.

TROUBLESHOOTING

Condition	Possible Cause
Squealing brakes	1. Glazed brake lining. 2. Saturated brake lining. 3. Weak or broken brake shoe retaining spring. 4. Broken or weak brake shoe return spring. 5. Incorrect brake lining. 6. Distorted brake shoes. 7. Bent support plate. 8. Dust in brakes or scored brake drums. 9. Linings worn below limit. 10. Uneven brake lining wear. 11. Heat spotted brake drums.
Chirping brakes	1. Out of round drum or eccentric axle flange pilot.
Dragging brakes	1. Incorrect wheel or parking brake adjustment. 2. Parking brakes engaged or improperly adjusted. 3. Weak or broken brake shoe return spring. 4. Brake pedal binding. 5. Master cylinder cup sticking. 6. Obstructed master cylinder relief port. 7. Saturated brake lining. 8. Bent or out of round brake drum. 9. Contaminated or improper brake fluid. 10. Sticking wheel cylinder pistons. 11. Driver riding brake pedal. 12. Defective proportioning valve. 13. Insufficient brake shoe lubricant.
Hard pedal	1. Brake booster inoperative. 2. Incorrect brake lining. 3. Restricted brake line or hose. 4. Frozen brake pedal linkage. 5. Stuck wheel cylinder. 6. Binding pedal linkage. 7. Faulty proportioning valve.
Wheel locks	1. Contaminated brake lining. 2. Loose or torn brake lining. 3. Wheel cylinder cups sticking. 4. Incorrect wheel bearing adjustment. 5. Faulty proportioning valve.
Brakes fade (high speed)	1. Incorrect lining. 2. Overheated brake drums. 3. Incorrect brake fluid (low boiling temperature). 4. Saturated brake lining. 5. Leak in hydraulic system. 6. Faulty automatic adjusters.
Pedal pulsates	1. Bent or out of round brake drum.
Brake chatter and shoe knock	1. Out of round brake drum. 2. Loose support plate. 3. Bent support plate. 4. Distorted brake shoes. 5. Machine grooves in contact face of brake drum (Shoe Knock). 6. Contaminated brake lining. 7. Missing or loose components. 8. Incorrect lining material. 9. Out-of-round brake drums. 10. Heat spotted or scored brake drums. 11. Out-of-balance wheels.

Troubleshooting Drum Brakes (cont.)

Condition	Possible Cause
Brakes do not self adjust	1. Adjuster screw frozen in thread. 2. Adjuster screw corroded at thrust washer. 3. Adjuster lever does not engage star wheel. 4. Adjuster installed on wrong wheel.
Brake light glows	1. Leak in the hydraulic system. 2. Air in the system. 3. Improperly adjusted master cylinder pushrod. 4. Uneven lining wear. 5. Failure to center combination valve or proportioning valve.

Appendix

General Conversion Table

Multiply by	To convert	To	
2.54	Inches	Centimeters	.3937
30.48	Feet	Centimeters	.0328
.914	Yards	Meters	1.094
1.609	Miles	Kilometers	.621
6.45	Square inches	Square cm.	.155
.836	Square yards	Square meters	1.196
16.39	Cubic inches	Cubic cm.	.061
28.3	Cubic feet	Liters	.0353
.4536	Pounds	Kilograms	2.2045
3.785	Gallons	Liters	.264
.068	Lbs./sq. in. (psi)	Atmospheres	14.7
.138	Foot pounds	Kg. m.	7.23
1.014	H.P. (DIN)	H.P. (SAE)	.9861
—	To obtain	From	Multiply by

Note: 1 cm. equals 10 mm.; 1 mm. equals .0394".

Conversion—Common Fractions to Decimals and Millimeters

Common Fractions	Decimal Fractions	Millimeters (approx.)	Common Fractions	Decimal Fractions	Millimeters (approx.)	Common Fractions	Decimal Fractions	Millimeters (approx.)
1/128	.008	0.20	11/32	.344	8.73	43/64	.672	17.07
1/64	.016	0.40	23/64	.359	9.13	11/16	.688	17.46
1/32	.031	0.79	3/8	.375	9.53	45/64	.703	17.86
3/64	.047	1.19	25/64	.391	9.92	23/32	.719	18.26
1/16	.063	1.59	13/32	.406	10.32	47/64	.734	18.65
5/64	.078	1.98	27/64	.422	10.72	3/4	.750	19.05
3/32	.094	2.38	7/16	.438	11.11	49/64	.766	19.45
7/64	.109	2.78	29/64	.453	11.51	25/32	.781	19.84
1/8	.125	3.18	15/32	.469	11.91	51/64	.797	20.24
9/64	.141	3.57	31/64	.484	12.30	13/16	.813	20.64
5/32	.156	3.97	1/2	.500	12.70	53/64	.828	21.03
11/64	.172	4.37	33/64	.516	13.10	27/32	.844	21.43
3/16	.188	4.76	17/32	.531	13.49	55/64	.859	21.83
13/64	.203	5.16	35/64	.547	13.89	7/8	.875	22.23
7/32	.219	5.56	9/16	.563	14.29	57/64	.891	22.62
15/64	.234	5.95	37/64	.578	14.68	29/32	.906	23.02
1/4	.250	6.35	19/32	.594	15.08	59/64	.922	23.42
17/64	.266	6.75	39/64	.609	15.48	15/16	.938	23.81
9/32	.281	7.14	5/8	.625	15.88	61/64	.953	24.21
19/64	.297	7.54	41/64	.641	16.27	31/32	.969	24.61
5/16	.313	7.94	21/32	.656	16.67	63/64	.984	25.00
21/64	.328	8.33						

Conversion—Millimeters to Decimal Inches

mm	inches	mm	inches	mm	inches	mm	inches	mm	inches
1	.039 370	31	1.220 470	61	2.401 570	91	3.582 670	210	8.267 700
2	.078 740	32	1.259 840	62	2.440 940	92	3.622 040	220	8.661 400
3	.118 110	33	1.299 210	63	2.480 310	93	3.661 410	230	9.055 100
4	.157 480	34	1.338 580	64	2.519 680	94	3.700 780	240	9.448 800
5	.196 850	35	1.377 949	65	2.559 050	95	3.740 150	250	9.842 500
6	.236 220	36	1.417 319	66	2.598 420	96	3.779 520	260	10.236 200
7	.275 590	37	1.456 689	67	2.637 790	97	3.818 890	270	10.629 900
8	.314 960	38	1.496 050	68	2.677 160	98	3.858 260	280	11.032 600
9	.354 330	39	1.535 430	69	2.716 530	99	3.897 630	290	11.417 300
10	.393 700	40	1.574 800	70	2.755 900	100	3.937 000	300	11.811 000
11	.433 070	41	1.614 170	71	2.795 270	105	4.133 848	310	12.204 700
12	.472 440	42	1.653 540	72	2.834 640	110	4.330 700	320	12.598 400
13	.511 810	43	1.692 910	73	2.874 010	115	4.527 550	330	12.992 100
14	.551 180	44	1.732 280	74	2.913 380	120	4.724 400	340	13.385 800
15	.590 550	45	1.771 650	75	2.952 750	125	4.921 250	350	13.779 500
16	.629 920	46	1.811 020	76	2.992 120	130	5.118 100	360	14.173 200
17	.669 290	47	1.850 390	77	3.031 490	135	5.314 950	370	14.566 900
18	.708 660	48	1.889 760	78	3.070 860	140	5.511 800	380	14.960 600
19	.748 030	49	1.929 130	79	3.110 230	145	5.708 650	390	15.354 300
20	.787 400	50	1.968 500	80	3.149 600	150	5.905 500	400	15.748 000
21	.826 770	51	2.007 870	81	3.188 970	155	6.102 350	500	19.685 000
22	.866 140	52	2.047 240	82	3.228 340	160	6.299 200	600	23.622 000
23	.905 510	53	2.086 610	83	3.267 710	165	6.496 050	700	27.559 000
24	.944 880	54	2.125 980	84	3.307 080	170	6.692 900	800	31.496 000
25	.984 250	55	2.165 350	85	3.346 450	175	6.889 750	900	35.433 000
26	1.023 620	56	2.204 720	86	3.385 820	180	7.086 600	1000	39.370 000
27	1.062 990	57	2.244 090	87	3.425 190	185	7.283 450	2000	78.740 000
28	1.102 360	58	2.283 460	88	3.464 560	190	7.480 300	3000	118.110 000
29	1.141 730	59	2.322 830	89	3.503 903	195	7.677 150	4000	157.480 000
30	1.181 100	60	2.362 200	90	3.543 300	200	7.874 000	5000	196.850 000

To change decimal millimeters to decimal inches, position the decimal point where desired on either side of the millimeter measurement shown and reset the inches decimal by the same number of digits in the same direction. For example, to convert 0.001 mm to decimal inches, reset the decimal behind the 1 mm (shown on the chart) to 0.001; change the decimal inch equivalent (0.039″ shown) to 0.000039″.

Tap Drill Sizes

National Fine or S.A.E.

Screw & Tap Size	Threads Per Inch	Use Drill Number
No. 5	44	.37
No. 6	40	.33
No. 8	36	.29
No. 10	32	.21
No. 12	28	.15
1/4	28	3
5/16	24	1
3/8	24	Q
7/16	20	W
1/2	20	29/64
9/16	18	33/64
5/8	18	37/64
3/4	16	11/16
7/8	14	13/16
1 1/8	12	1 3/64
1 1/4	12	1 11/64
1 1/2	12	1 27/64

Tap Drill Sizes

National Coarse or U.S.S.

Screw & Tap Size	Threads Per Inch	Use Drill Number
No. 5	40	.39
No. 6	32	.36
No. 8	32	.29
No. 10	24	.25
No. 12	24	.17
1/4	20	8
5/16	18	F
3/8	16	5/16
7/16	14	U
1/2	13	27/64
9/16	12	31/64
5/8	11	17/32
3/4	10	21/32
7/8	9	49/64
1	8	7/8
1 1/8	7	63/64
1 1/4	7	1 7/32
1 1/2	6	1 11/32

APPENDIX 225

Anti-Freeze Chart

Temperatures Shown in Degrees Fahrenheit +32 is Freezing

Cooling System Capacity Quarts	\<td colspan="14"\>Quarts of ETHYLENE GLYCOL Needed for Protection to Temperatures Shown Below

Cooling System Capacity Quarts	1	2	3	4	5	6	7	8	9	10	11	12	13	14
10	+24°	+16°	+ 4°	−12°	−34°	−62°								
11	+25	+18	+ 8	− 6	−23	−47								
12	+26	+19	+10	0	−15	−34	−57°							
13	+27	+21	+13	+ 3	− 9	−25	−45							
14			+15	+ 6	− 5	−18	−34							
15			+16	+ 8	0	−12	−26							
16			+17	+10	+ 2	− 8	−19	−34	−52°					
17			+18	+12	+ 5	− 4	−14	−27	−42					
18			+19	+14	+ 7	0	−10	−21	−34	−50°				
19			+20	+15	+ 9	+ 2	− 7	−16	−28	−42				
20				+16	+10	+ 4	− 3	−12	−22	−34	−48°			
21				+17	+12	+ 6	0	− 9	−17	−28	−41			
22				+18	+13	+ 8	+ 2	− 6	−14	−23	−34	−47°		
23				+19	+14	+ 9	+ 4	− 3	−10	−19	−29	−40		
24				+19	+15	+10	+ 5	0	− 8	−15	−23	−34	−46°	
25				+20	+16	+12	+ 7	+ 1	− 5	−12	−20	−29	−40	−50°
26					+17	+13	+ 8	+ 3	− 3	− 9	−16	−25	−34	−44
27					+18	+14	+ 9	+ 5	− 1	− 7	−13	−21	−29	−39
28					+18	+15	+10	+ 6	+ 1	− 5	−11	−18	−25	−34
29					+19	+16	+12	+ 7	+ 2	− 3	− 8	−15	−22	−29
30					+20	+17	+13	+ 8	+ 4	− 1	− 6	−12	−18	−25

For capacities over 30 quarts divide true capacity by 3. Find quarts Anti-Freeze for the ⅓ and multiply by 3 for quarts to add.

For capacities under 10 quarts multiply true capacity by 3. Find quarts Anti-Freeze for the tripled volume and divide by 3 for quarts to add.

To Increase the Freezing Protection of Anti-Freeze Solutions Already Installed

Number of Quarts of ETHYLENE GLYCOL Anti-Freeze Required to Increase Protection

Cooling System Capacity Quarts	From +20° F. to					From +10° F. to					From 0° F. to			
	0°	−10°	−20°	−30°	−40°	0°	−10°	−20°	−30°	−40°	−10°	−20°	−30°	−40°
10	1¾	2¼	3	3½	3¾	¾	1½	2¼	2¾	3¼	¾	1½	2	2½
12	2	2¾	3½	4	4½	1	1¾	2½	3¼	3¾	1	1¾	2½	3¼
14	2¼	3¼	4	4¾	5½	1¼	2	3	3¾	4½	1	2	3	3½
16	2½	3½	4½	5¼	6	1¼	2½	3½	4¼	5¼	1¼	2¼	3¼	4
18	3	4	5	6	7	1½	2¾	4	5	5¾	1½	2½	3¾	4¾
20	3¼	4½	5¾	6¾	7½	1¾	3	4¼	5½	6½	1½	2¾	4¼	5¼
22	3½	5	6¼	7¼	8¼	1¾	3¼	4¾	6	7¼	1¾	3¼	4½	5½
24	4	5½	7	8	9	2	3½	5	6½	7½	1¾	3½	5	6
26	4¼	6	7½	8¾	10	2	4	5½	7	8¼	2	3¾	5½	6¾
28	4½	6¼	8	9½	10½	2¼	4¼	6	7½	9	2	4	5¾	7¼
30	5	6¾	8½	10	11½	2½	4½	6½	8	9½	2¼	4¼	6¼	7¾

Test radiator solution with proper hydrometer. Determine from the table the number of quarts of solution to be drawn off from a full cooling system and replace with undiluted anti-freeze, to give the desired increased protection. For example, to increase protection of a 22-quart cooling system containing Ethylene Glycol (permanent type) anti-freeze, from +20° F. to −20° F. will require the replacement of 6¼ quarts of solution with undiluted anti-freeze.

Index

A
Air cleaner, 7, 93
Air conditioning
  Sight glass inspection, 15
Alternator, 50
Antifreeze, 226
Automatic transaxle
  Adjustment, 137
  Filter change, 26
  Pan removal, 26

B
Ball joints, 145
Battery
  Jump starting, 29
  Maintenance, 9, 55
Belt tension adjustment, 9
Body, 172
Body work, 172
Brakes
  Adjustment, 159
  Bleeding, 162
  Caliper, 163
  Fluid level, 18
  Fluid recommendations, 25
  Front brakes, 162
  Master cylinder, 159
  Parking brake, 169
  Rear brakes, 165
Bulbs, 126

C
Camber, 148
Camshaft and bearings, 64
Capacities, 20
Carburetor
  Adjustment, 111
  Overhaul, 109
  Replacement, 109
Catalytic converter, 106
Charging system, 47
Chassis lubrication, 27
Circuit breaker, 127
Clutch
  Adjustment, 135
  Replacement, 135
Coil (ignition), 41
Connecting rod and bearings, 64
Constant velocity joints (CV), 133
Control arm
  Lower, 146
Cooling system, 13, 67
Crankcase ventilation (PCV), 8
Cylinder head
  Removal and installation, 59
  Torque sequence, 60

D
Dents and scratches, 176
Distributor
  Removal and installation, 48
Door panels, 173
Driveshaft, 130

E
Electrical
  Chassis, 119
  Engine, 46
Electronic ignition, 37
Emission controls
  Air management system, 95
  Catalytic converter, 106
  Computer command control system, 100
  Deceleration valve, 104
  Early fuel evaporation, 97
  Electronic spark timing, 105
  Evaporative emission control system, 92
  Exhaust emission controls, 93
  Exhaust gas recirculation, 98
  Idle speed control, 105
  Mixture control solenoid, 104
  Oxygen sensor, 107
  Positive crankcase ventilation system, 91
  Thermostatic air cleaner, 93
  Throttle position sensor, 104
  Transmission converter clutch, 106
Engine
  Camshaft, 64
  Cylinder head torque sequence, 60
  Exhaust manifold, 62
  Front cover, 62
  Identification, 5
  Intake manifold, 61
  Oil recommendations, 22
  Pistons and rings, 64
  Rebuilding, 69
  Removal and installation, 56
  Rocker arm (or shaft), 60
  Specifications, 56
  Timing chain (or gears), 63
  Tune-up, 33
Evaporative canister, 92
Exhaust manifold, 62

F
Fan belt adjustment, 9
Firing order, 50
Fluid level checks
  Battery, 19
  Coolant, 19
  Engine oil, 16
  Master cylinder, 18
  Power steering pump, 19
  Steering gear, 19

INDEX

Transaxle, 17
Windshield washer, 19
Fluid recommendations, 25
Front suspension
    Ball joints, 145
    Lower control arm, 146
    MacPherson struts, 141
    Wheel alignment, 147
Front wheel bearing, 146
Fuel filter, 22
Fuel pump, 108
Fuel system, 108
Fuel tank, 116
Fuses and flashers, 127, 128
Fusible links, 126

G

Gearshift linkage adjustment
    Automatic, 137
    Manual, 130
Generator (see Alternator)

H

Half shafts, 130, 140
Hand brake, 169
Headlights, 125
Heater, 119
Hoses, 12

I

Identification
    Body, 5
    Vehicle, 5
    Engine, 5
    Transaxle, 6
Idle speed and mixture, 44
Ignition lock cylinder, 153
Ignition switch, 125, 153
Instrument cluster, 122
Intake manifold, 61

J

Jacking points, 28
Jump starting, 29

L

Light bulb specifications, 126
Lower control arm, 146
Lubrication
    Chassis, 27
    Engine, 24, 65
    Transmission, 26

M

Maintenance intervals, 23
Manifolds
    Intake, 61

Exhaust, 62
Manual transaxle, 129
Master cylinder, 159
Model identification, 5

N

Neutral safety switch, 135

O

Oil and fuel recommendations, 22
Oil change, 24
Oil filter (engine), 24
Oil pan, 65
Oil pump, 66
Oil level (engine), 16

P

Parking brake, 169
Pistons and rings
    Installation, 64
    Positioning, 64
PCV valve, 8
Power steering pump, 154

R

Radiator, 67
Radio, 120
Rear hub, 151
Rear suspension, 149
Regulator, 52
Rear main oil seal, 66
Rings, 64
Rocker arm (or shaft), 60
Routine maintenance, 7
Rust spots, 174

S

Scratches and dents, 176
Serial number location, 5
Shock absorbers
    Front, 144
    Rear, 149
Spark plugs, 33
Specifications
    Alternator and regulator, 51
    Battery and starter, 55
    Brakes, 169
    Camshaft, 58
    Capacities, 20
    Carburetor, 117
    Crankshaft and connecting rod, 58
    Fuses, 127
    General engine, 56
    Light bulb, 126
    Piston and ring, 58-59
    Torque, 58
    Tune-up, 34

228 INDEX

Specifications (*Continued*)
   Valve, 57
   Wheel alignment, 149
Speedometer cable, 124
Springs
   Front, 142
   Rear, 150
Starter, 52
Steering
   Linkage, 154
   Wheel, 151

T

Thermostat, 67
Tie-rod, 154
Timing (ignition), 42
Timing chain and sprockets, 63
Timing cover oil seal, 63
Tires, 20
Toe, 148
Tools, 2, 172
Towing, 28
Transaxle
   Automatic, 136
   Manual, 129
   Fluid change, 26

Troubleshooting, 189
Tune-up
   Procedures, 33
   Specifications, 34
Turn signal switch, 152

V

Valves
   Adjustment, 44, 61
   Service, 60
   Specifications, 57
Vehicle identification, 5

W

Water pump, 67
Wheel alignment, 147
Wheel bearings, 146, 151
Wheel cylinders, 168
Window glass, 172
Windshield wipers
   Arm, 121
   Blade, 15, 121
   Linkage, 122
   Motor, 122